PROFESSION ADVENTURER

PROFESSION ADVENTURER

100 of the World's Most Inspiring
Adventurers Teach You How to Turn Your
Passion into a Fulfilling Career

GLENN VALENTIN

TABLE OF CONTENTS

PART THREE: AIN'T NO MOUNTAIN HIGH ENOUGH

PART FOUR: I WANT TO RIDE MY BICYCLE

PART FIVE: SMOKE ON THE WATER

PART SIX: SNOW (HEY OH)

PART NINE: GO YOUR OWN WAY

BACK TO BASECAMP

Let's Start The Adventure!

Foreword by Karen Darke

This book is a collection of stories from people who have dreamed, and who apply passion, commitment and effort to turn those dreams into reality. I am privileged to be writing this foreword, to have the opportunity to inspire you with the essence of the stories that lie ahead: a sense of limitlessness. The biggest obstacles to us achieving incredible things together in this world are the limits we impose with our own minds. Our thoughts create our reality, and the more we work to weed out the unhelpful, disempowering and limiting thoughts and to nurture the expansive, blooming colors of possibility, the more surprising our lives can be.

Becoming paralysed at a young age taught me early in life to focus on our strengths and the things we are fortunate to have, and to pay no energy to what we struggle to do or don't have. Without that approach little of what has been lived through these stories would have been possible. At the root of this is a sense of curiosity and gratitude. Pursuing learning and growth, and taking time to reflect and appreciate sit in the heart of all of the people and their experiences that you will read about within these pages.

Very few people are born with a natural talent, but yet so many of us achieve surprising things by having courage to begin a path toward a vision, by caring enough to put in the hard work, and through facing fear and failure with a resilience that allows success to flourish.

A journey towards new possibilities inevitably involves obstacles and challenges. It is through navigating these that we recognize patterns in ourselves that in pursuit of our goals we will likely need to change. The obstacles life presents us with are an opportunity to drop old ways of thinking, break unhelpful habits and ways of being and open up to new possibilities for ourselves and the world we live in. The challenges of life offer us a gift: to discover how we can change ourselves inside, in order to change our world outside.

As you read these wonderful stories of ordinary people who have done some extraordinary things with their lives, I believe you will connect deeper with your own dreams and strengths. You will perhaps learn some tips on how to grow resilience and adaptability. Perhaps it will remind you to live in the moment and let go of fear about the future. I hope these stories will remind you that we can find freedom and peace in the fact that things are changing and unfolding, encouraging you to let go of futile worry about what will happen tomorrow. The people in this book have had to trust and rely on their team, a reminder of the importance of trust and being united together in the world. This needs to begin with ourselves: being committed to a cause or goal sufficiently to trust ourselves to work steadily towards it, and also relying on and supporting our teams, loved ones and the communities we live in. The 'we are in this together and we will get through this together' approach is a powerful force for action, change, and success.

These stories remind us that perception is an illusion. We all filter the world in different ways, and so what seems impossible to one person at a certain time, isn't even a grain of sand in the shoe to another. Our versions of what is possible are largely dictated by what we have become trained to believe: based on our childhood, our life experiences, our social and cultural environments and so on. From sport to business, the pattern is the same. Climbing the local hill to the supermarket is a version of Everest to some. Losing a few million in a bad business decision then gaining it all and more back again might be some people's version of a 'regular day in the office' but way beyond conceivable imagination to others.

When we are open to embrace a mode of curiosity, then we enter a zone of unknown possibilities. In my experience, we always learn and discover something new, and find the opportunity to change our world. Instead of allowing our left-brain logical mind to censor possibility and introduce all the reasons why things may not be possible, it is helpful to play with the question "How can we make that possible?", or "What else might be possible?". Life experiences combined with my fascination with the mind and how to use it to our advantage has led me to learn ways to strengthen myself to negative emotion. I use techniques to flick switches in my mind to imbue positivity, keep motivated and focused on creating and bringing dreams alive. Living a life with this 'possibility principle' approach seems to hold enormous power.

My first Paralympic Games was London 2012, for which the English artist Tracey Emin created a poster with these four words: Courage, Inspiration, Sweat, Love. I see these as vital ingredients for life and pursuing our dreams, and ingredients that are woven amongst the stories you will read here.

(1) COURAGE: We have to be bold and brave in facing new horizons, and willing to embrace the unknown, to face what feels like disaster or trauma but trust that ultimately we will arrive in a better place.

(2) INSPIRATION: We can be inspired by the experience of others, often by those who have lived through trauma or difficult times and have grown experience in resilience.

(3) SWEAT: We have to work hard to stay mentally, physically, emotionally and economically sane and healthy. If we want to create change, craft a desired future, then we have to put in the effort to stand for what we believe in or feel passionate about.

(4) LOVE: Connecting on a non-superficial level: seeking deeper, heart-level relationships with other amazing humans, and supporting each other through our challenges is the way that we will overcome things. When we pull together, surprising things will be possible.

Someone once told me, "ability is a state of mind not a state of body", and I believe that's true. Through my own journey, I've discovered the incredible power we have within us to change our thoughts, our emotions, and our energy. We can all learn to be our own alchemist, to transform unwanted emotions or experiences into gold, be creators of our reality and in doing so change our performance, our wellbeing, our world.

Preface: Grab every chance to live an epic life!

One of my first childhood memories is sitting in front of the television screen as a 6-year-old kid, in awe, watching how two of my countrymen were moving in a fairytale-like, never-ending white landscape. They looked like eskimos and their names were Dixie Dansercoer and Alain Hubert. I didn't realize it at the time, but I was witnessing how they broke the World Record for the longest expedition by foot and skis in Antarctica, covering 2438 miles (3924 km) in 99 days.

Fast Forward 22 years later. I was sitting in front of a screen again, in awe. On the other side of the screen: Dixie Dansercoer. This time I was directly talking to him, as a stepping stone for the book you're holding in your hands. I was terribly nervous before the interview; I would meet my childhood hero, the first person who made me dream about adventure, a national superstar, Grand Officer in the Crown Order of Belgium. But, there was no need for that nervousness; Dixie showed up as a bundle of humility and kindness, and seemed just as interested in my story as I was in his.

But honestly, my story wasn't that interesting at all until that point. I'd had an average upbringing in a small city in Flanders, my friends were normal people, I had won a couple of regional triathlon- and running races, I had a regular university degree and a conventional career as a physiotherapist. Although that might sound like a fairly successful and good life, I was deeply unhappy.

Ever since my first internship at uni, I knew that physiotherapy wasn't for me. Being stuck in a 10m² cubicle all day long, being forced to listen to complaining people 7-10 hours a day, sacrificing the health of my own back and wrists to help patients that don't make any effort to be healthy themselves, and having to fit in the – sometimes absurd – structures and regulations of the social security system. No, thank you. As a consequence, the question that haunted me for the following eight years was: "Well, then, what do you want to do?"

Further in this book, sailor Alex Alley refers to Alan Watts' famous speech titled 'What if money was no object?'. It's a speech I listened to hundreds of times during those eight self-reflecting years. Throughout all that time, my heart had known the answer to that question, but I hadn't dared to listen to my heart because, well, money is an object in this world. All those times I had secretly known that I wanted to be an athlete, I wanted to be an adventurer, I wanted to be an explorer. But how does one earn money from that?

At about the same time when the pain of dragging myself to work had become too intense to ignore my heart's preachings, the universe orchestrated the COVID-19 lockdown. Time became more abundant than ever before, so I decided to investigate the tactics and strategies of the people who had already built the career I was dreaming of. I set myself the goal to interview 100 "professional" adventurers, and what I got out of executing that process was beyond what I ever could have imagined.

I started this book with the focus on how to make a living out of adventure. But the core message the adventurers gave me was that it's not that much about how to make money, but about how to make an impact. As you'll discover reading through the next 476 pages, a fulfilling adventure career has little to do with being the best, the first, the longest, the richest or the craziest. A fulfilling career has much more to do with the unexpected kindness of strangers, the oneness with nature, the discovery of oneself and the hearts of people you touch.

Hundreds of other mindset-, business- and life lessons will be found in this book, and one of those lessons stands out to me. I want to share it here in this preface with you. Let's get back to being face to face with Dixie.

A couple of weeks after interviewing Dixie, I signed up for an introductory polar expedition course in the Swiss Alps in January 2021, led by Dixie. Shortly after signing up, I quit my job as a physiotherapist and decided to live off my savings in order to complete this book. But life is always more expensive than you calculate, and it became clear that attending the polar course would involve bringing my bank account literally down to zero. So a couple of weeks before I'd planned to set off to the Alps, I canceled the course and claimed a registration fee refund. I said to myself: "I can always do it next year."

A couple of months later, Dixie died after falling into a crevasse on an expedition in Greenland. I was devastated. It felt unreal; my childhood hero, the man I had been emailing just weeks before, the explorer who I hoped would one day mentor me, one of the world's most experienced and risk-averse polar guides, was no longer here.

But shortly after the initial shock came the realisation: "Dixie lived a fucking epic life". Dixie had started his athletic career as a pro windsurfer. Next, he dipped his toe in triathlon and trained with some of the world's best at the time. Dixie had also traveled all over the world as a flight attendant, and via his employer he got the chance to climb a 8000m-peak with professional mountaineer/explorer Alain Hubert. This Himalayan adventure was the beginning of an intense friendship between the two, and it brought Dixie to the Poles.

Dixie had put in the hard work to learn hundreds of business- and communication skills which enabled him to build a fruitful and passionate career as a polar explorer and polar guide. A career in which he shared the wonder for the beauty of our planet with his vigorous expedition partners, his adventurous clients, attentive public speaking's audiences all over the world, and mesmerized 6-year-old kids in front of the TV screen.

My bet is that Dixie died without regrets, because his 58 years on this planet have been so rich, so diverse, so intense, so deep, and so inspiring. Dixie had seen many chances in his life come along only once, and most of those times he had grabbed that one chance. If there's only one thing you take away from this book, please let it be this:

"Grab every chance to live an epic life."

Thank you Dixie for showing the way.

In Memoriam: Dixie Dansercoer

12/07/1962 - 07/06/2021

Being a Good Leader is About Listening to Your Team Members

DIXIE DANSERCOER started his career as a professional windsurfer. Later on, he would focus on triathlon and mountaineering. During an expedition on Cho Oyu, he met another Belgian explorer: Alain Hubert. A couple of years later, the two set off to break a world record for the longest distance covered on the Antarctic continent. Dixie continued coming back to the ice and became one of the world's most renowned polar explorers.

"I've always chosen the difficult path, it has never failed me!"

Adventure Inspiration

Young boy scoutism was my first encounter with adventure. Having to rely on myself as a kid, embracing the outdoors instead of being afraid in the woods, standing my ground in rough games, finding a way through the sadness of not having parents around... These experiences shaped me as a person, they fed my inquisitiveness and taught me to feel good when alienated from the cushy life in a western society. Scoutism laid the foundations in order to become a thirsty traveler, ambitious sportsman and curious adventurer.

In a later stage and while striving for grand goals, I always looked up to people who were better than me or who radiated an air of excellence. During my young years as a passionate bass-player it was Jaco Pastorius, athletics had me look up to Olympic medal winners in 5000 or 10,000m, in windsurfing it was prodigee Robby Naish, during my triathlon years I trained with my idol Wito De Meulder, in mountaineering I looked up to Reinhold Messner and finally it was the countless heroes from the pioneering years of polar exploration whom I revered.

Even though they took my breath away, I thought that these individuals were actually not unreachable, but merely people who had only two hands and two feet, just like me. They could have only become successful by following two possible pathways: either the privileged path of being an extremely talented person, or a path of hard work and zest for success. Gambling on getting it for free - the first option - was my second choice, so I cultivated the more difficult path, and it never failed me!

From Windsurfer to Polar Explorer

In my early twenties I dreamed of becoming a top windsurfer, so I booked a around-the-world ticket with Hawaii as my first destination. Pretty soon I found sponsorship in France and got the chance to compete in World Cups for three years. At the end of the third year, my contract stopped and I was forced to look for a job. Luckily, I have a good friend whose uncle was the CEO of *Sabena*, a former Belgian airline. This way, I found myself quite rapidly being a flight attendant, a job I would eventually hold on for 13 years. The great thing about it was that it allowed me to continue to discover the world.

During this period, I started mountaineering and competing in triathlons. In the early 90s, my employer *Sabena* was the sponsor of Alain Hubert, a belgian adventurer, who had planned an expedition to Cho Oyu, one of the very few 8000m peaks, on the border of Nepal and Tibet. *Sabena* organized a race for all of its employees, whereby the winner got to join Hubert for his climb. To my great surprise, I won the competition and thus got to meet Alain Hubert, the beginning of a fine relationship. In 1995 we crossed Greenland together and in the winter of 1997-98, we managed the integral crossing of Antarctica over a length of 4000 km in 99 days, by foot, ski's and kites. It was the longest distance people had ever covered the continent 'by fair means'.

Polar expeditions are very expensive, how do you find the budget?
I've always relied on private sponsorship. If you make use of governmental support, you can be sure to receive criticism. People would ask why their tax payments should be used for polar expeditions. I wanted to avoid that and, above all, I didn't want people to pay for my personal projects. For each and every one of our expeditions, we embraced a scientific goal. Because we were convinced that we should pro deo contribute to fill the hiatuses in Antarctic knowledge by collecting data. It's a job I do with heart and soul, being able to contribute to science as a by-product is something I do with pleasure.

If you approach companies to propose a collaboration, it's important to never sell your soul. You must give them a return on investment that feels right. What businesses are really interested in is your intellectual property, you need to have a story that's unique, a story that really appeals to them.

Another practical advice is to over-budget by one-third. If you do the math to calculate the total cost of your expedition, you can be sure that in reality, it will turn out to be even more expensive as there are always unforeseen costs. I've found that calculating 33% extra is a good rule of thumb to prevent getting into financial trouble.

If you want to become a certified IPGA polar guide (*International Polar Guides Association*), you have to give proof of first aid knowledge, crevasse rescue, glacier travel, gun handling... Today, thanks to my accumulated experiences, I'm one of the 13 master polar explorers in the world.

What are you afraid of?
I cannot say that I am really afraid of potential hazards, even if our destiny is written in the stars. But of course, on a subdued, conscious level polar bears, crevasses, cathedral-size waves and avalanches do instill fear. When you're an explorer, dangerous situations do inevitably occur. Luckily, I have always had this gut-feeling when danger announced itself as a red line that should not be transgressed and I have learned to be a conservative risk-taker. If I'm handed a bad hand of cards, it's in my nature to always try to find a solution, but I have also learned to immediately accept the inevitable when there is no turning back, when I have to face the foolstop. Developing my own defense mechanisms to limit danger has been a progressive learning curve that has kept me safe so far.

How does your mother deal with you being in dangerous situations?
My mom has lived through every stage of my life and has witnessed my growing ambition in an area where danger is apparent. I can only imagine the disbelief and concern that my mother expressed with every announcement of yet another expedition, but gradually she has accepted that my passions are who I am and that without them I would not be such a happy soul. I find it incredible that she has never demanded that I stop doing what I love and I am so thankful for that. By doing so, I have also become extra careful instead of reckless.

We lost a man and shot a bear
During the 2017 North Pole season, I was in good company of a very international team of accomplished adventurers, one of which was a Japanese woman 20 years young. She wanted to reach the North Pole as the last hurdle towards achieving *the Adventurer's Grand Slam*, which is climbing the highest summit on each summit plus a *Last Degree* to the South Pole and the *Last Degree* to the North Pole. On a very crispy and cold day, I was helping a Czech man repair his harness when our intrepid Japanese came running to us, shouting: "Dixie, Dixie, polar bear is running away with my sled!" I told myself that she was seeing ghosts after the early morning descent of a helicopter that picked up two of our team members with either slight frostbite or physical exhaustion. But, no joke, a bit further where the two female explorers had opened their sled to take out their lunch, I saw a bear pulling at the rope in an attempt to appropriate it. Seeing a polar bear running away with one of my sleds, that was a first! I could not let that happen, though, as the sled contained so many essentials, so I took out the flare gun and walked towards the predator.

It suddenly let go of the rope and made a move towards the other sled to get some of the salami out of that one, but before he reached it, he changed his mind and came towards us. We grouped together and when I fired a warning shot, the bear did not seem to be bothered so we shot again. Clearly understanding the message, the white king of the Arctic bounced away and ran off. I climbed one of those big compression ice blocks to have a better view and saw that the bear disappeared in the distance. We continued in the direction of the North Pole and kept to our routines that night…. That meant cooking dinner, mending whatever needed to be repaired and communicating. Usually, I am the only one with satellite phones and a link to the real world but in this case, our Japanese lady had also asked to recount the day to her manager who would then put it on the worldwide web.

The next day, to my big surprise, I learned that supporters and people anywhere in the world read the update of our Japanese client: "This morning, we lost a man and late this afternoon, we shot a bear!" Clearly, there was a missing out on language skills. Losing a man as well as shooting a bear means that both specimens are … dead. Better would have been 'one of our colleagues was picked up by helicopter' and 'we shot AT a bear'. Now, we can have a good laugh at it, but the consequences of such communications are pretty disastrous…!

What makes you a good leader?
Taking the time to dive into the souls of each team member to really try to understand them. Inviting everyone to show their weaknesses in order to be able to show empathy and

anticipate potential misunderstandings. Ask what the expectations of group members are, what they expect of the expedition, of others, of myself as the guide. The leader must delegate with trust when all is well, gives a helping hand when help is needed and is a fix-it-all in difficult situations. He also employs strict guidance to create clarity and avoid too many opinions when safety is at stake.

What does a typical day in your life look like when you're not on expedition?

Early-morning yoga - cup of coffee - enjoy the birth of the day - use the clarity of the morning to write (emails, documents, book, interviews) - breakfast - work on all aspects of the guiding business: maintaining and developing partnerships, PR & promo, ameliorating & customizing equipment, organizing stocks, communications,... Also physical or online meetings with clients, partners, our co-guides, retailers, providers, logistics partners, ... - Physical training: walk, bike, run, pull tires, kiteboard, indoor fitness - Aperitif and dinner with family - Evening relaxation: read, quality movie, ...

What does a pulling-tires workout look like?

It's training to mimic the conditions of polar expeditions. When I'm not on an expedition, we either live in Oregon -my wife Julie is American-, Switzerland or Belgium. In Belgium, there are no mountains, there's no snow. So what I often do is put a belt with car tires tied on it around my waist and go out in the woods. I always make it hard: I run some stretches, I go up and down the hills. And actually, it comes quite close to the feeling of pulling a sled on the ice.

Nothing is also OK

When you arrive in a polar environment, it's always a very abrupt change compared to the way of living at home. You can't escape the emptiness, the monotony. I try to mentally prepare for this by training in difficult circumstances -as with pulling tires- and by meditation. During the first days of an expedition, you often try to keep your mind busy. "Today, I'm going to count the clouds", "Today, I'm going to focus on the color of the ice", "Today, I'll try to spot polar bears"... but soon you're out of possibilities. After about 2-3 weeks your mind has drained empty of thoughts, it does not any longer want to stay busy. So that void implies accepting that thinking about nothing is also OK.

According to your wife Julie, what are three good and one bad personality traits that you have?

Good: we are alike, worldly and organized
Bad: I leave the toilet seat up (working on it!)

Do you agree with her?

Yes

What are you grateful for?

I am grateful for fate having decided to put me on Earth in the non-perfect, but safe harbor called Belgium. Happy that I was raised by wonderful parents who gave me space to be myself although they did not always approve out of concern. I am also amazed at what an adventurous spirit can do by opening up for the unknown. Thankful for my wife, children, the rest of the family, all the good friends and many more kind people who inspire me. Thankful for the good health that allows me to enjoy life to the fullest.

What are the biggest life lessons you're teaching your daughter?
Kindness over principles: if someone has a vision that runs counter to your own, it is better to first take a broader view instead of discussing with the sole aim to be right. Be kind to that person and try to understand his or her opinion, think beyond your own convictions. What's equally important is to help others, to be a good friend, and to give time to those who need it. Follow your passions, use your fullest potential.

Do you have any regrets?
I do not believe in regret when it means that you 'should have' or 'could have' done this or that. When something is in your own, personal power and you consciously decide to do something with it, only fate can contradict you. Even when you gamble and the outcome can be good or bad, there is only one person who is responsible for that moment of decision-making and there should not be any regret when it goes wrong. If negative forces outside our will impose unpleasant or downright disastrous consequences, then it is time to accept the unavoidable. Fate can be a bitch. But regret has no place in these kinds of situations. Secretly, I sometimes regret that I cannot feel what gracious birds must feel, soaring in the sky.

Thought experiment: In 2030, you drink an elixir which makes you live another 100 years. By the time we're in the year 2100, all 10 billion people on planet Earth have a chip planted in their head and are connected to a supercomputer. If you'd be given control over the supercomputer, which belief/conviction would you program into people's mind?
I would not want to be the person to dictate what humankind must do, feel, say or believe. If I could have a voice in a larger input, allowing for a democratic way of spreading a so-called dogma, it would be kindness, acceptance and good will.

A life well lived according to Dixie Dansercoer
Having tasted both the good and the bad and having used one to cure the other.
Knowing that you have enriched other people's lives.
Being the most loving being you can be.

Find out more about Dixie:
www.polarcircles.com
www.polarexperience.com
facebook.com/PolarExperience/
instagram.com/your.polar.experience
instagram.com/dixie.dansercoer

Ahimsa ... First Do No Harm

JULIE BROWN is the managing director of Polar Circles, the company she created with her partner Dixie Dansercoer. She's the project coordinator of Dixie's expeditions, as well as an author, organizational performance coach and keynote speaker. Every now and then, she joins Dixie on an adventure. The red line throughout all these projects: humor, honesty, gratitude and coffee.

"Laughter is a huge part of my life and nothing gives me more pleasure than to share a good belly laugh with Dixie in the middle of an intense expedition."

What have been the major sources of influence for you in order to become an adventurer?

I became a virtual adventurer via books from a very young age. The public library in my hometown of Perrysburg, Ohio served as my first travel bureau. One book in particular that sparked my interest in adventure was *Dove* by Robin Lee Graham. Throughout my life I've been influenced by countless sources of inspiration: personal encounters, books, movies, music and art. I tend to be profoundly touched by "extraordinary, ordinary" people. I'm hyper-aware of authenticity.

How does a typical day in your life look like when you're not on an expedition?

It starts with coffee! I would dare to say that coffee is the only consistent component in our "daily" life. Dixie and I have straddled the bizarre line between the extreme expedition atmosphere and "normal" life for over 20 years. Dixie is deeply passionate, highly determined, and has seemingly endless energy. Sometimes, these combined positive traits swirl into a perfect storm and suck the oxygen out of our shared space. When we're home together we work in an office with computers and mobile phones, we go to meetings, we give presentations, we work, we clean, we cook. But we always make time to sip an aperitif at Wine O'Clock.

When Dixie is out on the ice, I manage our home and our business so the days elongate and the tasks require more night work. When the kids were younger, I split my day into shifts and tried to establish family-time boundaries when possible. Homework - Healthy dinner with Dixie's photo on the table to represent him - Bath time/ bedtime stories - Pack school lunches. After Dixie's nightly phone call from the ice, I would then dive back into the office to record his position, write the web blog, and attend whatever professional tasks came with his daily update.

I often travel to the expedition locations as a project coordinator. Our youngest daughter Robin has accompanied me on many of those trips, which has resulted in her having been to all seven continents by the age of 15. I try to establish a familiar routine no matter where we find ourselves, coffee helps with that.

Humor and Gratitude

Laughter is a huge part of my life and nothing gives me more pleasure than to share a good belly laugh with Dixie in the middle of an intense expedition. I have managed our expedition communications for over 20 years and when Dixie is out on the ice I do my best to sneak in a good joke during his nightly calls.

During my first polar expedition as a participant, *Antarctica 2000*, I found myself laughing uncontrollably after a massive fail with a pee bottle inside the tent. Thank goodness it froze and cleaned up relatively quickly but the shared humor with Dixie in a potentially awkward moment still makes me chuckle.

I practice a short moment of gratitude upon awakening each morning. I'm grateful for life, for health, for warmth, for love, for a full belly, for a roof over my head, for water, for a breath of fresh air... Most of all, I'm beyond grateful for the health, wellness and safety of my husband, kids and all of my loved ones.

What makes you a good leader?

I'm not impulsive and I therefore take my time to make informed decisions. Once I finally do make a sound decision, I don't look back.

Financial Advice

The business of managing an expedition is like any other business ... It requires funding and funding requires sales. Many adventurers struggle with that reality. They confuse money with something that could potentially taint their "pure" adventure.

The corporate world needs inspiration. The world needs inspiration. Adventure, if authentic, has a valuable place in our global economy. That said, adventure is a choice, we must remain humble to the fact that we are asking for financial support for a choice, not an imposed necessity. Humility, honesty and gratitude have served us well in our relationships with financial partners.

Thought experiment: In the year 2030, you drink an elixir which makes you live another 100 years. By the time we're in the year 2100, all 10 billion people on planet Earth have a chip planted in their head and are connected to a supercomputer. If you'd given control over the supercomputer, which values would you program into people's minds?
Humility, honesty and gratitude.

If you would be obligated to live on an isolated island without any inhabitants, and you're only allowed to bring two people and five objects with you, who and what would you choose and where would you go?
Now that is a tough question ... I would prefer an island with a nice balance of sun and shade but not too hot ... A cool breeze would be welcome.
I would definitely want to share this experience with Dixie. The limit of two people implies the breakup of my immediate family which leaves me distressed. However if I have to choose, we're not yet finished raising Kid Number 4, so I would bring Robin along to finish the job.

The five objects I would choose are a giant photo of our kids and loved ones, a coffee machine, music for listening pleasure, paper & pencil for writing and sunscreen.

Favorite Books

Dove, by Robin Lee Graham. I read this book in 1974 when I was ten years old. I found it amidst the "new young adult novels" at the Perrysburg Public Library in Ohio and had to ask permission from the librarian to be able to check it out since I was officially too young. Her willingness to break the rules opened up my eyes to a world full of possibilities. This book started my fascination with travel and adventure and led me to consider the name Robin for our baby daughter.

Good Girls Don't Ski to the South Pole, by Liv Arnesen. This book revealed a then mysterious world of polar travel and ambitious expeditions. Liv sent this book to Dixie when he was preparing for his irst Antarctica expedition in 1997. (Read the interview with Liv on page 272)

Revolutionary Road, by Richard Yates. I read it in 2001 when I was pregnant with our daughter. It exposes mediocrity and complacency "in a drugged and dying culture." Heavy & initially regarded as pessimistic, I found this book to be a beautiful tribute to the pursuit of grand goals hidden within a cautionary tale.

The Diving Bell and the Butterfly, by Jean-Dominique Bauby. This was a life-changing read for both Dixie and me, humility on every page. There is no more room for any excuse once you read this true story.

Wild, by Cheryl Strayed. Raw, honest, real. Just read it.

The Sex Lives of Cannibals, by Maarten Troost. Unforgettably entertaining read while in -28°C Nome in 2005. What better way to endure the deep Alaskan cold than to be whisked away to the island of Kiribati in the equatorial Pacific.

The Art of Crossing Cultures, by Craig Storti. This book was given to me in 1999 as a wedding gift by a Delta Air Lines colleague. It is now tattered and torn and filled with tear stains on a few pages. How perceptive my friend Mari was to offer me this handbook when I was naïve enough to think that it would be a "piece of cake" to move from the United States to Belgium.

South, by Ernest Shackleton. Every corporate leader – or any leader for that matter – must read *South*. I read this book in 1999 in what I thought was preparation for my first Antarctic expedition. Instead, it whet my appetite to develop our first corporate leadership keynote ... and *Polar Circles* was born.

Wherever You Go, There You Are, by Jon Kabat-Zinn. Linda, my massage therapist girlfriend, gave me this book in 1998 when I officially became a Belgian resident. She was worried about me as I embarked upon my new role as a step-mother of three lively kids, a partner to a man who would be gone for extended periods of time, and a person about to participate in her first polar expedition. Mindfulness has been my guide ever since.

The Art of Happiness, by the Dalai Lama. The title says it all.

Silence in the Age of Noise, by Erling Kagge. Kagge is a Norwegian explorer, his book about silence is just WOW.

What are the biggest life lessons you're teaching your children?
I've tried to provide our daughter Robin and my three stepchildren Jasper, Evelien & Thijs with every opportunity to thrive. It has been deeply important to me to be a facilitator as a parent, someone who brings other positively influential people into our kids' orbit. I never wanted to be an overprotective mother, but rather someone who enables our children to trust in the many good people on this planet. It gives me enormous satisfaction to see our kids connect with and learn from other people.

A life well lived according to you, would be described as...
Ahimsa ... first do no harm.

Find out more about Julie:
www.polarcircles.com
www.polarexperience.com
facebook.com/PolarExperience
instagram.com/your.polar.experience

PART ONE:

RUN TO THE HILLS

There Are No Special People; There Are Only People Who Work Extremely Hard

MICHELE GRAGLIA is a professional ultrarunner. He won the Badwater 135, the Ultra Milano-San Remo, the Yukon Arctic 100, and the Moab 240, amongst others. He is also the World Record Holder for the fastest crossing of the Gobi Desert (1703 km in 23 days, 8 hours, 47 min) and Atacama Desert (925 km in 8 days, 12 hours, 46 min).

"One day in the library I stumbled upon the book 'Ultramarathon Man,' written by the legendary Dean Karnazes. I read a couple of pages and it blew my mind . . . since that moment Ultra Running became the central pillar in my life."

The Italian Dream

I grew up in a little village in the North-West of Italy, close to San Remo. My parents instilled in my younger sister and I a deep appreciation for nature from a very young age; in winter they took us skiing in the Alps, in summer we went hiking in the Dolomites. We also had a business in the export of flowers and traveled for work in other European countries like Scandinavia, Germany, and Scotland. As a kid I loved to get to know new cultures, to meet new people.

I was a very active kid, I spent countless hours playing at the beach with my friends. Though it wasn't until the end of elementary school that I started doing sports within a team; namely track and field. Track and field was a particular choice for an Italian guy, because soccer is our national sport. When you're 12-13 years old, you have to be very dedicated and committed if you want to be a good runner, because you have to spend many hours training alone while your friends are having fun at the soccer field. At that time my drive was not big enough, so when I was 15 I shifted from track and field to soccer. I played in a regional team for three years until I went to university.

I went to study Law in Italy, but pretty soon I dropped out. One, because I didn't like it. Two, because my father gave me the opportunity to come work for his business. I took the opportunity, had my first successes early on, and steadily grew as a salesman and entrepreneur. By the time I was 24, I had a decent income, a nice car, and a beautiful house. But then my long-term girlfriend broke up with me. I got over the break-up rapidly and said to myself that, now that I wasn't bound to a relationship anymore, it was the perfect moment to take another step in my personal development and to listen to the call for adventure I felt inside me. I said to my father that I wanted to go overseas, to Miami, to enrich myself and expand our business. He was very supportive, encouraging me to step into the unknown as he had done as a young man himself. If things wouldn't work out, he told me, I could always come back and join the business in Italy.

So only a couple of months after my break-up, I arrived in the United States. When I arrived, I stayed on the couch of a friend of mine, the time to ind an apartment for myself. One day when I was visiting properties, a heavy rainfall hit. I quickly entered the irst restaurant I could ind to shelter. It was a Johnny Rockets restaurant and while I was sipping from my *Coca-Cola*, I noticed an elderly, graceful woman gazing at me. After a couple of minutes, she stood up and walked up to me. She presented herself as Irene Marie, CEO of *Marilou*, one of the most famous model agencies at the time. She invited me right on the spot to her of ice and that same day I signed a modeling contract that would completely change my life.

Ultramarathon Man

When I entered the model world, I felt like the king of the world. I got a big paycheck, I was welcome at the most exquisite parties, and I was surrounded by beautiful women. It was a world of sex, drugs, and alcohol which you can only truly understand once you have been in it. Nevertheless, I slowly got to understand that it wasn't my world. Having pictures taken of me half-naked didn't give me ful illment, there was no sense of purpose.

I remember one particular night being paramount for me. I got invited to a private party in a giant mansion in Miami. We spent a wild night partying and I decided to stay there overnight. The following morning, I went to the bathroom and noticed the owner of the mansion lying in his puke, crying, completely destroyed. This man had a giant mansion, millions of dollars in his bank account, several sports cars . . . he met the picture of what people believe is ultimate success and achievement, yet he was miserable. I asked myself: "Do I want to ind myself in his position in 20-30 years, or do I want to be truly happy?" At that point, I decided that I had to make a big transition in my life.

My heart was telling me adventure was the direction I had to follow. So I made use of every second of free time – time I wasn't on a photoshoot or in the gym – to research adventurers. I read dozens of books about ocean rowers, long-distance swimmers, explorers . . . and although these were very interesting stories, it didn't feel like what I was looking for. One day, by chance, I stumbled upon a book titled 'Ultramarathon Man' in the library. On the cover was a picture of Dean Karnazes (read the interview with Dean Karnazes on page 46) and it appealed to me immediately. I grabbed it out of the shelf, read a couple of pages and it blew my mind . . . I knew that ultrarunning was the thing I was longing for, and ever since that moment it became a central pillar in my life.

The transition that followed wasn't easy. Giving up everything you have to chase a dream that has no guaranteed success is a scary thing to do. From 2010 to 2013, I juggled my career as a model with my revealed ambitions as an ultra marathon runner. In this time period, I already managed to win several races. 2014 was a magni icent year with a lot of very good results, the victory in the Ultra Milano-San Remo being the icing on the cake. Winning a renowned ultra race at my front door caused me to burst into tears of happiness at the inish line. The successes of that year got the ball rolling in terms of sponsorship and in 2015 I became an athlete in *La Sportiva's Ultra Team*, which allowed me to make a living as a pro athlete.

A Winning Lifestyle

On a normal day, I put my feet on the ground around 7-7:30 in the morning. Mostly I skip breakfast and go for a 20-25 km run. Next, I eat, work or read a bit, and do a stretching or yoga session. This is followed by a second run in the afternoon which takes an hour to an hour and a half. This is my schedule from Monday to Friday; during one of these days, I integrate some speedwork, most often in the form of a fartlek training. On Saturdays and Sundays I go out for long runs; in general 50 to 70 km a day, however, this can add up to 100 km.

I consider my nutrition just as important as my training. I've cut out all wheat in my diet and mostly rely on healthy fats, I'm probably the only Italian who doesn't eat pasta (laughs). I've relied on the work of Peter Defty regarding *Optimized Fat Metabolism (OFM)*. This is based on the understanding of the evolutionary process of humans. For the big majority of our history, fats were our major source of energy and the reason is that fats give us limitless energy. I like to compare carbohydrates with putting paper on a fire; if you do this you'll see a short, powerful spark arising. That's what carbs do in the body: they give you a short spark in energy. Fats, on the other hand, are like big blocks of wood on a fire: they can keep burning and burning endlessly. Besides choosing fat as my source of fuel, I've also asked myself the question of which micro-nutrients nourish and which ones damage the cells. This way, my diet has become more and more plant-based throughout the years, and I'm almost fully vegan right now. I eat a lot of vegetables, seeds, and nuts. The micronutrients in these foods nourish the cells, counteract inflammation, and improve my recovery.

Another thing I do in order to increase my body's efficiency is intermittent fasting. I skip breakfast most of the days and once a week I don't eat for 20-24 hours. Once every couple of months I do a 48h to 72h fast as a sort of big reset. Because my body is so used to burning fats nowadays, I'm not even hungry during those longer fasts anymore. Making the energy consumption of my body as efficient as possible has been a fascinating discovery. It's almost like discovering a new horizon. It has given me an edge over my competitors because I can keep on running even without food. If you rely on carbs, the moment you stop eating in an ultra, you bonk and you can't progress anymore. Besides, relying on carbs comes with a lot of gastrointestinal problems. The last advantage of my dietary shift has been that I rediscovered my taste buds; I can really appreciate the taste of a simple carrot or a piece of celery again.

Meditation: a Necessary Art to Learn

Another thing I'm doing almost on a daily basis is meditation. I see meditation as a necessary part of what I do. By meditation you learn to transcend the body, the focus goes within. That's a fundamental skill to be able to run for a very long time. Ultrarunning is a real battle with the mind. One of my favorite quotes is: "The brain is a great servant but a terrible master." What I mean by that, is that thanks to our minds, humans have amazing capacities. But at the same time, it's our mind that holds us back way too often. The brain dictates us to take the easy way out by inflicting fears on us and by making negative anticipations about the future. But actually, fear and thoughts about the future are not real, they aren't tangible, they are constructs we make up in our head. *The only thing that is real is the present moment.* Meditation helps me to be present. I think it's a necessary art to learn because it can free us from our brain and as a result override the fear that stops us from realizing our dreams.

My wife and I are now building a yoga and meditation retreat. For the last couple of years, I worked in such a retreat in Malibu for certain times of the year. It was an elite retreat. We would welcome famous film producers, celebrities, and entrepreneurs. All of them successful, yet miserable to the bone. But after seven days of spending time mastering their mind, they left us with a huge smile on their faces.

The last decade you've gone on an extraordinary inner journey of self-discovery which has allowed you to become who you really want to be. Do you think that everyone should go on his own inner journey?
I can't tell other people what they have to do, but I do recommend everyone to step out of their comfort zone and embark on a trajectory of self-discovery. In my opinion, too many people accept the status quo. The status quo tells us to do things that make us comfortable and safe, but the problem is that that is only a false sense of security, actual security doesn't exist and that's something that has become very clear with COVID-19. The blend of a security-seeking society and the insecurity brought by the virus resulted in the whole world freaking out.

When it comes to realizing dreams, there's a big misconception going on. People believe that only special people are able to do it, only special people can have an amazing lifestyle. Well, if there's one thing I've learned throughout the years, it is that there are no special people. The people at the top of their game are people who are working very hard and investing a tremendous amount of energy in their own development. People want to have fame and money, but that's a meaningless pursuit, it can't be the end goal. The goal should be to explore ourselves and the world around us, to venture into the unknown, and to find out what we really want. Once you have found your passion, you can work really hard and achieve excellence, and then fame and money can become the result of excellence. But on the other hand, if you have only fame and money without purpose, that's emptiness.

What's your goal in ultra races?
It has to be big enough, I'm always looking for a goal that's a bit out of my comfort zone, a goal that challenges me. The preparation for an ultra race is extremely daunting, it's very time-consuming and demands a whole lot of energy. You can only get through that hardship if your goal is big enough. I believe that it is possible to be 'just fit' by a daily training routine without a specific goal. But if you want to become 'ultra fit' you absolutely need to have a goal that pushes you to become the best version of yourself. I never race to win, I race to be the best. What I mean by that is that I don't compete to beat all the other competitors, but to be the best Michele on race day. How good the other runners will be is out of my control, so I prefer to focus my awareness within.

If given the chance, what would you put on a massive billboard in New York?
In general, people living in big cities don't give a shit about what happens elsewhere. All they want is "the good life". On a massive billboard, I would put a picture that shows them the

backside of the good life, a picture about how our comfy, materialistic society is destroying our planet.

How do you think that we as a species could shift towards living more in harmony with our planet instead of exploiting it?
That's a difficult question, but it's something I like to think about because I realize it's time for us to face our demons and acknowledge that the way we live isn't sustainable. I very much support the work of fundraisers and climate campaigns, yet I think we need something stronger than that if we want to make the transition that is necessary. The only way I see us doing that is by a shift in consciousness.

The dominant way of thinking in this world is one of disparity. We talk in terms of different religions, different countries, different cultures. Travelling has taught me that every individual on this planet is part of the same family. We have to rise from the chains of society that define us as part of a certain population group and understand that we are all bonded to each other and we are all bonded to our planet. Once we can come to that awareness, we'll understand that we have to respect and take care of each other and the planet.

If you would have the chance to go and eat a salad with three people dead or alive, who would you choose?
Sadghuru; that would be a guarantee for very deep, inspirational conversations. I would also want to reconnect with Dean Karnazes and Anton Krupicka whom I've met before. Dean stepped out of his secure, comfortable, wealthy life on his 30th birthday and became a figurehead in the sport of ultrarunning. Reading his book, I could relate a lot to his story. It made me believe that I could become a successful runner myself. Anton has also been very influential in my career, but in a different way. Anton experiences the sport in a very minimalistic way and puts a lot of value on freedom and connection with wild places. That triggered something in me, it's the way I wanted to experience ultra running too.

Recommended Books
Ultra Marathon Man, by Dean Karnazes. The book that changed my life.
The Power of Now, by Eckhart Tolle.
La fine è il mio Inizio, by Folco Terzani. The title means 'the end is my beginning', but unfortunately the book isn't translated into English. It's about an old man at the end of his life talking about what he has learned throughout his life. It made clear to me that our soul has a calling and it's up to us to take the initiative to listen.

If you could turn back time and relive one moment of your life, what would it be?
My victory in the *Badwater 135*. The feeling I had during the last 30 seconds of that race can't be put into words. As soon as I got into ultra running, *Badwater 135* represented *the* ultra, *the* challenge. I had dreamed about that moment for a decade.

What is your definition of happiness?
It's tapping into your inner child. Look at children, they are happy because they listen to their heart instead of their head. If you listen to your heart and go on the journey of self-discovery

and exploration, you get to know yourself and you discover what you are capable of. It's by rising above yourself and going beyond your limits that you can find meaning and happiness.

Find out more about Michele:
www.michelegraglia.com
instagram.com/mickeygraglia
facebook.com/MicheleGragliaOfficial

Every Time I Talk to Someone, I Learn Something More About Myself

RICKEY GATES is an artistic adventurer who uses running as his canvas. After a decade of high performance in the world's most renowned mountain and trail races, Rickey ran across the U.S. as well as every single street in his hometown, San Francisco.

"After running races all over the world, I figured out that actually, I didn't know my neighbors. Projects such as the 'Transamericana' and 'Every Single Street' allowed me to connect to, understand, and unify the people around me."

Rickey, at the end of the movie about your run across the U.S. you say: "What I learned is to be content with who I am, where I am, what I am, and with whom I am. That would have solved a lot of problems in the past." Can you tell me a bit more about your spiritual journey?

My quote can be condensed to one word: *mindfulness.* The only moment we have is right now. As humans, we have the ability to mentally transfer to another place and time. This allows for empathy. The other side of the coin is that we can worry about the future, have regrets about the past, and forget to be present in the now. I feel as I'm getting older, I tend to get better at appreciating the moment. I'm more aware when my thoughts shift away to places that are of no use.

I started meditating long ago. I noticed how my fellow runners got injured and how this was real torture to them. This was because running was the most important thing in their life, it was the thing they identified themselves with. I wanted to anticipate the day I would get severely injured and figured out I needed something just as important as running. Something for which I wouldn't need my body, only my mind. This way I started meditation. The form of meditation I execute up until today is Vipassana, in which you concentrate on the sensations in your body. It's a very basic, pure form of meditation unrelated to any dogma or religion. I try to meditate every day and I attend a ten-day retreat almost every year. Meditation is just like running, you have to do it almost on a daily basis if you want to stay sharp.

Full Circle

25 years ago, I started running in the first place because I was looking for friends in high school. It's only in college that I discovered trail running and mountain running. Our cross-country coaches encouraged us to not only train on tracks and roads, but to challenge ourselves in nature. I'm still thankful for that, cause it's by doing so that I truly fell in love with running. Besides, it turned out that my body was much more suited to running long distances than it was for the high-speed cross country races. In this period, my main motivation for

running shifted from making friends to using running as a way to connect to nature and – I have to admit – to feed my ego.

On top of this, I discovered that running was a great means to travel the world. I traveled to Europe to participate in trail- and mountain running races and I even went working as a dishwasher in Antarctica so I could run a marathon over there. Once *Salomon* started sponsoring me I had the chance to run in Asia and South America too.

As I got older, competition became less interesting to me. I started reflecting on the fact that I had traveled to so many countries, I had immersed myself in so many cultures, but I didn't really know my neighbors, figuratively speaking. That's how I came up with the idea to run across America. Not to break a record, but to understand what lives in the hearts and souls of my countrymen. Once I had finished the Transamericana, I took my philosophy a step further and decided to run every single street in my adopted hometown San Francisco. This way, my running career has come full circle. I started out with the motivation to get to know my peers and 25 years later I'm on the same mission again. But it's definitely not the end of my evolution as a runner and person. I hope to continue running for the rest of my life and to continue learning more about the world and myself.

What does a typical training week look like?
I no longer have typical training weeks, but I used to. Before, I would do one or two very long runs a week. One speed training session, one hill run, and casual training sessions on the remaining days. Nowadays, it's much more about consistency. I've built up so much muscle memory that I'm able to go out and do an ultra run at every moment, as long as I manage to maintain a certain endurance routine. These days I do a lot of mountain biking and skiing and I'm using adventures such as *Every Single Street* as a way of maintaining mileage.

What would you want to write on a giant billboard in San Francisco?
I would just put my hashtag, #everysinglestreet.
You know how big tech companies put strange, mysterious texts on billboards to attract the right people for a job? Because maybe only one out of 1000 people get the message and it's exactly that one person they want to get on board. My hashtag, #everysinglestreet would be the same, some people would look it up and find more about the vision behind it.

What have been some of the choices that made you the Rickey Gates you are today?
In my early twenties, I decided to quit college and travel on my motorbike all the way down to South America. Later, in Europe, I also joined a famous English runner at the time, Martin Cox, who was training in the Alps. Martin was a vagabonding mountain runner who taught me a lot. I copied a lot of his lifestyle; living cheaply, using running as a way to connect with nature, vagabonding . . . I think everyone who has the chance to travel while they are young should do so.

Another important choice has been to refuse to pay more than 200 dollars in rent. I did that for ten years in my twenties. If I couldn't find a residence I liked for less than 200 dollars, I'd sleep in my car. Most people spend a whole lot of money on rent, food, and drinks in bars and restaurants. I did the exact opposite. I would work hard for a few months a year, save up as much as possible and travel the rest of the year. I feel that this habit of economic living still serves me today. I'm still very happy with very little.

Although they are materialistic objects, both the motorbike and the VW van I bought as a young man have been some of the best investments of my life because they gave me so much freedom.

Do you see yourself first as a runner or as an adventurer?
For most of the time, running has been a means to go on an adventure. I think that the adventure aspect of what I'm doing is more important than the running aspect. If I wouldn't have been a runner I would probably still have been a cyclist or skier doing adventures. I prefer to use running as an adventure because it's accessible to almost anyone.

You're a very creative person, do you feel arts and sports lift each other up?
I'm very grateful that my running career has allowed me to expand my pursuits in an artistic way. It is very difficult to make it as an artist. By running, I had the luck that both an audience and sponsors started following and supporting me. Along the way, I shared more and more of my photography and writing with them. Now I'm lucky that they appreciate that as well.

At the same time, it's important to stay mindful if you combine several passions. Hamish Fulton is an artist who inspires me a lot. Fulton is known as *The Walking Artist.* He walks around the world and makes art in the different places he visits. But he never makes art while walking - and his walking trips can be anywhere from 12 hours to 21 days - because in his philosophy it's important to be present in what you are doing at the moment. If you are walking and doing something else at the same time, you aren't fully aware of what you sense during the walk and that's a shame. Hence mindfulness.

If you had the chance to grab a beer with 3 people dead or alive, who would you choose?
1. Polar explorer Robert Falcon Scott.
2. Writer Henry Miller (he's one of the most honest and raw artists I know)
3. A random person on the street. During my last adventures, I had so many interesting conversations with random people on the street, sometimes homeless people. Homeless people are very content to have someone noticing and valuing them and they can tell you exceptional stories.

When we're asked a question like this, we tend to want to pick people who are famous. I can tell you that most people who have achieved success have become different people. For example, today I have 50,000 followers on Instagram and I must say that it's a challenge to stay true to myself. I know that a lot of people in my position start acting according to what the 50,000 followers want, instead of what they want themselves. So it's often more interesting to talk to random strangers on the street.

Why did you say yes to my request to participate in this book? With 50,000 followers your inbox must burst at its seams?

I say yes to everyone. It is my job, and I feel very fortunate to be in this position, fortunate to have all these conversations. Every time I talk to someone, I learn something more about myself.

If you became the next president of the United States, what would your opening speech be about?

It would be about unity. In politics nowadays, there's not much effort done in bringing people together, quite the opposite. What brings people together is having uncomfortable conversations. If you only speak to people who share your ideas, then that's nothing more than an echo chamber for the ego. It will only convince you more that you are right. Therefore, in my first hypothetical speech, I would encourage people to go on the street and start a conversation with someone who has a different opinion than they have and try to see the world from that person's viewpoint, try to understand why that person thinks in that way.

What do you believe that most people think is insane?

Everybody is good.

What does happiness mean to you?

Not needing much.

Not inflicting ill-will on other people.

Taking fresh air and moving your blood.

Offering to other people without the intention of getting something back.

Find out more about Rickey:

www.rickeygates.com

facebook.com/rickey.gates.39

instagram.com/rickeygates

Back Yourself: You're Tougher Than You Think!

JENNY TOUGH loves nature, mountains, and physical challenges. She's mostly outdoors by foot or bicycle and makes some wonderful short movies about her adventures.

"I love that I have the ultimate freedom in my life, but getting to share that with others and inspire more people to explore the outdoors is so incredibly rewarding, and that's what keeps me going."

An Adventurous Childhood

The seed for adventure was planted when I was ten years old. My parents led the ultimate example by taking the whole family on two years of traveling and adventure on a sailing boat. After coming back, we moved to the foot of the Rocky Mountains, where I learned outdoor and mountain survival skills throughout my teenage years. I also started running as a teenager, but it wasn't by heart. I saw running as punishment for eating, a way to burn calories. Honestly, I hated my body and I hated running. But gradually over the years, enjoyment began creeping in. I noticed that the days I ran were the days I felt best, and so I started expanding myself. When I finished high school, I started traveling and I used running as a way of exploring the new places I found myself. At age 20, I ran my first marathon. The confidence boost I gained from crossing that finish line changed my entire attitude to my body and my health.

Jenny's adventures

Baltic Sea Cycle (2015): cycling 3800 km around the Baltic Sea
Run Kyrgyzstan (2016): 900 km, 25 days
Bikepacking the Balkans (2017): 2000 km, 3 weeks
Running the Atlas mountains (2017): 860 km, 22 days
Transcontinental race (2017): bike-packing race across Europe
TransatlanticWay Race (2018): 2500km across Ireland - 2nd place
Running the Bolivian Andes (2018): 600 km, 17 days
Silk Road Mountain Race (2019): 1800 km across Kyrgyzstan - 1st place
Running the Southern Alps New-Zealand (2019): 23 days
Atlas Mountain Race (2020) - 1st place

The Adventure-Lifestyle

I love my lifestyle in many ways. I can do what I want, I'm connected with nature, I have great encounters with people, I achieve big goals, and I use my creativity. It's a constant process of self-development and I experience ultimate freedom. Getting to share my adventures with others and inspire more people to explore the outdoors is so incredibly rewarding, that's what keeps me going.

The hardest thing is the lack of a 'normal life.' It's hard missing events with friends and family when you're traveling all the time. My family and closest friends are incredibly important to me. I'm very fortunate to have a group of individuals who support my lifestyle. On the other hand, establishing any sense of a regular domestic life is pretty difficult, but I feel at home in nature. It's kind of spiritual, nature. Mountains in particular are where I feel most calm and present.

My life also involves danger. Risks are an inherent part of stepping out of the comfort zone. The point is to always plan ahead, try to predict what dangers may exist, and then mitigate against them. I spend a lot of my time in big mountains, often solo, where risks are naturally high. However, I'm experienced and always make the most responsible choices I can in those situations. I've faced rockslides, altitude problems, storms, men with guns, high-risk areas... all of it. As long as I'm comfortable with the situations I put myself in and have a plan for how I'll take care of myself, I can justify these risks.

Do you make use of any mental techniques before or during the adventures?
I believe in the power of visualization combined with positive self-talk. As many of the biggest challenges I pursue are solo, these are great techniques I can take on by myself. Especially in crisis situations in the backcountry when I need to find a way to perform.

The most difficult aspect is fear. For the last couple of years, I've been working on a global project to run across a mountain range on every continent, solo and unsupported. Sometimes, that means I have to run for more than 1000 km. Facing such a challenge is very intimidating, I would often find myself thinking: "You can't do this, this is too much, this isn't for you." So, I had to learn to break down my adventures into stages; divide them into manageable chunks.

Another technique I use is *'be the expedition buddy you wish you brought'.* Sometimes, when things get hard, I can be pretty hard on myself. There's this negative self-chat telling me I'm a terrible runner, I suck...and so on. But if I was there with a good friend – an expedition buddy – they would never speak to me like that and denigrate me at difficult moments. They would say nice things, they would encourage me. So I've started to invent this imaginary buddy supporting me.

It's always mentally difficult to finish an adventure. You're used to being outside, to seeing new things all the time, and suddenly you're back inside, seeing the same things again. After my early adventures, the blues hit quite hard. I think these experiences have taught me that it's important to have new goals to look forward to, but not to push myself too hard too soon in training; instead take the time to recover, to sleep well, to reduce my mileage, to do a lot of yoga.

Characteristics and Personality Traits
[I asked Jenny to rank herself from 0 (not like this trait at all) to 10 (very much like that)]

Optimism: 10
Discipline: 6
Courage: 10
Resilience 10
Stubbornness: 6
Social skills: 7
Creativity: 7
Intelligence: 7

How to 'Jump off the Cliff'

Set the target for what you want, and then take out a pen and paper and make a list of the things that stand between you and your goal. What are the reasons you're not doing that thing now? The list could include money, skills, fitness, family, whatever it is... Just list out those things that are stopping you from being where you want to be. Then, with a different pen, figure out how to get around each one. How can you save more money? Do you need to go on a course to gain some skills? Can you take your family with you?? There's an answer to everything, if it's really important to you.

Back yourself: you're tougher than you think.

Find out more about Jenny:
www.jennytough.com
instagram.com/jennytough
facebook.com/jenniferjtough

You Are Allowed to Be Scared

KRISTINA PALTEN climbed Mount Aconcagua, ran 322 km in a 48-hour push on a treadmill. and alternately ran and kayaked from Turkey all the way home to Sweden. But she is mostly known for her inspiring run through Iran, which made 40 million people look at the country through a different lens. Despite the challenges Kristina faces, she's far from an adrenaline junkie.

"I've learned to deal with the fears. As long as the desire, purpose, and meaning of my adventure is worth the feeling of fear, it's ok."

Getting out of the "normal" life

The hardest thing about my journey was to let go. To let go of what I thought was "a normal life," my own supposition that I had to live like everybody else, the picture of having a husband, children, a house, a full-time job, being exhausted on Friday evening's and being satisfied with a bit of happiness during the weekends and vacations…

It was also hard to let go of financial stability. I was used to having a well-paid, full-time job and building a pile of money that I did not know how to spend. I remember sitting at the office, at age 44, thinking: "I want to see who I am when I am in full freedom." My partner calculated that, with the savings I had, I would be able to live for 4 years. So, at that moment, my curiosity and urge to do what I wanted to do – have adventures – had become stronger than the financial insecurity. I thought: "Even if I can't live in freedom for the rest of my life, I will have at least those 4 years." So, I quit my job as an engineer and project manager and went to Iran.

Running and Kayak

By the time I plunged into the big unknown in 2015, I had already completed a couple of challenges. I began running at age 31, starting off with 10km-races and from there on gradually building up the distance, each time out of curiosity to see what I was capable of. In 2010, I did my first 24-hour race, in 2011 I ran 750 km from Karlstad (Sweden) to Trondheim (Norway) and in 2013 I broke the 12-hour treadmill world record. Later that year, I ran with my dear friend Carina Borén from Turkey to Finland, good for 3200 km, and then kayaked the last 500 km home to Stockholm.

In February 2014, Carina and I had planned another kayak adventure: from Stockholm to Gothenburg. One day, there was a lot of wind and Carina preferred not to paddle. But I insisted, saying we could always turn back if the weather would get too bad. My ass, there was no way of turning back, we got into waves of 1,5m high. The wind was blowing at 45 km/hour and leading us in the direction of a rock wall. If our kayak would have tipped over, we would have smashed against these rocks and it could have meant the end… I do remember that I got extremely focused in the moment, and finally we managed to come ashore on a small island. We hugged each other for several minutes and then ate a whole bunch of nuts… But I felt so ashamed that I had convinced Carina to depart that morning, I had brought the two of us in danger... I offered her my excuses. Angel as she is, she forgave me.

Fear

A couple of days later on this kayak trip to Gothenburg, we encountered big waves again. I knew we could handle them easily, but because of what had happened I was shaking and feeling afraid. I let the feeling exist, even made a small song about it « Du får vara rädd, det är helt okej » meaning « You are allowed to be scared, it is totally okay ». I kept on singing that song again and again to myself until my body ceased trembling and I was fine with the waves.

Compared to many other adventurers, I'm no thrill-seeker. I'm actually a very cautious person. Once I was at a leadership training with a company. After hearing about my adventures, the students at that leadership program had to guess my personality traits. Everyone thought that I would be fearless, dominant, and extroverted, but the reality is quite the contrary: I am a bit shy, introverted, and humble. What the students failed to see was that I had found a way to handle my fears. I do this by observing and rationalizing them. For example: before my run through Iran I wrote all of my fears down, there were 22 of them. Then I gave them a severity score from 0 to 100, where 100 was what would make me extremely fearful. Then I defined what I could do to prevent them from happening and also what I could do if they really happened. This exercise made me feel much more confident.

I also try to be really conscious about the feeling of fear. We humans have a brain that is five times more sensitive to threat than to what makes us feel secure, so a lot of our fears are totally irrational. So what I try to do is to be really aware of what's going on in my body, and then ask myself if the situation is really dangerous. Often, it turns out that it isn't very dangerous and insecure.

Every adventure is a balance between longing and curiosity on the one side and fear on the other side. The perfect adventure for me is when the desire is slightly greater than the fear. I think it's unhealthy to let your life be run too much by fear, that's why I've made the decision to never let fear determine my life.

Inspiring 40 Million People

My two treadmill world record attempts, the 12- and 48-hour, were two moments of fear since I did them in the presence of hundreds of people in the gym, and 10,000 people following me on screen. But on the other side of the fear was the realization that I had a tremendous impact on a lot of people. And I could have this impact by doing what I love: running. I knew that I was inspiring at least some of them to start their own journey towards fulfilling their dreams.

With my solo run through Iran, I managed to reach even much more people. First of all, the local people. They were so generous. They invited me to sleep in their houses, they prepared meals for me, they offered a tremendous amount of gifts, lots of fruits... in the end, I had only spent half of my foreseen budget thanks to the kindness of the Iranian people!

I had a camera with me, and an Iranian photographer followed me for 8 days as well. With the footage, filmmakers André Larsson and Shamim Berkeh created a documentary. I gave them my material for free and never earned a penny from it. The trailer has been seen by 30 million people and the film has been shown in over 15 countries. Besides, the Guardian picked up the story and made their own film about it, which has been seen by 15 million people now. Although I didn't earn directly from the movies, I got quite some fame out of it, which created a lot of opportunities. For the last 4 years I've been earning my income thanks to giving lectures about my run through Iran, and the book I wrote about it. But even more important: my story influenced the way Westerners look at Iran and its inhabitants... By spending 2 months of time and 1200€, I've been able to reach out to more than 40 million people and give them an honest picture of the kindness and generosity of Iran, the contrary of what the mass media shows us. I'm very proud of that.

Listening Inwards

I've done several types of spiritual and mental training; Gestalt Therapy and Psychosynthesis, image therapy, releasing dance, attending tantra workshops... Nowadays, I do one hour of meditation every morning. I've also experienced that endurance running and being in nature in themselves are a form of mind training.

To me, personal development comes through challenges where I am stepping out of my comfort zone in various ways. That means that I also consider writing a book as an adventure since that was also stepping out of my comfort zone. I also consider therapy as a challenging adventure, because it is on the inside I find the biggest challenges and the biggest ups and downs.

The most profound, mysterious experience during all my adventures was when I was standing on the top of a small hill in Iran, experiencing truly and deeply that I was one with everything, and everything was one with me. The wind was blowing through me, yet I was the wind. There was no time, no room, just that moment and everything that existed right there and then.

When planning an adventure, I would say that the important thing is to be real, to be authentic, to be true to yourself. If you're looking for a sponsor, make sure they never let you do something that is against your own values. Make sure it is you who has the final word and that you're fulfilling your own dreams, not someone else's.

I've experienced that when I do what I love, money comes. It should never be the other way around, except in times of financial crisis. I am aware that I am talking out of a very privileged position when I am stating this.

Don't set targets out of the personal resources you have, that will never create any miracles. The reason is: most of us are unaware of our resources. By going out in the wild, by leaving your comfort zone, and confronting yourself, you discover your resources and you can create anything you want. To be able to do that, you have to let go and trust Life, God, The Universe, your own Inner Strength, or whatever you want to call it.

The advice I give young people is: "Be yourself. Love yourself. Listen inwards. Try different things. Travel. Expose yourself to new ideas, people, cultures, worlds, ways of living. That makes you get perspective on yourself. Evaluate what you like in what others are doing and creating, or in the way they are living, and adopt what you like."

Taking Responsibility

Before running through Iran, one man asked me how much it was worth to do this run. Was it worth the cost of my life? I thought about his question for several days and finally, I ended up with the answer: "Yes, it is worth dying for." My urge to contribute to building a world of trust, curiosity, and openness between people and cultures was so incredibly strong that I was willing to take the risk of dying. I thought: "What is the meaning of life if I don't live for what I believe in?" I did not want to crawl away like a coward just because of the fear of death. The moment I realized that it was ok for me to die while doing what I believed in, a new fear came. That was the fear of being a fundamentalist. I thought: "Fundamentalists are also willing to die for what they believe in, what is the difference between them and me?". That question troubled me for a couple of days until a friend of mine said: "Fundamentalists cause other people to die. The only one who is jeopardized in your adventure is you". Then I felt much better. It is ok to risk my own life as long as I don´t risk other people's lives. But then came up another question every adventurer has to deal with: "What responsibility do I have towards the people who love me?" Before my run through Iran, my sister Ulrika was worried that I'd get into trouble, she said: "What am I going to do with mom's and dad's sorrow if you never come home?" At first, her remark made me feel terrible, disgustingly selfish, ashamed. Until I realized Ulrika had projected her own worries on our parents. I came to the conclusion that my sister's worry is her responsibility and she needs to take care of that. However, at the same time, I made arrangements to comfort and reassure all my loved ones that I was safe: I borrowed a live GPS tracker, I did send regular messages home, saying that I was safe, I gave my whereabouts to the Swedish embassy in Iran, and an Iranian-born friend of mine closely monitored Iranian newspapers in order to inform me about potential dangers.

Words of Thanks

First of all, I have to thank Carina Borén, for always being there for me and loving me no matter which bastard I can be from time to time. My parents Inger and Fritjof Wikström for withstanding the fact that I am making them worried and still being able to cope with that. My partner Fredrik Lindblad for being my light, always supporting and appreciating me, and becoming inspired by seeing me fulfilling my dreams. Rune Larsson for teaching Carina and me how to run long distances and how to make multiple day journeys by kayak. Anders Lundh and Anders Mohlin for teaching Carina and me how to kayak and camp during wintertime and Anders Lundh also for always being positive and coming up with thousands of ideas about how to handle the challenges I meet. And my ex-husband Jan Rydberg for divorcing me so that I did not end up living a "normal" life.

Alone Together

Silence and solitude are necessary for my mental health. It is difficult for me to deliver high-quality lectures if I am exhausted from meeting too many people and being the center of attention all of the time. My best way to mentally recover is to go spend time in the kayak, preferably alone. I'm very lucky right now, I'm living 200m off the shore, so that makes it easy.

I think personal development comes from balancing time in solitude and being exposed to other people at the same time. Having good relations is the key to happiness, meaning, laughter, creating new, crazy ideas, and opening the mind. Actually, life as an adventurer is perfect for me. If I would be with my friends and family all the time I would become bored, if I would be doing adventures all the time I would be exhausted. It feels good to rest in the arms of loved ones after an adventure.

Find out more about Kristina:
www.palten.se
facebook.com/kristina.palten
instagram.com/kristina_palten

Don't Run at Night, Don't Get Drunk, Don't Have Sex With Local Women. If You Follow These Rules, You'll Probably Be Alright.

*After 12 years of working for an international communications agency, **JAMIE RAMSAY** wasn't happy with the direction of his life. The solution he came up with: running 17,000 km from Vancouver to Buenos Aires. It was the start of a professional career in 'doing what he wants'.*

"The most difficult part of my story was leaving my job and taking the plunge. From there on, everything took care of itself."

A Conversation Fabricated in the Mind

Like so many people, I had no idea what I wanted to do when I was 18 years old. So I did the usual thing, the thing society expects you to do: studying. Influenced by my father who was a businessman I decided to study economics. This way, after graduation, I stumbled into the typical city life in London: getting a car, buying a flat, paying a mortgage, working 9-to-5. For my job in financial communications, I felt no passion at all, but it paid the bills. And that's a dangerous deal because this way you get trapped in something you hate. That's why I looked for outlets; I went to the gym, started running races, followed by triathlons . . . but I went to the bar just as much as I escaped into sports. Spending entire nights in bars and clubs and getting shitfaced, in the World I was living in it's a common thing . . .

I remember one night I went out until about 4 o'clock and got very drunk. I said to myself I might just as well immediately go to the office, instead of losing time by taking a stopover at my apartment. So I slept it off and when I looked in the shower mirror at work the following morning, I said to myself: "This isn't going in the right direction, Jamie, you have to make some serious changes in your life." Sitting at my desk, I looked around me and said to myself that my colleagues are not at all who I want to be. But who did I want to be?... I tried to remember the last time I had been really proud of myself. That was when I had run 240 km through the jungle of Vietnam all by myself, a couple of months before. I knew this was what I had to pursue.

Looking back, I mainly chose the financial career path because I didn't want to disappoint people. I wanted to do what was expected of me, or at least what I thought was expected of me . . . When I left my job, I had a conversation with my dad about this. He said: "I never wanted you to do like me and work in the city, that's a conversation you fabricated in your own mind. I just want you to be happy." I think a lot of people do live up to perceived expectations about how to live a life, but in fact, most of the people around us just want us to be happy.

People Told Me I Wasn't Ready. They Were Right

When I decided to take the plunge, I came up with the plan to run from Vancouver to Buenos Aires. Actually, I didn't have enough money to run the entire distance, but I did have enough money to at least start the challenge. I calculated that I would probably have enough to make it to Panama City, and that would already make me proud. People think that an adventure like this is complicated to organize. But actually, it isn't at all. You need to have the equipment, the flight tickets, and the physical preparation. The most difficult part of my story was leaving my job and taking the plunge. From there on, everything took care of itself.

A second thing people told me was that I wouldn't make it, that it is impossible to run through the Atacama desert or across the Andes. And they were right: the Jamie that left in Vancouver wouldn't have been able to face those challenges. But by the time I got to the Atacama and the Andes, I had spent months alone, pulling a stroller, I had run thousands of kilometers in all kinds of circumstances. The Jamie that arrived at those places was a different, much stronger person. My advice to people is: "If you want to do something, don't overthink it. Just start, and as you push yourself, the mental, physical, and often financial part will follow automatically."

Adventure Isn't for Everyone

I think that a lot of our sense for adventure is in our DNA . . . Today, there's this philosophy of organizations like *Yes-Tribe* that say: "If you go on an adventure, you'll be happy" . . . I don't think that's necessarily true. I think you need to have a certain personality type in order to enjoy the discomfort and adversity. A lot of people like structure, they like a simple family life, a stable income, knowing what their future will bring . . . To me, this kind of predictable and comfy lifestyle was a struggle, it felt like a real sacrifice. I'm happy when I'm on an adventure, when I'm pushing myself, and when I'm in a space of discomfort. I feel a natural affinity for harsh environments. I crave those places, it's where I feel pleasure. It's just when I'm in a 'normal' society that I find it mentally difficult. It's also why you shouldn't believe the critics. If people tell you you're not able to complete a certain expedition, they're telling you because they think they aren't capable themselves.

The mindset of an endurance adventurer must be: "I'm going to do this thing until the end, no matter what happens." I'm very hard on myself. I have a lack of self-worth, so I need to prove to myself that I can do something, that I'm strong. I haven't found this by doing something academically, or by doing business. It's only by exploring my possibilities and pushing the boundaries during an adventure that I gain confidence. We all have a perceived ceiling of our possibilities. I have experienced that when you push through that ceiling, you find a massive amount of new possibilities. That's what has driven me to do these adventures again and again... I've now built a routine of breaking ceilings.

It's Good to Have Someone Who is Worried About You

I'm very lucky. I have two brothers and one sister and we are all very close. We never have arguments, there's no messiness. As soon as I started going on adventures, my father became one of my biggest supporters. Our relationship is much closer now compared to when we were both in business. His acceptance and encouragement are a big thing for me. I think all men want some kind of approval from their fathers.

My mother is just as important in my journey. I'm a mommy's boy, I always have been. You know, it's nice to have someone worrying about you when you're adventuring, this makes you remember that there's someone out there who loves you. It keeps me making safe decisions as well.

When I was running *The Americas*, the local people in Peru told me I shouldn't run through the desert, because there were bandits and this could make the situation dangerous. At that moment, I was totally fine taking the risk, I could accept the idea of dying. But afterward, I thought about the people close to me, and it would be a disaster for them if I'd passed away. Since then, I take this danger a lot more into consideration when I plan my adventures.

Our happiness is what makes the people around us happy, that's important to remember. Actually, it bothers me that the adventurers who put themselves in danger get paid the most for their stories. Getting into trouble and nearly dying isn't my definition of a good adventure. I've had traffic accidents, I've run out of water, I've climbed dangerous walls. These were potentially life-threatening situations, but they didn't come unexpectedly so I knew how to handle them.

In essence, there are some simple rules to keep everything safe: train well, prepare well, don't interfere with people's life along the road. I know that if I don't run at night, I don't get drunk and I don't have sex with local women, I'll probably be alright.

Doing What I Want

A big inspiration for me has been Alan Watts' famous speech 'What if money was no object?'. Watts asks the question of what you would do with your life if you didn't have to worry about money. "Then, do that", Watts says, "Because if you keep doing the thing you like doing, you'll eventually master it and you'll get paid for being a master." Me running *The Americas* was putting this into reality. It was such a transformational experience and totally changed the direction of my life…

When people ask me what I'm doing for a living, I tell them that my job is to work for brands by creating content, doing talks, testing kits … the work happens when I'm not on an adventure. Basically, I work to pay for my adventures, and I do my adventures to get more work. I'm always honest and authentic and this resonates with the brands I work with. I'm happy to have sponsors that don't ask me to do a certain adventure, they kind of trust me and are willing to follow me on the journey.

I don't do World's Firsts, I don't do records, I don't want to be famous. I'm doing this for myself. I choose adventures based on the criteria of what they're going to teach me, how they will make me grow, what they will present to me… I basically look for a combination of an experience that will be beautiful and will make me proud of myself. That's why I prefer to go solo. During an adventure in Iceland, I ended up running with other people. Therefore, I couldn't push it as hard as I wanted and was left with less satisfaction than usual.

Adventuring and traveling are hugely exciting. There's a danger that you can make it mundane, you can become bored. You have to be clever to make sure you're adventuring on your terms, for your benefits, not for the benefits of others. Because there's the danger of falling out of love with the wonderful world of adventure, that would be a very sad thing.

Lifestyle Design
I hate social media, but I understand the importance of it if you want to create a personal brand and get a following. Social media also allows me to stay in touch with my friends. I'm lucky to have a couple of friends who've always supported me, and thanks to technology we can stay in touch even while living far apart from each other.

I have the feeling that my experiences of adventure help me in day-to-day life. During COVID-19, I was living all alone in a house in Southern France, but I managed to keep a routine, stay productive, and not let watching TV and playing video games become my life.

When it comes to training, I'm doing a lot of cross-training. I'm never focussing on one discipline. I run, I hike, I cycle, I do yoga, and a lot of strength work as well. I want to be physically ready at any time to jump on an opportunity that comes along.

If I could give advice to people, it would be: "Get out of toxic environments as fast as possible. Whether it's a relationship, a friendship, or a workplace environment . . . it's very dangerous. It seeps into your soul very quickly."

It's important to be flexible, to be able to adapt to new circumstances. I know that I won't be able to stay an adventurer forever, one day I'll have to take a job again. But I'm confident that I'll find a job I like because I know how to adapt easily.

Setbacks
My biggest setback as an adventurer was Madagascar 2019. I had planned to run the island from north to south, and I wanted to celebrate my 40th anniversary on the trip. Three weeks before take-off, I twisted my foot in a rabbit hole during a run. It was bad, I couldn't stand on my foot. I didn't train for three weeks but left anyway because I thought I would be able to handle it. Besides, there were the expectations of my followers and the fact that I had put in the money. So I arrived in Madagascar and decided to do a test run without a backpack. My ankle hurt so much that I thought "What am I doing? Why am I here?" The good thing is, it taught me something, just like every setback. I learned that pride had made me make the wrong decision. If what you're doing isn't a learning experience, you're doing the wrong thing and have to change.

What's your advice to an 18-year old that has no idea what to do with their life?
Define your passions and make passion a massive part of your life. Either you try to make a full-time living out of your passion, or you play it safer and get a job to finance your passions.

What's the impact you want to have on the world?

I want people to be happy, I want them to be inspired, I would love it if I could enable other people to inspire them to go on an adventure. On a bigger scale, I would like to get into some kind of beach cleaning project.

Find out more about Jamie:

www.jamieramsay.net
facebook.com/jamieisadventuring
instagram.com/jamieisrunning

There is a Deep Desire Within Me to be My Best Animal

DEAN KARNAZES , a.k.a. Ultra Marathon Man, ran 50 marathons – one in each of the 50 United States – in 50 consecutive days. He has run 350 continuous miles without sleep and has run across the Sahara Desert as well as along the Silk Road. Dean also was the first man to run a marathon in Antarctica and he has won the Badwater 135, known as the world's toughest footrace.

"A life well-lived is simply being the person that you are. Shakespeare said it well: 'To thine own self be true.'"

Follow Your Heart and You Will Never Lose Your Way

I grew up as the oldest of 3 kids. My brother Kraig is one year younger and my sister Pary was 3 years younger than me. My earliest running memories go back to kindergarten. I didn't want to burden my mother with getting me home from school every day, so I started running. At first, I took the shortest way in between school and my home. But after a while, I started exploring alternative, longer trajectories. It didn't take long before I enjoyed running to school more than attending it. As I grew older I continued exploring and pushing my physical abilities. By the time I was eleven years old, I had already trekked rim-to-rim-to-rim across the Grand Canyon fully self-supported and climbed Mount Whitney, the highest mountain in the U.S. outside of Alaska.

In junior high school, I was on the track-and-field team. The training theory of my first coach was simple: "Whoever was willing to run the hardest, train the longest, and suffer the most would be the one crossing the finish line first." With this theory in mind, I progressed as a runner and eventually won a couple of races. Nevertheless, at age 15 I hung up my shoes and wouldn't run anymore for the next fifteen years.

My sister Pary died on the eve of her eighteenth birthday in a car accident. She was a very beautiful, radiant, vibrant girl and her sudden disappearance left my family in despair. A few years after her passing away, my dad started running. Though it was unspoken, I think it was his way of paying tribute to his daughter. I, however, kept active by mountain climbing, scuba diving, and most of all: windsurfing. After graduating from business school, I started working in the marketing department of a major healthcare company. I was making decent money and living the idyllic yuppie lifestyle. As the years rolled by, however, work was stressing me out. I felt hollow inside, something was missing. The advice Pary had once given me echoed through my mind: "Follow your heart and you will never lose your way."

On the day of my 30th birthday, I realized that my life was being wasted. I had succumbed to the trappings of the corporate world. Making a lot of money and buying useless stuff had taken over what was really important; friendships, exploration, personal expansion, and a sense of meaning. That night, after getting really drunk, I left my celebrating buddies behind in the night club. I went home, pulled off my pants and sweater, put on a pair of sneakers, and started running in my underwear in the streets of San Francisco. I covered 30 miles that night and never stopped running ever since.

Why did it take you till your 30th birthday – nine years after Pary's passing away – to listen to the advice she had given you?
There is a grieving cycle one goes through during great loss. At first, there was anger. I was mad at the Universe, at God, for taking her away from us. Then came denial, I simply refused to believe she was gone. This, of course, was delusional. Once I finally accepted her passing, I became consumed with sadness. After nearly a decade of hurt, I came to the conclusion that my behavior would not be something that made her proud. Upon that realization, I decided instead to live every moment of my life to its utmost to celebrate and honor her.

You are well-known to run a marathon before breakfast on most days. On top of this, you do a series of strength exercises in the afternoon. How do you stay driven to keep training that hard?
The fire is within. There is a deep desire within me to be my best animal. Though let's be honest, it also comes down to having the self-discipline and drive to motivate yourself. Not every day is easy.

Life Lesson
I've taught my children: "Dreams can come true, especially if you train hard enough."

If tomorrow you were elected as the first 'President of the World'; what would be the first thing you'd change and/or put your energy into?
My solution for world peace is that our leaders must meet and negotiate in the buff. Nothing is more humanizing than public nudity. Could you imagine Trump, Kim Jung-un, and Angela Merkel in a room together in their birthday suits? That would be a spectacle!

If you were an angel who had the ability to stick a post-it note on the desk of every unhappy businessman in San Francisco, what would you write on it?
Failure is better than not having tried.

What is your definition of a life well-lived?
Being the person that you are. Shakespeare said it well: "To thine own self be true."

Find out more about Dean:
www.ultramarathonman.com
instagram.com/ultramarathon
facebook.com/DeanKarnazes

Natural Spaces Provide Me The Opportunity to be The Best Version of Myself

DAKOTA JONES is a professional trail runner with side-passions for climbing, writing, and environmental protection. Some of his biggest athletic accomplishments are placing second and third place in two 'Hardrock 100' races and wins in the 'Transvulcania' and 'Pikes Peak Marathon'. As a climate activist, Dakota supports 'Protect Our Winters' and is the organizer of 'Footprints Camps', in which he brings academic experts and college runners together.

"Today, the focus of my career is to find an answer to the question of how we can run races and protect the places where we run at the same time."

An Adventurous Youth

I've been really blessed to have grown up in the mountains and to have a dad who had a big influence on me. From a very young age, he took me out into the desert and the mountains. We went climbing, skiing, hunting, cycling, camping . . . everything. My dad taught me a lot. Honestly, at first, I didn't like the mountains that much. I wished I could spend my weekends hanging out in town with my friends. That shifted when I was 15 years old and our family moved to Colorado. Up there I took a class called 'Outdoor Vacation'. We went skiing, mountain biking, and rock climbing . . . and learned how to do every activity technically correct and in a safe way.

That is where I fell in love with rock climbing and started dreaming about it. My desire was to go climbing all over the world, on rocks and mountains. The problem is that the climbing sport isn't super accessible. You need to find a group of climbers, you have to invest in ropes and gear, and there are a lot of technical things to learn. When I was 17 years old I went volunteering on the *Hardrock 100*, one of the most renowned ultra runs in the United States. That's where it sunk in that I could already have all the adventures I wanted simply by running.

How Running Led to Climate Activism

I guess that a big part of what drew me to trail running is that in the community, I recognized the same values my father had instilled in me. Trail runners highly value experiencing nature, feeling alive, and sharing experiences with each other. My dad too had taught me that being in the mountains is about living the best life you can. We can have a normal life in the cities, have our day job and other occupations, but in order to get the most in touch with ourselves we have to go to the backcountry. He also said to me: "Dakota, you can do everything you set your mind to." This belief definitely contributed to my ambition as soon as I entered the sport.

Nevertheless, competition has never been my main motivation. Racing was a fun side thing, but what was really important was the connection to the land and the people, as well as the process of self-development that comes with challenging yourself and setting big goals.

If your entire value system is based on experiences in nature and the people with whom you have those experiences, it doesn't take much thought to understand that if those natural places disappear, so will the experiences. So far as I can remember environmental issues have always been important to me. In the first years of my career as a professional trail runner, I flew thousands of miles overseas to run races in Europe and felt guilty about that every time. In 2014, I stepped out of the *Ultra Trail du Mont Blanc* because I felt that I shouldn't be there. I felt as if the race wasn't worth the carbon emissions my flight had caused. During those years, I always wanted to get in action to protect our environment, but for too long I felt as if I wasn't expert enough. I didn't feel qualified enough to talk about the problem. In 2016, when Donald Trump was elected as the new president of the United States, I realized the world was coming to an end if we didn't take massive action. That's where I really started my climate activism, just with the knowledge and experience I had at that time, and more importantly by aiming to learn as much about the topic as possible.

A Double-Edged Sword

Being an athlete and a climate activist at the same time is a big challenge, it is something I really struggle with. I want to be competing, I love racing, I want to be the best athlete I can possibly be. And I want to run the races I love; Europe has such cool races where I participated in the past and where I would like to go back and do better. But because they are so far away, traveling to the start line comes with a large carbon impact. Most of the time that's enough to convince me not to travel overseas.

Also in terms of relevance in the sport and being interesting for sponsors, being a climate activist turns out to be a double-edged sword. I don't travel that much, so I don't race that much and I don't win that much. It is difficult to maintain my place in the sport while also doing the right thing for the planet. My career now is really centered around finding the right answer to deal with this conundrum. Trying to find an answer is the reason I went back to engineering school. It is the reason why I study Climate Science and have set up camps to empower young athletes to make a change themselves. Unfortunately, I still don't have the answer right now, but it seems to be that my quest to find the answer is interesting and worthwhile to people. I think that a lot of people can relate to my situation. We want to travel, see new places, meet new people, but at the same time we don't want to harm those places and people.

If running a race and protecting the place where I want to run are contradictory, my personal choice is most often – not always – to prioritize protecting the environment over running. The best situation is when you don't have to choose. The *Pikes Peak Marathon* I won in 2018 was the perfect example of this, because I went to and from the race on my bicycle and was still able to compete at the highest level. Going there on the bike meant that I had to acknowledge right from the start that it could jeopardize my race and I had to be ok with that. I wanted to show the World that protecting the place where I run is higher in my value hierarchy than running at my peak ability. In reality, not going there by car didn't save all that much carbon, but it was a statement about the priorities I chose to demonstrate. Luckily, it turned out that cycling the 250 miles to the start line didn't have an influence on my performance. That's really cool because this way I showed people that you can travel to a race in a sustainable way and still compete at the highest level and – as was my case – even win the race. You don't have to choose between the two, so there's no reason to not try it out yourself.

I do also believe that incorporating climate change into the running and outdoor community is more powerful than just informing people by means of academic knowledge. Because emotionally we (outdoor athletes) feel connected to nature and thus want to protect it. If we can contextualize the solutions the scientific world already has figured out, in a passionate community, we can make a difference. That is why *Protect Our Winters* is so successful. They bring scientists and passionate outdoor athletes together. It is also what I'm trying to do with my *Footprints Camps*. I might be the organizer, but it's not my role to come up with new solutions to protect our landscape. It is my role to connect the people who already know solutions – scientists and academics – with the community of runners.

Would the world be a better place if adventure were an obligatory course in school?
That would be amazing! Adventurers and outdoor athletes don't feel separate from nature, they feel part of nature and feel that nature is part of them. As I said before, I am very grateful to have grown up in cities where we were within walking or cycling distance from wonderful natural places. The experiences in that environment made me feel connected to nature and thus willing to take care of it. A lot of children living in big cities don't have access to nature like I did. As a consequence, they don't build values around it because they don't interact with it on a regular basis. If we were to force kids to have a course in adventure, a lot of them would not be interested at first, because they don't have this sense of connection. But a large percentage of the kids that would take the class in adventure would realize that it is a really cool thing to do.

A class in adventure would also give us a strong sense of purpose. I don't like to use generalizations, but I think that a lot of people nowadays have forgotten what it means to struggle. Most people want to start something and be good at it right away. I believe that it's important for our well-being to meet a challenge and struggle with it, to become frustrated, but to keep on working on it and overcome it. Because overcoming something difficult gives us a strong sense of purpose, it validates us, it makes us feel proud and worthy. Overcoming obstacles and facing challenges is something that happens every time you go on an adventure, whether it's rock climbing or running or skiing, whatever. You get tired, cold, hungry, a little scared . . . but you get over it. The sense of worthiness that gives us is one of the biggest things I get out of the mountains, even more than the connection to nature in itself. As a matter of fact, it's the natural spaces that provide me the opportunity to be the best version of myself.

You are a professional runner, you are studying engineering, you organize *Footprints Camps*, you support other environmental organizations, and you're a writer. How are you able to fit everything into your schedule?
It is insane sometimes. You know, in this world everybody always seems to be willing to be busier and more productive than anybody else. I don't want to be part of that race, I don't want to be that guy who is busy all the time. At the same time, I'm ambitious. I want to

accomplish things and contribute to the world and that requires a lot of work. I admit that often I take on a lot of projects and at a certain moment they become too much. But throughout the years I'm getting better at asking for help. My *Footprints Camps* are a good example of that. I may be the organizer, but it's not my goal to be the center of attention. There are people working at the camps who are of more value than I am. The exact point of the camps actually is that I'm the one who brings people together, not the one who's talking and presenting and answering questions. My role is to bring environmental experts and athletes together and delegate tasks.

Running is something I really need. I have to exercise. If I don't exercise, I feel miserable, I feel like the worst person, I hate myself. It's an addiction in a certain way, I just have to do it and I always make time for it.

When it comes to my studies, that takes up a lot of time because I can't ask for help as much. I'm the one who has to do the homework. This also means that during the academic year I hardly get to write. But when the semester ends, a lot of time frees up and I get back to writing a lot more. So besides asking for help, chunking my time by focusing on one thing for a certain extent of time is another way to get my different areas of interest aligned.

If you were elected as the new 'President of the World', what would be the first thing you would change?

I think that would be the worst job imaginable. No matter what you do, people are going to hate you. Nevertheless, a president has a lot of power. A president can demonstrate very strong practices and push a lot of powerful agencies and organizations in the right direction. The opposite holds true as well, and that is what Donald Trump has shown us. Trump has used the power of the president to undo things, to separate, to ruin.

If I would be the president, climate change would of course be a big focus of my actions. But it wouldn't be the first thing I would tackle. The reason is that imposing all kinds of regulations to improve the protection of our natural environment is not necessarily a good plan in the long term. The president who'd follow me will have the power to change all the rules and actions I'd put in place. So my first job would be to improve communication and unify the people, that is really the foundation according to me. The U.S.A. is very polarized today, there are very opposing views in society. I think that one of the fundamental problems is that people feel unheard. As a result, there is a lot of anger and bitterness in society. If I were the new president of the U.S. or – hypothetically speaking – of the world, I would figure out a way to be able to listen and communicate effectively with the people and unify them. This is what would encourage them to take actions themselves in favor of our society and our planet.

What is the biggest gift someone can give to Dakota Jones?

A donation to an environmental cause. It's something my sister has done every Christmas for the last couple of years and I really like it. You know, I have enough gear. I can get stuff for free from my sponsors, repair things or even do without. I don't need more stuff, things are just things. Instead, a donation to a good cause is a real precious gift, because it makes you reflect. Let's say someone offers you a donation once a year, for Christmas or your birthday. This donation makes you ask the question: "Have I made the world a little bit better the past year?"

What has been the best compliment someone ever gave you?

Recently, I received a letter from a friend who has participated in the *Footprint Camps*. I had sent her a t-shirt and a bag of goodies and she replied with a note to thank me, including a quote that said: "The true value of a leader is not in the work they do, but in the work they inspire other people to do."

What has been the best advice someone gave you which you did or did not follow?

The first one is to make a long-term plan and follow it. I could have been more successful in my twenties if I could have thought multiple years in advance. I was just always more interested in the things that looked fun to do in the short term. But if you want to accomplish big things, you have to think far in advance and take a whole lot of small steps in order to get there. Kilian Jornet is a personal friend of mine and he is a real master in planning for the long term.

The second piece of advice comes from my dad actually. It is to be honest with people. In the past, I struggled with telling people the truth if I knew it would hurt them. Throughout the years, I think I've become better at being straightforward and telling people things they don't want to hear. It's difficult, I'm a nice guy, I want to make people happy. Nevertheless, I feel as if this genuity and authenticity are appreciated. I have the impression that it has given me a position in the sport where people trust me - to a certain extent anyway. Actually, often being authentic means saying "I don't know." If someone asks you a question and you don't know the answer, don't say some bullshit so people will think you are smart, but just honestly admit that you don't know the answer.

Book Recommendations

Amusing Ourselves to Death, by Neil Postman.

It's a book written in 1985, in which Postman explains how television has become the dominant form of dialogue in society. Television dictates the way people think and communicate with the world around them. Postman's core message is that television - by the way it is designed - will always be a way of entertainment and if we use this medium to talk about serious issues, these serious issues will stay very limited in their scope and we won't value them in the right way.

What Postman says about television is even more true in regard to social media today. Trump was the perfect example. He was the ideal social media president. He didn't say things that really matter, but things that get attention, that raise people's blood pressure, things that cause scandals. On social media today, people are rewarded – by likes and shares – if they cause a scandal and make people angry. Trump knew this better than anyone else and that is why he was so successful.

I read several books by Postman and I really appreciate his approach to our technological society. Postman doesn't say that we shouldn't be entertained, but he warns us that we should be careful to acknowledge entertainment as entertainment and that political discourses and other serious issues are discussed in a serious manner. So I think it is important for people to read this book to understand that social media, if used in the wrong way, can be a form of discourse that damages the integrity of our society.

What do you believe that most people think is insane?

I don't have a good answer for this. Because in my mind everything Donald Trump says is insane, he is an insane character. Yet, tens of millions of my countrymen still voted for him. I'm flipped upside down by that. Maybe what I'm thinking and doing is insane? Maybe most people think that running and climbing and skiing are insane things to do? Maybe most people believe I am insane? Maybe that's the answer to your question.

If given the chance, what would you put on a massive billboard in New York?

I would put a picture of a nature scene with a bunch of friends on it, obviously having a good time. The billboard would say: "You are beautiful. You are worthwhile. The world loves you." If we trust each other, love each other, and take care of each other, we would be more willing to make a lot of progress in issues that really matter to us.

What is your definition of a life well-lived?

I don't know, honestly. Maybe a life well-lived is a life in which you try to find a definition of what a life well-lived is? If you try to do enough things and see enough things so that by the time you're done you have an idea what a great life looks like?

I also think that a life well-lived can't go without contributing. Leaving the world a little bit better and having the people around you be a little bit better off, by having known you. Inspiring people to live their best lives and protecting the environment we live in, that's probably a part of a life well-lived.

Find out more about Dakota:

www.jonesdakota.com
instagram.com/thatdakotajones
facebook.com/thatdakotajones

PART TWO:

COME FLY WITH ME

Appreciate the Present Moment and Let the Little Magician do His Work

*In 2008, **OLIVIER PEYRE** left for a trip around the world with the firm objective not to use any motorized means of transport. By a combination of cycling, paragliding, and hitchhiking sailboats, he succeeded in his goal. Even more, after seven years of traveling, Olivier maintained sobriety, ecology, and freedom as some of his main values in life.*

"I've found that freedom is a difficult notion. For me, a lack of choice feels more like freedom than plenty of it does."

Boy Scouts

I had an adventurous upbringing. From a very young age, my parents took me and my siblings for hikes and bivouacs in the Alps. Sometimes, our hikes were close to mountaineering. That's definitely where the seed for my adventurous spirit was created. This seed got watered a lot thanks to the boy scouts. I absolutely loved the boy scouts, especially the yearly camp. Living independently, in connection with nature, for 3-4 weeks every summer was amazing! I especially remember the so-called 'raids'. During these *raids*, we left with a small group of five to seven youngsters for a couple of days of hiking. We were forced to help ourselves. For me, this was magical. I didn't want these camps to end, I hated going back to school.

Another key moment in my life was when I was 14 years old. My older brother had come home after a bicycle trip of several weeks. He was offered a book written by two guys who had traveled around the world on their bicycles. I robbed the book, read through it, and was amazed by their adventures. I promised myself that one day I would do the same: travel the world on a bicycle!

This dream always stayed in the back of my head. Though, more conceived important things took priority, not least my studies as an aeronautical engineer. During my studies, I convinced my good friend Luc to undertake this trip around the world with me after graduation. When the time of my graduation had come, I went to Luc and said: "Are you ready?" But Luc had a secure job and asked me to wait 1-2 years. So in the meantime, I decided to backpack through Australia and New Zealand. But when I came back and rang Luc's doorbell again, it became clear that he would relinquish our plan. After Luc, there were a few other people in my life – a couple of girlfriends for example – who showed interest. But in the end, every candidate turned his or her tail. At the same time, I wanted to work for a year or two as an engineer to validate my engineering diploma. After trying out the so-called 'normal' sedentary life for this period, I no longer wanted to postpone my dream of long-term traveling. I was finally mature enough to say: "If nobody wants to join me, I can go by myself and I will be perfectly fine!"

Zero Carbon

At first, I thought my trip would take me one year. The only model I had was the book I read as a 14-year old kid. Those guys had cycled across the world in one year. But then I got inspired by the book *Latitude Zero* by Mike Horn. Horn's pure, natural, slow way of traveling with absolutely no motorized means appealed to me. So instead of flying airplanes across the oceans, I decided I would try to hop on sailboats with people crossing the seas. At the same time, I had started paragliding so I added that to the equation as well. This way, my concept was born: '*En route avec aile*' (direct translation: "On the road with a wing", or "*Fly'n'Roll*" as the official English title). However, this meant that it would take me more than one year. When I kicked off in 2008, I had in mind to be back in France four years later. But after two years of traveling, I said to myself: "I am so happy during this trip and actually I want to enjoy even more time on this *longest holiday ever*." So I decided to double the whole duration, meaning eight years total.

In order to prolong my trip as long as possible, I had to shrink my budget as much as possible. I had to get by with about €5 a day, from which my health insurance was eating €1,5. Also, the regular bike repairs were costly. This meant that I had about 2-2,5€ for lodging and food each day. The first decision was quite easy to take: only wild camping (although I got invited home by people I met along the road quite often). No campsites, no hostels, no Airbnbs. This wasn't a sacrifice at all, actually. Quite on the contrary. Beforehand, I had invested in very good equipment: tent, sleeping bag, cooking stove, etc. So I felt really comfortable and I discovered that camping in nature to its fullest offers a new type of comfort; the aliveness you feel by interacting with it. Hearing the rain dripping on your tent, waking up and putting your bare feet in the dawned grass, seeing a wonderful sunset . . . it made me feel so alive, so intensely happy.

When it came to food, I also learned to get along with very little expenses. At the beginning of my trip, I met a couple of other travelers. When we decided it was time to go shopping, they said to me: "Don't use the main entrance, there's a back door as well." So we went on the backside of the shop and bumped into several bins full of food that was perfectly edible. This way, I learned to be what is called *a freegan*, someone who lives from a very simple, free diet. For the last three years of my trip, I got almost 100% of my food out of bins.

The passion with which you speak about sobriety makes me guess you continued the lifestyle after coming back to France?

Oh yeah! Let's say I'm still a freegan. I still have a budget of €5 a day. I chose not to get a paid job for the last five years. My girlfriend and I are now converting a van with the idea to live in it, so we can avoid paying rent. I nearly stopped passing at cashiers; no more shops, no more bars. I don't really enjoy bars anymore. It's just not my style of living. Sometimes, this may cause friction in social situations. That's why I have a small 'social piggy bank'. When I spend days with friends and loved ones, I double my daily budget. I allow myself to indulge to keep the group ambiance high. But when I notice I'm around people with whom I have to go way beyond my €10 budget, I try to point it out. I say: "Excuse me, guys. This is not my way of living." That is not always easy, it can lead to heated, but interesting, discussions.

I'm also a big believer in non-monetary exchange. For example, during my world trip, I went on board lots of big sailboats without having to pay money for it. This way, I could go from Europe to the US 'for free'. But I don't see this as exploitation or taking unfair advantage, because most often I went on board sailboats whose owners were retired people. I could offer them manpower, sailing, and navigation skills. This way, I was also beneficial to them. Another example; when I got invited to sleep at people's homes, I always offered to use the food I had with me for dinner. And I often gave a present. Mostly this was a self-created cooking stove made out of a small can that works by burning alcohol in it. It's original, it's cheap, and people always loved to see my demonstration of it!

I just try to get rid of my needs. Or better, I try to transform them. When I talked about the drink in the bar. That's just not giving me any pleasure anymore. Because I've found other ways of satisfaction that mean more to me and cost nothing. Things like a paragliding flight, a hike or an outdoor game in the mountains, time by the sea, or a good conversation over a cup of tea at home . . .

Freedom

Freedom is a difficult notion for me. I thought I would feel free on my trip, but actually, I never felt as constrained as during those seven years. I cycled 8-9 hours a day, then I had to look for a good spot to sleep, set up the tent, repair broken bicycle parts, fill in my travel diary, cook dinner . . . I never stopped working actually! Nevertheless, these were the consequences of my very own choice. And I had taken the freedom to make that choice. So in a sense, if you can fully deal with the consequences of a choice you've made, that means responsibility to me. And that responsibility is a form of freedom that is much more real than the typical holiday freedom, where you escape from all your worries at home for a couple of weeks a year. At least, that's my view on it.

I'm also aware that having less choice means more freedom to me. For example, in Turkmenistan, my visa request was refused. I researched how I could deal with this problem, and I found out that there was only one way to do so. It involved going down a rabbit hole of administration and negotiation, but it was my only chance. So I went full in and got totally captured by the tasks I had to do. I even found myself enjoying the discussion with the state officers. And I managed, very very luckily, to get the visa! Also in my life today I make the deliberate choice not to spend money (which I would have to earn in advance) on a whole lot of things. They just are out of the question. For me, saying 'no' to so many things is what offers me more freedom to do what I really care about.

What is your purpose in life nowadays?

Coming back home after my bike trip wasn't easy. I had to look for a new dream. After reflection, I knew my dream would be to share with others what this trip had done to me, what it had taught me. I do this in different ways. I wrote a book, I'm a public speaker, and I organize small adventures in which I take people paragliding, hiking, and/or sailing. These are small sources of income, but I'm mainly doing it because I love it and it makes me happy to share my values of sobriety and eco-responsibility.

What would be the first thing you'd change if you were 'President of the World'?

Hmmm, good question. Difficult question, too. There are so many things I would like to change, I could write a book about it, including many questions. I guess my focus would be on the environment. The way we're exploiting our planet today is my biggest concern. I think that my first action would be to try to instill some awareness that we are not different from all other living creatures on this planet. I would uplift the rights of non-human living beings. I think people have to relearn again that we are part of nature, instead of believing we're standing above it. Our atoms are the exact same atoms of bears and deers and trees for Earth's sake! After traveling the way I did, I really got to feel that connection to the Universe. I felt part of nature, I felt interconnected with everything.

What advice would you give to the 10-year old Olivier?

I would say nothing because I know he will discover it anyway. But yeah, maybe with the following advice I could have helped my 10-year old self somewhat: "Don't worry, everything is going to be alright. But don't wait until you're an adult to go on a discovery of the path you feel really appealed to."

I told you about boy scouts and how much I loved it. But then, as I grew older, I started believing that adventure isn't for me. That sailing isn't something for me. That paragliding isn't something for me. Actually, that was a real mental prison I was captured in. There's nothing worse than being held back by limiting beliefs. In my case, these limiting beliefs led me to step in my box on wheels in the morning when it was still dark, work eight hours at a desk, get out of the office and drive back home in my box on wheels. By the time I got home, it was dark again and I came to say to myself in the evening: "Again another day I didn't live." While in reality, all those adventurous activities, all those childhood dreams, were actually very accessible. That's why I'd encourage the kid Olivier to start exploring his interests immediately and keep on dreaming. No matter how crazy those dreams seem to be. *"Quand on veut, on peut."* [When you want, you can.]

What is your definition of happiness?

It's appreciating what you have at the moment. Your question reminds me of a question I got asked a lot during my world trip: "Which country did you like the most?" I always answered: "Here and now." It's something I learned on this trip. Stop having regrets about yesterday, stop worrying about tomorrow. Just enjoy the moment right here, right now.

To this I would add that you have to try to nurture the little magician in the back of your head. When you have certain tasks at hand, certain choices to make, ask yourself: "How can I make this magical?" Let me give you an example. When I came back from my world trip, my girlfriend Nadège wanted to settle down in an apartment. To me, this was like: "Oh my God, I don't want to be imprisoned by walls! I won't be happy living in an apartment." But ok, living in a couple was my next adventure. Since I care a lot about Nadège, I agreed to watch out for an apartment. But at the same time, I engaged the little magician in my head. This way, we found an apartment on top of a mountain. Now I can just step into my garden and take off with my paraglide to fly to my appointment in the city below. This way, the apartment doesn't feel so much as a constraint but more as an easy access to execute my passion.

Find out more about Olivier:
www.enrouteavecaile.com
facebook.com/peyreoli
instagram.com/enrouteavecaile

Above Everything: Dream!

ANTOINE GIRARD has been on the exclusive list of athletes invited for the Red Bull X-alps, he has paraglided above 8000m peaks and holds the World Record for biggest paragliding altitude gain (5854m). Despite this impressive list of achievements, Antoine considers the hiccups of his career as just as important.

"By failing I learned the most."

How did you become a professional adventurer?

As a young guy, I read some books about famous climbers and mountaineers such as Reinhold Messner. I got inspired and started rock climbing. It turned out that I had quite a bit of talent, so I evolved quite smoothly and eventually made it to the World Cup. I also really got into alpinism and climbed several 8000m mountains, one of which was a solo climb of K2 in 2006. The following year, I started paragliding and did some smaller adventures, at 2500m-3000m altitude. Because of family life, I slowed down my ambitions for a couple of years.

Then, in 2013, I entered a paragliding competition and it went really well. About a year and a half later I got in touch with sponsors and started my career as a professional athlete. At the same time, I broke up with my girlfriend. I don't really know whether my pro career was the cause or the result of this break-up . . .

What's the hardest part of your lifestyle?

There are a lot of difficulties: finances, practical organization, the dangers, social life . . . You have to know that for every achievement the people see, there have been at least 10 failures. The same holds true for financing: 90% of sponsors you approach will say no. As an adventurer, you have to be very perseverant. I've never lived full-time as an adventurer. I always kept my job as a staff member of the University of Grenoble. About three months out of the year I work at the University. It's a backup, a safety net. I'm glad I have it. Periods, like what we went through during COVID-19, can be lethal for explorers and adventurers. The other part of the year I'm abroad, living like a nomad. Having this lifestyle eight to nine months a year isn't easy, especially if you want to build a family, something that comes up more and more in my head. I would love to have children one day.

When it comes to danger, mankind freaks me out the most. In the mountains, I've encountered a lot of hazardous moments, moments where I could have died. But in these situations, there's almost always something you can undertake: look for shelter, change your course, turn back . . . Recently I was in Ethiopia and ended up in a situation where I was surrounded by a couple of armed civil warriors. I was powerless, they simply could have shot me if they felt like it . . .

Lifestyle and Preparation

Today, I work out 20-25 hours a week: running, climbing, and hiking. Of course, I also have to fly a lot to improve my technique. Physical training has become a habit. I have lived like an athlete from a very young age. The same holds true for nutrition; I eat merely healthy, without constraints. Being healthy is a lifestyle. Another big part of my success comes from visualizations. I spend a lot of time visualizing. Not only the flights, but the entire expedition . . . being alone, passing mountains, and overcoming obstacles. The most difficult part for me is the practical and logistical organization of every expedition, especially when there's paragliding involved. I spend entire evenings studying maps, months in advance . . . and it's always a hassle to get flying permits. Always.

The Beauty of Having Time

There was a period in my career when I preferred to go on solo expeditions. I did this because I wanted to discover my own boundaries. I wanted to push it as hard as I possibly could. Plus, I needed time to reflect. When you're all alone in remote places, hungry and thirsty, the core of yourself comes to the surface. You re-center. You ask yourself questions about what's really important, what you really want to get out of life. In our society today, there are so many distractions, so many opportunities to be busy, that we don't ask ourselves these questions. On expeditions, once you're dressed and you've tidied up your tent, there is this enormous amount of time in front of you. That never happens in "real life."

After every expedition, I experience some kind of depression when I come back home. And all my adventurer friends feel it too. In the beginning, it was really hard to cope with. The only solution I could find was to start planning the following expedition as fast as possible. Nowadays, I deal with it better, but it's still there every time.

True Success

I have a different definition of success than most people. For a lot of people achieving a summit, without getting into trouble physically and mentally, means an achievement. For me, that's a failure. It means that it was too easy. If I don't push my limits, what do I learn from it? On the other hand, I've failed to reach mountain peaks many times, but if I gave the best of myself, if I prepared everything in detail, if I persevered through hardship on the way, then that's a big achievement.

As a consequence, the biggest sense of accomplishment comes when I put in tremendous effort and do achieve the goal by inches; when the only way of achieving the peak has been by pushing my limits a little bit further. That's why I consider my crossing of the Andes as my biggest achievement as a paraglider. For the public, setting a world record by flying over Broad Peak (8051m) stands above everything. Not for me, since crossing the Andes was more difficult. It pushed me harder.

What advice would you give an 18-year-old kid that has no idea what to do with his life?

Dream! Dare to dream! It will be difficult, there will be many more failures than successes. So you have to be willing to work very hard. You have to be extremely perseverant, but never stop dreaming!

Find out more about Antoine:
www.antoinegirard.fr
facebook.com/antoinegirardfly
instagram.com/antoinegirardfly

Being in Business Was My Biggest Adventure

PETER WILSON was born in Zimbabwe in 1957, became a successful businessman in his late 30's, and learned to fly a helicopter in 1998. In 2014, he sold his companies and fulfilled his dream: taking up long-range flying and thereby raising awareness for sustainable development.

"In business, I had a track record of designing and implementing programs of transformational change in many sectors and now I'm doing the same with my adventure projects."

Three Journeys Round

My adventures of the last five years have been within my 'Three Journeys Round' project. I undertook three remarkable journeys by helicopter: *Round Africa 2016, Round the World 2017,* and *Round Latin America 2018/2019.* The purpose of my journeys was to raise awareness for *'a better planet through sustainable development'.* My research showed that sustainable development, climate change, and poverty were inseparable problems to solve. With my three journeys, I also had three objectives: to have an aviation adventure, to travel with a purpose, and to share the stories.

The Lessons of Business

I graduated in 1982 and worked as a Mechanical Engineer in Scotland. I founded *The Change Works* in 1992, co-founded *The Health Works* in 2004, and sold the combined businesses to GE Healthcare in 2014. Throughout this period, I gained tremendous life lessons. Actually, I consider being an entrepreneur as my first big adventure, and probably my most difficult. Being in business is where I learned and improved skills like goal setting, project management, leadership, people management, and work-life balance. I learned that a healthy body equals a healthy mind, which I have later relied upon. My *Three Journeys Round* project has been no different really: chasing sponsors, solving problems, relentless logistics, and endless administration while also finding the time to exercise. Very few life lessons were left after spending 20 years in business. However, I had to prepare myself for the massive challenge of aerial circumnavigation: the organization, pilot skills, technical detail, teamwork, and navigational and meteorological knowledge required.

People and Nature

You can't have a successful company if you're not valuing and understanding teamwork, you have to treat people fairly and understand that there is no such thing as a silly question. I've been lucky to have had great mentors and colleagues along the way. Through my business and personal life, I have always been a traveler, meeting people to engineer better solutions. This ingrained in me a passion for human geography. I also believe that we cannot continue infinitely consuming Earth's finite resources and assume all will end well! My father - a geologist - was clear that our rapid population growth wasn't evolution anymore: it was an explosion in resource consumption and waste production that would break the Earth's existing systems. Sustainable development would mean that we need to live within Earth's means. Nature is not free and capitalism needs to use it responsibly.

The biggest problem in this whole story is that people do not yet see the consequences of their collective actions on the Earth, in both developed and underdeveloped countries. And that's a shame because our planet is so beautiful! I've witnessed so many marvelous vistas. Some of my favorites include the water worlds of Llanos de Moxos in Bolivia, Pantanal in Brazil, and Okavango in Botswana, as well as Torres del Paine in Chile and the Sahara desert. But the most beautiful place on earth must, for me, be Ilulissat, Greenland with its immense icebergs.

Family

Being a business owner and adventurer also both mean that you're not seeing your family as much as you want. That's definitely one of the most difficult things to cope with. Actually, I have the impression that my family thinks I'm boring them if I constantly talk about my adventures. For various reasons, they don't come with me. I'm trying to enjoy encounters with people along the road as much as possible, but this feeling is hard to share with my loved ones.

Luckily, I meet a lot of warm, inspiring people during my travels and can tell their stories. One such person was Abdullah Munish. 20 years ago, Abdullah was involved in a car accident, which paralyzed him from the neck down. After the accident, he was helped by and then became a regional coordinator for *Motivation International*. This company provides mobility solutions for disabled people living in the developing world, thereby helping the most disadvantaged and vulnerable people to lead healthy, active, and full lives. When I met Abdullah in Kenya, he told me: "This wheelchair brought my life back."

Fear

For a pilot, changing weather conditions form the biggest risk of mortal danger. I've had several sweaty hand moments in my long-range flying career, due mostly to wind turbulence, mist, or heavy clouds. My most dangerous moment was when I was flying around Africa in 2016. I nearly killed myself by getting caught in a brownout at 7,500 feet above the Sahara between Tamanrasset, Algeria and Agadez, Niger. A brownout is when everything around you is dusty sand lifted into the air and you cannot see your horizon. I was frightened; I had no visibility at all and couldn't easily get radio contact. I tried to get a frequency with every device I had, but it was only after crossing the border of Niger that I got in touch with the Agadez controller. He guided me and after what must have been about two hours, the haze finally cleared up. This experience had scared me so much that I took some extra safety measures for my trip around the world the following year. I recruited a co-pilot and installed a two-axis autopilot in the helicopter. Honestly, I'm not afraid of dying but I would rather not! I do take a lot more calculated risks when I am by myself. Before every expedition though, I promised my sponsors that I would operate safely. However, you can never eliminate all risks from flying a single-engine helicopter over miles of rainforest, open sea, or desert.

Training

I've been in shape all my life. I achieved this through a combination of walking, running, gym work, and weightlifting for my various adventure sports. These sports have included skiing, scuba diving, windsurfing, and mountain biking. Nowadays, I still exercise hard, skiing in the winter. I exercise at least two days out of three. I don't do any kind of mental training. I am a realistic optimist and believe I can do anything I set my mind to. I have a very high level of self-motivation and determination to achieve the goals I set for myself, and I always have new goals ready for when I have accomplished the ones I'm working on. I'm flexible and in my experience, it is definitely about taking the memories and experiences rather than anything else.

The Importance of a Job

If you want to maximize the adventure in your life, there are two options. You can look for a normal job that allows you to be outdoors, something you like doing, and that pays the bills (journalist, travel guide, scientist, etc). Or you can try to become a professional adventurer. There are much more of the former than the latter, and trying to become a full-time adventurer involves way more financial suffering. I had to work very hard to get to a position where selling my companies would give me enough financial security to start fulfilling my aspirations as a pilot. But still, I have to rely on sponsorship to make my dreams possible. It's extremely hard to persuade others to pay for your 'fun'. I always try to approach as many companies as possible, and my background in business definitely helps me in this process.

Find out more about Peter:
www.threejourneysround.com
facebook.com/threejourneysround

Life is About Creating Memories

THOMAS DE DORLODOT – you can call him Tom – is a professional paraglider who competed 8 times in the Red Bull X Alps. Besides flying, Tom enjoys other outdoor activities such as running, cycling, and climbing just as much. He's currently traveling around the world on a sailboat, with his family, in search of beautiful flying spots.

"Throughout the years, my motivation has shifted. I am no longer interested in beating others in competitions. Today I'm really in search of exploration and a way to contribute to the world."

Learning From the Best

When I was 14 years old, a friend of mine started flying a paraglider. He invited me to practice on the soccer field, I tried it out and fell in love with it immediately. Because I was living in the countryside in Belgium and was too young to drive a car, I didn't have many opportunities to fly. Luckily my father was a farmer, so we had a lot of property on which I could play around and improve my versatility skills on the ground.

My father also helped me pay for my first paramotor, which at the time was an extremely dangerous instrument with an unprotected propeller. Any moment of losing vigilance could cost you a limb. Anyhow, pretty soon I started working in a paramotor school. Skilled as I already was by that time, I was hired to teach clients how to improve their skills on the ground. As a reward, the school offered me a couple of paramotoring flying hours per week.

At age 17 I started my first company: *Airshot*. The idea was simple. I went flying above villages and towns and took pictures of the houses beneath me, and every Saturday I went from door to door to sell the pictures. Since I was young and cute, it worked out rather well.

Next, I went to university in Brussels, where I studied Communication. Every moment of free time, I took my car and went to flying spots in France or Switzerland. I would eat very cheaply, sleep in my car, and do anything to maximize my time flying. Early on, I already understood that it would be a shame not to share my adventures with other people, so I wanted to improve my filming skills. I made my parents believe that the best school for videography was in Granada, Southern Spain. Of course, the real reason I went there was that it's an amazing spot for paragliding and some of the world's best paragliders lived there. I wanted to train with them. I got in touch with the paramotor phenomenon Ramon Morillas, who was the paramotor World Champion back then. I offered to take care of filming his expeditions and communicating to sponsors, press, and fans. In return, I got to learn from him and join him on some crazy expeditions. I was essentially his 'caddy' at the time. I prepared his equipment, took care of the logistics, and carried his gear. I became a better pilot and filmmaker though, so it was definitely worth it.

Your specialization is hike-and-fly, how do you train for this?
Honestly, I'm not a laboratory rat. If you want to train well, you have to be extremely motivated and disciplined or make it as much fun as possible. I'm someone who takes the latter approach. I hate gyms, so I'm training only outdoors. I run about three times a week. In my biggest weeks of training, this adds up to 50-80km. I try to get friends involved as much as possible as well, in order to hold me accountable. But my favorite type of training is micro-adventures. For example, recently I cycled from Brussels to Chamonix and climbed Mont Blanc afterward.

Over the years, my motivation has changed as well. I used to dream about winning races, but now I seem to have lost that competitiveness. I still love training, I still love flying, I still love making friends with other athletes on races, but beating them is just no longer interesting to me. Nowadays, it's much more about the inner adventure, about exploring and discovering. Paragliding is one of the rare sports in this world where you can still be a pioneer. There are so many places where nobody has ever flown before. Finding these spots attracts me a lot more nowadays than the competition does.

Besides the physical training, the mental part is very important as well. Especially in a technical and risky sport such as paragliding. One of the advantages of technology is that we have these little GoPro's nowadays. Whereas, 10-15 years ago, if we wanted to learn a new trick – helicopters, loopings, etc. – we went flying with someone who was already skilled in the trick. Then that person would fly next to you, watch how you're doing it, and give advice. Nowadays, we can just film our tricks while executing them, look at the recording and immediately see what we should do better next time. This way, these action cameras have caused a real revolution in the sport. Paragliders now learn tricks 3-4 times faster than we used to.

The real beauty comes when you combine this with the power of visualizations. Recently, I wanted to learn one of the most difficult tricks in the sport. I asked a friend of mine who had already mastered the skill if I could watch his recording. I looked at it over and over again, then visualized myself doing the sequence of steps exactly as he did. In only three days I managed to do the trick. My friend was amazed!

Another key to success is preparation. Before every flight, I spend a lot of time getting as much information as possible about the weather, flying lines, and mountains. And I also visualize what I will do in a worst-case scenario if things go very badly.

About Setbacks
I've had a couple of big accidents. In 2014, I was on a 3000km hike-and-fly trip with a friend. About halfway through our trajectory, while flying in Switzerland, my paraglide collapsed. I was at 20m altitude, which is really the worst height to find yourself when this happens. It doesn't give you enough time to open your rescue parachute, nor to unfold the paraglide. I crashed hard into a tree and for a few minutes, I was paralyzed from the neck down. That was a very scary feeling. Luckily, the sensation came back. I had broken my pelvis, hip, sacrum, some ribs, and some vertebrae. The doctors in Switzerland wanted to operate, put in screws and plates everywhere. They told me I'd probably never be able to run again. Somehow, I had a feeling I shouldn't get surgery. I took a picture of my X-rays with my smartphone and sent

them to all of my friends, asking them if they could ask for a second opinion from surgeons within their network. The evening of the day before my operation was planned, a very accomplished surgeon from Belgium called me up. He assessed that I would be able to recover without surgery. When the nurses came to bring me to the operation table the following day, I said: "Nope, I'm not coming with you." My sponsors and my insurance agency arranged a private medical plane for me to Belgium. Over there, I was forced to stay immobilized for five weeks.

Now I look at this event as the most extraordinary thing that ever happened to me. Because, while the world kept turning, I was forced to stand still. I had plenty of time to think about my life, my dreams, and the people around me. In this reflection, it became clear to me that I was living very egocentrically. That I was living way too fast, also. I was constantly running after the next project. I was unable to say 'no' to any proposal that came my way. There, in the hospital bed, I learned what was really important to me: spending time with the people I love, taking time for myself, and enjoying the present moment. When I started training again after a couple of months, I told my sponsors and business partners I would no longer be available in the morning. The morning is when I focus on training and taking time for myself. They never made a problem out of it and when I did my physical test for the RedBull X-Alps the following year, I had better results than ever before.

Another big accident happened in 2016. I was on an expedition with Belgian professional climbers Sean Villanueva and Nicolas Favresse. The idea was that I would mentor them while flying, and they would do the same with me while climbing. One day when we were about to climb a wall, I woke up and I intuitively felt something wasn't right. When we were 80 meters up the wall, I told them: "Guys, I'm not confident. I have a bad feeling about this wall." Sean and Nicolas asked me to continue on with them a bit higher to later rappel down. A moment after, a massive rock fell down on my hand. I had to be carried to the hospital and a crappy Greek 'butcher' operated on my finger, which left me with an index finger missing two cm. My insurance covered hand therapy in Belgium. I was expected to do silly exercises with 'Lego' blocks and things like that for three hours a day. After two days I had enough of it, bought myself a ticket to New Zealand, and decided that flyfishing would be a much more fun revalidation than *Legos*. One day, while fishing, I had kind of a spiritual experience; suddenly I felt healed, physically and mentally. There was no more resentment, no more shame, I was fully ok with the situation.

You Don't Buy Things With Money, You Buy Them With Time
Nowadays, I give speeches to big enterprises. I share the lessons of my adventures with them. One of the most important messages I like to share with them is that life is about creating memories. So many people are running after something their whole life long, just to keep up with the people around them. They always want a bigger car, a bigger house, a swimming pool.

I like to refer to a saying by the president of Paraguay: "You don't buy things with money, you buy them with time." For example, a lot of people want a nice, carbon bicycle. The price of their bike is the equivalent of their monthly salary. Why not buy a second-hand aluminum bike and enjoy 26 extra days of cycling? For me, life is really about appreciating the moment and enjoying it to the fullest, it's about experiences. The bicycle ride from Brussels to Chamonix I talked about, wasn't a big deal, it's not a very extraordinary adventure, but I felt so happy while doing it. In the end, that's the only thing that counts.

What advice do you give to people who aspire to have the kind of lifestyle you have?
We talked about a couple of things already. Search out people who are good at what you want to do. Don't be afraid to ask them for advice.

Ask yourself what is holding you back? Then, write down ways you could deal with these obstacles. If you're afraid of public speaking, for example, try to take acting classes, practice in front of family and friends.

The next point – it's a cliché but it's so true – is to step out of your comfort zone. By doing this you will notice that you're actually able to open doors, to break through walls. You will gain confidence. If you step out of your comfort zone, you turn from a thinker into a doer. You let the action speak for itself, this way you become immune to nay-sayers. When I was young and dreaming about becoming a professional paraglider, my parents used to jokingly ask me: "Do you really think you can make a living out of air?". . . but I had the confidence, and look what I'm doing today!

Maybe the most important advice would be to make as many mistakes as possible. In Europe, we don't have a culture of failure. Failing is something you have to avoid. In America, if someone has gone bankrupt three times, people say: "That guy must have experience!" (laughs) So yeah, take risks and make mistakes, especially if you're young. If you're 18 to 25, you don't really have responsibilities. Even if everything goes wrong, you can still find a couch to sleep on and you'll have plenty of time to recover. When you have a family, things get more complicated. That's where people get stuck. They buy a house way too big and have children early on. As a result, there's a bank waiting for a big amount of money at the end of each month. It's hard to get out of that situation.

The last thing would be to follow your intuition. Instinct is a primal thing, but intuition is based upon past experiences. As a result, it's almost always right. For example, in the mountains: if you have a doubt, there's no doubt. If you have a belly feeling things aren't quite right, turn back. But it also goes in the opposite way. If you feel you really want to do something, although it doesn't seem smart or logical, go for it. People are experts in making excuses. That's sad because life passes by quickly, and we need people who take initiative.

Real Connection
You experience how restricted we are by our society when you go traveling. If you think about it, we learn to sit still in school for eight hours a day, to listen to the teacher, and to obey. In essence, we are trained to be sheep. In my opinion, that's not a good thing. We need people who take initiative. By traveling around the world, you see how shitty the planet becomes, how humans are ruining it.

By going into the mountains or in oceans, you find a way to escape all the ties and regulations of society. These are the last places where you can fully express yourself, where nobody tells you what to do, and where you can feel free. Unfortunately, that is changing as well. For example, I spent six summers in a row in a small village in Pakistan. The first year I went there, they did not yet have electricity. There was an absolute serenity in the village, everyone seemed calm and happy. The second year, they had electricity for one hour a day, which was good because this way labor and education could be organized a bit more efficiently. In the third year, everyone in the village had a television. All of a sudden, they were in contact with the western world, Bollywood movies, and Shakira dancing. This disrupted the balance in the village completely. All the youngsters wanted to get out of there. They wanted to chase the wealth and temptations they were now aware of. In their full right, of course, but this way the sense of connection in the village was completely lost.

Another example is when I take a team with me on a sailboat. Day one, we still have phone coverage. Everyone's constantly looking at their screen, swiping Instagram, Whatsapp, Twitter . . . On the second day, on the full sea, we lose 4G and people start talking again with each other. By the third day, we are playing cards and having deep conversations . . . It feels like a real treasure, the rediscovery of true human connection. But then, as soon as the shore is on the horizon and we have phone coverage again, everyone is back on their little screen, sending pictures to family and friends. Of course, I'm no different. After a week on the sea, I like to see pictures of my son Jack as well . . . But these experiences do make me reflect on whether progress is always progress.

Do you look at life differently now that you're a father?

Yes, I do. I must be honest, it's intense. Having a child takes a lot of time, planning gets more difficult. I'm aware that I take fewer risks while flying as well. On the other hand, my wife Sofia and I haven't changed our lifestyle much. We're still living adventurously. Jack was only four weeks old when we started living on a boat. He literally learned to walk on waves. As a result, he has a great sense of balance! He's only one and a half years old now, but he has already experienced so much: he swam in the sea, he saw whales and dolphins . . .

Sometimes, other people who are concerned about the future of the planet tell us we shouldn't have children. But if everyone who's aware of our environmental and social problems nowadays stops making children, we'll have a big problem. We have to raise children who are aware and who are taught to take initiative, to look for solutions.

What is your biggest dream left?

As I told you, my motivation is shifting much more from competition to exploration and contribution. The next big project I will be working on will be an expedition boat. We want this boat to be as energy-neutral as possible, yet still be capable of going to rugged places such as Patagonia and Antarctica. The aim would be to invite people, mostly adventurers, for in-depth conversations about nature and the environment, in the hope that these portraits will inspire more people to live in a way that takes care of our planet and our society.

Find out more about Tom

www.thomasdedorlodot.com
facebook.com/thomasdedorlodot
instagram.com/tomdedorlodot

Failure Made Me Who I am Today

KRYSTLE WRIGHT is an adventure photographer and director. Her versatility led to her shooting some of the world's best surfers, climbers, kayakers, slackliners, BASE-jumpers, parasailers, and more. Above all, she's an absolute admirer of nature.

"The connection with nature is a feeling that is unique every time. The moments when wildlife has chosen to interact with me have created some of the most intense feelings of joy."

Heart Explosions

Growing up on the Sunshine Coast, I was naturally surrounded by an outdoor lifestyle which prompted me to participate in as many sports as possible. The first adventurous realm I was exposed to was the ocean and up until today, I love to free dive and play amongst the waves. One of the biggest pivotal moments of my career was when I was invited on my first expedition in 2010, which consisted of camping in the Arctic for a month with a group of BASE Jumpers from around the world. I was so far out of my comfort zone in the Arctic, but that experience was one of the strongest that has continued to resonate with me. It showed me the life and career I wanted to pursue.

Since the Arctic expedition, I've continued to search out other expeditions that take me far off the grid in unique locations. I've continued pursuing this lifestyle because there is so much beauty that is associated with it. In particular, the connection with nature is a feeling that is unique every time. I know that if I have a difficult day, I need to jump in the ocean as it always cheers me up. The moments when wildlife has chosen to interact with me have created some of the most intense feelings of joy. For example, I remember a group of Sperm Whales that swam within a meter of me in the Atlantic Ocean, an elephant seal pup who hugged my legs on the shore of South Georgia, and a small herd of baby goats and sheep jumping on top of my tent in Mongolia. I like to call these moments 'heart explosions' since the overwhelming feeling of joy completely consumes me. They are some of my favorite memories that I will carry with me to my grave.

Forehead Scar as a Reminder of Danger

When I am in the wild and in precarious situations, I feel fear instinctively. This instinct is my biggest asset in keeping me alive. I believe that complacency can be one of our greatest dangers in this lifestyle. I've faced dangerous situations and one in particular that involved a tandem paragliding accident taking place in Pakistan in 2013. Everything that day happened so fast. By the time I had a split second to see that we were about to hit a boulder, I remember only experiencing a succumbing feeling and thinking 'oh shit.'

Since I lost consciousness, I don't remember if I thought I was going to die in those moments. But by the time I regained consciousness, my focus had shifted purely to staying calm. The scar that remains on my forehead is a constant reminder of how quickly things can go wrong, and to listen not only to my surroundings with more acute awareness but also to listen to my gut instinct. I do believe there were signs that day warning me not to fly, but my drive and ego perhaps overshadowed and I took too great a risk that day.

What's the hardest thing about being an adventure photographer?
Pursuing expeditions is financially difficult. Unless there is support from a sponsor or several sponsors, it's tough to take on major expeditions as the costs escalate fast. I've also discovered that as I get older, and I take on more life responsibilities, it has also become difficult to dedicate long periods of time to these trips. Life is and will always be about balance. I do think this lifestyle is achievable, but it takes a lot of dedication and sacrifice to make it work. There's not a singular aspect that sticks out as the hardest thing since every trip demands different needs. I've experienced trips that have been financially very difficult, while other trips have been merely emotionally difficult.

About Failure
Failure to me has been the greatest lesson that has helped me evolve into who I am today. I've made so many mistakes but I always figured that if my career failed I could always come home and simply start again. It takes dedication to stick to your dream and then the patience and perseverance to see that out. Life really is short and there are no guarantees.

If you had to live on an isolated island for the next 10 years, and were only allowed to take 2 people and 5 objects with you; who and what would you take with you?
It's a romantic thought, but I'd like to think that I could bring a partner and without a doubt, I'd bring a dog as my second person. As for five objects, I'd have a leatherman, fishing line, fire-starter, large water container, and blanket.

How do you keep your mind and body healthy?
I wouldn't say that I live on a specific diet, but when I eat food, I eat for the soul. I try to eat healthy when possible but have never followed a specific diet. If anything, right now as we live through the strange times of the COVID-19 pandemic, it's been transforming to re-embrace moving slower. Perhaps that falls into the category of meditation, but I'm relearning how to enjoy the days of nothingness. This space gives me the chance to dream. I would consider myself a spiritual person. I believe in Mother Nature and I like to think about energy a lot and how that runs through the veins of every living thing. It's hard to explain something so personal but when I lost a friend many years ago on an expedition, I took comfort in the thought that he's not gone, but his energy that day transpired back into nature.

I do also believe in surrounding myself with a community that helps support me and in turn, I support them. It took me years to realize that I was draining myself with certain friends who abused that trust. I began to cut ties and made sure that I would only allow people in my life who uplift me.

What advice would you give to your 18-year-old self?
I wouldn't give my 18-year-old self any advice because I know that 18 year old to be incredibly stubborn and probably wouldn't listen to me anyway. But jokes aside, I really wouldn't because I think in life you need to take the path you're on and learn from your mistakes along the way. Sure there are a couple of situations I look back on and feel embarrassed by, but that's life and I feel good about who I have become today and excited for where I am going.

Sources of Inspiration

Trophy, directed by Christina Clusiau and Shaul Schwarz. This film challenged my preconceived ideas about conservation and opened my eyes further to a complex issue. The filmmakers also impressed me so much by how they were able to create a film without their opinion, which is extraordinarily difficult when these subjects stir a lot of passion.

Dark Emu, by Bruce Pascoe. This book has challenged my education and upbringing, and what I thought I knew about Australia's indigenous history.

The Empire of Illusion, by Chris Hedges. A heavy read that offers a fascinating insight into our modern-day society and the illusions we have created throughout so many facets of our lives and institutions. This book hit me hard emotionally but is one of the most powerful reads I've done in recent years.

Characteristics and Personality Traits

[I asked Krystle to rank herself from 0 (not like this trait at all) to 10 (very much like that)]

Optimism: 6
Discipline: 7
Courage: 7
Resilience: 9
Stubbornness: 10
Social skills: 6
Creativity: 9
Curiosity: 10

Find out more about Krystle:
www.krystlewright.com
instagram.com/krystlejwright

I Always Have a Great Plan A, as Well as a Great Plan B, Because Things Do Not Always Go the Way You Want Them to Go

*Swiss paraglider **CHRISTIAN MAURER** is a former Swiss and European Champion, who has won the Overall World Cup three times and holds the world record for longest triangle flight. Yet he is most known for his invincibility in the RedBull X-Alps, which he has won seven times.*

"I'm naturally a very competitive person. I really need challenges to get the best out of myself."

Born to Fly

I grew up in a small town in Switzerland called Adelboden. I got in touch with paragliding already as a toddler, when my father went to a paragliding school in our village. This way, I could see all these wonderful pilots fly like birds. When I was only seven years old, I did my first tandem flight. Two years later I started practicing by myself on the ground and flew some small distances. It was enough to get me hooked. As I lived in an environment where paragliding was all over the place, I already knew important things such as which material to choose, how to take off, how to read the weather . . . before entering paragliding school at age 15. Despite my insider knowledge, paragliding school is where I got to experience what it really means to fly. I experienced a sense of freedom, a total release of stress and problems. Flying meant the discovery of a new horizon, and I immediately knew I wanted to get really good at it.

As a young adult, I was lucky to be surrounded by a couple of more experienced, very accomplished pilots. I trained with them, learned from them, and joined them in competitions. My first competitions gave me a lot of motivation to get better and I made it a goal to get selected for the Swiss League and also the Swiss Championship. Once I achieved that, my objective was to participate in the World Cup. From there I tried to enter the European Championships. This continuous raising of the bar kept me very driven, it kept me very sharp. Nevertheless, I stuck to pure paragliding competitions for a very long time. In these competitions, the main focus is on flying very fast. Your physical condition isn't that important. As a young man, I was quite heavy and not very athletic. Because of this, I wasn't attracted to hike-and-fly competitions at all. Besides, at that time the equipment was very heavy. Hauling up a mountain with a 25kg backpack didn't sound fun to me.

But then in 2003, *Zooom* organized its first *Red Bull X-Alps*. The *RedBull X-Alps* is a 1000km race across the Alps, from Salzburg to Monaco. The participants complete this distance by a combination of hiking, running, and paragliding. This race immediately captured the imagination of athletes in the paragliding world. Pretty soon, competitors worked together with manufacturers in order to develop the equipment as light and fast as possible. This way, the sport became attractive to more and more pilots, but it wasn't until 2008 that I gave it a chance myself. At that time, my motivation wasn't to win the *RedBull X-Alps* or other hike-and-fly races, it was just because I wanted to improve my health and be able to follow my friends while running.

Now we are 14 years later and you're the RedBull X-Alps record holder with seven victories. What sets you apart from the others?
There are several factors, I think. I have a lot of experience, I know when to push and when to hold back. I also worked for eight years as a test pilot, testing out new wings and equipment. Thanks to this job, I got very technically skilled, especially in starting and landing. It also taught me a lot about risk management.

Another important element is tactics. A hike-and-fly race is like playing chess. You don't win by pushing really hard on the flights or by pushing really hard on the ground. You win by being in the air at the right time and place. This means you need to have a lot of knowledge about the weather and geographics, as well as the right instincts. The more you've practiced, the more often your instincts will be right.

On top of this, the *RedBull X-Alps* is, in essence, a team sport. Every pilot has a teammate with whom he has radio contact and who can help him with changing clothes, providing nutrition, hiking up the mountains . . . In most of my editions, my good friend Thomas Theurillat has been my teammate. Thomas is both a mountain guide and a psychologist. In the early editions, Thomas had a very important role regarding my mental state. Thanks to him I could stay ready, confident, and focused all the time. We worked a lot with checklists and reminders. I would write motivational words as well as tactical reminders on my gloves, for example. When it comes to tactics, Thomas and I always have a great plan A, as well as a great plan B, because things do not always go the way you want them to go.

About Risks
In 2014, I had a landing accident and broke my leg. This accident made me reflect on the way I was approaching paragliding. It made me realize that paragliding can be dangerous and that I was often taking risks that were not worth it. This doesn't mean that I've become more careful, but instead that I've become more focused.

Today, each time I ask myself the question: "Is the possible gain of this risk worth it?" If the answer is still yes, then I still do take the same risks as before but I'm sure to be one hundred percent focused while doing so.

How does a typical training week look for you?
It depends pretty much on the season and the planned competition. In autumn, I do quite a lot of power training in the gym. I want my body to be resilient for the volume of training that will follow afterward. In winter, the focus is on endurance training – mostly by ski touring and MTB – and focusing on acrobatics and downflights. In spring, I steadily increase the volume of hiking and running, which I do almost always with a backpack to mimic the competition. It's

also the season where I focus on thermal flying, start and landing skills. Before the *X-Alps,* I do a couple of big cross-country flights to really get my body and mind prepped for the competition. Overall, this means I'm doing 8-12 hours per week of physical training in autumn and winter, this goes up to 25 hours in spring. On top of this, I fly almost every day the weather allows me to.

Do you ever lose the motivation for competition?
No, actually. I feel as if I'm still learning as a pilot and that I'm learning most by competition. When you fly for more than 20 years, there's little that a solo training session can teach you. But when you're with 20 pilots in a thermal, in the stress of competition, that's where you still learn. This doesn't necessarily mean you still become a better pilot, but you can learn how to better communicate with your supporter in stressful circumstances, for example.

Besides, I think I'm just naturally a very competitive person. I really need challenges to get the best out of myself.

If you hadn't become a professional paraglider, what would you be now?
I think I would be a truck driver. I worked as a bricklayer from 1998 to 2001, before I became a test pilot. Thanks to my job as a bricklayer I learned how to drive a truck and I really enjoyed that actually.

If you could grab a beer with three people, dead or alive, who would they be?
First of all, Roger Federer. Federer is one of the top tennis players for so many years, despite several injuries. I would be interested to have a chat with him about how to continuously keep improving and staying motivated as an athlete.

Secondly, an important influencer in the world of social media. I could use some help with social media myself and I'd be eager to share some ideas about the use of social media back and forth.

Thirdly, someone who's able to be content without having anything. A homeless person for example. In my opinion, most people work too much and have too much money for what they really need. I think that people without possessions could teach us a lot about the famous expression 'less is more.'

In your experience, has social media changed the sport?
When I was starting out, we only had big cameras with a small film angle. About a decade ago, *GoPro* action cameras with wide angles became mainstream. All of a sudden, we could film our acrobatics and immediately see what we did right or wrong. This in itself has transformed the sport already. Thanks to social media, we've been able to share our insights, and this way we learn from each other. In that sense, social media definitely contributed to the evolution of the sport.

On the other hand, I think that 90% of what we can find on social media is bullshit. It's spam, it's trash. I think that we as athletes and adventurers must be really conscient about what we share on social media. Social media shouldn't be used to uplift the ego, but instead to contribute to the community and to portray an honest image. For example, I did base jumping recently from a paraglider and made some nice shots about the experience. I decided not to share it on social media because it shows me in a crazy moment which could be dangerous for people trying to copy me. I could have shared the video on social media, but only if I would have talked about precautions, limits, and dangers in the post. Another example is a video I posted where I'm doing a take-off from a mountain peak in crazy conditions, but only after failing several times. I didn't just share the successful take-off– in order to show how good I am – but I also showed all the failed attempts because I want other pilots to understand that hard and difficult work is needed to succeed.

What's the biggest gift someone can give you?

I feel very rich already. For me, a perfect day is when I go out for a hike and fly in the morning, and have quality time to spend with my two sons in the afternoon. And you know what, that's the life I'm living! Of course, there's a lot of work people don't get to see. I spend many hours at a desk; calling sponsors, doing interviews, and preparing projects. But still, I have enough money and time to do what makes me happy: spending time with my family and paragliding in the mountains. There's no bigger gift than that.

Find out more about Christian:

www.chrigelmaurer.ch
facebook.com/chrigel.maurer1
instagram.com/chrigelmaurer
instagram.com/teammaurertheurillat

Live Lightly

*Highline, parapente, base jump, or wingsuit, **JULIEN MILLOT** loves and masters all of them. The dare-devil, who is based in the French Alps, is one of the founders of the Flying Frenchies, an ensemble of unique and original adventurers who lifted aerial sports into an art.*

"Every individual of the Flying Frenchies has his own talents and brings his own flavors to the group. Our main goal is to have fun and to live lightly. There's no pressure to perform at all."

Late Bird

As a kid, I did a lot of bike and motor trials, but I started very late with aerial sports. I was 24 when colleagues of mine took me out climbing for the first time. It wasn't until four years later that I discovered highlining. Base jump and wingsuit followed later. During my engineering studies, I was mostly occupied with music. I wasn't doing sports at all, at that time. Nevertheless, as soon as I went climbing, I recognized the same requirements as I needed for trial: balance and technique. These are my strengths. All my life, I've been someone who has difficulties building muscles, but on the contrary, I'm very technically skilled. That's why climbing and highlining appealed that much to me, I guess.

When I started the highline, I got to know Tancrède Melet. The sport was fairly new in France, Tancrède and I were amongst the first ones doing it. This has been our luck, since this way our videos became immediately quite popular, we got invited to do acts and to give interviews everywhere. We didn't consciously decide that this was what we wanted to make a living off of. The success more or less just happened to us. In the small world of highline at the time, we quickly got to know Antoine Moineville and Sébastien Brugalla. Together we went on an expedition where we highlined on the Dent du Géant, a famous 4000m peak in the Alps. This was actually the first adventure movie filmed by Seb Montaz, who by now has gained a lot of fame as the director of Kilian Jornet's films. This expedition is where everything became more serious. We got our first sponsor contracts, we were filmed by a professional filmmaker for the first time, and had our first real marketing campaign.

Making it a Profession

After meeting Tancrède, he quite rapidly convinced me to start base jumping. He had a lot of ambition, a lot of drive. I didn't have goals as big as he did, but jumping off a cliff sounded like a fun thing to do. So I joined Tancrède, liked it a lot, and with that came the intrinsic motivation of wanting to become better. We realized that the combination of highline and base jump was unique. This shaped the idea of another film called 'I believe I can fly'. For this film, we went to different places - Chamonix, Verdon, Paris, Norway - to do stunts that were a combination of highline and base jump. This film became a real buzz and opened a lot of doors for us.

As we became more and more popular, *the Flying Frenchies* - at that time we were still called *'the Bad Slackliners'* - became my major source of income. However, it was never my idea to make it my profession. From the four of us, it was only Tancrède who had the ambition to make this his sole job. The rest of us wanted *the Flying Frenchies* to stay a hobby, a passion, a way to make fun with friends. We wanted to keep it light. At the time I was working for a company that constructed and sold slacklines, Antoine was a mountain guide, Freddy was a rope access professional. These were our jobs, not *the Flying Frenchies*.

From 2012 on, I started to take some more distance from *the Flying Frenchies*. I did fewer projects, only when I truly felt like it. Today, I'm in the process of becoming a paragliding instructor. I see that as a real professional career. *The Flying Frenchies* nowadays generates only a small part of my income. I think that this way, without pressure, *the Flying Frenchies* stays more genuine, more spontaneous. We do a project because we feel like it, not because it is the most interesting from a marketing point of view. Typically one of us comes up with just a silly idea. Little by little, the group engages in it, and months later this silly idea has turned into a big, challenging project. For example, Arnaud Longobardi, who is a speedrider (speedriding is a combination of paragliding and skiing), had the idea to fly at the speed of a wingsuiter. The group picked up the idea, worked on it and we came up with the plan to form a V-formation with Arnaud in the middle, two wing-suiters at the left of him, two at the right of them. All five of us had to hold hands in the air. It's an insane idea. Normally speeriders and wingsuiters don't fly at the same speed, they have different lines, a different finesse ... But we were curious to see whether it was possible and started practicing. We invested tremendous time and thoughts into the realization of this project, which was basically nothing more than five dudes holding each other's hands in the air. But we just felt like doing it. After a lot of practice, we managed to execute a perfect V-formation, a world's first.

In January 2016, your friend Tancrède Melet died during a project with *the Flying Frenchies*. How did this impact you?

Tancrède was in France with some other guys from our group. I was in Tahiti at the time on a solo adventure. Tancrède was doing a stunt for which he hung under a hot air balloon. All of a sudden, while standing on the ground, one of the balloons took off and embarked Tancrède. He fell down when the balloon was at 20m altitude and died. When I heard the news, on the other side of the planet, it was a hard pill to swallow.

Tancrède and I had been very close from 2008 to 2011. Since 2012, our ways have split more and more. Our connection was less profound, emotionally. At the time of his passing away, he was much closer to other team members of *the Flying Frenchies*; they had a hard time getting over his death. For me, the acceptance came quite rapidly. After all, ever since I started aerial sports, I was aware that death is always around the corner. We've heard many stories of people dying in our industry. So you know that one day it may impact someone close to you, if not yourself. Tancrède's death was devastating, but I found my own way in the mourning process and it didn't impact the way I executed our shared passions afterward.

You know, I love being alive. I have a great girlfriend and two amazing daughters. I absolutely love to be outdoors. I want to spend many, many more years doing my passion and being with my loved ones. That's why I minimize the risks to the fullest. But in our industry, this is a difficult equilibrium to find, there's a thin line between safety and recklessness.

How do you prepare yourself mentally and physically?

I do a lot of visualizations. More and more actually, especially for base jumping, wingsuiting, and paragliding. I notice I profit from them. I'm also doing a lot of breathwork, without following a certain stream or executing a particular pattern. As a highliner, I just learned that if I get conscious of my breath, and try to breathe deeply and out of my belly, stress tends to decrease. Today, it's a natural reaction I have as soon as I feel nervous.

When it comes to the physical side, it's difficult. With a family and a daytime job, it's hard to find the time to do a lot of exercises. I try to hike as much as I can, every now and then I go running and climbing. And I want to do a minimum of 100 base jumps and 100 paraglide flights a year, this way it stays a habit and I never lose the feeling for it.

How would you describe your character in three words?

Haha, is this a job interview? I really have no idea. Energetic, probably. But rather in a sense of endurance. I'm quite calm, but when I have a goal in my mind, I'm unstoppable. That's my notion of being energetic. As a second characteristic, there's no one word to describe it, but I try to live like I'm on a holiday all of the time. I want to evoke this feeling you have when you're feeling without worries, as if life is good. Sort of as much as possible remembering that life is a miracle and not a follow-up of problems. And thirdly, I would say that I'm caring about others. Empathetic might be the right word. I want the people around me to be happy, to have a good time.

Live Lightly

I have two daughters, seven and four years old. I encourage them to live lightly too. Be zen, don't stress out. And if they really have a problem, to talk about it openly. If you look at the course of my life, you understand that it's important to me to give them freedom. Freedom to experiment, freedom to play, and freedom to make mistakes.

What advice do you give to young people who want to maximize adventure in their life?

Be patient. It takes time to reach the lifestyle you really want. People might think that a lack of money is what is holding them back, but I don't think that's necessarily true. For example, if you want to become a paragliding instructor, but you have no money, then try to find a job as a cashier in a sports shop where they sell paraglides. This way, you'll get specific knowledge about paragliding, you'll have the possibility to build a network of passionate paragliders, while at the same time you're putting money aside. At the moment you'll have the budget to follow your passion, you'll be ahead already. If your dream is to be a professional climber, then go live in a van. Get a seasonal job in winter and go climbing as much as possible during summer. You really have to immerse yourself into the environment where you want to flourish. And when I'm saying 'be patient', I don't mean 'postpone'. If you want something, you have to go for it now. Don't wait until you're 50. Channel your focus and energy.

At the same time, I'm someone who doesn't have really clear goals in my life. Because you never know what you will feel like in the future. For example, today I'm really into paragliding, while I'm a bit done with highline. But maybe in five years time I'll feel like highlining again and will be bored of paragliding. Another advantage of not having very clear long-term goals is that it leaves the door open for spontaneity. Often, you meet someone who sparks a new interest in you, or an opportunity passes by and you have the freedom to jump on it.

Summarized, I'd say: create a life in function of your passion. Don't hesitate, don't be afraid to make extreme choices, don't be afraid to fail. It will be a process of trial-and-error. That's guaranteed.

What's your definition of happiness?
At dawn, a base jump on a beautiful spot, followed by a nice meal at a restaurant with my family at noon. At dusk, some paragliding with a bunch of friends or my daughters. Watching the sunset with people I care about.

Do you get to have a lot of these happiness days?
Oh, yes! And the great thing is, if you have a lot of these days, you're happy on rainy days too. Because that means you can finally rest a bit (laughs).

Find out more about Julien and the Flying Frenchies
www.flying-frenchies.com
facebook.com/flying.frenchies
instagram.com/flying.frenchies/

PART THREE:
Ain't no mountain high enough

Don't Worry About What You Don't Have

When **JAMIE ANDREW** got stuck by a storm on Les Droites in the Alps, he was a 29-year old industrial abseiler, passionate rock climber, and experienced mountaineer. It would take five days and five nights before the storm calmed down and the French rescue team could save him. By that time, the -30°C temperature and extreme winds had not only turned Jamie's feet and hands into blocks of ice, they had also taken the life of his best friend. Despite having to carry on with four amputated limbs, Jamie came back as a climber.

"Take one step at a time, be patient."

Storm in the Alps

When the accident happened, in the winter of 1999, I already had 13 years of experience. I started rock climbing at age 16 and mountaineering at age 18. I had done a lot of famous routes and walls: El Capitan, Half Dome, several 4000-meter peaks in the Alps . . . My climbing partner Jamie Fisher was a very good mountaineer as well. We were flatmates and climbing partners for years, and the route was very well within our abilities. When we left Monday morning, the weather was great. We had planned to be back in the valley by Wednesday evening. Monday, we progressed real quickly and made our bivouac (temporary camp) halfway up the face. Tuesday we continued, and when we were about ¾ of the way up, snow unexpectedly started falling. The snowfall turned into a blizzard, but we didn't panic and continued climbing. It was well after dark when we finally reached the Breche des Droites, the narrow notch in the summit ridge from where the descent down the other side begins. We were now facing a 1000m cliff down on both sides of us . . . and weather conditions that made it impossible to descend. The storm would rage nonstop for three days . . . too much for Jamie. When I noticed that Jamie was dead, on our fifth night on the mountain, I closed my eyes as well. I knew I wouldn't open them anymore.

Second Chance

I was given a second chance. The PGHM had done one of the most spectacular rescue operations in history to bring me to the hospital in Chamonix. I knew that, if Jamie would have been given a second chance, he would have grasped it with enormous enthusiasm. So, in order to honor my friend, I had to do the same. During the rehabilitation, the lessons I had learned through climbing came in useful: set big goals but take one step at a time, stay focused, don't worry about the capacities you don't have, don't try to do everything by yourself, instead make use of the support of others . . . This way, I made small progress every day. I also was lucky; my two bosses offered me a management function in the company. I became the leader of the industrial abseiler training company. One and a half years later, I left the company. It was time to teach others what the accident had taught me.

A French TV station invited me to fly on a helicopter above the Breche des Droites exactly one year after the accident. At that moment, I realized that it wasn't the mountain to blame, this had been a human tragedy. There was no reason to feel resentment for the mountain. Shortly after shooting the French television documentary, I started rock climbing again. Despite the enormous grief of Jamie's death, I still had the same passion for the mountains. I wasn't ready to turn my back on them, climbing is who I am.

Dream Big, But Take One Step at a Time

The first thing I did after resigning from my job was writing a book about the accident and my rehabilitation, called *Life and Limb*. I also started doing speaking engagements, today this is my main occupation. I've traveled to more than 50 countries as a speaker. My main message is what I learned through this entire project: "Dream. Take it step by step. Be resilient. Make use of the capacities of yourself and the people around you. Be patient as well, confidence and strength take time to develop." I've got three teenagers at home now. I try to give them the same life advice. The best thing I can do as a father is to inspire them to be confident and pursue their passions and dreams, so I hope I succeed in that.

Since my accident, I've set myself a series of personal challenges as well. I started surfing, I've sailed the North Sea Yacht Race with two other amputees, I've completed a full-distance triathlon. I've found it very powerful to pursue new, big goals like this. In 2007, I also founded a charity called *500 Miles*, together with inspirational amputee Olivia Giles. *500 Miles* provides prosthetic treatment for countless children and adults in Malawi and Zambia. I'm no longer involved in the organization, Olivia is leading everything now. Today, I'm on the board of a couple of other charities, both in the world of sport and adventure, which are making a difference for disabled people.

Matterhorn

The hard thing about climbing without limbs is for sure the absence of hands. The prosthetic legs we have today are great, they won't let you down. I can walk with them, I can run with them, I can cycle with them, without any problem. But I'm born one generation too early to really profit from bionic arms. The models we have today are still too much of a hassle. There's limited battery life, they can't stand cold, they can't stand heat. Besides grasping and pinching they're still very limited in function and they don't give you any sensory information. Wearing them is much more of a limitation than a benefit. That being said, climbing with stumps instead of hands is extremely difficult, not only the specific act of grasping the rock but everything: opening carabiners, rope techniques, opening snickers, going for a pie . . .

My most beautiful experience as an amputee climber has probably been the ascent of the Matterhorn. The Matterhorn is one of the world's most difficult mountains to climb, so at first, I thought it would be impossible. But then, I approached it like every other challenge: one step at a time. I got the right people involved, progressed in training, and searched for the right equipment. It was very difficult to get to the foot of the mountain, but once there everything went perfectly. The climb was pure joy, it felt almost easy.

Support

I am very lucky to have wonderful people around me. My parents have always supported me, just like my wife Anna. The accident also meant a handicap for her. We had to go through the same challenges together. I have great friends, lovely children … Also, Jamie Fisher is still important to me, up until today. The first months after the accident, I felt a lot of anger, a lot of guilt. But I changed these negative emotions into something positive. I wanted to honor Jamie, therefore I had to take responsibility and grasp this second chance to make the most of it.

Find out more about Jamie:

www.jamieandrew.com

You Can Change the World

DAWA STEVEN SHERPA summited Mount Everest three times as an expedition leader. He's also the owner of a chain of resorts, a gastronomic restaurant, an oxygen bottling company, and a climbing wall in Kathmandu. He's one of the strongest forces in the efforts to clean up Mount Everest, organizer of an ice skating event, and a novel skydiver.

"I believe you can do almost everything you set your mind to, it all starts with a single step in the right direction."

Parents as Role-Models

I grew up in Kathmandu as the son of a Belgian mother and a Nepali father. My father grew up in a village called Khumjung, which is on the way to Mount Everest. Both of my parents have been big role models for me. My mother was very caring and very engaged in the upbringing of my two brothers and me. My father was an example as a mountaineer and businessman. In 1982, he bought a trekking company called *Asian Trekkings*, which grew over three decades to become the premier service of mountain expeditions in the Himalayas. In Nepal, my father became a public figure. He was involved in a lot of tourism associations, politics, and socioeconomic development projects. As kids, we were used to seeing ministers and well-known businesspeople at home. I wouldn't consider our family to be rich, though. Financially, we were doing well, but this wealth was created by the hard work and perseverance of my parents.

At age 18 I left Kathmandu to study abroad. First, I applied for an Erasmus program in the Netherlands. But because of the slowness of the Nepalese post service – this was the era before the internet – my application letter didn't reach the University in time. Luckily, I did manage to enroll in a Scottish University instead. Actually, I had many interests as a young man, and didn't know which direction to choose: archeology, history, architecture, piloting, business . . . My father finally pulled me over. He said: "If you study management, you'll still be able to go in every direction and create a business in any field you want to."

Everest Bakery

When I look back, I think I have to admit I've been a businessman from a very young age. I was only 12 years old when I set up a small shop at school with some friends. It didn't make us rich, but we had fun and earned some pocket money. In 2006, after coming back from Scotland, I went on my first expedition on a mountain exceeding 8000 meter above sea level: Cho Oyu. Over there, I noticed that the mountaineers were very territorial. I would try to go and talk with people in other camps but didn't feel welcomed. I didn't like this ambiance; I thought it would be much more enjoyable if people from different camps and nationalities would socialize.

This way, I came up with the idea to create a bakery in Mount Everest base camp. When I spoke about my idea with others, some people laughed at me. They didn't believe it would be possible. But at the same time, other people said it was a great idea and they wanted to help me out. One of my company's old expedition cooks was interested in becoming our baker and even did the necessary training in Kathmandu before the climbing season started. We had to figure out the right dimensions for our gas oven, since baking at 5500m altitude isn't the same as it is at sea level. After a couple of days of trial-and-error, my baker found the exact formula to be able to bake amazing bread at a high altitude.

I started this bakery with the intention to connect people – not to make money – but it turned out to be a huge success. You have to know that a lot of hikers do the Everest base camp Trek. Starting at the village of Lukla at 2800m above sea level, they hike up to base camp in 8-10 days. Before I set up the bakery, they would arrive at basecamp, take some pictures and go back down to the nearest village to grab a drink or a snack. There wasn't any provision at the camp and mountaineers wouldn't share their small food supplies with these trekkers, of course. Our bakery changed this; people started spending more time in basecamp, enjoying a coffee and an apple pie.

After the first year, I started using the money I earned with the bakery to set up cleaning programs on Mount Everest, paying sherpas to bring down the garbage that could be found on the mountain. At the same time, the National Park services started to bother me. Rangers would come to the bakery and tell me I didn't have the right to set up a commercial enterprise over there. I would answer: "I'm selling bread, not for my profit, but to clean Everest. I'm actually doing what should be your job." This was 2008, the year in which my father handed over *Asian Trekkings* to me. As I now became literally responsible for the lives of our clients, it became very difficult to keep the bakery as a priority, especially because of the political constraints. So I tried to hand the bakery over to the youth club of a village down the valley. However, these youngsters didn't have the logistical and management skills to carry on the project and the bakery died a silent death.

Seeing Opportunities

When it comes to business opportunities in the Himalayas, we haven't even scratched the surface. There are so many options. I'm a real idea-generator, I used to write down all my dreams on paper. When sharing my dreams, a lot of people told me I'm crazy, but I've accomplished most of them. Often, accomplishing one dream opens the gates to other ones. For example, I'm also the owner of an oxygen-bottling company. As a result of being the CEO of this company, I got in touch with skydiving. In the last couple of years, high-altitude skydiving has become popular. In the early days, the skydivers who aspired to jump out of an airplane at 8000 m above sea level were looking for oxygen bottles and someone who knew the mountainous area well. So I jumped in to fill this market demand which, in its turn, got me involved in a project in which we try to recuperate and exploit unused airfields in Nepal.

Another project our team worked on last winter was the organization of an ice skating event on Valentine's Day. We invited famous ice skaters (a 3-time Olympic Champion, an American National Champion, a Russian National Champion, an Indian National Champion . . .) and organized a competition on a frozen mountain lake. It was magical. The common belief in

Nepal is that tourism is a summer thing because the mountains are too harsh to climb in the winter. But I believe that there are tremendous opportunities to encourage tourism in the winter as well. Especially because a lot of rich Indians are living close to the border of Nepal.

On top of this, our team is working on the construction of comfortable lodges on the way to Everest base camp. We've already built four of them. The idea is to generate jobs in the small villages on the way up to Everest and to offer a place where mountaineers can find comfort and good, healthy meals. Finally, my girlfriend is involved in an organization that provides meals for homeless people. They provide 400-500 meals a day. I also offer a helping hand to her.

Being involved in so many projects, you must be very efficient in your time management?
Honestly, my time management could be a lot better. You have to understand that Nepalese people aren't Swiss machines. It's hard to get a reunion starting on time, schedules aren't very strict. If you want to be a successful businessman in Nepal, being flexible is imperative. Also, because I have a lot of contacts abroad, I regularly have to get up at night to make a phone call or join a Zoom meeting.

I have to admit that running so many projects has taken a lot of time away from physical training. I used to go to the gym six days a week, but since the massive earthquake in Nepal in 2015, I can't free the time anymore. After the earthquake, we've gotten a lot of money donated by the Belgian citizens. These donations were used to build 700 houses for people whose homes were destroyed. Since then, the busyness of my life never stopped. But at the same time, I'm still moving from one place to another all day long, and I still spend two to four months a year in the Himalayas as an expedition leader. This keeps me fit.

What skills does a good manager need?
It all comes down to trust. Employees need to be able to trust you, and you have to be able to trust them. When I'm leading expeditions, there's very poor or even no internet connection in the mountains. I have to be able to trust the fact that every employee in Kathmandu is taking responsibility and doing his job. *Asian Trekkings* employs more than 100 people. Taking into account all the sister companies, we're a team of approximately 200 people. I think we manage to trust each other a lot. Many of my employees have been in the company for 20-30 years. Remember my baker in Everest Base Camp? He's still involved in the company. To me, trust is also the most important aspect of leading a mountaineering expedition. In essence, there's not that much difference between leading a group of mountaineers in the Himalayas and a company in the capital Kathmandu.

Trust also comes down to having the space to make mistakes and learn from them. However, I do really expect people to learn from their mistakes, I can't bear it very well if someone makes the same mistake twice.

Which mistakes did you have to learn from yourself?
Oh, I made a lot of mistakes. The most difficult learning curve I had to go through was in my communication with clients as an expedition leader. Most of our clients are very head-strong and it's not always easy to find the right approach to handle every individual. I had to learn

not to communicate with every person the same way. People from different cultures, women and men, experienced versus beginners . . . I had to learn that you can't approach every mountaineer the same way.

If you had the power to plant one belief in all people's minds, what would that be?

One person does make a difference. A lot of people tell me: "Dawa, I would never be able to do all the things you're doing." The problem is, most people don't even start. I'm just an ordinary guy, but my belief system says: one step will take you a thousand miles. My parents always taught me that you can achieve anything you want – with the premise of doing what you love – but you have to be willing to work hard. So yes, I would make people believe that they can make a difference, that they can change the world.

What is your definition of happiness?

My definition of happiness is: "being able to fall asleep within five minutes of hitting the pillow." Because if you manage to do so, this entails that you're free of guilt. It means that you're living lightly, that your consciousness doesn't hunt you, because you're following your heart and helping others.

Find out more about Dawa:

www.asian-trekking.com
facebook.com/AsianTrekking
instagram.com/asiantrekking
instagram.com/dawasteven8000m

Nowadays, I Can't Leave Her Behind on a Glacier Anymore

When **STEF MAGINELLE** wanted to organize a Belgian expedition to Gasherbrum I and II in 2013, **SOFIE LENAERTS** literally came knocking at his door, asking what the project was about. On this adventure, Stef would become the first Belgian to peak two 8000m summits without supplementary oxygen in a single expedition. Sofie didn't make it to any of the summits.

"After this failed expedition, I asked Stef if he wanted to become my personal trainer. Two years later, he became much more . . . "

The Long Path to the Big Mountains

Sofie: I've been very adventurous from a young age. I've jumped with parachutes, I did motorcycling, scuba diving, skiing . . . But it wasn't until age 24 that I started climbing. In Flanders, there are no climbing rocks, so I started in a gym . . . little by little I came to challenge myself more and more. At first, I went rock climbing in the Ardennes. This was followed by a via ferrata in Italy, then I took my first steps in mountaineering in the Alps. This led to climbing Mount Elbrus in 2009 and Aconcagua in 2010.

Stef: I underwent a similar gradual process as Sofie did. I started indoor climbing as a student. From there it went to rock climbing, later on, a couple of mountains in the Alps . . . I was about 30 years old when I had my first experience with high altitude climbing, where I really found my thrill.

Sofie: Before meeting Stef, I went to Mount Denali in Alaska as a test to see if it would be possible for me to join the team to the Gasherbrums the year after. Although at that point I had already climbed mountains like Mount Elbrus and Aconcagua, accomplishing *the Seven Summits* had never been in my mind. This seed only got planted when I had the opportunity to climb Mount Everest.

Climbing as a Couple

Stef: In 2013 we went with a Belgian team of five people to Pakistan with the goal to climb Gasherbrum I (8068m) and II (8035m). At the time, Sofie and I weren't lovers yet, and my only goal was to reach the summit of the two mountains, which I did. So to me, the expedition was a success. I felt extremely euphoric, but Sofie was disappointed.

Sofie: After an acclimatization round we needed to go quickly up for a summit push and I was too slow for the team. I had to stay behind in Camp 1 and during the second weather window, we got hit by a storm. I went down instead of being patient and trying again. I believe we learn just as much from our failures than from our successes, and the lesson I took with me from that day was that I had to prepare myself better, physically and mentally. So I asked Stef, who's a physiotherapist and physical trainer, if he wanted to coach me. We won't tell you the details, but over the years we crossed the borders of our coach-pupil relationship . . .

Stef: When we were at the Gasherburms, I left Sofie behind on a glacier because she was too tired to continue and decided to get back to the camp. It never came into my mind to stay with her, I was there to reach the summit of Gasherbrum I. Ever since we became a couple, dynamics have changed; we do really take a lot of care of each other now. A couple of years ago, we went to Ama Dablam, a famous mountain in Nepal. We wanted to climb fast and light, so we cut down on our clothing. However, there was a lot of wind on the ascent. Sofie got terribly cold and at 300m separated from the summit, we decided to turn back and descend. Summiting alone and letting her go down was no option for me.

Sofie: Being a couple doing expeditions together has its advantages and disadvantages. On the one hand, we might get too worried for each other sometimes, on the other hand, we do really have the routine down. Besides, we enjoy ourselves a lot. When we're stuck in a camp for several days because of bad weather, we never get bored.

Stef: Both of us are very optimistic and flexible people. In 2004, years before I got to know Sofie, I was with a friend on Mount Denali. We were waiting for a window for five consecutive days in the highest camp, at 5300m. A lot of teams quit their expedition, while we spent those days having fun and laughing.

Sofie: The same happened to me when I was doing a solo expedition on Khan Tengri in 2015. I was in Camp 3 when bad weather struck. Everybody ceased their climb, and I decided to go to Camp 2 where I would be safer. A lot of people gave up the summit attempt and headed back to basecamp, thereby dumping their gas and food in Camp 2. I saw this as an opportunity "Great, with the food and gas I can stay here for a while," was my reaction. The next day, new teams arrived at the camp, I easily made friends and spent the evening laughing and dancing.

Choosing Experiences Over Prestige
Sofie: Stef climbed Mount Everest in 2007, I summitted it in 2016. Both of us came back with the idea that this wasn't our preferred way to climb mountains; sherpa's doing all of the work, being amongst rich business people that know nothing about mountaineering, dragging up heavy oxygen bottles, having to wait in line on the climb . . . it's not our cup of tea. So, after my Everest experience, we decided to attempt Lhotse in a team of two; just Stef and me, no sherpa's, no supplementary oxygen, no expensive fees . . .

Stef: Sofie looks at this Lhotse expedition as a failure because we didn't reach the summit. But for me, it's the project that makes me the proudest. We were there, all by ourselves, experiencing pure mountaineering, and making it just above 8000m without any external help.

Sofie: The commercialization in mountaineering bothers us. It's not just a phenomenon on Everest, but on smaller, famous mountains as well. The Mont Blanc, Matterhorn . . .

Stef: People pay to hire a guide that brings them up these mountains, just for the prestige that comes with reaching the summit. A lot of these people know nothing about mountains. I think that's a sad thing, you can never have much satisfaction out of these experiences. If you learn the skills yourself, if you go out to more savage mountains, if you learn to be self-reliant, then you'll get much more pleasure and satisfaction out of it. You'll have to do it for yourself, for the fun of mountaineering, not for ticking off a list of popular mountains.

How do you train for mountaineering in a country with its highest point being at 694m above sea level?

Stef: I'm a physiotherapist and physical coach. In our cabinet, we have a high-altitude training system. We've been experimenting with this since 2013, in order to find a good training protocol. Concretely, in practical terms, we do interval training for 45 minutes. Depending on our season and goals, this goes from zero to one to several times a week. This interval training can be running, stepping, or cycling. We simulate altitudes of 4000 to 6000 m. Scientists still don't agree about the effectiveness of high altitude training, but we definitely feel that it enables us to adapt to the altitude on our expeditions.

Sofie: Besides the high altitude training, we try to prepare ourselves as specifically as possible, this means a lot of endurance work. We do a lot of long hikes with a heavy backpack, and Stef likes trail running. Sometimes, I walk up and down a stepper in our living room for hours in a row. I remember doing this while watching a documentary about Mount Everest before flying to Nepal in 2016. It was really useful, once I was on the mountain I knew exactly which section was about to come. For me, physical training is a difficult part of being an adventurer. I'm working as a police officer and it's hard to put in the effort to put in the amount of exercise we need in order to be ready for our expeditions.

Stef: For me, physical training isn't really an issue. I find that the only thing that is really hard about our projects is finding the money. Nowadays, nobody is willing to sponsor people just to get to the summit of a mountain.

Sofie: Actually, we still meet people on our expeditions who simply received sponsorship like that, but we don't understand how they do it. We literally had to knock on 1000 doors to get one opened. And you always have to deliver something in return; an article, a movie, a speaking engagement . . . For me, in order to finish *the Seven Summits*, I had to finance the expedition to Mount Vinson myself. I approached a number of companies, but in the end, only found one sponsor who offered me a rather small budget, the rest came out of my own pocket. I left for Antarctica bankrupt. The good thing is, if you don't have any expectations from financers, there's less pressure and you climb more liberated.

Ueli Steck

Sofie: I once got into a small avalanche in the Vosges in France. The cornice was called *secteur des avalanches*, so I was warned. While going up, all of a sudden I felt a plate of snow disappearing underneath my feet and I slid down a couple tens of meters. I got out of it without trouble, but it made me realize that death can come any time . . . We've known several people who didn't come back from their expedition, like the regretted Ueli Steck. A couple of years ago, the famous Swiss mountaineer was in Brussels to speak at an event. The organizer of the event had asked me if I could tell my story as an opener to Ueli's one. I made use of the opportunity to have a nice chat with Ueli. In May 2017, we met him again in Lhotse base camp.

Ueli had the plan to break the record of climbing Everest and Lhotse in one push, together with a high-level sherpa. However, the sherpa got frostbite so Ueli decided to go to Nuptse, a mountain nearby, to do some extra training before his attempt. On Nuptse, he slipped, fell down hundreds of meters, and died. When the news reached us, we were deeply affected. Ueli's personality and mountaineering philosophy were an inspiration to us. Of course, he was doing it on a much higher level and taking a lot more risks than we do.

The Mental Side

Stef: Apart from visualizations, we don't really make use of mental training techniques. As we've said, we're both cheerful and optimistic people, which helps a lot in the mountains. I don't need any methods to reduce the stress. Quite the opposite, it's only when I'm in the mountains that I feel relaxed.

Sofie: Actually, I've rather noticed the opposite effect: our experiences in the mountains help us throughout life with more flexibility and confidence. Having to wait in a basecamp for days without the distractions of the modern world has taught us to be comfortable and happy by ourselves. To me, this effect really got clear during the COVID-19 epidemic. People who had been stuck in the same life pattern for years lost their coolness during the imposed isolation. They got bored, they complained all the time . . . these people lacked the mental flexibility to see opportunities and stay positive in every situation. That's something adventure has taught us.

Find out more about Stef and Sofie:

www.sofielenaerts.com
facebook.com/8000unlimited
instagram.com/sofie_lenaerts_8000unlimited

Working as a Sherpa is Physically and Mentally Very Challenging

*From 1990 to 2011, **APA SHERPA** climbed to the summit of Mount Everest 21 times, becoming the record holder for most ascents of the world's highest mountain until 2017. Nowadays, Apa lives in the United States and empowers the educational opportunities for today's generation of Nepalese children through the Apa Sherpa Foundation.*

"I have been terrified for every expedition, but I had no other choice than to be a sherpa because I had to provide income for my family. Today, I want to give Nepalese children the chances I never had."

The Hard Life of a Sherpa

I grew up in a poor family in a small village called Thame, in the Solukhumbu District of Nepal. Since my family was poor, I had to help my family make a living already at an early age. I would go to Tibet, crossing the Himalayas with my uncle to trade for salt and other commodities that were not available in my village. When I realized I could make money in the tourism industry, I jumped in and became a porter, although I was only a kid. One year, a Danish group of trekkers I was helping out said that I should quit working and go to school instead. They promised me a scholarship and so I joined Khumjung school (built by Sir Edmund Hillary's *'Himalayan Trust'*) with an ambition to become a doctor. I had to walk three hours to school and three hours back home. This left no time to study or do homework. My dad passed away when I was 12 years old and my mom was left with six kids and no income. I had no other choice but to give up on my dream to become a doctor, quit school, and go back to working as a porter. Later on, I became a trekking guide and finally a climbing sherpa. I went to the summit of Mount Everest for the first time in 1990, as part of a team with the legendary Rob Hall and Peter Hillary, the son of Sir Edmund Hillary.

For every expedition, I was terrified, and so was my wife. Mountaineering is a risky business. In one of my expeditions to Annapurna I, eight fellow sherpas and I narrowly escaped death. Our tent, gear, and clothing all got swept away by an avalanche. We were able to rush into an ice cave and survived with minor injuries. The nine of us had to huddle together in that cave all night to keep ourselves warm. We were able to get back to base camp the next day. I was so scared because of what had happened. The thought that if I died in the mountains, there would be no one to support my family, was even more frightening. I wanted to quit mountaineering, but that was no option. I had no education so I would not be able to provide a living for my family, I had to swallow my fear and continue climbing.

The life of a sherpa is very tough. Our first task starts at base camp: setting up the camp. We then have to carry loads up to each following camp to set up the tents and install the camps. We have to haul climbing equipment, food, and other necessities to each camp. We have a responsibility to train our clients and guide them safely on the mountain. We have to make sure we have fixed-line ropes all the way to the summit. We help our clients get to the summit and back to basecamp. When they leave, we have to go back up and retrieve everything; tents, gear, trash, ropes … Working as a sherpa is physically and mentally very challenging.

Experiencing the hard life and the dangers of being a porter and sherpa have been the motivation to create *'The Apa Sherpa Foundation'* which supports schools in Nepal. I want the Nepali kids from today to have a choice when they grow up, to have the option to follow an education instead of being forced to become a porter.

In your mountaineering career lasting over 25 years, what have been some of the most remarkable changes you've noticed throughout time?

Back when I first climbed Everest, the mountain was covered with a lot of ice and snow. Now it's mostly exposed rock. It has become very hard to climb with crampons. Equipment-wise, things have improved a lot. We can buy lighter and better quality climbing suits. Back in the day, I used to put on four or five layers to keep me warm.

Communication and weather reporting have improved a lot. In the early days, we had to send handwritten letters. It would take months for that letter to get from the north side of Everest to our family down in the valley. Nowadays, mountaineers can surf the internet on the mountain, they can use cellphones and satellite phones on Everest. I remember that in 2010 I made a phone call from the summit to my family in the U.S.A. Also, the number of climbers coming to climb Everest has increased quite a bit over the years. With the increase in tourists and climbers, the local economy has become better. People are able to open tea houses, lodges, and shops to earn a living. With that income, they can send their kids to school.

The Most Remarkable Anecdote

I had to rescue a Ukrainian climber from an altitude of 7000 meters on the north side of Everest. He was over six feet and I am only five feet four inches. I carried him all the way down to base camp. His legs were being dragged on the ground. It was very challenging, I will never forget that day.

Are you rather optimistic or pessimistic about the future world your children have to navigate through?

I always wanted to provide my kids with a good education so they could have choices in their lives. I was able to do that in America, where we have lived since 2006. The three of them are all college graduates. I am very optimistic; their life will be much better compared to mine.

If you were given 10 million dollars, how would you spend/invest it?

I would spend that money to improve the education infrastructure of rural Nepal.

Who have been/are the most important people in your life? Who do you want to thank?

I had so many people who have helped me to get where I am today. It's hard to narrow that list down, I am thankful to them all.

Growing up in Nepal and currently living in the US, what are the biggest life lessons Nepali people can learn from Americans and vice versa, according to you?

Americans have a very good work ethic and they value time very much. I think it is something Nepalese people should learn from them. Nepali are very compassionate people, we respect and help our neighbors and our elders. I think that is something Americans can learn from us.

What is your definition of a life well-lived?

If you have worked hard enough to serve your community.

Find out more about Apa:

apasherpafoundation.org
instagram.com/apasherpafoundation
facebook.com/apasherpafoundationorg

Being Aware of Your Limitations is the Only Way to Become Limitless

JOYCE AZZAM speaks five languages, has three master's degrees and one Ph.D., is a celebrated speaker and architect, and became the first Lebanese woman to climb the Seven Summits. Still, her family will only see her as truly successful when she'll settle with a husband and have kids. But Joyce has different plans, she wants to clean Mount Everest and complete the Explorer's Grand Slam.

"It's in my DNA to chase big goals, you have to do what's in your DNA."

Growing up in a Bunker

I was born in one of the Northern suburbs of Beiroet during the Lebanese civil war that took place from 1975 to 1990. I was the fourth child out of five, and the first six years of my life were spent in a bunker. My first life memories are people dancing in a bunker while there's a war outside. I think that shaped my resilience. I developed an ability to stay positive in any circumstance.

The post-war phase was probably even harder than the war itself. Society had to build up again out of a state of chaos and confusion. People had no idea what to expect from the future. My household was a typical lower-middle-class family. We were always in survival mode; if you just did the minimum as a child – going to school and helping out at home – that was enough. There was no permission to dream further. As a result, during my whole childhood and adolescence, I had no idea about the existence of life as an adventurer.

I was 21 years old when I did the first hike of my life, together with friends from University. It was a disaster! You have to know that I have hypermobility syndrome. As a teenager, I could hardly run because of the pain in my knees. I got bullied, I got called an alien. But I was determined to show my peers what I had in me. My brother George, who studied Physical Education, taught me that I had to become more muscled. So every day I would run, on my own, on the school's playground. I tried to add a little bit of distance every day. Little by little I gained strength and even started basketball at age 15. But then, years later, on this first hike with my friends, I got into trouble again. We were walking on muddy terrain, I had painful knees and I just couldn't keep myself from falling every few minutes. On the other hand, I totally enjoyed the experience, being in nature and feeling free, it felt great! I wanted to go back outside as fast as possible and asked George for some training advice once more. That's where my adventurous lifestyle began.

The Seven Summits

From that moment on, I went full speed. I lived close to the sea and close to the mountains. So from age 21 to 25, I tried a lot of different sports; swimming, skiing, rock climbing, caving, mountaineering. I got in touch with other outdoor-minded people and my life got really structured around sports. The first time I heard about *the Seven Summits* was in 2006. There was a documentary on national television about Maxime Chaya who had become the first Lebanese man to climb the highest peak of each continent. I was 22 years old at that time and had just started my adventurous life. At that moment I didn't see the possibility of me completing *the Seven Summits* one day. It didn't seem possible until 2012 when my boyfriend at the time invited me to join 'Team Lebanon', a project where we would try to find sponsorship to climb the highest peak on each continent with a small group of mountaineers. *Team Lebanon* held only two women, and the first one dropped out after the first expedition, leaving me as the only female climber.

Team Lebanon was the first time I got in touch with gender inequality in the world of adventure. Every time I wanted to give input about our projects, I was seen as being bossy and aggressive, as if a woman shouldn't have her own opinion. This made me feel as if I was used for improving the team's image and attracting sponsors, nothing more, although I was just as strong as the boys physically. Eventually, we climbed Mount Elbrus (Europe), Carstensz Pyramid (Oceania). and Kilimanjaro (Africa) together. In 2014 I left the team because I planned to do my Ph.D. in *Landscape and Environment* in Rome, Italy.

Harry

A Ph.D. is really, really hard. You have to be extremely focused. It's like climbing another big mountain. So, for two years I put *the Seven Summits* out of my head, although I continued mountaineering in the Apennines and the Alps. Eventually, in August 2016, I arrived in Seville for an exchange project. While I was there, I read in an article that Raha Moharrak had become the first Arab woman to climb Mount Everest and was now heading for *the Seven Summits*. This made me really upset and, without Raha knowing, she had evoked a healthy sense of competition in me.

I felt like being the first Arab woman to complete *the Seven Summits* was something that belonged to me. So in 2017 I continued my pursuit and climbed Aconcagua (South America), Denali (North America), and for a second time, Kilimanjaro (Africa). Only two mountains were left for me to complete: Mount Vinson (Antarctica) and Mount Everest (Asia). The one problem: these two expeditions are extremely expensive, about €80,000 each. So I had to pitch for sponsors, but nobody seemed to believe in me. You know, I look very feminine, I love to dress very well, and sponsors couldn't understand. They doubted my potential. They were thinking "If a woman wants to do this, she should look very athletic, almost masculine."

At the same time, I did a couple of small jobs to cover my living expenses, I had to train very hard and finalize my Ph.D. It was hell. After a while, I started losing confidence in the project myself and started applying for jobs in Europe. I got in touch with a professor I had met in Seville who offered me a job in the Netherlands. I was ready to sign the contract when all of a sudden I received a message that went like this: "Dear Joyce. My son Harry loves your projects as a mountaineer. At school, he and his classmates have to give a presentation about their heroes. Harry chose to talk about you." This message changed everything. I laid aside the job offer in Europe because Harry made me understand that what I did had indeed an influence on the community, which has always been my mission. I call Harry one of my 'angels'. My 'club of angels' consists of people that seem to come out of nowhere and offer me their help. This includes people I met at a dinner party who gave me 50 or 100 dollars because they like what I'm doing and want to support it, or people bringing me into contact with sponsors without any personal interest. My physical trainer is an angel as well, for years he guided me without ever charging anything, just because he believes in me and gets inspired by what I'm doing. It's wonderful!

Death and Life on Everest

Finally, I managed to get my expeditions to Mount Vinson and Everest sponsored. The landscapes in Antarctica were wonderful, just like they had been in Alaska when I climbed Denali. But Everest definitely tops every expedition. Climbing Everest takes a lot of time. I was away from home for two months, totally disconnected from the world. It was a true physical and mental struggle. All this hardship opened a path to self-discovery I had never gone through before. Besides, I got confronted with death from nearby. At first, there were the bodies of dead climbers along the way. At Everest, you often have to wait in line because there are that many climbers. Sometimes you're standing only a couple of meters from a dead body. I remember a moment where every time the fixed rope moved, I saw a female climber's limbs moving. I couldn't grasp what was going on with her and asked my sherpa if we shouldn't help her. "She's dead," he answered.

I must say, I hadn't been prepared for these experiences. They made me ask whether it was worth the risks we were all taking. But on the other hand, I knew how well I was prepared, I knew I had chosen a strong team and I had a very strong reason to climb this mountain. Nevertheless, the panic caused by seeing the dead bodies had made me inhale more rapidly. As a consequence, arriving at a place called 'the balcony', I ran out of oxygen. *The balcony* is a very steep ridge at 8400m altitude. My Sherpa Gabee was climbing very fast because he wanted to pass *the balcony* before the crowd of climbers behind us caught up. I had no choice but to follow his pace, which was essentially too fast for me. When my oxygen bottle got empty, I suddenly lost all sensations in my hands and felt kind of unconscious . . . like when you're super drunk . . . it took a while for Gabee to understand the severity of the problem. He switched our oxygen bottles and after a couple of minutes I felt normal again. From that moment on, I could climb at my own speed, which I call the turtle-way; I'm taking very slow and small steps without getting out of breath. This way, I rarely have to rest and I still arrive at the summit quite rapidly after the fastest climbers. During the last 500m of the climb I prayed the rosary, it got me into a flow state and before I knew it, I had arrived at the summit. It was such a blissful moment, I had so much gratitude for being on the top of the world.

The way down wasn't without incidents either. Going down, you have to use the same fixed rope as people who are still walking up, and you attach two carabiners to this rope. Each time you're crossing someone going up, you detach one carabiner, re-attach it below him and then detach the second carabiner and let him pass. The problem is, a lot of people are stressed out, they want to go up as fast as possible. At a certain moment, I had to cross a climber going up, and the guy detached one of my carabiners at the same time as I was detaching the other one. In an instant, I realized that I wasn't safe anymore and in a reflex, I put my hand in this guy's harness, which created a weird interaction, hahaha! Now I can laugh about it but at the moment I was really scared.

Once we got back safely to basecamp, I felt an extreme sense of joy. I didn't just feel the happiness of climbing Everest . . . I felt it 7 times because I had just completed *the Seven Summits* as the first Lebanese woman in history!

How to Deal With Adversity

If you hear my story, you can understand that I had a lot of adversity. If you're being born in Lebanon during the Civil War, there's no indication at all that one day you'll make it to the summit of Everest. As I told you, physically it was very hard. Up until today, I've been struggling with my hypermobility syndrome. Walking down Mount Everest was extremely painful. My quadriceps had melted away because of the deprivation of the entire expedition. When I got back to Lebanon the week after, I wanted to do a small hike with my friends and I didn't even manage to walk down a small hill. Luckily, there was my brother again who gave me the advice to start building up muscle with electrotherapy, which totally relieves the knee joint.

As I said before, finding financial backup for all of my expeditions was extremely hard as well, but the biggest adversity by far has been socially. My friends often asked me why I was wasting my time climbing mountains instead of pursuing a career and building a family. My father said I was a gambler in life, he compared my passion for the mountains with being a drug addict. My mother said that no man would be interested in a woman like me, who dressed in these thick, colorful alpine clothes and who didn't want to build a family. In our culture, getting married and raising children is the definition of success. After climbing Everest, I called my parents from basecamp. They were very proud, but only a couple of weeks later my mom told me it was now time to think about children . . .

I think I'm super determined, quite stubborn as well. And I'm always optimistic when faced with adversity. I think that with every mountain you climb, with every big goal you set for yourself, you're training your resilience and you become a better person. Besides, the more experience you gain, the better of a leader you become, you get more assertive, you take more responsibility . . . But still, I'm shocked when people tell me they see me as a super confident and strong woman because I still bear a lot of insecurities in me. I think we all do, even the best explorers in the world. But I also believe that it's a good thing to be aware of your insecurities and limitations, that's the only way to become limitless.

Getting Over the Blues

Coming back from Everest, I had a very tough time. Everyone around me was super happy for me and very proud of me, but I felt bad. It's a chemical thing in the brain. After a big achievement, you have to adapt again to a normal life, and your neurotransmitters drop again to normal levels. Adrenaline, dopamine, endorphins . . . all of these chemicals have been extremely elevated for weeks or months in a row, thanks to the extreme emotions that come with an expedition. What happens after is what I call *'the mountain-blues'.* After Everest, I experienced *the mountain-blues* like never before. I came back without a next goal in mind, so I ate and drank as much as I wanted and rapidly gained weight, which made me feel terrible. In the end, I saw a therapist to help me adapt to a normal life again and to set new goals for the future.

Now I'm super excited again. I'm working on several projects; I'm guiding people who never have been to the mountains with their first adventures, I've started an environmental project to clear all waste from Everest base camp and engage climbers to be much more eco-responsible, and I've set another goal as an athlete: going to the North and South Pole and this way completing the Explorer's Grand Slam (*the Seven Summits* + expedition to the North and South Pole)."

Final Advice

I'm very grateful for what I've been able to experience during the last decade. My biggest sense of fulfillment comes from seeing that I've evoked a change in the belief system of other women. When I was climbing Kilimanjaro the second time in 2017, I did it with three young Lebanese girls aged 13, 14 and 16. They had no clue about mountaineering. Today, the oldest one, Rawan Dakik, has climbed six peaks of *the Seven Summits*, and she's just 20 years old! I also believe that adventurous women from the Middle East have to support each other as role models, instead of competing. That's why I give a lot of thanks to Raha Moharrak, because she really inspired and pushed me.

My advice to everybody is: "Dream. Fight for your dream. Take responsibility for your dream. It's never the fault of someone else if you fail; it's not the fault of your parents, your teammates or the sponsors you didn't find. If people don't support your dream, who cares? Accept failure and have the faith to keep on dreaming. If you put all your passion and energy into one goal, and never give up, you have a 100% success rate. Have faith in this fact, it's a scientific equation."

Find out more about Joyce:

www.joyceazzam.com
instagram.com/joyceazzam7s
facebook.com/JoyceAzzam7s

Life Shouldn't Be Too Easy

*On the 17th of May 1993, **REBECCA STEPHENS** became the first British woman to reach the summit of Mount Everest. The following year she went on to become the first British woman to scale the Seven Summits. Since then, her wide variety of interests has led her to lead treks in the Himalayas and Africa, as well as becoming a leadership coach and successful public speaker.*

"When I finished the Seven Summits, I felt a combination of euphoria, relief, and sadness. But I didn't suffer from the well-known post-adventure blues because there are so many different things in life I draw pleasure from."

Curiosity

I grew up in a safe, comfortable, grounded household. I don't think I would have been considered a particularly adventurous kid, at least not for that time period. These were the late 60s, early 70s. Children had a lot more freedom than they have nowadays. This was the era before safety belts in cars and mobile phones. I was free to roam as I pleased, as long as I was home by a designated time. To sum it up, I would say that my parents gave me the freedom to explore, while at the same time ensuring emotional security.

I have two daughters now, aged 17 and 13. When they were younger, I gave them the freedom to explore, to discover. I let them climb trees and ride horses, actually, I encouraged it. Some parents might consider these activities dangerous, but I believe that you have to let kids take some risks and make mistakes, that's how they learn. Yes, my daughters fell off sometimes, but they always got back in the saddle – that's a lesson for life.

I went to university and then into journalism. I guess I was a typical student; mostly occupied with studying, having fun with friends, and going out. In the late 1980s – working in London at the time – I read an article in The Times about a British team of mountaineers planning to climb K2, the second-highest mountain in the world. They were giving a lecture and I went along to hear about it. It turned out that to help fund their expedition, they were inviting members of the public to trek with them to the base camp - something that appealed to me but was too expensive. I suggested to one of the climbers that I might write about the expedition to cover my costs, something that didn't materialize.

Then a couple of years later, this same climber was off to Everest to attempt a first ascent of the North East Ridge and asked if I would like to write about it. Of course! This time I was commissioned by the Weekend Financial Times to write a series of articles on the base camp, from a layman's point of view. It was one of the most enriching experiences of my life. I had never climbed before, never been involved in the mountaineering community. But I had always had a deep love of landscape, particularly mountains. As children, we would go on holiday to Dartmoor, the Yorkshire Dales, and once to Switzerland.

Traveling through the Himalayas, and hanging out at the case camp on the Northern side of Everest for some eight weeks or more, surrounded by the highest mountains in the world, I had a strong feeling of coming home. My job of course was to write about the experience, and the burning question in my head was 'why do climbers climb?' Why do they risk life and limb to climb a lump of rock? Curious, I decided to climb to the first camp on the North East Ridge, a small tent atop a buttress at some 7,100 meters. The majority of the climbers on the expedition were reticent, concerned that I might get acute mountain sickness or an injury. But one wonderful Sherpa, Chhwang, was supportive and lent me all his kit: crampons, ice axe, harness. With one of the climbers on the team, I made my way up mixed terrain on fixed ropes, to a small tent high on the North East Ridge. I looked over the ridge into an expansive, empty valley. I looked up along the ridge, to the Pinnacles, and beyond to Everest's summit. I was hooked. It was the most explosively joyous moment of my life. That same day, I decided I would come back one day and climb to the summit of the highest mountain on Earth.

Seven Summits

When I came back to the U.K., I started climbing. I started with London climbing walls, then traveled further afield. I was lucky in that I was taken under the wings of some very experienced mountaineers who shared the same goal of climbing Everest. A lot of my weekends and holidays were spent training in the mountains of Scotland and Wales. The leader John Barry was responsible for training and logistics, and the only obstacle to our dream to climb Everest was the money. There were a worrying few weeks after I had signed my 3-month notice to resign from my job in order to go to Everest and yet we still had no sponsorship in place. Only at the eleventh hour, DHL stepped on board and made it happen. I will admit I was worried – actually, heart-stoppingly scared – throwing away a perfectly good job when I had a mortgage to pay in the middle of a recession, but in my heart, I had little choice. I so badly wanted to climb Everest and had already ventured a long way along the path; it would have been more difficult to watch the opportunity pass. My parents always encouraged me to follow my heart, and that's exactly what I did by going to Mount Everest. On the 17th of May 1993, I did what I had promised myself four years earlier: I found myself on the roof of the world.

Everest is of course the highest mountain in the world, but in the context of *the Seven Summits*, it is just one of seven, the highest in Asia. A couple of years earlier I had walked up Kilimanjaro (the highest in Africa) with a friend, and the previous year our Everest team had climbed Denali (the highest in North America) as a training peak. Climbing Everest meant that I had climbed three out of the seven. What better way to spend the next few years than traveling around the world and climbing the remaining four? Unfortunately, it wasn't quite as simple as that. I needed sponsorship. Brilliantly DHL was good enough to agree to sponsor me . . . but on one condition. I had to be the first British woman to climb the seven. There was another British woman, Ginette Harrison, also climbing *the Seven Summits*. She was a mountain ahead of me, so I had to abandon any dreams of casually ambling around the world, climbing mountains, yes, but also exploring their respective continents and writing books. Instead, I must run.

I had four mountains to climb in five months and was obligated to climb Aconcagua out of season in October, in dangerously cold temperatures and high winds. Other than Everest, it was the toughest by quite some margin, but we made it. From Aconcagua, we went straight on to climb the last of the seven, Vinson in Antarctica. I remember standing on the summit and the tears running freely – tears that were a combination of euphoria, relief, and sadness, that a colorful chapter of my life was at an end.

Experiential Learning

After finishing *the Seven Summits*, I had no job to return to, and actually haven't been an 'employee' as such, since climbing Everest! But my journalist experience enabled me to write freelance articles and books. I also discovered a new way of communicating – for me, at least – which was public speaking. I honestly had no idea there was such a market. After Everest, I was invited to speak about it by various institutions – schools, theaters, corporations – and continue to be invited today. Most of my work is through referrals.

Besides this, I have written several books including one title, *The Seven Summits of Success*, which I co-authored with business guru Robert Heller. This explores leadership lessons from climbing mountains, that can be translated into the business context to improve performance in the workplace. Through the years I gained more insights into the business world. This has led to hosting leadership workshops on teams, diversity, resilience, decision-making, and communications; as well as 1-on-1-coaching.

Another thing I love to do is to lead treks in the Himalayas – in Nepal, Tibet, Bhutan, and Ladakh – as well as in Africa, most recently in Ethiopia. As well as leading treks essentially for the joy of being immersed in these beautiful places, I also organize treks with an additional 'experiential learning' element to them. For four consecutive years, I worked together with the Rotterdam School of Management (RSM) on an initiative called the RSM MBA Kilimanjaro Project. This was an MBA module that women could elect to attend, on the mountain. In total, I accompanied 70 women on the mountain, the large majority of them to the summit. Although reaching the summit wasn't the main objective. The aim was to develop leadership skills and explore the idea of women relying on women, and working as a team. The focus was on the manner in which we achieved things, not just the achievement itself. The women found that they learned at a very deep level about themselves and others, about the need to trust and respect one another. Many grew in confidence and all developed a network of friends and colleagues for life. The project was a huge success. More women signed up to do an MBA at RSM as a result, and still, I constantly receive emails from students telling me how much this trip changed their lives.

Shackleton

One of the workshops I facilitate is on the navigation of organizational politics. It's a tricky subject. The vast majority of employees steer away from it because they see it as manipulative, or they feel their intellect and ability should speak for themselves. But the reality is that it is important to be politically active within organizations in order to get things done. And it can be done in an ethical manner. The teaching I deliver (based on research conducted by organizational behaviorist Professor de Luca) brilliantly reveals to people how they can be 'wise owls', gather support, and get things done in an entirely ethical manner. It's important to see the big picture; to put the good of your organization above your own gain, to communicate effectively, and most importantly, to be trustworthy. I talk a lot about the trust equation:

Trustworthiness = (Capability + Reliability + Intimacy) / Self-interest. You can't be an ethical leader if you don't care about your people.

On the subject of leadership – and in particular Resilient Leadership – I often refer to the guru of emotional intelligence, Sir Ernest Shackleton. I have sailed to Antarctica in a small boat and crossed the island of South Georgia in Shackleton's footsteps – and know his story inside out. There is so much to learn about leadership from his example. During the COVID-19 lockdown, I wrote an article about the specific lessons we can learn from the story of his *Endurance* expedition of 1914/16. These lessons were helpful in isolation. The first lesson was optimism. Shackleton always stayed positive – even if feeling fearful inside – and successfully ensured his crew was motivated. He also provided structure; he ensured everyone had something purposeful to do every day and ensured that work time was compartmentalized and separate from time to relax and play. This is an important lesson, particularly when people are working at home. The third and most important lesson on leadership from Shackleton was that of compassion. Shackleton was tolerant of people's anxieties and concerns; he understood they were fearful and found solutions to deal with them. For example, one of the crew was hyper-anxious about running out of food, constantly squirreling food under his pillow. The rest of the crew was extremely irritated by his behavior. However, Shackleton understood and put this man in charge of the food supplies, so he would have a sense of control and be less fearful. Such empathy and understanding go a long way when people are working under stress.

Which books about leadership and adventure do you recommend?
Shackleton's Way: Leadership Lessons from the Great Antarctic Explorer, by Margot Morrell and Stephanie Capparell

Giant Steps: The Remarkable Story of the Goliath Expedition From Punta Arenas to Russia, by Karl Bushby. I recently interviewed Karl Bushby. 23 years ago, Karl set off from Punta Arenas, Chile, without any money, with the goal to walk around the world. He skied and swam across the Bering Strait (together with Dimitri Kieffer, read his interview on page 289), walked through Asia, and is now almost at the end of his journey.

Up: My Life's Journey to the Top of Everest, by Ben Fogle. I know Ben in person. He is a very nice guy, an explorer and TV broadcaster.

Beyond Possible: One Soldier, Fourteen Peaks - My Life Beyond the Death Zone, by Nirmal Purja. Nirmal Purja is a Nepalese climber who climbed all the 14 of the 8000 meter peaks in one season, 189 days to be specific. The previous record was almost eight years. He's a guy who gave up his job and a secure pension in the special forces to fulfill his dream. He used crowdfunding to get his project funded, and then corporate sponsors came on board. I confess that like most people I didn't believe he would fulfill his ambition . . . but he did, and remarkably so.

What are you grateful for?

Oh, I would need pages to complete the list of things I'm grateful for. Most of all, my two kids. I'm blessed to have given birth to two healthy children at the ages of 40 and 45. I'm also blessed that I'm still very healthy. I'm blessed that I have had a solid, safe upbringing. And I also count the lucky stars that I'm an optimistic person, which is probably genetic but has gotten stronger through life experiences.

What does a life well-lived mean to you?

A life well-lived, for me, means finding fulfillment in different areas of life: family, work, creativity, adventure. A life well-lived would also be a life in which I have given more than I have taken. Life shouldn't be too easy. It's the difficulties that allow us to grow and develop as people. It's by this growth that we can start thinking beyond ourselves and be of value to our family, community, and even the world on a bigger scale.

Find out more about Rebecca:

www.rebeccastephens.com

If We Detach Ourselves From the Things We Think We Need, It's Easier to Take a Risk and Do Something More Meaningful

HAZEL FINDLAY is a professional climber. She was the first British woman to climb a route graded E9 (8c+/5.14C) and the first woman to free climb El Capitan. While living in her van, Hazel traveled all over the world to climb the most impressive walls. Hazel is also a mental coach and host of the 'Curious Climber Podcast'.

"If I didn't have flow experiences I don't think I would be as happy as I am. If I couldn't climb anymore, I'd definitely search for flow states in other activities."

Becoming a Professional Climber

I started climbing when I was only seven years old. During my teens I had an up-and-down relationship with the sport; sometimes I loved it, sometimes I didn't. After secondary school, I took a gap year and went traveling around the world to climb in the most amazing spots imaginable. Before leaving on this trip, my plan had been to go to University to study Philosophy followed by a Master in Law as soon as I got back. But the trip was so amazing that it got me very much attached to climbing. When I got back to the UK and entered Bristol University, I found myself constantly thinking: "Should I be here, shouldn't I be climbing?" I nonetheless obtained my Philosophy degree, despite thinking about giving up several times during my studies. About the same moment as my graduation, I got a sponsorship deal with *The North Face*, which basically allowed me to climb full-time. As a result, I forgot about the once planned Masters in Law. Later on, during my professional climbing career, I took several courses in the intriguing field of Psychology. These classes led to me becoming a mental coach for athletes as well as business people, musicians, and artists.

The Right Choice?

Looking back, it might seem as if choosing climbing over studying Law was the right choice. I think we can never know whether our choices in life have been the wrong or right ones because we don't have a second life in which we can try out the options we left aside. I don't know what I would have been if I'd not chosen to focus on climbing in my early twenties. I might have been just as successful and happy in a different career.

You got shoulder surgery in 2015 which forced you to stop rock climbing for a while, how did you mentally deal with this setback?

I injured my shoulder in 2009 while climbing a 5.13b route in Utah. This had caused what is called a SLAP-tear and the pain got progressively worse over the following years. After the operation, I noticed that my mood was very low since I couldn't climb. I decided to go on a meditation retreat in India and hike up several mountains in the Ladakh region. During the meditation retreat, I asked myself why I needed climbing to be happy and came to the realization that I actually didn't. If I was mentally resilient enough, I could cultivate inner happiness without the need for climbing. I feel very fortunate that I was able to do this trip, which allowed me to learn a lot about myself. I probably would not have done it without the injury. So, actually, I have to say that this whole process of having the injury, going through a period without climbing, and traveling to India has been a massive mental training in itself.

Van Life

I bought a house in Wales in 2019 and actually, that was the first time since the start of my professional climbing career that I settled somewhere properly. Beforehand, I lived the van life for many years. I recommend living on the road to other climbers. Not having to pay rent is one of the best things you can do for your bank account and having a van also allows you to follow the weather. After all, a climber needs dry rocks and boulders.

Flow and Happiness

I am a level-3 coach at *The Flow Centre*. *The Flow Centre* teaches techniques for easier access to the powerful *'flow state'*. The flow state is when we are absorbed in the moment and apply ourselves in an optimal and effortless manner. When you're in a flow state, it's difficult to feel emotions because you're so absorbed in the present moment. But when you get out of the flow state, you feel very happy, positive and sometimes ecstatic. After a deep flow state, this sense of happiness can even last for days. You can feel happy even if you didn't succeed in your goal (reaching the top of a mountain, winning a race, etc) as long as you've been in the flow state.

I don't think that having regular flow states is necessary for happiness, but it definitely contributes. If I wouldn't have flow experiences I would not be as happy as I am now, I think. If I wouldn't be able to climb anymore, I'd definitely search flow states in other activities. Talking about the relationship between flow and happiness, it also works in the other direction. If you're in a happy, optimistic, present state of mind, it's easier to tap into the flow state.

What advice would you give to the 12-year old Hazel?
The 12-year old Hazel didn't feel great in her skin. So I would tell her: "Don't worry, it's going to get better."

Which advice would you give to someone who feels stuck working in an office and dreams of being outdoors more often?
There are two options: either you change your mindset towards the work you're doing in order to become happier at doing it, or you have to change your work. If you spend so much of a lifetime at work, it has to be meaningful. I know it's a cheesy thing to say, but we only have one life. I think people can be happy working in an office if they are able to find flow states and joy in what they're doing. If they try to do that but don't manage, it's best to change. Taking a different career path is difficult, but if we detach ourselves from the things we think

we need, then it's easier to take a risk and do something with our lives that is more meaningful.

What is your definition of a life well-lived?

A life well-lived entails you being engaged in personal development; you're becoming more kind to the people around you, you become less selfish, you keep on challenging yourself... Basically, a life well-lived is when you're always making efforts to be a better person in order to increase your own happiness as well as the happiness of the people around you.

Find out more about Hazel:

www.hazel-findlay.com
facebook.com/hazelfindlayathlete
instagram.com/hazel_findlay

Be Bold, Humble, and Creative

GRAHAM ZIMMERMAN is a professional climber and co-founder, film director, and film producer at 'Bedrock Film Works'. As the host of the 'REI Wildfire Podcast' and lead of the CLIMB riders alliance at 'Protect Our Winters USA', Graham is also one of the leading voices in climate advocacy in the outdoor world.

"If there's one advice I can give to people who try to juggle different pursuits in life, then it is to regularly retreat in wide-open places with pen and paper. That's where you find the headspace needed to gain clarity about what you have to focus on."

Climbing as the Center Point of Life

My parents lived in Kansas, which is flat as a pancake. Being adventurous people, that wasn't the environment they were longing for, so they decided to move all the way down to New Zealand. I have to praise them for taking such a huge risk because growing up close to wild places definitely affected me. When I was 4-5 years old, we moved to Seattle where it was also easy for me to get exposed to the mountains. Skiing and snowboarding were my first passions. Soon I built a whole community, and even a big part of my identity, around skiing and snowboarding. After a while, I started looking for technical terrain in the backcountry, and this involved hiking up mountains. I discovered that I actually really liked the uphill part of my small adventures. This motivated me to start climbing in the gym at 14 years old and I fell in love with it right away. My parents, on the other hand, were not at all into the idea of climbing. They registered me for a course in which I would learn how to climb and belay properly and safely in the outdoors. In the back of their minds, they hoped that this course would convince me to stick to more reasonable, less dangerous sports. But unfortunately for them, it had the opposite effect; the course only gave me more ideas about what I could do in the mountains.

When I was 18 years old I went back to New Zealand to study Glacier Hydrology at University. Being at the front door of the Southern Alps, it was the perfect occasion for me to cut my teeth in alpine climbing. After finishing my studies in 2008, I went on my first big mountaineering expedition and since then it has never stopped. Throughout my twenties, climbing has been pretty much the center point of my life. I had a variety of jobs and lived in a lot of different places, which was the result of trying to shape my life as much as possible around climbing. For many years I worked as a geologist 4-5 months a year in different places around the world, notably Kenya, Eritrea, Ethiopia, the US, and Canada. These jobs earned me enough money to climb for the rest of the year.

A couple of years ago, a combination of factors made me decide to settle in Oregon. First of all, the relationship with my wife who has a stable job. Secondly, I got involved in several projects related to conservatism, for which it is more practical to have a home base. Thirdly, by going from expedition to expedition, I noticed that I was losing some of my technical climbing skills. I figured out that if I wanted to continue climbing difficult routes for many more years, it'd be better to focus more on training at the detriment of traveling.

Once the decision was made to settle down, the question that followed was: "What do I want to do?" Although working as a geologist had been nice, it wasn't the career I dreamed of. Thanks to my jobs in that field, I had gained quite some experience as a project manager. By the time we wanted to settle down in Seattle, I had also completed several film projects about my expeditions. As a result, I decided to merge my experiences as a project manager and as a filmmaker and to co-create a film studio called 'Bedrock' with my friend Jim Aikman.

Do you feel as if your different pursuits as an athlete, filmmaker, and conservationist push each other forward in some way?
Yes, definitely. Actually, I like to compare my life with a big climbing expedition. Mostly, what people get to see from big climbing expeditions is a couple of pictures of a mountaineer climbing an impressive wall. But that is only a very small detail of that expedition, there is so much more involved than technical climbing skills; researching the country and the region, choosing the right equipment, flying to the country, walking to the foot of the mountain, knowing how to act on snow and ice, knowing how to rescue and how to get help, effective communication skills, nutrition, decision-making . . . You have to manage all those elements in order to be a successful mountaineer.

In my life, in order to be successful, I have to manage the aspects of mountaineering, the aspects of my creative pursuits, and the aspects of climate conservationism. If I'm able to do that, I can have those different projects intersect and lift each other up at a certain point. Let me explain that in a more concrete way: the message I want to share with the world is the one of climate change, and in order to do so I have to tell stories. Filmmaking is the way I like to tell stories. Climbing gets in the picture because mountains are the setting where I personally get confronted the most by the results of climate change. So I am at the top of my game if I can tell a captivating story about climate change through the lens of climbing.

Wanderlust
If there's one piece of advice I can give to people who want to combine a lot of things with the risk of getting overwhelmed, it's this: go to wide-open spaces to sit with nothing but your own thoughts, pen and paper. One thing I love so much about expeditions is that during several weeks there are no Instagram notifications popping up, no inbox I have to check, no phone exploding with messages in my pocket. This gives me the headspace to reflect on life, put things in order, and come back from those expeditions with a clear view of what I have to focus on and which actions I have to take.

You climb quite often with older mountaineers, what are the benefits you get out of that?
Indeed, I climb often with Steve Swenson and Mark Richey who are in their sixties. The benefits are about 'standing on the shoulders of giants'. Starting out with all the knowledge and experience of the generation before allows for building on a baseline that's much higher compared to starting from scratch. It doesn't only allow you to climb routes that are harder, but it's also very important in terms of decision-making.

Take Steve Swenson for example, Steve is no longer able to lead climbs on hard technical routes, that's my job and the job of other young climbers. But what Steve brings to the group is 20 years of experience about the Karakorum: experience about the population, the culture, the mountains, the way to get to the mountains, the weather . . . This way, his presence helps to avoid mistakes and that's extremely important because mistakes can make you lose time, or can put you in danger and get you killed. I don't like losing time and I don't like risking my life. Even if you don't have the chance to go on expeditions with people from an earlier generation, you can learn a lot by talking to them or even by reading adventure stories.

What are the biggest lessons you learned about yourself in the past 20 years?
Make sure that the thing you do is something you do only for yourself. Don't do something to please sponsors or impress a girl you want to date. If you're high on a mountain and get caught by a snowstorm, the decision to go up or come down can't rely on whether the summit will give you extra income, exposure, or other external bene its.

Another lesson is that alpine climbing takes a lot of time to learn. The pace of our current society is very fast and that's re lected by climbers who want to learn mountaineering in a very short period of time. They start from zero and want to do the most dif icult things imaginable in one or two years. In my opinion, you don't achieve greatness in a short time period, mountaineering has to be a long-term lifestyle. If you look at the world's best mountaineers, you'll see that their achievements are spread out over one, two, three decades. People who are fast-tracking adventures get themselves in trouble.

If you could go and grab a beer with three people dead or alive, who would you pick?
Chris Wright, Steve Swenson, and Mark Richey. I climbed Link Sar in the Karakorum with them in 2019, we had a great time.

Shanon
I often praise my wife Shanon, she's a very important factor in my life. It's like we have a double relationship; on the one hand, the romantic one, on the other hand almost a professional one. She has an amazing ability to provide me feedback on the things I'm working on. She's also a former double World Champion ultimate frisbee player. This topsport career has made her gain a lot of experience in dealing with teams. As a result, she helps me out with my teamwork nowadays. She is also much better at Olympic weightlifting techniques than me – squats, pull-ups, things like that – which is very useful if we go to the gym together.

Recommended Books
The Art of Freedom, by Bernadette McDonald. It's a biography of the Polish mountaineer Voytek who has an amazing attitude to climbing.

The Quest, by Daniel Yergin. Yergin is a petro-historian and has written several very good books about climate change and the role of energy supplies in it. The Quest is a good one to start with.
Doom Novel Series, by Dafydd ab Hugh and Brad Linaweaver. I love reading science fiction.

Foreign Devils on the Silk Road, by Peter Hopkirk.

If you were invited to give a college commencement speech, what would your message be?

I would encourage the students to be bold, humble, and creative. Bold, because it's important to be brave, to be adventurous, to take risks. Humble, because it makes you a kind person, it makes you take the right decisions and thus stay alive. Creative, because it makes you ask the question of how you can handle problems in different ways and tell stories that have an impact.

I leaned into boldness, humility, and creativity in climbing, business, and policy work and I think I can argue that it has led to success.

What is your definition of success?

Coming home safe. Having a good time with friends. Having climbed/done the thing you had the intention to do. In that order.

You are the leader of the climber's alliance of *Protect Our Winters USA*, what is the biggest dream you want to achieve with this organization?

There are two dreams. One is to give athletes the tools that enable them to create stories that can craft change; this way they can create meaning out of their adventures. The other dream is to find a middle ground in which we can communicate with other subgroups, most importantly policymakers.

Are you optimistic or pessimistic about the future of our planet?

I am optimistic because I think there's no other option. If we are pessimistic, we'll give up and we'll fail in everything we try to do as a species.

In your opinion, how should and shouldn't outdoor athletes and adventurers use social media?

I think we have to use it to set an example of how we want others to act. That can be by sharing useful messages about how to make safe decisions in the mountains, how to do something for the environment, etc. Besides, I think it's important to keep something for ourselves. Not everything should go on social media. We have to really ask ourselves the question "What is for me, and what is for sharing?" I believe that is necessary for our mental health and also to leave space for self-reflection and for making decisions by listening to our heart instead of outer influences.

What does a life well-lived mean to you?

Finding the balance between different passions, being curious, and having a positive influence on the people around you.

Find out more about Graham:
www.grahamzimmerman.com
instagram.com/grahamzimmerman
facebook.com/grahamgzimmerman

Adventurers Who Know How to Tell a Story are a Gift for Me

BERTRAND DELAPIERRE *is a French alpine climber and filmmaker. Growing up in Chamonix, he was captivated by the surroundings. His career as a filmmaker was launched by going in the mountains with some of the world's best alpine climbers who lived in his village. Today, Bertrand is complimenting his work in the mountains with shooting documentaries to raise awareness for environmental protection.*

"I am grateful to have been able to turn my passion into my job. My definition of happiness is simple: being at the right time at the right place with the right people."

Chamonix

I've been lucky to grow up in Chamonix, where there are amazing opportunities for all kinds of action sports: rock climbing, mountaineering, paragliding, mountain biking . . . As a kid, we went skiing twice a week as part of the school curriculum. In my young years, I did a lot of cross-country skiing in competitions. Because I was very focused on this sport, I didn't start rock climbing until my adolescence. Around that same time, my parents offered me a small action camera which allowed me to record my first mountain ascents. Once I went to University and started my Engineering studies, I stopped filming. But, due to having grown up in Chamonix, I had become a close friend of Marco Siffredi who was a world-class snowboarder at the time. He was the first person to have snowboarded down the North slope of Mount Everest, in 2001. After graduation, I worked only 3 months as an Engineer. Because Marco was a big name in the world of adventure, he opened a path for me that pretty soon led to a lot of opportunities as a filmmaker.

Today, I still live in a village close to Chamonix. Chamonix is a real hotbed for adventurers, so it's very easy to find people to go into the mountains with. It's also probably one of the very rare places on Earth where you can do mountaineering in half a day because we have a funicular taking us up to almost 4000m altitudes. That comes in handy especially now that I have kids; I can leave home in the early morning, climb a challenging alpine route and be back in time to have lunch with the family.

Danger is Part of the Equation

In 2002, one year after snowboarding down Mount Everest, my friend Marco died in the Himalayas. I made a film about his life called *'Marco, l'étoile filante' (translation: Marco, the falling star)*. I've been in the adventure film business for 20 years now, and unfortunately, I lost more friends along the way. I'm very aware that danger is an integral part of my job, it's part of the equation. We try to limit the risks as much as possible, but we can never bring them down to zero. Especially when snow is involved, a significant unpredictability always exists. Despite the tragedies, I never considered putting an end to my career. This being said, because now I carry the responsibility of having a family, I stay away from certain situations I would have put myself in as a 25-year-old. I no longer film at places with seracs for example.

The last couple of years, I've been filming a lot at sea, within the framework of a scientific, environmental documentary. It's a project that involves much less risk but is exciting in its own way. Nevertheless, every time, as soon as I come back home and look through the window, I want to go into the mountains.

Healthy and Ecological

I've got the feeling that my 10 years as a young competitive cross-country skier are still paying off. They laid a foundation of endurance capacity for the rest of my life. Ever since I stopped skiing in competition, I never followed a strict training regimen. I don't do vigorous interval training, for example. I'm just spending a lot of time outside.

As we've been talking about dangers, I do actually think that in our risk analysis, our physical state is very important to take into account. If you've been sitting on the couch for a couple of months, then you can't expect to complete a difficult alpine route right away, even though you've done the route in the past. You could get through – if you're riding on the highway at 250 km/hour you could get through as well – but it's risky. You really have to adapt the challenge you undertake to the physical state you're in at that moment.

Another important aspect of staying in shape is nutrition. In our family, most of our meals are made out of natural products, with very little meat. My wife and I try to teach our children that what we choose to put on our plates has consequences for both our health and the environment. We eat as seasonal as possible – often vegetables out of our own garden – and buy a lot of eco-friendly products.

Egos are Important

When I started off as a filmmaker, there was a rather small group of ambitious adventurers looking for a cameraman. With the rise of social media, there's big democratization happening. Today, everyone can put pictures on Instagram and call himself an adventurer. It has become harder to distinguish true adventurers from people that like to put themselves on a pedestal. It happens that I get a proposition for a new project which seems impressive and professional, but once on scene, there's actually not that much happening. This being said, I think that for filmmakers it's a gift that some people have a big ego because often it's the ego that propels people to do big things, a lot of egocentric people have inspired others. Nevertheless, the ideal subjects to shoot a film about are the adventurers who can be vulnerable and who know how to tell a story. There's little interesting about robotic ego-driven heroes.

Smile Capital

My definition of happiness is quite simple: being at the right time at the right place with the right people. I've been so lucky to be able to discover amazing places in the world, thanks to my job. Above this, I got to experience these places with incredibly talented people, as well as very hospitable locals.

In my opinion, happiness isn't necessarily found in the extremes. You don't have to climb Mount Everest to experience it. Most often, simple moments in nature, in the company of good friends are the experiences that elevate our 'smile capital' the most. For instance, a couple of years ago I shot a film with some amazing slackliners in Polynesia. One evening, a friendly local fisherman offered us fish after having seen us coming down a hill with our headlamps. We had a wonderful evening eating and laughing all together. That simple moment was pure happiness.

Find out more about Bertrand
facebook.com/bertrand.delapierre
instagram.com/bertranddelapierre

Happiness is Doing the Things You Love With the People You Love

*After a severe accident while rock climbing in 2001, two-time World Champion **LIV SANSOZ** decided there is more to life than competition. She went back to where it all started: love for the mountains, whether that's by hiking, climbing, skiing, paragliding, or mountaineering. The highlight of her 'second career' was the ascension of all 82 peaks above 4000m in the Alps in 2017 and 2018.*

"This was a really difficult goal I had set for myself, I learned a lot about myself during this challenge."

Falling in Love With the Mountains

I had my first encounters with the mountains at a very young age. I grew up in Bourg-Saint-Maurice, a village at the doorstep of the Alps. My parents were passionate about nature, the mountains, and hiking. I was only five years old when they took me out camping in mountain cabins. My grandfather was a goat herder and as a kid, I would spend the entire summer helping him out in the fields. This only increased my love for the outdoors. When I was ten years old, I asked if I could join my father and his friends on a ski touring trip. After some hesitation, he agreed. For several years, I would go ski touring with this group of adults.

Since there were also climbers in the group, I got curious about that activity. So at 14 years old, I started climbing with the small club in my hometown. There's no climbing wall in Bourg-Saint-Maurice, so we went outside every time. I've been very lucky to have had a trainer in the club who was very passionate and did everything he could to transfer his passion to us. I remember that we went climbing once in a region called the Calanques, near Marseille in the South-East of France. The Calanques is a wonderful reserve where you literally climb walls out of the sea. I remember thinking on that trip: "This is it, this is what I really want to do!"

Soon after, I started competing in wall climbing and it went quite well. In 1992, only one year after I'd started climbing, I surprised myself by ending up third in the National Championships, one day after I had climbed Mont Blanc with my dad. That's where it became obvious that I could become really good at the sport! But then I would have to be able to train more often in a climbing gym. Since there wasn't a climbing gym in our village, I asked my parents if we could build a wall at home. To my surprise, they agreed and by practicing on the wall at home I made a lot of progress. From there it went really fast. I went climbing a lot in the U.S. with other top-level athletes, I competed in international competitions, and eventually would win 3 World Cups and 2 World Championship titles before I got a severe climbing accident in 2001.

New Doors Opening

One of the biggest lessons I learned in my career is that if you have to change paths, whether you're forced to or you choose to, new doors open. In 2001, my belayer let go of the rope while I was warming up to climb a route called 'necessary evil'. I fell down on the ground, broke a vertebra, and damaged a nerve. This meant I couldn't compete anymore that season, I couldn't try to win a third World Championship title. It was a hard period that led to a lot of reflection. I realized it would be a shame to dedicate my whole life to competition while there are so many cool things to do, it made me long to go back to where it all started: the love for the mountains.

In the rehabilitation process, I started base jumping. Unfortunately, this led to another big accident in 2009. I broke my sacrum and pelvis and had to stay in bed for three months. The following years, I was so fragile that I kept on breaking things: my ankle, my meniscus, wrist, shoulder, my two heel bones, and finally I had a head contusion. Instinctively, I did a lot of visualizations in these difficult years. I visualized myself running, climbing, or walking time after time. Actually, I never lost confidence that one day I would be back.

In 2017, after five years full of setbacks, I started to feel good again and wanted to test myself. The goal I set myself was to climb all the peaks above 4000m in the Alps – 82 in total – and I wanted to do it in less than one year, without the use of any lifts. You can imagine that I started with a lot of doubts after all the injuries of the years before. It would turn out to be an extremely hard challenge physically and mentally. It taught me a lot about myself and my climbing partners. Despite having to spread the challenge over two summers due to getting frostbite halfway, it gave me back a lot of confidence in my abilities. It also taught me again how much I love to be in the mountains and how much I love to share the moments out there with others. This motivated me to start preparations to become a mountaineering guide.

Liv's Bubble

I don't see the utility of meditation for me personally. If I'm in the mountains, I'm forced to be hyper-vigilant anyhow. I have no choice but to be aware and in the present moment. I don't think that meditation before an expedition could give me much of a surplus. On the other hand, when confronted with difficult situations, I need to go into my bubble. I need to switch off the input from the surroundings to recharge my batteries and come to a clear insight into what I have to do.

How would you describe yourself in three words?

Determined

Perfectionist

Human

I'm a perfectionist in the sense that I aim to be perfect. When I make a plan, it's a plan for perfect execution. Of course, in reality, you hardly ever manage to do everything perfectly. I've come to have enough self-knowledge nowadays to be able to let go of the desire to be perfect. I am able to be content with my accomplishments as long as I'm doing my very best, even though it's not perfect.

What's the best advice someone ever gave you?

'Believe in yourself'. It's an American climber and friend, Shelley Dunbar, who said this to me when I was 17 years old. Naturally, I wasn't very confident. Shelley saw my potential, her advice changed a lot. Shelley and I are still friends today.

Which role do you see for adventurers in society?

I think it's our responsibility to sensibilise people to take care of our planet. And not only by sharing this message to our fans or followers, but also by engaging in conversations with sports federations.

Favorites:

Rock climbing or mountaineering? Mountaineering

Valley or summit? Summit

Suffering or comfort? Comfort

Refuge or tent? Bivouac, which happens mostly without a tent for me.

Hot chocolate or champagne? Champagne

Parapet or ski? Ski

Becoming climbing World Champion or summitting all 4000 m'ers in the Alps? Both

Freedom or Security? Freedom

Facebook or Instagram? Instagram

Book or Film? Book

What would you talk about if you were invited to give a University commencement speech?

I think I would encourage them to get to know themselves. In my opinion, this self-knowledge comes by putting yourself in uncomfortable situations, that's where the growth happens.

What does a perfect day look like for you?

Every day is perfect. The days where you wake up in the morning in the mountains with a beautiful sunrise are the most perfect of them all.

What is your definition of happiness?

Doing the things you love with the people you love.

Find out more about Liv:

www.livsansoz.net

facebook.com/LivSansoz

instagram.com/livsansoz

A Life Well-Lived Involves Connection and Purpose

SIEBE VANHEE is a professional rock climber who specializes in big wall expeditions. He has opened over 50 routes all over the world. In 2018, Siebe had a climbing burn-out which led to deep introspection.

"I asked myself the questions 'What do I really want?' and 'What gives me energy?' The answer was simple: climbing. Climbing, but only in the way that is in line with my heart."

Eight Years Old and Obsessed With Climbing

I had a very traditional upbringing. Doing my best at school was highly valued, but I was quite a difficult boy. Siebe and school were two things that didn't go together at all. When I was ten years old my parents sent me to a Steiner school and that was a very good move from them. Over there I learned to be very responsible. My natural curiosity was supported, the rules were less strict, and I was allowed to relate most of my school tasks to climbing, which had already become a true passion by then. When I was only eight years old, my parents let me go to a climbing camp during the school holidays. That was a good thing for them because with my energy levels I was quite a fatiguing kid. But as it turned out it was also a very good thing for me because I got obsessed immediately and became extremely motivated to become really good at it. The following years, during two-week school holidays, I would often do exactly the same climbing camp each week. In the second week, I had the same instructors and we did the same activities as in the first week, but I didn't care, as long as I could climb.

I have one brother and sister who are nine-and-a-half and ten-and-a-half years older than me. By the time I was a teenager, they had left home. I was left alone with my parents who had a lot of fights. In my opinion, they should have divorced then. Luckily, by that time I had a very close relationship with one of the trainers of my first climbing team: Jorn Van Roy. I had gotten to know Jorn when I was 13 years old and soon he became a mentor and father figure for me. Jorn also had the guts to talk with my parents, told them that my home situation was an unhealthy environment for me, and suggested to them that I live by myself. My parents agreed and so I went to live alone in a tiny apartment. I was a very responsible teenager and never misused this position. I went to school every day and invested a lot of energy in becoming a better climber. The Steiner school supported me in my ambition. If I had to go abroad to compete and missed out on one or two days of school, they never made a problem out of that. Another great thing about Steiner schools is that there's a very supportive, enthusiastic ambiance. I never ever felt a sense of jealousy because I was allowed to skip courses to go climbing. I guess that is because every student had his own thing he was passionate about and got supported to develop that passion as much as possible.

Jorn

Jorn has been of enormous importance to me. In my teenage years, he contributed a lot to improve the confidence I had in myself. He also helped me in making hard decisions. When he noticed I was losing motivation for sport climbing, he advised me to follow my heart and focus more on trad climbing and the adventurous aspect of the sport, rather than competition. When I was 18 years old and hesitated between doing higher education or focusing on climbing, he motivated me to try the latter. This way, I decided to leave on a road trip to the coolest climbing spots in the United States and Canada. At first, I looked for someone to join me. But then, again, Jorn said the right thing to me: "Go alone, it will be good for you."

Jorn was right, it was an amazing experience. The two months of road tripping were so intense that I felt as if adventurous climbing trips were what I was supposed to do with my life. Going back to Belgium and studying felt so wrong. At the same time, there was so much social pressure to do it, especially from my father's side. In his family, a good education comes with a lot of prestige. My brother and sister both went to University. I indirectly felt the pressure to do the same. Nevertheless, my experience in the US and Canada had been so strong that I was able to resist the social pressure and decided to save up for another big climbing trip.

For several months I did a lot of shitty jobs in Belgium. When I had earned enough money I returned to the US for a second trip. I immediately bought myself a van and traveled around for a period of seven months. I traveled around with the idea to just enjoy my time before I would go studying after all. But then on the very last day of this trip, an American climbing friend – who was also a bit an idol of mine – planted a seed in my head. He said: "Siebe, we're planning an expedition in Venezuela next year. It'd be cool if you could join us." That simple line shifted my entire planning. Even though this expedition was not yet a certainty, it made me think: "I can't jeopardize the chance to go on this expedition because I'll be committed to following courses." So I went working again to save up enough money for the expedition which shortly after got confirmed to take place. Unfortunately, my best friend and mentor Jorn died of cancer just before I flew off to Venezuela.

Failing and Succeeding to be Free

In the preparation for Venezuela, I tried to find support from companies. I managed to get a deal with *Petzl*; they agreed to pay for my expedition in exchange for six lectures. I saw this as a huge opportunity, so I did my very best to make great footage of our trip. I edited a short movie and gave excellent presentations. At the exact same period, *The North Face* searched for a climber with my profile living in the Benelux. I made a resumé as a pro climber and sent it to *The North Face* agent of the Benelux. It worked out, they were interested and I became a local professional athlete! Only a few months later I was dealt a good hand by meeting a friend of a friend of mine. He was a professional climber belonging to the international *The North Face* athlete team. He introduced me to the sponsorship decision-makers of *The North Face*'s international team. I showed those people the movie and presentation I had made from my Venezuela expedition. They were charmed by it and gave me a chance. At first, I could join all kinds of projects from *The North Face* without a real sponsorship contract. The proposition for a fixed contract – with salary – came after a couple of months. But I laid it aside because by then I had finally started higher education and wanted to focus on that. So for four years, I focused on getting my diploma, while *The North Face* still provided me equipment and engaged me in several of their projects. At the end of my studies, their manager asked me straight: "So what do you fancy doing now, Siebe?" I replied: "I guess I'll focus on climbing now." Apparently, that was all he wanted to hear and so I signed the contract that made me a professional climber.

Two years later, I found myself spending my days watching Netflix. I started working as a bricklayer and I canceled a climbing expedition to Pakistan. I just couldn't deal with the responsibility that came with the freedom I had been offered. I had all the time in the world to do what I wanted. I had enough money to live comfortably and to pursue my passion, yet this freedom was too hard to handle. I felt as if there were too many choices and I put way too much pressure on myself. It had led to a burn-out and a long process of introspection. At the end of this internal journey, a combination of factors made me decide to anyhow continue my career as a climber. At first; the practical question: "If I no longer accomplish things as a climber, how will I earn money?" Secondly, I admit, a sense of longing for recognition, I wanted to be someone in the world of climbing. But what was really decisive were the questions "What do I really want?" and "What gives me energy?" The answer was simple: climbing. Climbing, but only the way that is in line with my heart. That involved climbing with new conditions; only projects that really appeal to me and no more wasting energy in marketing.

At the beginning of my career, I found the social media and marketing aspects of climbing challenging. After a while, it tired me and it set me up with a bad feeling. I didn't like selling myself, I didn't like putting out content only to flatter my ego or to make the sponsors happy. That's why nowadays I work together with a marketing manager who gives me a lot of advice, makes decisions, and takes action in dialogue with me. This way, things such as budget management, contacting sponsors, deciding what to share on social media, etc. are things that no longer drain my energy.

Looking for Purpose

Another good thing that came out of my burn-out was the desire to look for a deeper purpose in my life. I asked myself how my skills, my knowledge, my personality, and my network could contribute to others? This way I got involved in two organizations: 'Unicorn' and 'Escalando Fronteras'. Unicorn is a Belgian organization with the mission to close the knowing-doing gap; they put science into practice when it comes to everything that has to do with leadership. I work there as a coach, which implies that I lead management teams in outdoor activities. This way I guide them through challenges for which skills such as effectiveness, implementing good habits and good fights, trust, dealing with fear, etc. are required. This way they can transfer the lessons from the field into their professional career.

Escalando Fronteras is a Mexican non-profit organization that develops climbing-related programs for at-risk youth in underdeveloped areas of Monterrey. Their goal is to get children off the streets by giving them a healthy alternative hobby and broadening their social network outside of their neighborhood. My biggest contribution to this organization is my position as a climber. I can bring *Escalando Fronteras* into contact with companies that might be interested in financially supporting their programs. I also plan to climb a big wall with the three eldest climbers and make a film about it in order to put the organization in the spotlight.

Which advice would you give to an 18-year old who dreams of building a life around climbing and traveling?

It depends. If it's clear that he or she is someone with a lot of potential and ambition, I'd recommend investing as much as possible in their physical condition until they are about 25 years old. Try to become really good at sport climbing and bouldering before focusing on climbing expeditions. I say this because I might have started focusing on expeditions too early. I have a few regrets for not having invested more time in technical training when I was younger because I believe that would have allowed me to do more difficult routes today. If I look at the Dawn Wall of El Capitan for example, there are a couple of sections graded 9a. I don't think this is impossible for me, but I have to invest in several years of intense hard sport climbing and training for this difficulty. If I'd have invested more in becoming a first-class sports climber and boulderer in my early twenties, I might have been able to climb that route today. On the other hand, when I was 20-21 I made use of the opportunity that *The North Face* searched for someone like me to do climbing expeditions. If I'd have kept on focusing on sport climbing, the opportunity might not have come back later on in life. I went with the flow and I believe the flow is what you have to follow.

The advice I would generally give to the 'average' 18-year old is to discover, to try out a lot of things. There is little to lose when you're young. Also ask yourself what it is that your heart tells you to do, independent of the influences outside of you. What do you really want? What is your intrinsic motivation? And what are the extrinsic factors that make you move, maybe those are not the right ones.

What is the role of humor in your life?

I am a thinker, I have a tendency to be in my head too often. On the one hand, that's a strength, because it keeps me critical and honest about what I accomplish and contribute. But the danger is that my thoughts can shift to the dark side; I'm prone to taking life too seriously, too heavy. In those moments humor is of extreme importance to me. I relate humor to immersing myself in a group of people where I am 'Siebe, the friend' in the first place and not 'Siebe, the climber'. A group of people in which I can just be myself spontaneously.

Humor is also important on climbing expeditions. When you're climbing, you have to be extremely focused. It's fatiguing, sometimes you're cold, you're hungry, you have doubts. Humor is a way to relativize everything and to go back to enjoying what you're doing. That is why it is important to leave on an expedition with the right people. You need to choose people with whom you can have fun, but also people you trust and with whom you feel safe. It can be tempting to leave on an expedition with someone who's sponsored by the same company. Or with someone who has a lot of prestige or is very strong, but with whom you don't get along that well. It took me a while to be able to say no to those proposals because they can become dangerous. A climbing partner you don't like can reduce your confidence and cost you energy and that's not what you need when you're hundreds of meters above the ground. Climbing partners should always give you energy, not take it. Nowadays, I compare going on an expedition with people I don't like with having a broken leg. I don't go on expeditions with a broken leg anymore . . . This quote is inspired by Hansjörg Auer, a dear friend of mine who died in the mountains in 2019.

Out of Comfort

'Out of Comfort' are three words I keep repeating when I give public talks because they are tremendously important. Going out of your comfort zone leads to introspection, it humbles you, it makes you look at your skills in an honest way. That is the gateway to personal growth. Going out of your comfort zone together with others also improves your communication skills and empathy. Going out of your comfort zone also contributes to our happiness, according to me. Because overcoming a big challenge is such an amazing feeling. Lastly, it improves creativity, you have to be creative about finding solutions to problems you have never faced before.

The comfort zone also shifts. For me, a 9-to-5 job or starting a relationship with a woman is something more out of my comfort zone than climbing a big wall, for example. For me, the driving factor for stepping out of my comfort zone is curiosity. In my opinion, it's very important to always stay curious and to be willing to learn about things that are unknown to you. As soon as you're feeling that you're getting into a rut, it's important to ask yourself the question if you shouldn't discover a new environment, new people, a new style of living?

If you could turn back time and relive one moment of your life, which one would you choose?

I would pick the trip to Venezuela because it was such a big step into the unknown. We were four climbers with very little experience, yet we chose to climb a wall that would keep us attached to it for 16 days. We were very badly prepared; we had too little food and had heavily underestimated the wall's difficulty level. Yet, because we had such an amazing composition of personalities and an enormous drive, we managed to persist and accomplish. I think it's just because we were that unprepared that it has been such a strong experience. I'd be curious to see how different the experience would be if we would do this expedition again today, having much more experience and with better preparation.

If you were elected as the first 'President Of The World', what would be your first point of attention?

Giving people the right information. Media today is too focused on sensation and on negativity, while there are so many good things happening in the world. There are a lot of inspirational individuals on this planet. If we gave them the bandwidth they deserve, I think whole communities would be inspired to follow in their footsteps and make their own positive impact on the world.

If you'd be given the chance to grab a beer with three people dead or alive, who would you choose?

Paolo Coelho; I love his books so much. Secondly, Stephen Covey, the author of *The 7 Habits of Highly Effective People*. This book had a big influence on me, it led to several important reflections and new insights about life. Thirdly, Jorn of course.

What insights did *The 7 Habits of Highly Effective People* give you?

A lot, I give you the first ones that come to mind. The book underlined that what we think and how we act is highly biased by our upbringing, environment, and social climate. It showed how important it is to take an objective look at those influences and ask yourself what it is that you really want yourself.

Another principle Covey talks about is 'Begin with the end in mind'. You need to have a direction in your life. A kind of end goal for where you want to be in 1, 5, 10 years . . . but at the same time, you have to understand that this ambition has to be flexible. We change as human beings, the goals we have today may no longer be relevant a couple of years from now.

What is your definition of a life well-lived?

It's mostly about connection and purpose. Having taken the chances that were available, having had the courage to try and fail, having had the courage to build deep connections with people, having acquired insights about who you really are and what you truly want, having accepted who you are, having had a positive influence on other people's lives.

Find out more about Siebe:

instagram.com/siebevanhee
facebook.com/siebevanhee

Leadership Skills Learned From Ernest Shackleton

WIM SMETS *is a Belgian freelance consultant who creates strategic visions and roadmaps for transformational change in companies. His free time goes towards climbing big mountains. He has been on the summit of five 8000m-peaks and completed the Seven Summits.*

"I apply a lot of lessons from mountaineering into my management coaching, as well as the other way around. The two worlds have a lot of similarities."

How a Safari Led to Climbing Mount Everest

As a kid, the holidays with my parents were often spent hiking in the Austrian Alps. Throughout the first decades of my life, I always kept traveling and stayed physically active. Boxing was my main activity, but a dislocated shoulder made me decide to let it go. Around age 25, the curiosity to go back to the mountains came up again, so I completed a 3-week group trekking of the Annapurna Circuit in Nepal. During this trek, I turned out to be the only group member who didn't have problems adapting to the altitude. This stirred up the desire to start mountaineering.

About five years later, I had the idea to do a Safari in Africa, and I looked on the map to see whether I could combine this trip with the ascent of a mountain. This way, I ended up in Tanzania and climbed Mount Kilimanjaro. On this trip, I also met Douglas Beall, a radiologist from the US, with whom I would continue climbing for many years. In 2002, Douglas and I went to Aconcagua. There we ended up in a team with Dave Larson and his daughter Samantha, who was only 13 years old at the time.

Two years later, the four of us went to Denali, the highest mountain in North America. By reaching the summit of Denali. I had scaled three peaks of *the Seven Summits*. Yet doing all of them still wasn't a goal to me. This only came when Dave, Douglas, Samantha, and I found ourselves in a bar in a small Alaskan village after climbing Denali. The combination of euphoria and beer led us to make a pact: we would attempt to climb all of the Seven Summits as a team.

Completing the Seven Summits

What followed was the ascension of Mount Vinson in Antarctica in 2005 and Mount Everest (Asia) and Carstensz Pyramid (Oceania) in 2007. At that moment, Samantha was only 18 and became the youngest person to have conquered *the Seven Summits*. She took advantage of this turning point to start higher education and stopped her expeditions for a while. Also, her father Dave quit the team. While they had finished their own Seven Summits, I still had to climb my last mountain: Mount Elbrus in Russia. I did it one year later and thus became the third Belgian to have climbed *the Seven Summits*.

Honestly, I must say that I'm lucky to have had a well-paid job right from the beginning. But still, climbing *the Seven Summits* involved saying 'no' to certain luxuries: I live in a small house, I don't have a television, I don't buy unnecessary stuff . . . Most of my income goes towards adventure. And even my high income wasn't sufficient to go on expeditions to Everest or Mount Vinson, which are extremely expensive. For these projects, we absolutely had to find sponsorship, and that wasn't easy. My way to convince companies to invest in me is by giving them a worthwhile return. I organize events, I give inspirational talks, and I offer posters of my expedition to decorate their offices.

Two Similar Worlds

I'm primarily a transformation manager and an adventurer during my holidays. That's one of the reasons why I've always experienced that my job is actually harder than mountaineering. But if I would have to climb mountains most of the time and be a transformation consultant some of the time, then it would probably be the other way around. No matter what you do – even if you love it – doing it day in and day out makes it feel like a job.

Since Dave, Douglas, and I are all very busy professionally, we never had the time to prepare for expeditions, other than physically. We always enrolled in organized expeditions that took care of all the logistics and paperwork. This meant that we could focus on getting in shape and the actual mountaineering without having to worry about logistics.

My experience on K2 was the hardest. There were no sherpas and the climb was technically challenging. Despite not reaching the summit, it was probably the climb I enjoyed the most in my entire career, exactly because it was different and challenging. I experience that a lot of climbers are very goal-driven, they perceive their expedition to be successful only if they reach the summit. For me, it's just as important to enjoy the process. The same happens in business.

Perseverance is important. Not only in moments where the action is necessary but also when you can't do much. When you're climbing an 8000m peak, it sometimes happens that the weather doesn't allow you to leave basecamp and the only thing you can do is wait. At these moments, you have to stay positive. You have to keep on making fun, laughing, and enjoying yourself.

In a company, as well as in a climbing team, it's important to know and accept the weak sides of your team members and your own weaknesses. You have to communicate honestly about your weaknesses and compensate for them with your strengths, just as the others must be able to compensate for your own weaknesses. You also have to give your team members confidence, and that's a lot easier with sufficient self-confidence.

You can't be the executor in everything, but you can always be the controller. For example, my strength during the climbs was the physical work; dragging up ropes and bags. But I'm not the fastest when it comes to rope techniques. So I let other team members tie knots, yet each time I check whether they are well done.

I do quite a lot of visualizations of success. I visualize reaching the summit when I'm mountaineering, just like I visualize happy customers and managers when I'm transforming. I really believe that visualizing what success feels like works. But be careful: visualizing failures works just as well in causing failure.

Another tool for success is looking for supporters. Something I do before every summit attempt is check messages from people wishing me good luck. When the going gets tough, I think back on these messages and it helps me get through the toughest moments. It's equally important to be a supporter of others. In our team, I got nicknamed 'the mother' because I was always making sure everybody was doing fine and encouraging them.

Books That Have Changed Wim

The 7 Habits of Highly Effective People, by Stephen R. Covey
A lot of the principles Covey presents have been useful in my management career. One of the aspects I've experienced to be very much true is 'the circle of influence', which states that you should only bother about what you can control. The more you do this, the bigger your circle of influence will become.

Guns, Germs, and Steel, by Jared Diamond
This book explains why Eurasian and North African civilizations have survived and conquered others, while arguing against the idea that Eurasian hegemony is due to any form of Eurasian intellectual, moral, or inherent genetic superiority. To me, it just showed me how lucky we are to have been born in Europe. If I would have been African, my life would have been completely different.

Endurance, by Ernest Shackleton
This is one of the greatest survival stories of all time. The incredible thing about this story is that not one single person died during months of extreme cold, fatigue, and deprivation. And all of the crewmembers attributed this to the great leadership skills of Ernest Shackleton.

Overcoming the Fear of Changing Your Life

What the story of Shackleton shows is that humans are extremely flexible and resilient. This is a message I try to share with people when I'm doing speaking engagements or management coaching, as well as in my book '*The Only Way Is Up*'. A lot of people start a job in their twenties, and at that moment they like the job. But after a while, it becomes a rut, the enthusiasm dissipates. I've been there as well; I started in an IT company called '*EDS*'. It was an engaging job, well-paid. But in 2008 HP bought the company, and as a result, I experienced less pleasure and fewer learning experiences. So, I wanted something different and decided to start as a freelance consultant. This was in 2016. And nowadays it happens that I meet old colleagues of mine who stayed in the company and are now worn out.

There are so many people in their 40s or 50s who are stuck in a job they don't really like. But they don't dare to change because they're not sure it will work out. To them, I say: "You've gone through kindergarten, then through primary school, then through secondary school, and then through University. All of these steps meant a big change in environment and tasks, and you got through them safe and well. Why wouldn't you be alright this time?" You can decide to count down your days to retirement, stay five, ten, fifteen years in the same rut and then all of a sudden get fired, leaving you in a position where it's much more difficult to find a job you're going to enjoy. I think it's better to take the initiative yourself to quit the job.

Find out more about Wim:
www.wimsmets.com
facebook.com/Wim-Smets-361763363872995/

PART FOUR:

I WANT TO RIDE MY BICYCLE

For 10 Years, I Had to Live on Rice and Beans, But I Was Okay With That

Bike-packer **LAEL WILCOX** *won the Trans Am Bike Race against all-male participants, holds the female world record of the Tour Divide and had the fastest known time on the Baja Divide. Besides racing, Lael runs a non-profit which motivates girls to start cycling, grants out scholarships to girls, and created a 500km bicycle trail around Bogota, Colombia.*

"After 12 years of cycling, I still love it just as much. But what makes it really interesting is to share the sense of happiness and freedom with others."

The Road to Becoming a Bikepacker

As a kid, I was always active. I played a lot of soccer and basketball. I grew up in Anchorage, the biggest city in Alaska. Since my parents weren't very outdoorsy, I actually didn't discover adventure until I went to high school. During this period I went hiking and camping with friends, but the bike was not yet involved in our escapades. It wasn't until I was 20 years old that I discovered biking when I searched for a convenient way to cover the 6 km between my home and my workplace. I bought myself a simple bike, and only one year later, after University graduation, I found myself cycling across the country. This voyage only motivated me to keep on exploring parts of the world by bike. For the next seven years, I found myself working six months a year only to save up enough money to bicycle the other half of the year. I had discovered a bottomless well full of possibilities, each trip made me dream about where else I could go the next time.

On one of these trips, in Israel, I discovered there was a 1000-mile long bike-packing race organized across the country. I said to myself: "Why not take part now that I'm here anyway?" I was the youngest participant, the only woman, and had a very basic bike. Nevertheless, I finished at the front of the pack, and really enjoyed the race. When coming home I bought myself a better bike and decided to cycle from my hometown, Anchorage, all the way down to Banff – an over 2000 miles long ride – only to get to the starting line of the Tour Divide, a 2750-mile race from Banff to the border of Mexico. That first Tour Divide has been a key moment in my life. I was sick for days in a row. Every day I said to myself: "If tomorrow I don't feel better, I'll quit." But, I never quit! If I would not have finished that race, I might have never gone back to another long bike-packing race again.

Living on Rice and Beans

For ten years, I was dirt poor because I loved cycling, and wanted to do nothing else but that. Working half of the year was the only sacrifice I wanted to make because it was necessary to provide for my basic needs. I worked for $10 per hour, as a bartender, and saved up half of what I earned. I didn't want to do anything else other than riding my bike, so I just stubbornly stuck to it for a decade. Although that meant I had to live on rice and beans, I was okay with that. Looking back at this period, it seems like it was the right thing to do. But, during those difficult years, I sure wasn't thinking: "One day it's gonna get better, and I'll be a successful, sponsored athlete." I didn't see why someone would pay me to do what I love.

Looking back today, I'm happy I had this period in my life. It made me realize that having very few living expenses can be very liberating. One of my biggest expenses was paying off the student loans from my studies in Chemistry and French (even though I was not using my degree at all).

The biggest problem of living on a bike is going to a city. When you're in the countryside or the mountains, you can easily set up your tent somewhere. But in a city, you need to find someone who can offer you a place to sleep for free. I discovered *"Warmshowers,"* a platform where bicycle travelers host other bicycle travelers. The problem with *Warmshowers* is that you can't just ring on people's doors because you want to visit their city, your ride has to be embedded in a longer trajectory. In the end, I just avoided going to cities. This is a shame because there are so many interesting things to do and see in them. Another problem of living on the bike is bad weather. I remember cycling in the Netherlands, Belgium, and Northern France for four weeks and having rain non-stop. This means that you have to put on wet clothes every day, try to keep your sleeping bag dry, and sleep in a humid tent. After this trip, I started organizing my travels based on where I would find the sun.

Things started to shift in 2015 when I got equipment sponsorship. Until then I had always paid for my bike, gear, and clothing myself. In 2018 I got a sponsorship deal with *Specialized,* which allowed me to become a professional athlete! I admit that life has been much easier since then. There are a lot fewer worries, but my wage is still very modest. No one in the bike industry is gonna get rich I guess (laughs).

When it comes to sponsorship, I've experienced that the new model is not that much about results anymore. You can win all the races, but if nobody outside the world of bikepacking knows about you, sponsors won't be interested. What you have to be able to offer them is media exposure. You have to share your stories by means of films or social media. I am very lucky that my girlfriend, Rue, is a professional photographer and filmmaker. She manages to translate my adventures into amazing storytelling by means of films. Thanks to Rue, and my sponsorship contract, I've been able to share my stories with so many more people.

You have over 90,000 followers on Instagram, and your movie 'I Just Want to Ride' has been seen by one million people on Youtube. How has this big following impacted your life?

I think I am still the same. Social media has definitely made my life better, and weirder at the same time. I get a lot of messages from people who got inspired by me, and started their own bicycle challenges. These messages have left me with mixed feelings. It's cool to know that you have an impact. On the other hand, there's not much more that I can give than a cheering comment in the sense of 'Wow, great!' . . . Of course, I could start a conversation with that person, but I can't do that with everyone because I only have so much to give . . .

Sometimes there's also criticism. And yes, that affects me, I am a very sensitive person. But then I remind myself that it's much easier to criticize than to create, and I just go back to doing what I love: cycling. What's sad is that some people base their self-esteem on their popularity on social media. Really great people who feel bad about themselves because they only have so many followers. What does it matter? You're still an awesome human being!

Despite the downsides of social media, it has helped me to connect with a lot of people, and it has shown the world that women are capable of winning races even against men. But for me, it's really not about beating the other sex. All I do is try the hardest I can. I'm aware there's another generation coming who will soon beat me, and I hope there will be some girls amongst them too. Imagine there's a 15-year-old girl who got inspired by me and will break my records in a couple of years. How great would that be?!

Nasty White Fox

When you're doing long-distance bicycle races, a positive mindset is imperative. You need to look at the bright side of things, try to see the humor in difficult moments. One of the funniest things that happened on my adventures was during my first *Tour Divide*. One night, I heard sounds around my tent. I looked outside and noticed a white fox. This happened several times. The following day, I noticed that all my food had disappeared; salami, cookies, chips, everything . . . Instead of cursing, I burst out in laughter . . . that nasty white fox had stolen it all!

Who have been the most important people in your life?

My family, my girlfriend Rue, and my best friend Christine. But overall, meeting incredible people has been one of the best aspects of bikepacking.

What's the best gift someone can give you?

Something I didn't know I needed. In 2016 my mom gave me a smartphone for Christmas. At that time, I didn't think a smartphone would improve my life, but it really did!

What is your definition of a happy life?

Getting to do the things you like every day. This means that most of my days, I'm happy because I get to ride my bike. But what keeps my bike riding interesting is to share the experience. I'm involved in a community program that puts girls on the bike, I grant out scholarships to girls, I've developed a long-distance bicycle trail. This way I manage to have a direct impact on people's thinking and way of living. Because I do not only want to experience freedom myself, but have as many people as possible experience this feeling.

If you were invited to give a college commencement speech, what would your message be?

Go after your dreams with urgency. Don't push off your dreams, chase them now.

Find out more about Lael:
www.laelwilcox.com
instagram.com/laelwilcox
facebook.com/lael.wilcox

Don't Worry About What Might Happen, Just Deal With the Shit When You Face It!

VEDANGI KULKARNI has cycled across the Himalayas, the length of the United Kingdom, and around the world. She accomplished all of these feats before her 21st birthday. In 2020, Vedangi started her own expedition management company 'The Adventure Shed', and is making big plans for upcoming adventures.

"As a kid, my parents taught me that if I want something, I have to ask for it. If I ask for something, generally people will help me. If they help me out, I can make progress and step up to the next level."

Growing Up in India

I was born near Mumbai and grew up in a city called Pune. My father has had a lot of influence on the development of my adventurous soul. He used to be keen on traveling when he was in his 20's and he also spent a lot of time abroad for work. I hung on to his words every time he told me the stories of his adventures and travels. Because of his job in the oil and gas industry, long periods abroad were alternated with long periods at home. During the periods he was in India, my parents took me on road trips all over the country. This way I learned things about history and geography which most kids only see in textbooks. We also traveled as a family to different countries in Europe and the Middle East.

As good as family life was, so bad was it at school. I had difficulties fitting in, I was 'the weird kid', annoying to everyone and spending a lot of time alone. But at the same time, I was quite courageous and would just step up to other kids and ask them: "Why don't you like me? Why do you find me annoying?" I never really got a good answer to those questions . . .

In my teens I discovered that I liked football and used that as a way to integrate and make friends. The role I was most suited for was goalkeeper because I wasn't afraid at all to jump high and fall back down hard, I wasn't scared of throwing my body in front of a ball or scraping my skin . . . I broke several bones during that period. Thanks to this fearlessness, I made it to a professional level. Nevertheless, I didn't excel at the technical aspects of football and I also wasn't really happy with the team dynamics. So I decided I might be a better coach than an actual player. With this idea in mind, I went searching for scholarships abroad and managed to receive a grant for studies in sport management in the UK.

A couple of months before leaving India, I had cycled across the Himalayas all by myself, a 500-mile long trip. Shortly after arriving in the UK, I made a plan to ride the length of the country. Well, actually, I didn't really make a plan; I just took my bike and left the front door with that idea in mind (laughs). I had no tent, no sleeping bag, no mattress, not even warm clothes. My "plan" was to knock on people's doors and ask to sleep there and igure everything else out along the way. I must say: it was a steep learning curve. A lot of things went wrong, but in the end, I made it. When I was sitting on a bench at John O'Groats, looking out over the ocean, I said to myself: "Wow, look what I've been able to do! I cycled the length of Britain without actual preparation and actually enjoyed it! Wouldn't it be possible to cycle around the world too?"

The Power of Being Naive
Shortly after, I set myself a big goal: I wanted to cycle around the world in 100 days, which would mean beating the *Guinness World Record* for the fastest woman to circumnavigate the globe on a bike. Looking back at it, just as before my trip across the UK, I was way too naive when I set myself that objective. But you know what, I think there is power in being naive. If you don't research everything to the smallest detail beforehand, you're less likely to stop yourself because of fear, you simply don't know what to be afraid of. For example, if I would have been super prepared for my trip around the world, I might have freaked out about passing through Canada where bears are living or I might have stressed out about not finding food in certain areas. What happened is that I just arrived at those places with bears or without food. Yes, I got uncomfortable and a bit afraid, but I dealt with it because I had no other choice.

This being said, one thing I've been way too naive in was my route tracking and navigation. First of all, I didn't even know that you can enter your route in advance with a GPS and then just follow its instructions when you're on the road. Instead, I was constantly reaching out for my phone to check which direction I had to go. This has obviously cost me a lot of time. On top of this, often I would just shut off my tracker to save its battery or because I was afraid people would follow me or because I was riding on endless straight roads, where using a navigational device was useless. The problem is that you need to have data from your entire route to send to *Guinness World Records*. I naively thought that if I explained why I hadn't used my tracker on some parts of the route, they would simply believe me. But things don't work that way.

Reconnecting the Dots
In the end, it didn't matter that much because I finished my trip around the world in 160 days, while at about the same time Jenny Graham broke the *Guinness World Record* by cycling around the world in 124 days (Read the interview with Jenny Graham on page 159). But what shocked me is how many comments I received on not having tracked my entire route, people thought I had cheated. I remember receiving an insulting email from a complete stranger on the day of my 20th birthday – when I was halfway through my route – accusing me of having skipped certain parts of the trajectory. Happy Birthday! Also when I came back home people kept on questioning my integrity to the point where I started becoming paranoid. I consulted a psychologist and explained to her that I was sure that I had cycled around the world, but that at the same time I was doubting it because everyone else was.

The psychologist hung up a big world map on the wall and asked me to draw my entire trajectory. So I drew a line across Australia, New Zealand, Canada, Portugal, Spain, France, Belgium, The Netherlands, Denmark, Sweden, Finland, Russia, Mongolia, China ... Next, she asked me to put a random dot on the trajectory, which I did. She asked me how far I was on my trip the moment I got to the point that matched the dot and if I remembered something that happened over there. I could almost tell exactly what day I had been there and how it was. Then she asked me to draw another dot, and again I could give a detailed description. We repeated this for several more dots until she asked me to close my eyes and tell the story of the entire journey from A to Z. I started telling everything I could remember and the moment I finished the psychologist said: "Now you know that you have done it and you don't have to prove it to others."

What I learned that day is that the only thing that really matters is what I think about what I'm doing. It's something I've applied to other situations many times since then. For example, lately, I started running and sharing my training sessions on *Strava*. On the platform, I noticed how fast other people were running compared to me and that made me feel bad. I reminded myself of the lesson learned at the psychologist and set to myself: "Vedangi, you're running for yourself. It's a challenge you've set yourself to become a better person, it's nonsense to compare yourself to others."

You are only 22 years old and you have already moved to Europe all alone, you have cycled across the Himalayas, across the UK, and around the world and you have started your own company. Where does your boldness and confidence at such a young age come from?
Given the culture in which I grew up, I could be expected to be a shy girl. Luckily, my parents have always stimulated me in the opposite direction. I've talked about the trips we used to do as a family, well on those occasions they always supported me to find a way to contribute to the journey; as well in preparational work as financially. I remember that one day I had the idea to collect objects we had at home and go out on the street to sell them. When my parents found out about that afterward, they weren't happy about it, but I sure had gained some audacity that day!

I also remember a particular journey in Switzerland when I was nine or ten years old. My mom carried a dictionary with her, which allowed us to translate simple sentences such as "Excuse me, madam, what's the time?" into German. This way, she pushed me to step up to people and ask them for help in broken German. Being a small kid, that was a very scary thing to do! But the lesson was that if I want something, I have to ask for it. And if I ask for something, generally people will help me. And if they help me out, I can make progress and step up to the next level.

Reaching Out to Mentors
Sumit Patil is a friend of my parents who has cycled the *Trans Am Bike Race* and knows a lot about mountaineering. He was the person who made me believe that I was capable of cycling across the Himalayas and who helped me prepare for that challenge. Since that first adventure, I've asked him for advice countless times, so I consider him to be a true mentor.

In the meantime, I also have a bunch of people in the UK who I could call mentors. When I arrived here I wanted to find out how the adventure community works in the country. I put my childhood lesson into practice and sent out a bunch of emails to people like Mark Beaumont,

Ben Saunders, Jenny Tough, and Megan Hine to ask them for advice. Today, I have a whole list of phone numbers of accomplished adventurers and feel as if I could call them at any time to ask for advice. Some of them have even become friends.

Knowing Who You Want to Be

I write a lot. I have plenty of notebooks lying on my shelf. One of the journaling exercises I do every now and then is writing down which kind of person I want to become. I want to be someone who gets along with everyone without being a pushover, I want to be someone who knows how to set boundaries and can say no in a polite way. I want to be an adventurer who has no doubts raised about her accomplishments. I want to be someone who gives importance to the expectations of others but not to the extent that it creeps into my mind and makes me feel insecure. I also want to be someone who doesn't feel guilty about thinking about herself, nowadays I too often put other people's interests first. I think that if you want to be successful it's necessary to be a bit egocentric at times.

It's funny because recently, I had a discussion with other female adventurers about this. They said to me I should be happy with who I am, that I should stay true to my nature instead of trying to change myself. I don't know if I should listen to them, maybe . . . What's for sure is that I'm a work in never-ending progress. I will always keep on learning and trying to become a better person.

During your world trip, what have been the biggest lessons you learned about yourself and the world?

The world is really kind, with the premise of believing that. I have learned that if I expect people to be kind, they will be. If I expect drama and rude people, that's what I'll find too. It seems to be that the story I make up in my mind becomes reality.

I learned that I should trust my intuition. When I was in Spain, I wanted to make up for lost time and decided to ride during the night. One particular night I had a bad gut feeling. My intuition told me something was about to go wrong, but I decided to go for it anyhow. A couple of hours later I found myself in a hold-up with a threatening knife at my neck . . .

I also learned that I'm stronger than I thought. I had days in which I rode a total of 400 km. I spent nights with very little sleep. I pushed through pain I couldn't have imagined before. I also learned to be patient; because nobody gives a fuck if you're impatient. If you're at a border and need a visa, nobody really cares about that.

Waiting for a VIsa

When I was in Helsinki on my world trip and applied for my Russian visa over there, I heard that it would take one week to receive the visa after application. At that moment I had spent several weeks cycling in the heat and thus felt like going somewhere very cold. I took the farthest flight north and from there I took the bus that went as far as possible in the Arctic direction. Then I spent a couple of days hiking in the snow before coming back to Helsinki. It was fun!

Recommended Books
Becoming, by Michele Obama
Anywhere But Home, by Anu Vaidyanathan
The Biography of Steve Jobs, by Walter Isaacson

How would you describe yourself in three words?
Bold, adventurous, and curious.

Where do you see yourself 5-10 years from today?
I really want to beat the *Guinness World Record 'fastest woman to cycle around the world'* and do it in 100 days. So I'm sure gonna give that one another try, this time much better prepared.

Another adventure seed in my mind is an Arctic expedition in which I want to meet indigenous people, see how they live, figure out how climate change affects them, and see what I can do to help them.

I hope that in 5-10 years from now I'll be an established public speaker and that *The Adventure Shed* is a flourishing company that creates a firm, stable income. I want to give back something to my loved ones, especially my parents. All I can offer them now is my time, I would like to support them financially as well.

What advice would you give to girls your age who want to go on an adventure but have too much fear holding them back?
Open the door and get outside. Don't listen to the naysayers, don't worry about what might happen in advance, just deal with the shit when you face it!
But at the same time contact my company so we can do your risk assessment. (laughs)

What is your definition of happiness?
A walk in the woods without worrying, just being fully engaged in nature. Or sitting around a fire with friends, because that's where good, deep conversations take place.

Find out more about Vedangi
www.vedangikulkarni.com
www.theadventureshed.com
instagram.com/wheelsandwords

I Still Wish I Could Be More Normal

RACHEL YASEEN is a full-time gypsy adventurer, citizen of the world, meditator, cyclist, trekker, chef, scuba diver, yogi, mother, blogger, and vlogger. Her passion is the journey to self-discovery through meditation and adventure. 5 years ago she gave away nearly all of her belongings to live a nomadic lifestyle. This lifestyle, though, came with a lot of sacrifices.

"In order to make my adventures possible, I had to put an end to certain important relationships; the one with my husband, but also with my mother."

The Definition of Adventure

For me, adventure is putting myself into a situation where there is an element of surprise, unpredictability, and risk. It is about jumping into something without knowing how it will end. In 2006 I had a child, Wexler. That was and continues to be an adventure. It's probably the hardest thing I have ever done; raising this little human in a world that does not mirror my values or even understand my basic priorities.

The adventure that would take my life for the biggest turn began in 2015 when I walked the Camino de Santiago. I left home alone and took the flight to Madrid. From there I took the bus to St. Jean Pied de Port and started walking nearly 1000 miles to Santiago. When I returned back to Arizona months later, I was not the same person. I realized that I could do so much more than I ever could have imagined. A week after my return, I asked my husband of 25 years for a divorce. I loved him, but I wouldn't be able to follow my dreams together with him. I knew in my heart that this was the only thing I could do but I had absolutely no idea what my life would be like from there. And this is where the true adventure began.

Saying 'Yes' and 'No' to People

The hardest part about building this lifestyle was mental, for sure. The shame of not living up to family's, friends', and societal expectations. I still wish I could be more normal. In order to make my adventures possible, I also had to put an end to certain important relationships; the one with my husband, but also with my mother. I had to say 'no' to living in a stable community. However, for most of my life that had only been a dream anyway. I live in my own little world. I'm not in touch with many people. But of course, I meet a lot of strangers along the road, their hospitality and kindness have always been profound; in remote villages as well as cities.

I'm now traveling with my new partner, Rene. He's Danish. We met each other on the way to Santiago. At the end of the Camino, we had to fill in a form in order to receive a certificate. When asked about our occupation, Rene answered: "traveler." I bursted out in tears. Traveler, that was what I wanted to be as well . . .

A couple of times a year, I go on an adventure with my son. I think every parent should cultivate patience and perseverance in their children, and adventure is one of the best ways to do this. We completely underestimate our children's capacities. Wexler has done so many incredible things. We worked on a reforestation project in Haiti, he learned Spanish in Guatemala, he went to school in Peru, we walked part of the Camino de Santiago together, and many more adventures. Last year Wexler and I did a hike through the night. When we finished, he said he never wanted to do that again. But this year, he asked me to do another hike at night, and he wanted to bring his friend JP with us. Disclaimer: I am not particularly good with children. But Wexler insisted that his friend was quite strong. While this was encouraging, walking through the night involved a lot of challenges: we had to be able to navigate in the dark, we would get very tired and we would be crossing streams, some waist-high. We started at 6 pm and finished at 7 am. Most kids have walked one, two, maybe three hours, but few have walked 13 hours, let alone in the dark! It was hard, but they did it. They walked through the night with grace. They were awesome. It was a fantastic accomplishment.

Some of the Most Beautiful Experiences
- Scuba diving in East Indonesia is truly world-class.
- Cycling eight hours for only 34 km on a very steep and muddy hill in Thailand. And then, during the downhill, facing a wild elephant as a reward.
- Cycling at night during the summer in Australia to avoid the heat, with the danger of kangaroos bumping into us, but with the upside of seeing a beautiful sunrise every morning.
- The hospitality of farmers on the Indonesian Flores island; we spent entire days swimming with kids in the river, learning about local traditions, and eating delicious food.
- The euphoric feeling of accomplishment at the end of every hard cycling day.

Training Body and Mind
I eat a lot of food! I notice that I need to keep sugar to a minimum; I am best with real meals instead of crappy snacks. Sleep really affects my mood, I try to get eight hours in each night. The physical training happens on the bicycle, on the journey. Maybe even more important than the training is making sure to take time for rest.

I began to meditate about 20 years ago. Depending on my situation, I meditate for anywhere from five minutes to several hours a day. In 2018, I did a 21 days silent meditation retreat in Myanmar.

Books That Have Influenced Rachel
Siddhartha, by Herman Hesse. I read this in 1991 and it had a profound impact on me. It is actually a story about the Buddha. The idea of leaving all known comfort behind, denying myself of material possessions and physical needs, was incredibly exciting. It lit me up. I finished the book and told my boyfriend that I wanted to put our things in storage and start traveling. He was way too practical and responsible to participate in my plan. And because I was in love, I tucked this dream into the back of my mind. It would take another 25 years before I could make it a reality!

Rowing the Atlantic: Lessons Learned on the Open Ocean, by Roz Savage. Roz Savage rowed across the Atlantic Ocean all by herself. This was such an inspiring story because it demonstrated that a single woman can achieve such a great accomplishment. Her story made me feel that I was invincible. It illustrated for me that each of us can do so much more than we can possibly imagine (Read the interview with Roz Savage on page 197).

Swimming to Antarctica: Tales of a Long Distance Swimmer, by Lynne Cox. Lynn Cox does ocean and lake crossings in extremely cold water. She crossed the Bering Strait - five miles in 3°C water, wearing only a swimsuit, bathing cap, and goggles. I think this is the first book I read about a female adventurer. At that point, I did not see myself as an adventurer but I was inspired to consider that there was so much more out there than I ever dreamed possible.

Characteristics and Personality Traits
[I asked Rachel to rank herself from 0 (not like this trait at all) to 10 (very much like that)]

Optimism: 5 (depends on the situation)
Discipline: 5 (depends on the situation)
Courage: 9
Resilience 9
Stubbornness: 5
Social skills: 3
Creativity: 3
Intelligence: 5

We Are All Adventurers
We are all adventurers. The difference between most people and me is that I focus on making it a big part of my life. I think I have a couple of personality traits that make me feel so good in this kind of life: flexibility, the propensity to a nomadic lifestyle, a yearning for change and movement, endurance . . . For me, the most important thing about adventure is allowing for the unexpected, I often fight it. What helps is listening to more adventurous people who do bigger things, via podcasts like *Tough Girl* and *Wild Ideas*. Then I think: "If they can do that big thing, I can certainly do the little things." Rene also pushes me. I do live my life based on faith, faith is what I need to be my truest self, to embrace uncertainty, unpredictability, and risk.

My next adventure will probably be to motivate other people to follow their passion. I would like to make people think alternatively, I want to shake things up, I want to make them think big. People have so much more potential than they can possibly imagine. I want to motivate them to do something scary, without worrying too much about finding the right people, the logistics, or the money. Just go out there and try the thing you want to do, you will figure it out.

Find out more about Rachel:
www.rachelyaseenworldwide.com
facebook.com/rachelthetraveler
instagram.com/rachelyaseen

Just Get Started!

FRANK VAN RIJN has been traveling on a bike for 50 years, good for more than 600,000 km pedaling. During this half-century, he wrote 15 books about his bicycle adventures.

"A writer who's always traveling doesn't find time to write, and a traveler who's always writing doesn't get to traveling, so a 1:1 distribution turned out to be the best solution for me."

Traveling Writer

Very early on, as a kid, I discovered that taking bicycle trips is much more interesting than doing homework. This didn't always lead to the desired result, at least not when it came to my grades. But it led to another desired result: having a lot of time for my hobbies, of which cycling was the main one. In 1971, I decided to go on my first real bicycle trip. The plan: one month in Belgium, France, Switzerland, and Germany. I had never set up a tent, nor baked an egg before, so I started off with quite some doubts about the success of this trip. Luckily, it turned out to be a big adventure and a successful experiment. The freedom I experienced was a real epiphany.

The following years (while studying at the University of Delft) I would spend all summer long cycling. In 1978, I met a French cyclist in Algeciras, at the Southern tip of Spain. The man had taken the ferry from Tangier after a 3-year long bicycle trip. This encounter inspired me to undertake my first very long trip. As soon as I graduated as an electrical engineer, I bought myself a ticket to Southern Peru, from where I rode all the way up to Denver, Colorado. On this 9-month adventure, I discovered the beauty of famous tourist spots such as Machu Picchu, as well as simple agricultural villages far away from civilization. The landscapes of the Andes, the Sierra Madre, and the Rocky Mountains were breathtaking. After finishing this trip, I went to work as a physics teacher. Having to keep myself in line to stick to a tight timetable, as well as 25 pupils having a purpose different from learning physics, turned out to be a much more difficult challenge than cycling 24,000km over 5000m-tops in South America.

At the end of this year, I decided to take one more gap year. Just one, before starting a 'serious' life. I went through the Balkan, Turkey, and the Middle East towards Cairo, and from there to East Africa and down to Cape Town. Again, I was delighted to experience the adventure, to discover the true hinterland of Africa, with its different cultures, religions, and traditions. After this year, history repeated itself: I went working once more in a school as a physics teacher, again with tight timetables and uninterested students. My evenings were spent dreaming about another adventure and studying maps of where this next adventure would lead me: Asia. So when this school year came to an end, I cycled all the way from the Netherlands to Bali. In the meantime, I had also started earning a small income from writing books and giving lectures about my bicycle travels. This way, I transitioned from being a cycling teacher to a traveling writer. I had to figure out how to combine writing and cycling, because a writer who's always traveling doesn't ind time to write, and a traveler who's always writing doesn't get to traveling, so a 1:1 distribution turned out to be the best solution for me.

Did cycling across the world change you?

Every trip I've done has changed and shaped me, slowly, to some extent. I used to see things as simple and clear, and I was always right. Now I can see that everything is relative. Other people and other cultures think differently, believe differently, and act differently. Today, I understand that and respect the differences.

After my third trip across Africa, I felt as if I had become too much African for Europe, but that I was still too much European for Africa. That's another reason why it suits me to spend 50% of my time amongst other cultures, often in 3rd world countries, and 50% of my time at home writing about these cultures and countries.

Escaping Death

I've been in some very dangerous situations during my 30 years of traveling. Every busy road is a big risk, especially because there are a lot of people combining alcohol with driving. I've been attacked by bandits a couple of times. The worst time was in India, where 20 bandits armored with pitchforks and axes chased me. The axes lew around my head, but I could escape. Another danger occurred in India, where I had a severe accident riding downhill. My front fork broke and I smashed my forehead on the asphalt.

Who have been the most important people in your life?

Definitely my parents. They grew up during wartime and never had the chance to travel while being young. My mother encouraged me when I was doing my first trips, she said: "Grab the opportunity now, while you're young. When you'll be old, you will no longer have the chance to do this kind of adventure." She was right, so I took thc opportunity. My father was more skeptical in the beginning. He believed my only chance to experience a good future was by taking a good job. Later on in life, he admitted that I had made the right choice by traveling and writing about my travels. He has always supported me during my trips, for example by sending me spare parts from the Netherlands to where I was in need for them at a certain moment and place in time, or by doing my tax declarations while I was on the other side of the world.

How do you get your projects inanced?

I manage to make a living out of my books and lectures. For the last couple of years, I can profit from a pension. I think it's very difficult to find sponsorship these days, it helps if you first cycle around the world 10 times.

I have a fairly simple lifestyle. I think that our society today wastes way too much: energy, clothing, cars, televisions . . . Stuff that is still useful gets thrown away and replaced by something that's fashionable. If we no longer like the color of our kitchen, we throw out everything and give it another style. Two years later, we're bored again and we do it all over again . . .

How do you stay in shape?
Nothing special. When I'm in the Netherlands, I usually write in the morning and do a little bike ride in the afternoon.

What advice do you give to people who want a life full of traveling and adventure?
Just get started!

Find out more about Frank:
www.frankvanrijn.nl

I Still Haven't Figured Out What Happiness Means

CHARLIE WALKER cycled 43,000 miles around the world, skied the length of the Ural Mountain Range, paddled the Congo and the Ural rivers, and walked across Mongolia, the Gobi desert, and Papua New Guinea. He tells stories about his adventures through the means of books and public talks for people of all ages.

"Adults want to hear about people and culture. Children, on the other hand, are much more interested in animals. They want to hear stories about that time I woke up next to a snake or saw a crocodile in the Congo river."

Around the World on a £100 Bicycle

I grew up in a small village in a rural area of the UK, with one brother and two sisters. As kids we were quite active; running around, climbing trees, building little fortresses. Summer holidays with the family were mostly spent in the south of the country. It wasn't until the end of high school that I discovered what traveling really means. I took a gap year and went to Southern Africa and East Africa. Over there, I became fascinated by the people, the cultures, and the landscapes. I began studying English Literature at University, but the following summer I went back to the African continent. This time to the West. I was hooked on travel and the seed that had been planted one year earlier just kept on growing.

When I was 20 years old, a friend of mine convinced me to go cycling and hiking in the Nepalese Himalayas. That's where traveling started shifting into an adventure. I experienced the satisfying feeling of traveling under your own steam. Whenever you get to a beautiful spot, you feel as if you really deserve it. I also felt extremely healthy and fit. This trip gave me the thirst to do more of this purist kind of travel.

With my interest in both literature and travel, the dream to become a travel writer formed. I figured out that the best way to become a good travel writer would be to have as many extraordinary adventures as possible. After one year of working as a staff journalist, and sleeping on a lot of sofas, I had saved up £12,000. The most economical way to have many experiences on this rather small budget was to travel by bicycle. I bought myself a second-hand bicycle for £100 on eBay and soon after took my first pedal strokes of what would turn out to become a 43,000-mile journey.

Financial Limitations

These days people send me a lot of questions about how to organize an adventure. The most common is: "How do I get my expedition financed?" It's difficult to provide a universal answer because everyone has different desires and needs. Nevertheless, my main tip is to ensure you don't need a lot of money. You don't need to start big or go far right away, you can easily start with micro-adventures just around the corner.

In fact, if you're creative enough, it's even possible to find ways to earn money while traveling. I managed this when I was cycling the length of Sweden. Over there, for every bottle you recycle, you receive a small amount of money. I noticed that many bottles and cans were strewn along the roadside. So I started collecting them and exchanging them for money at supermarkets in the scattered towns I passed through. This way I managed to cover the food costs for my entire journey, and then even save up. You're allowed to wild camp for free in Sweden so I didn't have any hotel costs. I actually made money while traveling there, while at the same time doing something beneficial for the environment and the country.

Universal Goodness

I've been to over 80 countries now and I've noticed that people are quite similar everywhere. Of course, there are the interesting, superficial things that make different cultures unique – things like art, music, food, faith – but aside from these, people are more or less the same around the world. No matter where you go, the vast majority of people are friendly, caring, and looking out for each other. And they are welcoming and polite to bicycle travelers.

The Stupidest Thing Charlie Ever Did

When I was 23 I cycled across Tibet in midwinter. Foreigners are not allowed to travel there independently. To get across the border I cut a hole in the fence of a military base at four in the morning. During the following month, I sneaked through six more military posts in the middle of the night, until I eventually got caught. All that time I had footage of the first military post saved on my *GoPro*, so I could easily have been accused of espionage and put into prison. Luckily I hid the camera deep in my many layers of clothes and it wasn't discovered. Nevertheless, this Tibetan adventure was a foolish and dangerous thing to do. I put my life on the line: the military posts were manned by soldiers with rifles and aggressive military dogs that could have attacked me. I also could have frozen to death during the nights when the temperature dropped as low as -40°C.

How do you deal with loneliness?

Loneliness is a difficult challenge. It's the thing I struggled with most during my 4-year long bicycle trip. In certain regions, I didn't see a single person for several days. In Tibet, I spent 3 weeks without talking to anyone. I've found the best way to deal with loneliness is to stay stoic about it, to remind yourself that it's a temporary problem. Accept the fact that this is just a tiny period in your entire life where you don't have the possibility to talk with people. Remember that there is light at the end of the tunnel; you'll soon see the people you love and you'll be with your friends again.

If you could turn back time and relive one day of your life, which one would you pick?

The day I arrived back home after my four-year-long trip. Embracing my family and friends at the finish line felt so good, especially in combination with the satisfaction and pride at what I had accomplished. The party that night was great too. (laughs)

Recommended Books

The books I like to read depend very much on whether I'm on an adventure or at home. At home, I like to read literature that teaches me something. As a result, I read almost solely non-fiction, often adventure stories. When I'm on an adventure, on the other hand, I look for some kind of escape. When you're lying in a hammock in a humid, warm jungle, surrounded by thousands of mosquitoes, the last thing you want is to read some adventurer's biography.

I love to read the adventure stories of Redmond O'Hanlon. O'Hanlon is a biologist and ornithologist. And he looks like a bumbling 19th-century professor. But he's traveled to the most remote jungles in the world and got himself into all kinds of trouble over there; which makes for good reading. Another favorite is Benedict Allen's '*Mad White Giant: a Journey to the Heart of the Amazon Jungle*'.

About Storytelling

I've written two books about my four-year bicycle travels: '*Through Sand & Snow*' and '*On Roads That Echo*'. Compared to magazine articles, writing a book gives you a wonderful amount of freedom. In articles, you only have so many words to express your experiences and feelings about the journey. As a result, you're mostly limited to facts, brief observations, and swift descriptive narrative. In a book, on the other hand, you can go deep. You can truly express your thoughts and feelings and explore more complex ideas.

Another way of storytelling for me is public speaking. In a normal, Covid-free year I usually do over 50 speaking engagements; for businesses, literary festivals, book clubs, schools, etc. I've spoken for audiences ranging anywhere from 10 to 1,300 people. I like the creative challenge of adapting my story to a specific audience. Adults want to hear about people and culture. Children, on the other hand, are much more interested in animals. They want to hear me talking about that time I woke up next to a snake or saw a crocodile in the Congo river. As a result, when you have people from 5 to 80 years old in a single audience, it's an exciting exercise to make your talk interesting and understandable for everyone.

Today, I make my living solely from public speaking and book sales. This means that I officially carry the job title 'adventurer', and that still sounds weird to me.

What does happiness mean to you?

Tailwind on a bicycle. (laughs) No, I'm afraid I can't give you a good answer. I've thought about the concept of happiness quite a lot but still haven't really figured out what exactly it means to me. I guess happiness has a different focus at different times. For example, in the present moment it means the absence of suffering, it means having food, shelter, and good company. This is called Type One fun. But I've also retrospectively experienced tremendous happiness from moments in which I suffered, where I was hungry, where rain poured down on me, and where I felt extremely lonely. It's miserable at the time but you look back at it fondly. I suppose it's formative and character-building. This is known as Type Two fun. I need both types!

Happiness over a lifetime is yet another thing. If I continue my style of living, I think when I'm older and look back on my life I will be happy. Despite experiencing a whole lot of miserable moments, even moments where I came close to death. Because I'll have learned a lot from these experiences. And also, hopefully, people will have enjoyed these experiences through my work. I suppose in that regard vanity and ego are also a part of happiness.

Find out more about Charlie:
www.cwexplore.com
instagram.com/cwexplore
facebook.com/cwexplore

Every Project is Like Building a Start-Up

*In 2008, **MARK BEAUMONT** broke the World Record for cycling around the world un-supported. He covered 18,000 miles in 194 days. Nine years later, Mark repeated his feat, this time with a support team backing him up. With an average daily mileage of 240 miles, he circumnavigated the planet in 78 days. But Mark is more than just an extraordinary cyclist.*

"I've got interest in innovation, in investments, in property, in filmmaking, in storytelling, in writing . . . my life is far more interesting than being a professional bike rider and completing races."

How did you get into adventure?

I grew up on a farm in the Scottish Highlands with my parents and two sisters. We had quite an active childhood; we were homeschooled but spent most of the time on the farm. Every day we had to milk 60 goats and collect eggs from 200 hens before breakfast. Activities like riding ponies, climbing hills, and camping were my first contact with what you could call adventure.

At age eleven, I decided to go on my first sort-of expedition. The idea was to cycle from Lands End to John O'Groats (874 miles across Britain). But mum suggested I should try something smaller, so we ended up cycling from Dundee to Oban, 140 miles from the East to the West coast of Scotland. With this adventure, I was already fundraising for charities and I enjoyed telling the story in the local newspaper. This first adventure was a great learning experience and gave me a big buzz of motivation to do more adventures and storytelling.

Shortly after this trip, I started high school and that was quite a shock. Until then, my 2 sisters had been my only buddies. Arriving at high school, I was pretty socially inept and terrible at the most played sports: football and rugby. But I was a good student and at the end of high school, I applied for Harvard. I got through all the entrance exams and interviews, but our family simply couldn't afford the University costs, so I ended up studying Economics & Politics at Glasgow University instead. Four years later I was all set for the classic city career in finance. Nevertheless, since my first cycling as a 12-year old boy, I had also developed a parallel path as an adventurer. I just felt like doing one more expedition before starting my professional career, with the idea: "What do I have to lose?" That's how I decided to break the around-the-world bicycle record and make a film about it.

About People, Money, and Happiness

My mum, Una, has been a huge support for me. First of all, because of our home-schooled education. Later on, she worked with me full-time for 12 years with my business.

I've got a small home where I'm perfectly happy, a beautiful wife, two great daughters, and a dog. I've got a life I enjoy. For me, the most important thing in life is choice; having the choice to do the things you love. Material wealth is important up to a certain level, but there comes a point where you don't need more. I wouldn't trade the last 15 years for millions of pounds, because I got the fortune to travel to 135 countries and experience so many unique things.

I'm most known for my achievements in cycling, but I'm also an ocean rower and a mountaineer. The connection with nature on these expeditions is wonderful. However, I do prefer projects where I'm connected with people over these wild, off-grid adventures.

Comparing my two around-the-world trips, the first time was a much better adventure in the true sense of the word. I was on my own for 6 months, figuring out where to sleep each night, where I would take my next meal . . . The same holds true for when I was cycling from Cairo to Cape Town. In these unsupported expeditions, you're totally connected with the world around you. That's my favorite kind of adventure . . . seeing the world as a slideshow.

There have been a lot of setbacks over the years: people dropping out, sponsors not following through, big accidents. But I've never lost the big picture. I've always been conscious of the impact that I can have as a storyteller. Having this in my mind makes me pretty resilient.

You learn a lot when things go wrong. You learn a lot when people fail around you. You learn a lot when people don't do what they've promised. I'm pretty thick-skinned these days . . . but it's still ambiguous. I'm always looking for the best in people – still trusting them a lot – but I also want to get them to prove themselves more. I guess over the years I've gotten better at assessing people and knowing whether or not I want them around me.

Combining adventure with a family and social life is a constant interaction. There's no steady state. You have to communicate at all times and be willing to learn to listen and tweak continually.

The Hard Thing About Hard Things
The hardest part of every adventure is by far fundraising. Getting people to back your ambition before the start is incredibly difficult. Lots of people with endurance capacities are aware of it. But they don't master the business part of being an adventurer, so most projects don't make it to the start line.

Being an entrepreneur in the field of adventure brings a lot of insecurity, but I accepted that long ago and got used to it. Nobody sees the psychological rollercoaster you have to go through before every expedition. Every project is like building a start-up: you start from scratch, you build the team, you build the finances.

When it comes to the physical aspects, the hardest are the many months (and sometimes years) you're preparing for the big trips. When you're training many, many hours alone, in all kinds of circumstances, without any security whether you'll eventually achieve your goal. Or even going to find the fundraising to start the project.

I'm very much single-minded. I put myself in the driver's seat and don't wait for other people to promote me. Also, when I make a decision, I tend to stick by it.

You've got to be able to suffer well, push yourself hard, and have incredible discipline.

You have to be able to communicate well. You have to convince people to get on board, get them to share the dream and passion with you

Training your mind and spirit is not a classroom exercise. It's going out there, showing responsibility, and learning from setbacks. My entire life I've pushed my comfort zone. I've constantly pushed my boundaries.

The Most _____ Expedition

Difficult:
Cycling around the world in 80 days in 2017, averaging 385 km a day, which makes my first around-the-world record look like kindergarten (In 2008, Beaumont cycled around the world in 194 days, unsupported). As an athlete, fully-supported races where you ride 16 hours a day and hardly sleep, are really next-level. The resilience you need for these challenges is extreme.

Beautiful:
Difficult to say, I've experienced so many. I always love desserts. I love the wide, open spaces. I love meeting people in these remote places, so often ready to help unknown travelers. Riding alongside giraffes and elephants, and rowing near polar bears and walruses, these certainly rate highly.

Dangerous:
Capsizing on the Atlantic Ocean. Our team was 28 days into our Atlantic Crossing by rowboat, thinking we would smash the World Record, and capsized. We spent 14 hours in trouble before getting rescued. It's the only time I really thought I would die on an expedition. I've found that when I get into dangerous situations, I get very analytical and processed-driven, completely focused on survival. The mental difficulty comes afterward. Other members of the team have shut down in urgent situations. That's incredibly scary. In Western societies, most people don't face their mortality until later in life. I've been in dangerous situations several times at a young age. I've had that thought that I was going to die. These kinds of experiences made me pretty pragmatic, I've got everything arranged for if I'd pass on in the next adventure . . .

Advice to Aspirational Adventurers
It's not about beating everyone, it's not a competition. It's about expressing yourself and building an audience. So whether you are a professional athlete, or you're looking after a brand or a business, the best expression of yourself is taking your interests in a different direction. I'm clearly not the best bike rider in the world, but I'm successful because I'm backing myself. Of course, being a proper endurance athlete is an important element of my success. But I'm also backing myself with good preparation, physically and practically. And I

surround myself with the right people. That's the interesting point, it's far more interesting than being a bike rider and completing races.

The biggest key to success is building a habit of being furiously invested in your interests. You need to have a healthy dose of obsession. This simple habit of giving everything that's in you, committing to a task, and expecting yourself to learn and excel will undoubtedly open doors . . . things like money will take care of themselves.

I've got a portfolio of interests. This way I spread my risk. I'm interested in innovation, in investments, in property, in ilmmaking, in storytelling, in writing . . . This range of interests gives me freedom, it allows me to take on my adventures and travel. In the end, my expeditions only account for about ¼ or ⅓ of the time, because my wife, my kids, and other work are also important for me as well. I'm not one of these people who can switch all of that off and live like a nomad.

I have a lifestyle business now, but that has taken over a decade to build up. You can't just break records, write books, and make ilms out of nothing. You wouldn't have the credibility. I always say to people: "Shoot for the stars, but learn your trade, do your apprenticeship. Build up systematically. You can't try to become big in one moment, you'll fail. You have to set yourself up for success by having the right foundations and building blocks."

I'm eating clean food, mostly plant-based. I'm often sleep-deprived because I work late in the evening and get up early, but I need at least 2 big nights a week to catch up. You recover when you sleep, so it's an important thing for me.

I don't have to be the fastest racer, I just can't break down or get injured. So consistent training is really important for me, going out every day. I do a lot of all-around training: running, gym work, core stability, cycling, etc. I'm not a specialist, I want a body that's really strong to take on many sports in many different disciplines. I want to be fit and mentally alert my entire life. I want a body and mind that are resilient and adaptable.

Find out more about Mark:
markbeaumontonline.com
facebook.com/MarkBeaumontAdventures
instagram.com/mrmarkbeaumont

The Older I Get, the More I Feel I Can Be Myself and That Being Myself is Awesome!

JENNY GRAHAM is the fastest woman to have circumnavigated the world on a bicycle. In 2018 she cycled 18 thousand miles in 124 days. As a member of The Adventure Syndicate and Global Cycling Network, Jenny shares her passion for cycling and adventure with others.

"I love to see others breaking down barriers. But it goes in two directions, I often get inspired by the clients I work with too."

An Unusual Path

I didn't grow up as a typical sporty girl. I hated gym classes and didn't like team sports activities, but I loved adventure. I loved climbing trees, building huts, and exploring. As a teenager, I became an army cadet. Each weekend we would go into nature and do cool, adventurous things. But until that point, I still looked at adventure and sports as two different things. The only possible adventurous career that I thought was possible was joining the army, something I wasn't willing to do. Besides, I had my son, Lachlan, when I was only 18 years old. As a result, I took a step back from adventure for a couple of years and got what people call a normal job and a standard life.

When my son started going to school, the mating call of the outdoors rang harder again, and I enrolled in a college course that taught the basics of adventure. In 6 months we learned to ski, climb, navigate with a compass; those kinds of things. This course planted a big seed in my head. I knew this is what I wanted to do as much as possible in my life! After the course, I started contacting outdoor companies asking if I could volunteer for them. Time after time, I got turned down because I didn't have any qualifications. Until one day a guy called Ron Woodark agreed. Ron was organizing adventures for youngsters and could use some help. Actually, I could say Ron became my mentor for many years. I learned a lot from him.

From that point on, I started taking courses and getting qualifications in the field of adventure. I mostly fell in love with the mountains. I went hiking as much as I could in my little spare time. After putting Lachlan to bed I would go to the mountains to walk with my headlamp on. It would take some time before I discovered cycling and it was only when Lachlan was a teenager that I started bikepacking. As soon as I heard that it's possible to take a tent and camping gear on your bike and escape into nature, I knew I would fall in love with the sport.

The Adventure Syndicate

Nowadays I'm able to make an income out of my passion for cycling. I work for *Global Cycling Network*, as well as for *The Adventure Syndicate*, a nonprofit organization that uses the inspiring stories of women adventuring by bike to encourage people to push their perceived limitations. I really love it. *The Adventure Syndicate* was founded by two friends of mine, Lee and Emmely. At first, I just helped them out every now and then. Subsequently, they helped me out a lot with the funding of and giving a voice to my around-the-world bicycle trip. By the time I got back from my trip, Emmely had decided to follow other pursuits in life and Lee asked me to replace her. I didn't hesitate much.

The Adventure Syndicate uses the written word, talks, films, podcasts, informal ride-outs, training camps, and skills courses in order to encourage and enable cycling women to take on their own challenges. I'm a real people person and I absolutely love to see how I can plant seeds in people's minds, how I can change their ideas about what's possible, and see them break down barriers. But it goes in the opposite direction as well, often women I meet through *The Adventure Syndicate* plant a seed in my head and make me shift my own mindset.

Being a people person, how difficult was it to cycle around the world with a speed-record breaking time frame in mind?
In the beginning, it was not easy. I tried to be strict but more often than not I didn't manage to. I would start a conversation with someone, get totally caught up in it, and look at my watch half an hour later thinking "Oh my God, I gotta go!" In the beginning, I would be upset that I'd lost half an hour, but I realized that kind of conversation actually refueled me and made me go faster for the next couple hundred kilometers.

The further I went on my journey, the more tired I got. After a while, I just didn't have the energy anymore to talk to people. I would step into a bar to drink or eat something, head down, thinking to myself: "Please don't talk to me." I would then call my family and ask them for an explanation: "What's wrong with me, I don't like talking to people anymore?!"

Would the world be a different place if adventure was a compulsory course in school?
Wow, what a beautiful thought. For sure school focuses on the wrong things. There's so much judgment based on qualifications. Adventure definitely isn't valued enough in our society, while nature is the place where we come to the best version of ourselves. A course in adventure at school would definitely teach children some valuable lessons such as how to deal with adversities. It would give them a perspective on life, open up headspace from which too much is taken up by their screens right now.

Can you give a moment during your adventures where you came to a deep insight?
When I was cycling through Siberia during my around-the-world record attempt, I met some young Russian girls who spoke fluent English. I asked them if they planned to go traveling or studying in the U.S.A. or Great Britain or so, but they answered that simply wasn't a realistic option for them. This made me realize how many choices we have as Westerners, and that we aren't valuing this choice enough. We're valuing money and possessions instead. And honestly, it's hard to value the most important things in life if almost everyone around you seems to do the opposite.

Which life lessons do you teach your son?

I try to make him understand that he's capable of doing everything he wants if he has the patience to do so. Every realization of a dream is a step-by-step process, there are no shortcuts. Some people are more efficient than others in putting the pieces of the puzzle together – I certainly wasn't very efficient myself – but everyone has to work hard anyway.

I also want him to just be happy. He used to have a job that paid well but made him unhappy. I said to him that it makes no sense to do something which doesn't make him smile. Better to have a job that pays less but gives you fulfillment. At the same time, I think there's a lot of pressure on youngsters to find their passion. I'm a very passionate person, his father is a passionate person, I guess that's a weight not too easy to carry for Lachlan. That's why I tell him he'll discover his passion along the road as long as he stays open to it.

What's the advice you would give to the 15-year old Jenny?

"You're OK." When we're growing up as teenagers, we constantly want to fit in. But the older I get, the more I feel I can be myself and that being myself is just awesome!

I think that for youngsters today the pressure to fit in is probably even higher than it was for my generation, because of social media. Recently, I installed an app on my phone that tells me how much time I spend on Instagram. It turned out that I was watching Instagram for about one hour a day. At first, I said to myself that's reasonable. As an adventurer, social media is a means to sell yourself in a way, after all. Then the app calculated that in a five-year time period I would spend 90 entire days on Instagram. That's such a scary thought, I am wasting so much life on a screen!

You know, I'm a woman who cycled around the world, I had a child at age 18, I've gone through so many ups and downs, and I still care too much about and spend too much time on social media. If it still affects me, how must it be for a 15-year old who still has to figure everything out in life?

Adventure is a way of life and in my opinion, social media should be used as a window to show other people this way of life, to show them what can happen if you think out of the box and if you bring a bunch of extraordinary people together. It shouldn't be used to show off and pump up your ego.

By the way, another piece of advice I'd give the 15-year old Jenny would be: "Go and get a bike, girl!" (Laughs)

What would you want to put on a giant billboard in New York?

"Plant more trees." It's basic, but vital.

What's a quote you live your life by?

Tomorrow's goals are made by today's actions.

If you were forced to live on a desert island and you could only take 2 people and 5 things with you, who and what would you choose?

Lachlan.

Can I take my dog instead of a second person?

5 Objects: my trainers, my bike, a packraft, a ball-launching stick to play with the dog, lip balm (I'm addicted to it)

What do you believe that other people think is insane?

The monster of Loch Ness exists. I know, I live at the lake.

What's your definition of happiness?

It's having a balanced life. I feel like I need to have something to push myself towards in order to be happy. At the same time, I need to feel the contentment of where I'm at already. I'm the happiest if I'm experiencing variety and balance at the same time; if family, adventure, tranquility at home, friends, traveling, and eating healthy are all present in my life, without one taking the upper hand.

Find out more about Jenny:
www.theadventuresyndicate.com
facebook.com/jennygrahamis
instagram.com/jennygrahamis

If You Want to Go Into Adventure, Don't Even Bother Looking for Sponsorship. First, Do a Very Big Thing, Get an Audience, and Prove Yourself to the World.

JONAS DEICHMANN cycled from Portugal to Vladivostok in 64 days, from Alaska to the most southern point of South America in 97 days, and from Cape North in Norway to Cape Town in South Africa in 72 days. He became the fastest man ever to cross Europe, Eurasia, North + South America, and Europe + Africa on a bike, without external support. With four cycling World Records in his pocket, Jonas explored his limits even further and completed a triathlon around the world consisting of 450 kilometers swimming along , 21,000 kilometers on the bike and 5,060 kilometers running across Mexico in 2021.

"I'm just a person that doesn't feel drawn to hotel vacations, lying on the beach and spending €100 a night in clubs."

Following a Different Path

I grew up in a small village in Germany. We spent a lot of time camping and playing outside. Adventure has always been an important value in our family. My grandfather was a snake hunter in Africa for 30 years, and my father got out of the corporate world to follow his dream. He laid down his job as a CEO to become an artist and today he's preparing to sail around the world. My granddad and my father always motivated me to be adventurous, to be entrepreneurial, and to try new things.

After my childhood and adolescence, I went to business school. After graduation, I cycled around the world and visited 64 different countries. This trip made me realize that I didn't want to follow a normal career path. But choosing to live the life of an adventurer wasn't easy. Almost all of my former co-students and friends went into highly-paid corporate jobs. They have a very different opinion about what people should do with their free time . . . But I simply want to live my own life. I don't feel drawn to hotel vacations, lying on the beach and spending €100 a night in clubs.

This different vision of life required me to end certain friendships and even romantic relationships. For me, it's simply not possible at the moment to be in a relationship with a woman who doesn't support my adventurous lifestyle and absolutely wants to start a family life.

Confidence as Security

I chose a career path without any security. To overcome the opinion of others I had to set another definition of success. Success for me is not money or prestige. It is to do what I want to do and to be happy about it. Also financially it wasn't easy. When I started out, I hadn't heard about a single person in Germany who was living full-time as an adventurer. Yet, I had the confidence I would be able to do it . . . The first year and a half were really difficult. I experienced the biggest setback after my first two World Records, the unsupported cycling records of Europe and Eurasia. These accomplishments yielded me a firm fan base, so I approached potential sponsors. I simply wanted to earn a living and expected companies to be enthusiastic to support me in exchange for the exposure they would get in return. But this was just an illusion. A lot of companies were willing to offer me plenty of cycling gear for free, but no one wanted to provide money . . . At that moment I knew I had chosen a difficult field to succeed in. It was after breaking the Panamerican highway speed record in 2018 that I finally found the financial support I needed. I can now live full-time as an athlete, in combination with speaking engagements, books, and paid articles in magazines. But I'm still living extremely cheaply, I don't have a home, I essentially live on my bike year-round.

Resilience by Hardship

The World Record attempt of cycling Eurasia made me grow the most as a person. Before, I had never cycled more than 1,000 kilometers in a race, and now I wanted to try to keep the same pace I had during these shorter races for more than 14,000 kilometers. Achieving this meant a great mind shift. From that moment on I knew that basically, everything was possible.

The record I'm the proudest of is the Cape to Cape (Norway to South Africa). The reason is that I went through so much hardship on this trip. In Africa, something went wrong every single day. In Egypt, the police stopped me. They were afraid of terrorist attacks, so they proposed to drive me to the next hotel. But of course, I was on a human-powered World Record attempt, so I couldn't accept it. I had to cycle every single meter . . . That's how I ended up spending a night in the local prison. In Sudan, I had to ride more than 300 kilometers without meeting a shop or restaurant for several days in a row. A couple of times, I ran very short in food and out of water. Luckily, I always found local people eager to help me. I also got food poisoning, and just at that moment I drank unfiltered water and that made me extremely sick. Despite this, I survived and still beat the World Record by 30 days.

If you want to break a record, you have to believe in it 100%. If I set a challenge, I do it. Breaking records is 5% physical ability, 95% mindset. The best training for your mind is to always be successful, to always go to the bottom in order to reach your goals. If you give up at some point, the thought of giving up will come up easier the next time . . . In training, it's all about being outdoors a lot, doing the mileage, no headphones, just focussing on yourself. Every now and then I just put my bike on the rollers and cycle for 10 hours without rest . . . This really helps me to learn to focus in a quite analytical way.

Beauty and Danger

The most beautiful expedition I completed is definitely the Panamerican Highway. It runs through so many climate zones: from the Arctic landscapes in Alaska to the Atacama desert and then back to the cold and icy Patagonia. On the way, you cycle through a lot of wonderful

164

mountain areas. In these kinds of remote places, I sometimes have really spiritual experiences ... moments where I get a very clear mind and come to profound insights. The Panamerican highway was just the most beautiful ride you can imagine, because of the diversity of the landscapes and the friendliness of the South American people. However, saying that, I also encountered a couple of dangerous situations in Mexico and Honduras, where gangsters were ready to rob or even kill me. Another very dangerous moment was in Ethiopia – during the Cape to Cape – where I ended up in a kind of civil war. 100 people died that day in the conflict at the same place where I was. In Eastern Siberia, I had one moment where I thought I was going to die. It was so cold that I couldn't sleep because I was convinced I wouldn't wake up again ... so I spent all night long shivering in my tent. How did I deal with it? You've got to stay positive. In every dangerous situation I encounter, I rely a lot on my instincts and try to find a practical solution. Anyway, I'm not afraid of dying. For me, it's not important how old I get, but what I get in my life. That being said, I hope I'll still walk around for a while ...

If You're 18 and Have No Idea What to do With Your Life, Do This:
Go abroad, get out of your comfort zone and see a different perspective on life. I also believe that, if you want to get really good at something, you have to be very passionate about it.

If you want to go into the adventure business, don't even bother looking for sponsorship. Just do a very big thing, get an audience, and prove yourself to the world. Then, you can look for sponsorship for your second big thing. So, in the beginning, don't even ask yourself the question: "How am I going to earn money with this?" but focus on spending less and having a minimalist lifestyle.

It helps when you're the best at something, but it isn't enough in itself ... you really need to have great content. You need to have a great story to tell.

Find out more about Jonas:
www.jonasdeichmann.com
facebook.com/jonas.deichmann.7
instagram.com/jonas_deichmann

There Are Always a Thousand-and-One Reasons Not to Leave, You Just Have to Find The One Reason to Do So Anyway

*In 2006, a divorce and dissatisfaction at work made **GREGORY LEWYLLIE** decide to turn his life in a completely new direction. He booked himself a ticket to Paraguay and cycled for more than 2.5 years through Latin America. The trip ignited the adventure fire in Gregory. A couple of years later he participated in the Suntrip, a solar-panel-driven bicycle race from France to Kazakhstan. In 2018, Gregory tested the limits of technology even further by cycling 30,000 km on a solar bike made out of bamboo.*

"Life is like a high-speed train, and there are only a couple of stops where you can jump off. Don't postpone your dreams."

Finding the One Reason to Leave

In 2006 I had just gotten out of a difficult divorce and also at work, I didn't feel good anymore. Intuitively I felt I had to do something completely different. I then read about a man who had cycled all over the world and this way found my longed-for adventure. When I announced to my surroundings that I would be cycling for more than two years, the people around me reacted skeptically. I wasn't really known as a sporty person, so some friends thought I'd be back in Belgium after one month . . . They'd failed to realize that I am the kind of person that goes 100% for everything he decides to do. Once I had made the plan to travel on the bike, all obstacles became insignificant to me. One of those obstacles was the money. I traveled on a very small budget, but that never felt like a real problem for me. I think that a lot of people dream about doing what I'm doing, but are scared to follow their dreams because of the practical steps to take, a lack of money, or something else. There are always a thousand-and-one reasons not to leave, you just have to find one reason to do so anyway.

This being said, if you want to be an adventurer you need to be carved out of the right wood. You have to be able to live with very little stuff. You have to accept that luxury is not more than a refreshing shower or a nice meal and that days will pass even without these simple luxuries. Something we experience as normal in ordinary life becomes heavenly during bike travels. You also have to be open to what the world will offer you, let yourself be guided. Once you're able to do so, you'll be given back a lot. Successful adventurers also need endurance, a sense of perspective, and faith in the fact that in the end, everything will be alright.

How do you train yourself physically and mentally?

Before my bicycle trips I actually never properly prepared myself physically. I have never executed a special training plan. I have neither followed a diet nor done some form of mental training. I just know that every trip will involve difficult moments. Life just so happens to be a sequence of ups and downs and travel isn't different. I almost always set off for at least 15 months of cycling, that's why I think it's not very useful to get perfectly fit at the starting line. I build up my fitness level during the first weeks of cycling automatically. I believe that, when you're having high enough motivation and confidence in the success of your project, everything follows by itself.

The Downs of Traveling

By far the hardest moment during my bicycle travels was when my second wife sent me a Whatsapp message saying she wanted to end our 12-year-long relationship. This was during my last trip in 2018. For the first time in my life, I realized that I no longer had a place to 'come home'.

In Brazil, I got dengue fever. The dengue virus is a variation of malaria, though more dangerous. I had to sweat it out for several weeks but luckily I got through it safely and sanely.

During my last trip, I broke my collar bone and had to shut down my plans for two months.

I got robbed twice. The first time in Costa Rica, the second time in Russia while I was asleep. Each time, it took a while before I found myself able to trust people again. I would take more distance, would be on the guard for everyone. After one week, this caution was resolved. By traveling a lot, I experience I'm more and more able to evaluate the danger in certain situations. I also rely on the opinion of locals, they are in the best position to tell you whether or not you should take a certain road. Another piece of advice for other solo travelers is to pretend that you have a buddy who is a couple of kilometers in front or behind you.

Often, there's a positive thing that comes with setbacks, especially in case of material problems. Because when misery comes along, you inevitably have to rely on the help of local people. This often brings you to unfamiliar places and leads to unique encounters.

About Social Media

I almost never get homesick. Nevertheless, when you're on the road for one to two years without a break, seeing your social circle fading away is a natural process. Thanks to social media, we can nowadays stay very close in touch with our friends and family. That's definitely a wonderful thing. On the other hand, being reachable at all times and places diminishes the feeling of adventure. I've noticed that during my latest travels, I've been too busy sharing my experiences with the homefront by means of Instagram and Facebook. In the future I want to limit this, I want to go back to the basics of traveling.

What is the best investment you've ever made in your life?

Buying a good touring bike, without a doubt. The bike has allowed me to push my limits; geographical, social, cultural, and psychological limits. The bike has taught me that we can do with very little. It has shown me it is the best and maybe only way of transportation allowing us to travel 'behind the scenes' of countries.

How do you finance your bicycle trips?

I work as a civil servant, more specifically I'm a teacher in adult education. This regime comes with a lot of advantages in Belgium. I do have the right to take unpaid holidays for 5 years during my career, with the assurance of keeping my job each time I get back home. That's a luxury I'm very well aware of. Although I did rely on some form of sponsorship in the past, my job finances the big majority of my travels. I think that nowadays it's very hard to get valuable sponsorship. Nobody is still impressed if you're announcing – with all trimmings – that you'll cycle around the world. Not even if you do it with a solar panel-driven bike, as I did.

Many companies are overwhelmed by sponsorship requests. If they can't get marketing value out of your expedition, you won't get supported. It's that easy. You can ask yourself if that's worth the effort. Sponsorship also involves some kind of return. Often you have to invest time to put yourself on the radio, television, or the internet. And often supporting companies want to have their say in the adventure you're doing, you have to ask yourself whether you're willing to adapt your plans for them.

A Special Memory

The most profound travel experiences are the encounters along the way. The spontaneous, hazardous run-ins are what really colors the artwork I make while traveling. Each and every person has his or her own story. Each and every encounter is a moment in time that leaves indelible traces on my vagabond soul. One meeting I'll never forget was with an Englishman who had just finished traveling for two months with his family through South America. As icing on the cake, the father had decided to travel on his own for two more weeks, in order to reflect on the future. While we were sitting together around a campfire in the Bolivian jungle, I witnessed how he realized for the first time in his life that his career had prevented him from seeing his children growing up. He acknowledged that he hadn't been brave enough to set the right priorities. Life had passed before he had figured out what was really important to him. Ambition and money had kept him away from what life has to offer us. He admitted that he had put children on earth, but never had been the father they deserved. It was very confronting to see this man I barely knew confessing that he hadn't really lived and realizing he couldn't get a second chance.

What advice would you give to an 18-year-old who has no idea what to do with their life?

Follow your dreams, don't postpone them. Life is like a high-speed train – remember the English father's story – and there are only a couple of stops where you can jump off. My father loved to travel, he's definitely the one who gave me the bug. But the sad thing is that he died very young and passed away with a big bucket list of unrealized projects and adventures. His passing made me realize it's important to live 'in the now', every day could be your last . . .

I'm convinced that everyone should build their own road in life, knowing that it will be a bumpy one, but one far more interesting than the road society has paved for you.

If you want to make adventure a big part of your life, don't hesitate, fear is the worst advisor. Get out the front door, use your senses and let yourself be carried away by all the beauty life has to offer. After your first big trip, you'll come back home as a different, more mature person. You'll see the world with different eyes. You'll never ever regret it, I promise.

Find out more about Gregory
www.solarbiketour.com
facebook.com/gregorylewyllie
instagram.com/gregory_lewyllie

PART FIVE:
SMOKE ON THE WATER

I Would Rather Be a Superb Meteor Than a Sleepy and Permanent Planet

DAMIEN CASTERA *traveled from the glaciers in Alaska down to the sea by snowboard, packraft, kayak, and surf. He also went on remote surfing expeditions in places such as Liberia, Namibia, and Mexico. Even more than moving through magnificent landscapes, Damien finds meaning in the collaborations with other adventurers and the encounters with local populations.*

"I am an adventurer animated by poetry, a certain form of romanticism, and the taste of understanding. The encounters that happen during traveling allow us to think beyond the trivial things, to transform the experience in consciousness."

The Thirst for Freedom

As far as I can remember, I've always been fascinated by adventure stories. Stories about long-term travelers exploring vast mountains and distant oceans, outer space, or even simply the hearts of people. As a child, I remember getting nourished by all kinds of travel tales, from Shackleton's polar expeditions to the ones of aviator Antoine de Saint-Exupéry. Even more than the physical challenge and the courage of those adventurers, it was their thirst for freedom that I fell in love with. Behind their scientific, political, or athletic motivations, I recognized in their grand voyages an unerring way to suck the marrow out of life, to grasp the delicious vertigo of the unknown.

I also owe my love for the outdoors and wild territory to my parents. From a very young age, my parents transmitted to me the beauty of nights under the starry sky, the love for the sea, and the curiosity for ecosystems. Over the years, they educated me in the classification of species and the name of rocks and seashells. They taught me how to dive and catch fish with the purpose to feed ourselves, prohibiting me from looking at it as a trophy.

Years later I became a surf champion. Although competition gave me the chance to travel, it also limited me in terms of discovery and adventure. In 2011, just after having won the European Cup longboard and while being 5th on the world ranking, I decided to put an end to my competitive career in order to concentrate on exploration. Places such as Alaska, Namibia, and Papua became my new playgrounds. The goal became to discover unexplored waves by reuniting surf and adventure. Bivouac, hiking, surfing, and the encounters along the way are therein not the end products, but a pretext and reward at the same time. The end goal is sharing impactful stories about those adventures, either in written form or in film format, with the world.

The Hardest Part About Being an Adventurer

The preparation for each expedition, more specifically the quest for financing, is most often the longest and least enjoyable part of it. For example, for *Odisea* (an adventure on which snowboarder Mathieu Crepel and myself followed the stream of water from the source in the Alaskan mountains to the sea) we had to work more than one year in order to get the finances together and prepare all the necessary logistics.

At the same time, preparation is a fundamental phase of every adventure, which also gives you the chance to immerse yourself in the travel world, even before taking off. On top of that, I've been lucky enough to have been well-known as a professional surfer. Thanks to this career I have gained credibility and professional relationships that facilitate the search for sponsorship.

What did you have to say 'NO' to in order to live an adventurous life?
I never really had to make big concessions. I have the fortune (or misfortune, who knows?) to be single and childless. I take advantage of that position to realize as much adventure as possible. If in the upcoming years I meet my soulmate and we start thinking about a family, it might become time to slow down a bit and settle down. But at this present moment, I can only say that I'm incredibly lucky to be able to live my passion by a mix of surfing, adventure, film projects, and writing.

It's All About People
I'm a very curious person and that's the driving force behind me pushing my boundaries. I'm not the kind of adventurer motivated by performance. I'm not interested in breaking records. Instead, I am an adventurer animated by poetry, a certain form of romanticism, and the taste of understanding. There's no better way to go on a quest for those concepts than traveling. The encounters that happen during traveling allow us to think beyond the trivial things, to transform the experience in consciousness. From the Papous in New Guinea to the Tlingits in Alaska, man realizes that certain populations can teach us much more about the world than the simple scrolling of landscapes.

In the vein of what I just said, I'm someone who prefers to focus on what brings people together, opposed to what sets me apart from the others. I love to be inspired by other people's work and even more so to share my feats with adventurers who have other specializations than me. I've gone on adventures with snowboard champion Mathieu Crepel, with the teams of *Nomade des Mers*, *Lost in the Swell* (read interview with Ewen Le Goff from *Lost in the Swell* on page 207), and will soon do so with *Solidream* (read interview with Brian Mathé from *Solidream* on page 300). Each one of those collaborations has been and will be enriching in many ways.

Besides my adventure companions, there are people helping me out behind the scenes too. My parents are my biggest supporters. They always had confidence in me and encouraged me to go all the way to realize my dreams. I'm extremely grateful to them, just as to my friends Mathieu, Titi, John, Mika, and many others who've offered me a lot of helping hands in my projects. And of course, I can't express my gratitude to my sponsors, without them all the amazing adventures would never be possible.

The Adventure That Marked Damien the Most

The trip to Liberia in 2018 with fellow surf champion Arthur Bourbon has impacted me the most as a human being. We got in touch with former child soldiers who had created the country's first surfing community. Being confronted with the sad reality of a country that has been destroyed by 15 years of war has been something not easy to deal with. We produced the movie *"Water Get No Enemy"* about this adventure. It's definitely the film I'm most proud of.

If you could go and drink a beer with five people dead or alive, who would you choose?

French writer and adventurer Joseph Kessel. He was well known for getting drunk in a legendary way, as well as for his straightforward comradeship. Besides I'm sure he'd be capable of taking me into a gypsy festival from which he was the only one knowing its secrets.

Jim Morrison, the rock star from the '60s. He would be able to assist me in opening the gates of perception.

Explorer Fernand de Magellan, because I'm curious to hear about his world trip.

Poet Blaise Cendrars, so I could enjoy a live performance of his masterpiece "La prose du transsibérien"

But quite frankly, if I'd really have all the options open, my first invitee would be Kristen Stewart . . . just because it's Kristen Stewart.

Recommended Books

Army of Shadows, by Joseph Kessel
Night Flight, by Antoine de Saint-Exupéry
The Roots of Heaven, by Romain Gary
The Star Rover, by Jack London
The Count of Monte Cristo, by Alexandre Dumas
Crime and Punishment, by Fyodor Dostoevsky

Favorite Quote

By Jack London: "I would rather be a superb meteor, every atom of me in magnificent glow, than a sleepy and permanent planet."

What advice would you give to the 18-year-old Damien?

Continue and don't be afraid!

Find out more about Damien:

instagram.com/damiencastera
facebook.com/DamienCastera64

There's Not a Single Place on Earth Where the Impact of Humans Isn't Visible

*In 2014, sailboat 'Maewan' left the coasts of France for a 7-year-long trip to the world's most remote places. On this adventure, skipper **ERWAN LE LANN** and expedition leader **MARION COURTOIS** invited 100 high-level athletes to develop environment-related educational programs in 45 schools and make five movies aimed to sensibilise the viewer to show respect for our natural resources.*

"We see ourselves as adventurers of the future. If we want to keep traveling for the next 50, 100 years, the only way to possibly do so will be if we can do it with respect to the environment."

Maewan

Erwan: I got to know Marion 15 years before we started the *Maewan*-project when I organized an event for climbers on which she came to present her knowledge as a naturopath. Afterwards, we stayed in touch. Although that was rather sporadically since we were both traveling a lot. I went on expeditions as a mountaineer and Marion was a humanitarian in conflict areas.

Marion: Exactly, I've worked for several NGOs at different places in the world for 12 years. It was very hard work, mentally and physically. After a while, I noticed that the same problem came back again and again: the lack of resources which forced us to stop or scale back the mission. This was discouraging, I felt as if I wanted to be at the root of the problems instead of having to intervene at positions where the damage had already happened. At the right moment, Erwan disclosed to me the crazy idea he had about traveling to some of the most remote places in the world on a small sailboat, in order to raise awareness for the environment.

Erwan: When I was traveling by plane for my expeditions as a mountaineer, I realized that flying doesn't allow us to understand what's going on underneath. We can't relate to the people and environment 8000 meters below us. I wanted to discover what traveling in its purest form is, I wanted to create interactions and bonds with the societies along the way. *Maewan* was really the coming together of this desire, the discovery of sailing as a new passion, and the involvement of my network of high-level athletes.

Has Maewan changed you as a person?

Erwan: Maewan is a very small boat – less than 11m in length – as a result, we have to be very careful with the resources. This way we really get to reconnect with them. We need to have a lot of respect for the water, the energy, the food we have . . . we can't let anything go to waste.

Actually, I see ourselves as adventurers of the future. If we want to keep traveling for the next 50, 100 years, the only way to possibly do so will be if we can do it with respect to the environment.

We've been in the most remote areas of the Earth (the Arctic Ocean, Greenland, Patagonia, etc.) and there's not one single place where the impact of humans isn't visible. Seeing how much damage has already been done, definitely has motivated me to share our philosophy and insights with others even more.

Marion: I agree with Erwan. For me personally there's also a huge difference in how I experience 'the life in preparation for' and 'the life during' the actual expedition. Our 7-year project is divided into smaller expeditions. In between each expedition, we go back home to refuel and to prepare for the next mission. When we're at home in France, we're tempted to go into our own little bubble of comfort. That's just not possible on the boat, where we're living with five people together all the time, without any private room. This really reinforces the sense of sharing and connection and leads to a lot of deep introspections and reflections, for us but also for the athletes joining us.

Turning Adversities Into Enrichments

Erwan: Many years ago, I had a severe base-jumping accident. I smashed against a rock, broke my two feet and a couple of teeth. I had to stay in a wheelchair for two months. The experience made me learn so much. It gave me a better understanding of myself, I changed my approach to risk-taking, and it made me understand what life as a handicapped person must be like. In my wheelchair, I saw the mixed look of compassion and perplexity of strangers looking down at me. And then, having to learn how to walk again, that was an amazing experience. It was literally a realization of how far one step at a time can bring you. To me, this accident and its recovery have been a confirmation of how true the saying is that we learn from our mistakes.

Marion: The only way to make no mistakes is by trying nothing at all. I've experienced so often that every adversity, every setback, every wrong decision is a learning moment. The most painful setbacks for me have been the moments where political or personal agendas have led to decisions made opposed to the collective interest of a community. It's hard to deal with these kinds of situations (which I encountered both as a humanitarian worker abroad as well as in peaceful villages in France) where the discussion with people in power is biased in advance and the needs and desires of the locals are neglected. But even in these extremely difficult situations there is always some kind of solution, there is always a positive element or consequence to find. This way I really think that adversity makes you look at life in general with a more positive attitude.

Which moment in your life made you feel most alive?

Erwan: There have been so many, I can't pick one. Actually, it's the moments where my life has been in danger, where you have to think correctly to stay alive, where you have to be hyperreactive. I've had moments like these while climbing mountains, while base-jumping, while facing storms on the sailboat.

Marion: I agree with Erwan, but I can also feel very much alive when I sense the environment very vividly. For example when I'm alone at the deck of the boat in the middle of the night and feel a breeze on my face. That's feeling 100% connected to the surroundings, that's feeling alive.

How do you feel about combining adventure and a social life?
Marion: Traveling often facilitates the sorting, for sure. I now have a very small circle of close friends and family, but with them I do have a very strong bond. Our loved ones also see how adventure makes us blossom, which makes them respect our choices all the more.

Did you ever have to choose between a lover and adventure?
Erwan: No, we found the love for adventure. And on the adventure.
Marion: Surprise, we're a couple!

Haha, I wasn't aware of that. How would you describe your partner in three words?
Marion: Erwan is visionary, empathic and passionate.
Erwan: Rigorous, passionate as well. Let me think about the third one . . . do you know the word 'creek'? (Laughs)
Marion: Hé! Calm down, you!
Erwan: Just joking. Marion is rigorous, passionate, and free.
Marion: I really have to thank my parents for the latter. They really gave me the freedom to do whatever I wanted to do. I never had to deal with the constraint of them saying "You should be . . ." or "It's impossible to do that . . ." Their unconditional love allowed my free spirit to flourish.

If you ever have children, which lessons will you teach them?
Erwan: "Everything is going to be alright." I would also encourage them to have an open mind for the possibilities in life, and convince them they can do big things if they believe in themselves.
Marion: I would encourage them to look for the connection with nature and the connection with themselves. I have higher education degrees in psychology, public health and naturopathy. It's the latter one that serves me the most in my everyday life. If you connect to nature and to your spirit, you're so much happier and healthier. At the same time, I think we must be careful with the pressure we put on our children. I sometimes hear people say that the children are the solution to the problems we face. But that shifts away our responsibility, doesn't it? I think that as parents we must be the best possible guides in showing our children how to find solutions.

Would the world be a better place if 'Adventure' would be a course in primary school?
Erwan: There should at least be a cluster of courses related to the environment.
Marion: I would like to see some naturopathy in primary school, actually, teaching the kids how to connect with their own nature and the natural environment. A course that develops curiosity, in general, would be great as well. Adventure can indeed be a means to do so, because, in essence, adventure means leaving without knowing what you'll encounter. This way you get to discover so much, not at last about yourself.

If you'd be offered one billion euros, how would you spend it?

Erwan: I would refuse to accept. I think that money has a bad influence on people.

Marion: This time, I don't agree with Erwan. Because more money would allow us to develop more projects, to make more people conscious about our limited natural resources, to inspire society even more to take care of the climate, to maybe have 100 *Maewans* impacting people's lives for the better.

What's the best gift someone can give you?

Erwan: time

Marion: a smile

Erwan: and chocolate! (both laughing)

What's your definition of happiness?

Erwan: Freedom is a big part of it. Having challenges that lift you up too.

Marion: Being able to design a life according to what you believe in.

Find out more about Marion, Erwan, and *Maewan*:

www.maewan.com

facebook.com/maewanadventurebase

instagram.com/maewanadventurebase

On Any Day I Would Choose Trying and Failing Above Not Trying at All

*In 2013, **DARCY GAECHTER** became the first woman to kayak the Amazon river from source to sea. Together with her partner Don, she is the owner of a kayak guiding company in Ecuador and in her free time, she goes skiing, running, and mountain biking too.*

"I really need to be outside a lot. Nature is where I feel the most comfortable, it's where I can release pressure."

Falling in Love With Ecuador

When I went to Ecuador for the first time in 2001, it immediately kind of felt like home. There were amazing whitewater opportunities everywhere, the surroundings were stunning, and the people were friendly. That first time, I spent six weeks on the water. The following year I came back for the whole season, lasting 4-5 months. Since then, I have kept on doing this every year. After a couple of years, my long-term partner Don and I took over *"Small World Adventures,"* our kayak guiding company. Luckily, Ecuador is a country that is really open to foreigners who want to start a business. On the contrary, tax regulations are extremely complicated here. We hand everything over to a local accountant.

What has been the hardest thing in building this adventurous lifestyle?

The beginning was quite hard. I first started kayaking at age 19 and I really sucked at it. That was very unusual, until that time I had been good at almost everything athletic-wise. Once I had struggled through this difficult initial phase, the kayak community motivated me to go traveling. That really opened my world and motivated me to get better at kayaking.

Today, the most difficult aspect of our lifestyle is financial insecurity. We don't have the assurance of getting a comfortable pension. Sometimes, it crosses my mind that I could take a normal job that would give me this security. But there's just no job that would feel like a passion. I just can't imagine myself working 9-to-5 at a desk. The trade-off of increased security at the cost of decreased happiness just isn't worth it, for me anyway. If I gave up on my true passions and chose the path of security, I would feel it would not be a good use of my time on earth. But by this, I don't want to judge what others do with their time when I know nothing about their own struggles and motivations. I completely understand the draw for security.

Did kayaking the Amazon change you as a person?

Yes. It forced me to spend a lot more time on the mental side of kayaking. Kayaking the entire length of the longest river on the planet takes a lot of time (148 days), this challenges you in many ways. You have to boost yourself up day after day. You have to be able to communicate well with your team members. You have to be able to continue paddling although you're very fatigued . . . I think this experience definitely made me more confident. I see things more from a positive point of view. Today, I feel as if I can deal with difficulties more than beforehand. I see every obstacle more as a fun challenge to overcome.

Actually, the follow-up adventure, writing the book about my Amazon descent, might have been even more challenging than the actual expedition. It was something completely new for me. I knew nothing about writing and publishing a book. I had never even heard about literary agents. My first drafts really weren't good. I was just describing the facts of the day: we got up, we took breakfast, we went kayaking . . . quite boring, actually. When I showed the story to people, they said: "Nobody reading the book will relate to your adventure. Nobody is going to kayak the Amazon River, you have to write about you! Put yourself in the story!" The result was that I had to dig inside myself. I had to confront my issues and my doubts and put them on paper. That was really difficult for me, but in hindsight, it has been a very helpful process. I feel that it has made me someone who's better at communicating what's going on in real life. It also made me more patient with other people. I'm now better at respecting that others have their own agenda as well instead of trying to push through what I want at all costs. And it definitely made the book a lot better!

1+1=3

My boyfriend Don and I have been in a relationship for 17 years. We're very compatible as a couple. For example, when it comes to decision-making, I'm someone who pulls the trigger fast, according to my intuitive feeling. Don on the other hand will think through every step meticulously before deciding to go for it or not. As a kayak guide, Don is a stronger kayaker. He can definitely bring more skills to the river than I do. My talents are endurance (I can keep going), I can keep other people's energy levels up for a very long time, and I'm also someone who likes to do the logistics.

How would you describe yourself in three words?
Determined, focused, and hardworking.

What is your relationship to nature?
Nature is where I feel most comfortable. I freak out when I'm around a lot of people, I really hate to be in crowded places. Nature is also the place where I go to release pressure. If I feel stressed out, I jump into my kayak on the river or I go running 20 miles.

20 Miles, That's a Long Run
Yes, sometimes I'm very stressed out. (Laughs)

Listen to Your Intuition
I'm doing a lot of visualizations if I have to kayak a difficult rapid. I imagine the line I want to take several times in my head before I go. A remarkable thing is that sometimes when I try to visualize myself running the rapid, things go wrong. If that happens, I know I shouldn't do it. I take the kayak on the shoulder and walk around. However, it hasn't always been like that. When I started out, there were very few female kayakers. At rapids that felt risky to me, I felt that I couldn't just get out of the water and walk around. That would damage the image of female kayakers. I wanted to show that women are skilled and courageous as well. But I

learned my lesson the hard way one day in California. We had planned to go whitewater kayaking with a team of three: Don, his brother, and me. When I woke up, I didn't feel good. But I said to myself that it would be safer to go with a team of three instead of letting the two guys go alone, so this is what we did. The first rapid of the day looked very difficult, too difficult for me. I decided that I would just take the entry (the first part of it) and walk the rest. But after taking the entry, the kayak got very badly stuck in a hydro line. I swam out of the kayak and got carried away in the rapid. Honestly, this has been the only time in my career I thought I would die. I remember thinking: "You have to do something, Darcy, or this is going to be the end." I grabbed a boulder with all my strength and managed to climb up and escape from the rapid.

What advice would you give to the 18-year-old Darcy?
I would tell her not to worry about what other people say. So often, we do something that others expect of us. In my experience, getting accolades for something I don't care about doesn't really give me pride. Nobody cares about some things that felt like the biggest accomplishments for myself, feats that personally made me proud and made me grow. In the end that's all that is important.

I am a vegan, I'm very short, I look a bit wimpy; for a lot of people, it's unimaginable that I'm a strong kayaker. Over the years I've gotten some negative feedback based on the first impression people got of me. People tell me I shouldn't aim too high because I don't have the right body type. In society, this happens so often. People are masters in holding back other people's dreams, and actually that's just because they believe they can't do it themselves. They're projecting their own fears onto others.

Every big success starts with a belief that it's possible. You need this belief in order to take the first step. But most people don't believe in their capacities, so they never take that first step. That's a pity because when you start acting, your confidence grows and you'll take another step, which leads to more confidence again . . . it's a positive vicious circle. I guess people are just too afraid to fail. But failure is indispensable, failure makes you learn, and if you keep learning this will eventually lead to success. Personally, on any given day I would choose trying and failing above not trying at all.

Book Recommendations
The River Why, by David James Duncan. It's a story about a young flyfisher in his quest for self-knowledge and the connection of people with nature and one another.

Thinking Fast and Slow, by Daniel Kahneman. I'm reading this book right now, it's about human decision-making. It talks about how two parts of our brain act differently in decision-making. The fast way of decision is the snapshot we make, our first impression. The slow way of thinking involves more reasoning, more thinking, more work. In life, we mostly don't make the effort to engage this part of the brain. The eye-opening aspect of this book is that our fast, snapshot decision-making system is most often wrong, as in the example of people judging my kayak skills based on my appearance.

Who are and have been the most important people in your life?
Definitely my family. My parents are really awesome, I would say that they have supported me for 90% in my life choices. Of course, they also have some worries about my financial security in the long term, yet they never held me back in following my passion. I know people who have parents who are much less supportive and I know that that makes it so much more difficult . . .

Of course, there's Don. We've been together for 17 years now. We support each other in all our projects and dreams.

At last, there have been some very important role models when I was young. 15 years ago, Nikki Kelly was the female figurehead of whitewater kayaking. She really made me believe it was possible for me to do incredible things. Another person I looked up to is Ruth Bader Ginsberg, former head of the Supreme Court Justice. She was a brilliant mind and did a lot of good work to improve the equality laws for different minority groups.

What would be the first thing you'd change if you'd be 'President of the World'?
I would erase the 'thinking in categories' of people and the world. I wish people would have an open mind, especially about who they are themselves. Wouldn't it be amazing if people, instead of trying to fit in, would try to stand out by being who they really want to be?

Social media: improvement or disimprovement?
Definitely disimprovement. I don't like it, but I'm forced to use it to promote our company and to build my own 'Amazon Woman' brand. I see it as a distractor of human connection. Of course, it helped me to reconnect with high school friends and things like that. But this didn't lead to much more than liking each other's Facebook posts, not to really deep reconnecting.

Another example of the negative influence of social media is what we're experiencing in Ecuador. When we arrived here for the first time in the nineties, everyone was having good conversations. If someone had a problem everybody worked together to find a solution. Today, everyone is looking at his or her screen, the conviviality has decreased a lot.

What is the best gift someone can give you?
Their time.

What is your definition of a life well-lived?
Following your own path. Giving back as well, helping the ones in your community who can use it. For me, this translates into a contribution to river conservation – mainly to the Ecuadorian Rivers Institute – and animal protection.

Another aspect of a life well-lived definitely is to nurture good relationships. When I was young, I had a tendency to cut relationships in order to spend more time on the water. Luckily, I figured out quite soon that life without tight relationships is an empty existence.

Find out more about Darcy:
www.darcygaechter.com
www.smallworldadventures.com
facebook.com/darcy.gaechter
instagram.com/darcygaechter

It Is Important to Accept and Embrace Fear

JILL HEINERTH is one of the world's most accomplished cave divers. She is also a polar explorer, author, writer, speaker, filmmaker, and climate advocate, and she inspires children to face their fears and follow their wildest dreams.

"I compare cave diving with swimming in the veins of Mother Earth, there's nothing more beautiful than that to me."

The Cave Calling

As a kid I was very outdoorsy, exploring all the time. We lived in Canada's Great Lakes region. Swimming and especially canoeing were activities we did quite a lot with the whole family together. I remember seeing Jacques Cousteau on television and being inspired by his team. That's probably where the secret obsession in the back of my head got planted.

Throughout my youth, I stayed very active outdoors and dreamt about diving. I saved up money for several years to buy my first set of equipment and enroll in an open water scuba class at University. During my first dive, I knew that underwater is where I belonged and that diving would become a passion. During this scuba diving class, we had the chance to dive to shipwrecks and see beautiful fish and our instructor led us into a cavernous rock grotto. This first experience in an underwater cave was a magical, transformative, almost spiritual moment to me.

Why?

People ask me all the time why I am doing this. I've lost over 100 diving friends, why do I still take the risks? The only answer I can give is the fire I feel inside. It's about passion. Diving is essential for me. I compare cave diving with swimming in the veins of Mother Earth, there's nothing more beautiful than that to me. Each and every time I go cave diving I feel that is what I'm meant to do. I'm a true believer in the fact that there is something in all of us that drives us more than anything else. And if we would all be doing that thing that attracts us the most, the world would be a happier place.

How would you describe yourself in three words?

Drive, integrity, curiosity. Curiosity is my keystone. I've never been bored for one minute. Curiosity helps one to explore and discover, but also to collaborate and discuss with others and to try to understand their point of view. This way, curiosity contributes to open-mindedness, and open-mindedness is what pushes society forward through discovery.

The Obstacles Along the Way

Few people understand my dream. When I was a young woman and told my parents this was what I wanted to do for a living, they were full of doubts. "How are you going to make money? That's too dangerous. It's not something for girls." Also in relationships, it can be very challenging to have a risky, non-conventional career. My husband has PTSD from his military career. It sure doesn't help him that I go diving in the world's most remote places. We talk a lot, are open about our desires, emotions, and doubts. We even share our conversations on our podcast. Talking honestly helps a lot in dealing with fears.

Another difficulty is acting in a man's world. I'm often the only woman on the boat. There have been times where I've not been welcome in diving teams, I've been overlooked unintentionally in the organization of expeditions, and I had to deal with overt sexism and bullying too.

If you were invited to give a College commencement speech, what would you talk about?

Fear and the different ways to deal with it. A lot of people are running from fear instead of accepting and embracing it. But it's so important not to let fear stand in the way of following your dreams. If things go wrong in the pursuit of your dreams, all I have to say is: "Skin your knees, put a bandage on, and try again."

In my work as an inspirational speaker, I tend to gravitate towards working with children. I see many fears holding them back. The fear of being different, the fear of making wrong decisions about the direction of their life, the fear of breaking family norms . . . When I work with kids, I talk about fears, bullying, daring to be non-conventional, and following your dreams. I coach them to build their own brand on social media, about what interests them and represents them, to picture an authentic, original image of themselves.

How do you deal with the fear that comes with diving?

It is important to accept and embrace fear. You have to share your fear that is born from real risk and choose to dive with other people who experience fear, too. You have to be really open about this because this way you'll take care of each other. One skill that helps me a lot is visualizing. Mental rehearsal is something I do all the time in preparation for an expedition. Right before every dive I close my eyes and visualize everything that could go wrong. Then, for each scenario, I visualize what I can do to repair the situation. This way, if something does actually go wrong underwater, you don't stress out and you know exactly what to do to fix it. As I get older, I also get more mature in my risk-taking. If my instincts or my rational thinking tell me the situation could be dangerous, I'm much more willing to turn back compared to when I was younger.

What advice would you give to a 15-year-old girl who wants to become a cave diver?

It doesn't really matter what you're going to study. If you keep a sense of critical thinking, open-mindedness, and curiosity, you can get there regardless of what studies you choose. It's going to take patience, but I'm convinced that you can achieve everything you set your mind to. I also like to use the saying 'innovators don't wait for permission'. Twenty years ago, if I wanted to get my movies on television, I had to deal with certain gatekeepers or persons of authority who made decisions about whether an expedition would be seen on *National Geographic* or not, for example. Nowadays, everyone can make their own movies and distribute them on YouTube. Everyone can be an innovator and be the one making maps for others to follow.

As an adventurer, it's also important to have several literacies. I studied *Fine Arts and Visual Communication* at University, and it serves me well in my career as a diver. I'm able to tell my stories by means of paintings, illustrations, photography, and films. Writing, coding, foreign languages, budgeting, mechanical abilities, and scientific analysis are other useful literacies.

Nowadays, it's important to show potential sponsors a lot of material. If you pitch an idea to a foundation, request a grant, or apply for a project, the first thing a potential commissioner or employer will do is Google you. By Googling you they should find a website, movies, photos, articles . . . that represent who you are and what you stand for.

What has been the best advice someone ever gave you?
When I just started out, I had less patience and got easily frustrated when things didn't go my way. One day my brother told me: "You're going to be stressed if you're busy all the time, and you're going to be stressed if you're not busy too. Don't try to get it all done, go with the flow and enjoy the moment." Now I realize that the best parts of life are those journeys as you reach for new goals.

What has been the most beautiful experience in your career?
There have been so many exceptional moments. If I have to pick one, it would be diving in an iceberg in Antarctica. I was the first person to ever do this. It was magnificent, I think it's something that comes close to traveling to another planet.

If physiologically it would be possible to live underwater all the time, how would you divide your time under and above the water?
That would be magical, I would like that. But at the same time, I don't want to miss my husband too much, and he's not much into diving. So 50/50 probably.

If you were given the chance to grab a beer with 3 people dead or alive, who would you choose?
Three strong women: Michele Obama, fiction writer, and futurist Margaret Atwood, and the Prime Minister of New Zealand, Jacinda Ardern.

What is your definition of happiness?
Contentment, a sense of peace, doing what you are meant to do. Having empathy for people and the planet, and making the planet a better place.

Find out more about Jill:
www.IntoThePlanet.com
instagram.com/jillheinerth
facebook.com/jillheinerth
facebook.com/JillHeinerthAuthor

The Only Solution for Our Environmental Challenges Is Sobering Our Lifestyle, All the Rest Is Marketing

FRED BUYLE is a freediver and underwater photographer. In the nineties, he broke four freediving World Records. Currently, Fred combines his photography work with scientific collaborations to help protect underwater wildlife.

"You know that sperm whales' cortex – the brain's area dedicated to cognitive abilities – is much more developed than the ones of humans? I sometimes joke that if extraterrestrials would come to Earth, they wouldn't try to connect with people, but with sperm whales."

Being an Athlete

I grew up in Brussels, the capital of Belgium. Not exactly the dream spot for freedivers. Luckily, every year I was spending 2 to 3 months on the family sailboat with my parents. I remember that during those voyages, I was constantly looking down over the side of the boat to try to see what was happening under the surface. Since I was four years old, I have wanted to explore the underwater world.

When I was 7 or 8 years old, I began diving with a mask and snorkel during those family trips. From there, I progressed little by little in the freediving sport. When I was 19 years old, I established a freediving school in Brussels, and in my early twenties I broke my first World Record. You can compare freediving with athletics, there are a lot of different disciplines. The record I broke was called "Variable weight, still water." This meant that I went down with the help of a weight (51 meters for this record) and had to swim back up with fins. One year after my World Record, the first freediving competitions got organized. From then on, each season I focused on the World Championships and/or on breaking a World Record. I managed to become World Champion once and broke three more World Records.

In the beginning, my athletic career was very exciting. I was part of the first generation of athletic free divers, the first generation to approach free diving as a true sport. This meant that there was no blueprint for training. We had to figure everything out by ourselves, a process I've found very interesting. But once you're at the top of the world in your discipline, it means you have more or less figured out the best methodology, at least for that time period. As a result, I found myself repeating the same things, the same training strategies. After a while, that started to get boring and it became psychologically very demanding to maintain the motivation. In some sports, the fact that you can make a very good living probably helps to cope with that. But as this is not the case with freediving, it didn't help me much in keeping the spirits high.

Shifting

A lot of athletes coming at the end of their careers have difficulties finding a new direction in life. If you have put the vast majority of your time and energy into your athletic ambitions, having to face that and being forced to do something completely new can be a stressful period. I have been lucky because I never had to deal with that state of mind. Two years before I stopped freediving in competition, I had bought myself an underwater camera. The aim was to take pictures of my friends diving amongst the natural beauty of the ocean and gather some competition's memories. It turned out I was the only freediver who was filming underwater. I managed to take different kinds of pictures than traditional scuba divers with heavy equipment do. People liked my work and I quickly started to sell. This way I quite naturally shifted from being a competitive freediver to becoming an underwater photographer.

My development as a photographer was quite similar to the one as an athlete. In the beginning, I had to find my way, try out several things, and develop an efficient method. I always find that initial phase very gratifying. But naturally, I got to a certain level of competence and reached a plateau again. For me, that was the sign I had to shift gears once more. I was again very lucky that this happened organically because I showed up on the radar of scientists. As a freediver, you can help them with the fieldwork. As a result, I started working together with them and today my contributions have become a regular part of my activities.

Looking back at my career, it's interesting to see how freediving turned from a goal to a tool for photography, and how photography subsequently turned into a tool for conservation and science.

Do you feel as if your life is more meaningful now compared to the period where you did freediving just out of a competitive motivation?

No, not really. I believe that as a human being you need to go through a natural progression. First, you live for yourself. Then, you learn how to live with others. In the end, you live to make things better for others. At first, you have to construct yourself and that construction is a meaningful process. Once you know yourself you have to learn to cooperate with other people in order to achieve better results than you possibly could achieve alone. Thereafter, you start looking for ways to contribute as much as possible to society and eventually the planet.

Adapting the Body

When I was an ambitious competitive athlete, I trained 6-7 hours a day. In the morning, I would do one hour of yoga and stretching. Then I would head to the pool to swim and train freediving. In the afternoon I went to the gym for strength training and stretched a second time afterward. Sometimes my pool training got replaced by cross-training in the form of cycling, running, or mountaineering.

For the last 15 years, I no longer train at all, yet I still feel as if I'm at 80% of my maximal potential. That's because I spend a lot of days in the water for my job. Thereby diving for several hours on end, which is, of course, a good training in itself. On top of this, my body's physiology has adapted as the result of decades of diving. There are even some things I'm better at nowadays than before. For example, today I can stay still for five minutes at 15m deep to wait for an animal, something I couldn't do during my athletic career because that was something I didn't train for. But as a photographer you have to be able to lie still for several minutes in order to take a good picture, so that's what my body learned to do.

Creativity

Creativity is the motor of everything. Even when I was a competition diver, creativity was what I needed in order to find new ways to surprise my body. Because if you don't surprise your body with new stimuli, it can't adapt as well. As a photographer, creativity became even more important. Creativity reaches its peak when you're in the company of other people from different backgrounds. That's why creativity also plays a crucial role in science. By individuals throwing back and forth ideas in a group, the group comes to new insights and solutions. For example, when I entered the scientific world as a diver, people were using very clumsy gear to tag sharks. The scientists told me they had been using the same system for 20 years. I proposed to them a tagging methodology based on what I had learned during my spearfishing years, a method much less invasive and using more efficient gear.

Aging Makes You Less Courageous, But More Efficient

Aging makes you less courageous, but more efficient. When you're 15-20 years old, you don't know or listen to fear. You dive as deep as you can and you face sharks without really thinking about it. As you grow older, your instincts are more present and you get better at listening to them too. I've noticed that most people – myself included – do stupid things until they're 30-35 years old. It seems to be the time period necessary to gain the experience that enables a balance between risk-taking and living peacefully. But that balance remains a difficult thing to maintain. Experience also makes you waste less energy on the less important stuff, and instead helps you focus on the essential things.

How important is communication if you want to be successful?

Communication is a necessary evil. You need to invest in communication in order to obtain sponsorship and get exposure. Throughout the years, networking has become easier, but at the same time more difficult. Easier, because platforms such as Instagram, Facebook, and even email have made it possible to reach out to everyone. More difficult, because it has become so overwhelming that it's challenging to get your voice heard for something that really matters. Before, sponsors used to be mostly interested in the values you brought forward. Nowadays, the number of Instagram followers is amongst their most important criteria. The growth of social media also sets us up with too much input. You get messages each day and if you don't answer within 24 hours people get annoyed . . .

Is man the most or least intelligent animal on our planet?

Probably the least intelligent. Social media is only a reflection of how our society has evolved over the last decade. We always want more, always faster. Thereby we forget what is actually important. Our natural environment pays a high price for our instant gratification behavior. Humans have been on this planet for only 200,000 years and we've been able to cause more damage than any other species has ever done before. And most of that damage has been done in the last 100 years.

People have been very mad at COVID-19, while actually, we're functioning in exactly the same way as a virus: we multiply very fast, we progressively damage our host, and eventually kill it. For me, that's not intelligence, because intelligence means being able to be in balance with your environment. For example, sharks could be defined as very intelligent: they have been here for 400,000 million years because they are able to keep a healthy relationship with their environment. Also, some animal species will adapt the reproductive behavior if their food source is dropping or if the conditions aren't good enough to sustain their population and protect the species. It seems that humans aren't smart enough to do so.

All mammals living in the ocean are extremely smart. To give you an idea; sperm whales' cortex (the brain's area dedicated to cognitive abilities) is much more developed than those of humans. I sometimes joke that if extraterrestrials would come to Earth, they wouldn't try to connect with people, but with sperm whales. They are very intelligent animals and just as orcas and other whales, they have a very developed culture, social system, and language. One of the best days of my life was when I witnessed the birth of a sperm whale. Labour is the moment in which a mother whale is most vulnerable. My fellow divers and I were very careful and a bit concerned that she might want to attack us to protect herself and the newborn. But the opposite thing happened. The mother whale immediately understood that we were there to observe, not to do harm. After birth, she pushed the baby towards each member of the group, almost like a ceremony during which each individual can welcome the baby. When we were there, the mother pushed the baby towards us. She wanted to make it clear to her newborn that we were part of a group. We felt like we were considered friendly fellows. It was a magical moment.

Are you pessimistic about the future of the planet?
No, I know that the planet will take care of herself, she's very resilient. But I am pessimistic about the future of humankind. I'm afraid that we will take a lot of other species with us in our downfall. Thanks to my career I've seen environmental changes happen in front of my eyes. Most people don't get to see those changes, they're too self-focussed. Without a connection to nature, they don't really care about the changes our planet is going through. People also have too much faith that technology will save us. If you look at history, most major technological inventions have brought lots of environmental problems. If you look at electric cars, for example, they are supposed to be a solution to reduce CO2 emissions. But, they require a lot of raw materials, very polluting battery technology. On top of it, how will we be able to generate enough "green" electricity to power hundreds of millions of such cars? The only solution for the environmental challenges we are facing is embarking on a much more frugal lifestyle, everything else is just marketing.

What advice would you give to the 18-year-old Fred?
"Don't change anything!" Everything has worked out very well, I've managed to listen to my intuition and follow my dreams. That doesn't mean everything has been sunshine and roses all the time. I faced a lot of challenges and difficulties, but that's part of life.

I think that everyone has a lot of things which interest him or her. But you can't develop all of them. If you try to do too many things you'll risk getting into trouble or you won't be able to enjoy what you're doing. So you have to pick one or two things that stand above everything else. If you put everything in place to follow the path of those passions (even though you don't know where that path will lead towards)you'll ind contentment in life.

Find out more about Fred:
www.nektos.net
instagram.com/fredbuyle
facebook.com/fredbuyle

It is Important to Have Cheerleaders in Life!

SARA HASTREITER sailed the Volvo Ocean Race as part of a women-only team, has sailed 'the Seven Oceans', summitted three of 'the Seven Summits' (Kilimanjaro, Mount Aconcagua, and Mount Elbrus), and was forced to turn back close to the summit of her 4th one: Mount Denali. Her goal is to become the first woman ever who sailed 'the Seven Oceans' and climbed 'the Seven Summits'. At the same time, Sara studies Performance Psychology at Harvard.

"People don't understand how I can push things forward all the time, but you simply can't have a balanced life every day of the year if you want to make big dreams come true. It takes everything you have."

Being a High-Achiever

Already as a child, I was very disciplined, a perfectionist, very curious as well. Curious about nature, animals, and exploring. I grew up on a small farm and I grew up with the understanding that hard work is a part of life. Throughout my teens, I always stayed a very disciplined, perfectionist girl. Later I began to actually appreciate that part of myself. Today, I would like to be able to say that, by gaining life experience, I've become more forgiving and more gentle with myself. But honestly, that's not the case. Recently, one of my best friends had a conversation with my step-father. He said to her: "Make sure that Sara has some fun too." But I'm just the kind of person that needs a whole lot more type-2 fun than type-1 fun. My friends and family can't understand how I can push so hard all the time (and actually, I can't understand it myself) but that's just what it takes to be a top-level performer. You can't have a balanced life every day of the year if you want to make big dreams come true; it takes everything you have.

My understanding of balance is on a broader scale. For example this year with COVID-19. I was in France when the whole world went into lockdown. I was supposed to be sailing, to hit the gym several hours a day, to negotiate with sponsors . . . I had to understand that it wasn't the time to beat myself up because I wasn't working as hard as I had foreseen. Besides, my family started dealing with a lot of health problems; some severe illnesses, and death. I had to come to terms with the fact that the situation was already difficult enough and I shouldn't look for more challenges. I decided to use this period as a mental and physiological recovery. I literally texted my friends: "Hey, I'm planning to have two months of type-1 fun, let's do something together." This way, I went on camping trips, hiked up mountains, and went stand-up paddling on the Colorado River, just for fun. There was no real physical exhaustion and no element of risk on those trips. That was an entirely new experience for me. I was in the outdoors just to enjoy being in the outdoors, not to train hard or to reach a training objective to become stronger.

After two months, when the health situation of my family members was stable again and my world began to feel more normal, I went all-in on my goals again. I would say that I'm still working to be a high-achiever as before. I still have very high expectations of myself, but I've become more flexible in when and how I want my dreams to be realized.

What did you have to say 'NO' to in order to become who you are today?
Throughout all of my life, I've made a lot of sacrifices. Very often I prioritize my goals over a social life, for example. But saying 'no' to things became a real necessity two years ago. I had so much going on that I felt pulled in too many different directions. This way, my energy got spread out to things that were not that important, and often without compensation. From that moment on I learned to say no to a lot more things, especially to doing too many 'favors' or spreading myself too thin with social relationships.

You were forced to say 'no' to some volunteering, yet with your adventures, you're still raising money and awareness for several good causes. How important is it for you to not just do adventure for yourself?
It is one of the most important reasons, for sure. Many people in the world have a difficult life not by choice but by a matter of chance or circumstance. What most people in first-world countries don't regularly acknowledge is how privileged we are. We open the faucet and get clean drinking water. That's something we consider normal, but in many places in the world that is a luxury. By wanting to cross seas and climb mountains, I make my life difficult. It's my choice and that in itself is a privilege. I don't do it to get attention; but because adventure makes my heart full. If I can link my endeavors to good causes, it has the double benefit of increasing my motivation and raising awareness for the ones who are less fortunate.

Bring us back to your first sailing and mountaineering experiences. What were they like?
I'm not afraid to take direct paths to my bigger objectives, so my first real sailing experience and real mountaineering experience were both big expeditions. When I was in my mid-twenties, I lived in the Caribbean and began sailing there. Because of my love of adventure and the inherent nature of curiosity, I wanted to take on the scariest thing I could imagine. That was sailing across an ocean. I found out about the *Atlantic Race for Cruisers (ARC)*, which traverses the Atlantic Ocean, and I discovered that several boats were looking for extra crew to hold watch for crossings. I didn't hesitate and approached participating teams and found myself a boat. In exchange for chipping in with food and fuel and holding watch, I was afforded an amazing opportunity to sail from the British Virgin Islands to Portugal, and then onto Greece. So the first time I spent 24 hours on the water was actually the first day of an 8000-mile trip.

My first mountaineering experience was in 2006. I was doing an internship with an HIV/AIDS clinic in Tanzania. This beautiful East African country is home to the biggest mountain on the continent of Africa: Mount Kilimanjaro. I decided that after I finished my internship, I would attempt the summit of Kilimanjaro. A week before the planned climb, I became very ill and entered the hospital with a malaria infection. After a week in the hospital, I still felt very weak and seriously doubted any attempt on the climb would be successful. The expedition had been paid for and the best I could do was delay it one week, refunds were not possible. As a result, only 10 days after being discharged from the hospital I began my climb of Mount Kilimanjaro.

My idea was to attempt the first 2 to 3 days, with no real anticipation of making it to the summit. However, once I was on the mountain I found myself very determined to get to the summit, and I did. Actually, looking back at that expedition I'm almost happy that I got sick beforehand because this way reaching the summit felt like a huge achievement. Kilimanjaro in itself isn't a technical mountain to climb, so if I would have done it while being in great shape, I might not have felt as grateful for reaching the top.

The Summit Is for the Ego, the Journey Is for the Soul

In the year 2019, my big objective was to climb Mount Denali. I had prepared for it for an entire year, following my knee surgery, and it was a huge investment of money and time from myself and my sponsors. But bad fortune happened when I got a chest infection during the expedition. At an altitude of 19,000 feet, only 1,300 feet below the summit, I felt that I was bringing my health in danger. I made the very hard decision to turn back and go down. I was very disappointed, after all the efforts that had been done to make this a success. As I turned away from the summit, my guide whispered in my ear: "The summit is for the ego, the journey is for the soul." He was so right. Indeed, for my World Record attempt of becoming the first woman to sail *the Seven Oceans* and climb *the Seven Summits*, reaching the summit was the only thing that counted. But for me as a human being, the journey is what counts, not the summit.

Back to School

Following Denali, I turned back to sailing. We began a campaign for offshore sailing for the Paris Olympics in 2024. In June of 2020, I was fired from my campaign to be replaced by a better female driver . . . That was a hard pill to swallow. Especially because I didn't feel that the decision of the coaches was justified. Actually, it was just the opinion of one coach who had the conviction that I had started too late with sailing to get to an Olympic level of driving. In his opinion, you need to start at age eight to ten, and I discovered sailing when I was 26 years old. If the coaches would have done some data gathering and testing on my driving and based their decision on the measurements of that test, I could have lived with it. But now I was just defenseless.

Because I'm someone very goal-driven and need to feel as if my life is constant in forward progress, I decided to use the end of my Olympic dream as the start of a new pursuit. I started studying *Performance Psychology* at Harvard University, something that had been in my mind for a very long time. With the world being on hold due to COVID-19, it was the perfect moment to enroll in this program. Planning expeditions was very unsure at the moment, sponsors were not at all interested in investing in athletes. So instead of just waiting until we could go out exploring the world again, I decided to take the first steps in my future career. I'm really looking forward to being a performance coach for high-achieving individuals.

If you were invited to give a College commencement speech, what would your message be?

It would be twofold. First, I would say: "Give yourself permission." A lot of time, we're looking outside for permission. A lot of people don't feel the permission to not have kids, to build a life full of travel, to chase their dreams. It is really up to us to give ourselves permission to do what our heart wants us to do. Especially if that is something that is not convenient in society.

Secondly, I'd tell the students that things don't just happen because you want to. An amazing life doesn't get handed to you just like that. People won't turn up, knock at your door and present you with an opportunity. You need to get your ass off the couch and go ask for what you want. If you want to play life the big way, you have to expect a lot of work.

Dried Fruit Dipped in Chocolate

My parents have been the same as most people and for a long time I felt social pressure applied by them too. Having kids has been an issue for a long time, just as the question: "When are you going to stop sailing and have a normal career?" But I've been able to sustain the adventurous lifestyle for so long now that I think they finally understood that I will never live the convenient way. This being said, without the support from my family I never would have been where I am today. They have always been very cheerful and excited about my dreams too. For my expedition to Denali, for example, my mom helped me to pack all the gear and we spent hours preparing expedition food, dried fruit dipped in chocolate for example. That means so much to me.

If you were given the opportunity to go and grab a beer with three people dead or alive, who would you choose?

Ernest Shackleton; to learn about his tenacity and leadership skills.
Éric Tabarly; one of the pioneers of sailing who inspired me tremendously.
Melinda Gates; I really love the humanitarian work that she does.

What is the best compliment someone has ever given you?

Telling me I've inspired them.

What is the biggest gift someone can give you?

The gift of support, loved ones backing me. It's important to have cheerleaders in life.

What is your definition of a life well-lived?

Having the space to chase the things that are most important to your own fulfillment and happiness.

Find out more about Sara:

www.sara.blue
instagram.com/sara_hastreiter
facebook.com/sara.hastreiter

Be the Kind of Woman That When Your Feet Hit the Floor Each Morning, the Devil Says: "Oh Crap, She's Up!"

ROZ SAVAGE is the first, and so far only, woman to have rowed solo across the Atlantic, Pacific, and Indian Oceans. She accomplished these feats after having left behind a secure life as a management consultant in her mid-thirties. Roz is also an author, speaker, environmental advocate, and thought leader on the big existential questions of the 21st century.

"About twenty years ago I started making more decisions with my heart instead of my head. I've found them to be better decisions, and more independent of others. Listening to my heart has made me be who I truly am."

Two Obituaries

I studied Law at Oxford University and that's where I discovered rowing. But once I graduated and got a job, I didn't pursue any rowing ambitions anymore. I built up a fairly conventional life. I became a management consultant in the heart of London, got married, bought a house and a little red sports car. I had everything we are told we need to be happy, but I didn't feel happy. Every day on the way to my office I was wondering if this was what life was about. One day I sat down and wrote two versions of my obituary. The first one was the kind of life description of people I looked up to: risk-takers, adventurers and explorers, brave people. People who had tried a lot of things and didn't let failures stop them from achieving their goals. People who had followed their dreams and didn't seem to give a damn about what other people thought of them. The second version was the obituary I was heading for: a pleasant life with some moments of excitement, but for the majority of the time ordinary, safe, and easy.

Being confronted by the two life lines I had written down on paper, I knew I wanted the first one to come true. But when you have a husband, a secure job, a house with a mortgage, it's not easy to give up everything. At first, nothing happened. The gap between the two scenarios seemed way too big. Becoming 'Roz the adventurer' looked like an impossible dream. I tried to forget about it, but you can't unsee what you have seen. I had asked the question to my soul: "Why am I here?" My soul had replied: "I thought you would never ask!" Then it showed me the life that was waiting for me, if only I could find the courage to embrace it.

About one year after the journal exercise, I quit my job. Sometime later my marriage ended. Financially, things got wobbly at that point. From the outside, it looked like a disaster. If I would never have written down my obituary, right then, it would have felt like a disaster too. But in reality, it felt liberating; as if I was getting out of a cage I had been imprisoned in for too long.

Breaking Down Fears

What helped me in taking the big jump was breaking down my fears. Often we run away from our fear because we think it's a giant monster. But if we would just turn around and face the fear, we would realize that we have been deceived. We have been running away from a giant shadow of what we thought was a monster. But, by looking the fear in the eyes, we realize that the monster is actually smaller than we are. What I mean by that is that if you'd just write down your fears, you'd see there is actually always a way to handle them.

In addition to breaking down your fears, you might also try presenting your goal as a hypothesis to your mind. The human 'ego-mind' wants to protect itself, it doesn't like change. When I came up with the idea of crossing the Atlantic Ocean, my heart was saying: "Oh yeah, that's what I want!" while at the same time my ego-mind was freaking out. So I changed my approach and made the adventure a hypothesis. I took my journal and wrote down: "If I would row the Atlantic Ocean, I would have to learn X, I would have to contact person Y and Z, I would have to have this and that equipment . . . " This way I let my heart communicate with my ego-mind. By writing down all the steps I would have to take, I showed my ego-mind that it would actually be possible to fulfill my dream . . .

How did you deal with the financial insecurity that came with choosing a new life path?

It has not been easy, for sure. Worrying about how to get by is probably the most important reason people don't dare to listen to their hearts and take risks. But I've noticed that life and I always figure a way out. For example, my biggest stream of income nowadays is public speaking. In spring 2020, when the world went into lockdown, I saw all my conferences canceled. The vast part of my foreseeable income vanished into thin air. For four days I was really scared. What was I going to do? Then I remembered that over the last 20 years I've had a lot of moments of financial insecurity. But I never starved. Either I rolled up my sleeves and found a way to make money, or some unexpected things happened that provided me with some sort of revenue. 2020 has not been different. Out of the blue I got invitations for writing jobs. A fan of my blogs insisted on offering me a donation. I published a book called 'Gifts of Solitude' to advise people how to deal with the solitude experienced during COVID-19. The book is based on my experience of spending months alone at sea, as well as the experiences of incredible people I interviewed who have spent long times in solitude and uncertainty.

Of course, in some way, I have been privileged. I was lucky enough to get a great education without my parents having to pay anything, and I have a good enough brain. But on the other hand, my family isn't wealthy. Throughout my career, there has been no one who could support me financially, so I had to learn to be self-reliant early on. I just believe that once you fully commit to the life you really want, you always figure a way out to make things happen. I've lived in some strange places, including in an office and on a boat. I've resided free of charge in a small flat above a shop. At various times many strangers have popped up to help me out or even mentor me. What helps also is that if you don't have a job, you have time. Many times, I would start a conversation with someone I met, and because I had all the time in the world I would continue talking for a long time. By the end of the conversation, that person would come up with a solution for one of my problems. It's really easy to make friends when you have time, actually. Nowadays, people put so much pressure on themselves to be busy and productive and do things all the time. By all this rushing around they miss a lot of opportunities. I wish I could offer one year of free time to all the people doing a job they don't like. That would give them a lot of time to think and to have long conversations with other people. I expect that one year would be enough to get them to start chasing their true purpose in life.

This being said, there are also times when I'm just hustling on a project. I need both yin and yang in my life; times to be really driven and full-in on something I'm passionate about, alternated by times of not-doing, just being. I really value having the space to reflect on what's really important and recalibrate my compass. Honestly, how often does it happen that our busyness actually isn't connected to our long-term goals?

Your life story is the typical hero's journey. The call to adventure, the initial resistance, deciding to live your legend, mentors showing up, setbacks along the way, looking for a deeper purpose (namely the improvement of human connections and environmental protection). Do you think that everyone should go on their own hero's journey?
I don't like to tell other people what to do and I definitely do not recommend everyone to spend three months alone on the ocean. But what I do think is that everyone should listen to their heart. In British culture, most people spend too much time in their heads. It's in our upbringing to think rationally. When I was young, I most often made decisions with my head and that resulted in conformist behavior. I was copying others. About twenty years ago, I started making more decisions with my heart. I've found them to be better decisions and more independent of others. Listening to my heart has made me be who I truly am.

In which way is solitude a gift?
In my twenties and early thirties, I was around people all the time. This way, I was mostly reflecting on who they are. I was always in a position relative to them: the daughter, the colleague, the friend, the wife . . . By being alone on the ocean I got to know and accept myself. I got to know my strengths and my flaws and be totally ok with my flaws. Due to the advertising that is everywhere around in society, we are made to never feel enough: not rich enough, not beautiful enough, not lean enough . . . By being alone, I came to peace with the fact that I'm not perfect and that's ok. I found out that I actually liked myself quite a lot just as I am.

We often worry about what others think about us. But actually, most people don't really bother, they're more interested in their own lives and worrying about what others think about them. On top of this, the people who really love you and care about you just want you to be happy. Even if you make a choice that is not convenient, they will support you. By having completely changed my life and doing what really gives me happiness and fulfillment, I did not lose one true friend, while I made a lot of amazing new friends.

Most Influential Books
Recommending books to people is difficult because for a book to be influential, it's just as much about the individual and the period in the life of that individual as it is about the book itself. Nevertheless, if I have to choose three books that have been the most inspiring to me, they would be:

The Celestine Prophecy, by James Redfield. Maybe not a great piece of literature, but I read this at a very formative stage of my life and it changed the way I make decisions. I now trust my instincts much more than my head and keep the faith that everything is exactly as it is meant to be.

Ishmael: An Adventure of the Mind and Spirit, by Daniel Quinn. This book changed the way I see humankind's relationship with our planet, and why our current path is unsustainable.

Conversations with God: An Uncommon Dialogue, by Neale Donald Walsch. It made me change the way I look at comfort and fear. What is comfortable isn't necessarily good, and what makes us afraid isn't necessarily bad. Quite the opposite, we are here to learn and evolve, and the biggest growth happens when you face your fears and step out of your comfort zone.

(Find out a more expanded list of books Roz has loved to read on her online bookshelf: www.rozsavage.com/about/favourite-books)

Hypothesis: It's the year 2023. As a consequence of the worldwide COVID-19 pandemic and with other global problems such as climate change, inequality, and wars facing us, today's world leaders decide we need a 'President Of The World'. Roz Savage, you get elected. What would be the first thing you'd decide or change?
Haha, difficult question. I would like to organize a big global party where everybody loves each other. But I guess you can't force people to love each other, so I have to think more pragmatically. In my opinion, we have a financial system that indirectly encourages us to exploit the planet and other people. That's why I would introduce other currencies that would encourage good behavior. Currencies that would reward people if they take care of nature and each other. These currencies would also need to have a built-in system that prevents people from accumulating wealth so that the rich don't get richer and the poor get poorer . . . Alternative currency is a subject I'm diving into already actually, even before becoming President of the World (laughs).

Actually, your question reminds me of a commercial for Heineken. It's a commercial where individuals say who they are and what they stand for. For example, the first person would say he is against gay people, the second person would say he's gay . . . then the opposing pairs are put together and sit down to talk over a Heineken beer. After half an hour, everyone loves each other. So maybe, as President Of The World, I'd just have to figure out a way to have everyone grab a beer with someone they see as different, bad, or evil. Polarization is one of the biggest problems nowadays. We see ourselves as separate from the other. This makes us lonely and less kind and loving. I'm now actually working on a doctoral dissertation for which I research ways to change this narrative and bring humans together. If you have an idea I'd be glad to hear.

(watch the Heineken-ad Roz talks about here: https://www.youtube.com/watch?v=dKggA9k8DKw)

A question I've asked other adventurers is: "Would the world be a better place if adventure were an obligatory course at school?" , because I believe that this would make us feel more connected to nature and, by overcoming obstacles together, more connected to each other.

Wow, that is beautiful. Indeed, nature is such a big teacher in humility and it's also so important for our health. There is indeed a lot to say about our educational system. If I were to be President Of The World, that would be my second subject of attention. I feel as if our educational system pays less and less attention to what is really important. I would like to see courses like critical thinking, creativity, communication, and psychology included in the curriculum. Or maybe we should indeed just send our kids into nature and let them work together in adventurous activities. Maybe then we wouldn't need a curriculum at all . . .

What is your favorite quote?

Be the kind of woman that when your feet hit the floor each morning, the devil says: "Oh crap, she's up!"

If you were a magic fairy who could enter all the offices of management consultants in London, what would you write on a post-it to be stuck on their desk?

You have only one life, live it!

We started with your obituary, let's finish with your funeral. What do you hope people will say about you while they're putting you in the ground? (I'm sorry for the question)

I like to connect people, so I hope there will be some people up there who'll tell each other: "Without Roz, we would not even have known each other." I hope they will say that I've been a great friend and that the world is a better place thanks to Roz. And then I hope they'll say, "Let's go to the pub and raise a glass to her!"

For me, by the time I'm breathing my last breath, I hope (and I think) that I will be able to say that I did my very best in this life, and have no regrets.

Find out more about Roz:

www.rozsavage.com
facebook.com/RozSavageFan
instagram.com/rozsavage

If You Swim for 50 Hours Without a Break, You Have to Let Go of the Ego

CAMERON BELLAMY swam the Seven Oceans (seven of the toughest channel swims in the world), circumnavigated Barbados (96km), and swam from Barbados to Saint Lucia (151,7km). On top of this, he rowed across the Indian Ocean and the Drake Passage. As if that isn't impressive enough, Cameron is also a software entrepreneur, a physics student, and founder of the NGO "Ubunye," which develops educational programs in South Africa.

"I'm very lucky to be surrounded by amazing people helping me out. Before a big challenge, all I have to do is focus on training."

Ubunye

I grew up in the 80s and 90s in South Africa, in a beautiful house in a neat suburb of Cape Town. As a very young kid, I thought that all children were growing up in this luxury. But pretty soon I saw that there's a lot of poverty and tragedy in South Africa. I noticed that there are a lot of children who were less privileged than me and I made the vow to one day make a difference.

But then life passed by and this idea moved to the back of my head. I started rowing for the national team. My father was a very accomplished sailor at the time, but his motivation was mostly ego-centric. Besides, I grew up in the macho society of South Africa. These influences made me use rowing as a means of uplifting my ego. I wanted to beat others, to show off. That was quite a destructive mindset, actually.

Meanwhile, I studied economics and computer science. I got a job in finance in Beijing when I was 26 years old and worked in China for three years. During this period, I always felt the attraction of adventure and endurance sports. After three years, I decided to resign. I bought a bicycle and cycled all the way down from Beijing to the most Southern part of India. It was a solo trip of 6,500 km, in which I had a lot of time for introspection. It really felt as if I was born to do this kind of athletic endeavor. However, I no longer wanted to do it just to flatter my ego. I reminded myself of the vow I had made as a kid. That's where the seed was planted for my charity, *"The Ubunye Foundation." Ubunye* is the Zulu word for unity.

After the bicycle trip, I went back to London where I had worked before. I told a couple of friends about my idea. Sure enough, we started planning our first adventures; swimming the English Channel and rowing the Atlantic Ocean. At the same time, we had to figure out ways to organize actions in Africa; how to fundraise, how to do marketing and PR . . . Honestly, in the early stages of *The Ubunye Foundation,* we were just a couple of headless chickens running around. Today I'm the only one of this bunch of friends who are still involved in the charity. But, I've been very lucky to have attracted some amazing people along the way who put their heart and soul into the foundation. This way we've set up different successful educational programs in South Africa. Actually, all I have to do now is swim and row. The rest of the team takes care of logistics, management, and communication.

Too Hard to Describe in Words

In 2012, I completed my first endurance challenge: swimming the English Channel from England to France. It was a tough one. I had never really swum before, so I prepared myself in only eight months' time and the actual challenge was a close call. I remember that it was extremely cold and I got more tired than ever before. At one moment I was ready to give up when my mom screamed: "Cameron, you won't get into this boat before you're in France!"

Circumstances made me switch my plan of rowing the Atlantic to rowing the Indian Ocean. We had an incredible team on that row and even broke the speed World Record. Thereafter, I completed the Seven Oceans, which is the swimming equivalent of climbing the Seven Summits. I swam around Barbados, the longest swim around an island ever done. In 2019, I swam 151,7 km from Barbados to St. Lucia, the longest Channel swim ever completed. I was also part of the first rowboat crew to cross the Drake Passage, in between South America and Antarctica.

In my opinion, long ocean swims are some of the toughest things you can imagine. Swimming from St. Lucia to Barbados took me 56 hours, and swimming was actually the easiest part of the adventure. As it is described in the rulebook, you aren't allowed to touch the boat. This means that even while resting to eat and drink, you're still kicking your legs in order not to sink or drift away. This means you actually don't have a single second of rest. It also means you have to deal with sleep deprivation. But the toughest part of the challenge was the jellyfish and the saltwater. I got stung by jellyfish early on in the swim. That was extremely painful. Maybe even harder was the pain caused by the saltwater, especially at the lips and tongue. It started to get really painful after 30 hours of swimming. At that point, you know it'll only get worse. Honestly, it's hard to describe in words how difficult a long ocean swim is. After swimming from Barbados to Saint Lucia, rowing the Drake Passage almost felt easy.

Who are the most important people in your life?

Years ago, I wanted to swim the Strait of Gibraltar because it is a part of *the Seven Oceans*. If you want to swim across this channel between Spain and Morocco, you have to book a boat and its captain. The problem is that it's almost always extremely windy over there and the captain was only available to us for a short amount of time. After seven days of waiting for calm weather, I asked our captain: "Can we still do the challenge next week?" The captain told me that the boat was booked by an American couple, Steve and Amy. If they would agree I could swim with them. So a couple of days later I got to meet Steve and Amy and it clicked immediately. We decided to cross the strait with the three of us together. During the actual swim, we had great weather, and Steve and I even started to talk about business.

Steve and I stayed in touch and a couple of months later, Steve told me: "Cameron, I want you to come to San Francisco and set up a company with me." I took the risk, flew to the US, and created a software company with Steve. It all worked out well. Steve became a close friend and training partner. After a couple of years, I said to him that I wanted to take a step back and concentrate on rowing and swimming more. He respected my choice and has always stayed very supportive. Actually, I see Steve as a second father.

Another father figure to me is Kevin Jennings. Kevin grew up in extreme poverty but made it to study at Harvard. He became a high school teacher and climbed the academic ladder until he became the assistant deputy secretary of the U.S. Department of Education. Kevin got inspired to support *Ubunye* because he knows what it is like to grow up in poverty and wants to give other children the opportunities to get out of poverty as he did himself. I know I can count on Kevin every moment of the day.

Both my mom and dad have always supported me too. My dad was a famous yachtsman, who always organized his expeditions to the finest details. My mom is the opposite, she loosely floats through life. She's in her seventies now, but she still looks like she's 40. She's still horseback riding, she goes ice fishing in Greenland, she travels the world with a backpack. She's awesome.

I've lived in quite a lot of places around the world: Cape Town, Beijing, London, San Francisco, and Brisbane now. I'm lucky to have friends all over the world who are willing to help me out. So often someone offers me free lodging for a couple of weeks, others join me at the pool when I have to train the whole day long. A friend of mine, Kristina Evelyn, helps me out with marketing . . . I'm truly blessed by having these amazing people around me.

Back to School
I do have a lot of interests. I'm an endurance athlete. I worked in sales, software development, and security. I want to contribute to the community in South Africa. One other thing that has always fascinated me is physics. Recently, I went back to University in Brisbane Australia because I discovered a formation that's totally in line with my interests. But I must admit that it's very hard to get back to the subject matter after 15 years . . . I spend ten hours a day studying now.

This doesn't mean that I'm done challenging myself athletically. Actually, this year (2020) I had planned to swim the 180 km long Issyk-Kul Lake in Kyrgyzstan. This would have been a Guinness World Record for the longest uninterrupted swim ever done. Because of COVID-19, I had to cancel the undertaking, but I'm still planning to do it as soon as possible. It will probably be my very last big swim. I'm also working on a massive rowing expedition in a couple of years, but I prefer to keep it a secret what it's going to be for now.

One of the team members while rowing the Drake Passage was Colin O'Brady. Colin has become a real phenomenon after breaking the speed record for the Explorer's Grand Slam and by crossing Antarctica solo unsupported. He is a master in marketing and is one of the rare adventurers who has been able to leverage his feats into financial wealth and build an amazing lifestyle. As a result, a lot of people in the adventure world are jealous of Colin and this has caused some criticism. But to me, he's really a great guy and an impressive athlete. Maybe later on I will try to follow his example and try to make some income out of my athletic accomplishments. One idea I have is to simply travel around the world on a bicycle and write down my stories in a journal which then can become a book. But for now, I just love to be busy with the software company I've created in San Francisco and my University studies. Every now and then I'm invited as a public speaker, but the money I earn from that goes directly to *The Ubunye Foundation*.

I don't like bragging about myself on social media either. Honestly, I'm posting nothing at all on Instagram. It's Kristina Evelyn who voluntarily posts in my name. To me, social media is boring. For years, Kristina has been pushing me to make a personal website, but now I've found a friend who's willing to do the job for me.

What are the similarities between your athletic, academic, and professional careers?
It's all about hard work. The last five weeks before my big swims, I spend nine to ten hours in the pool almost every single day. When I built a company, I put in 10 to 14 hours a day. Nowadays, I'm studying 9 to 12 hours a day . . .

If you could choose to grab a beer with 3 people dead or alive, who would you choose?
Werner Heisenberg, one of the most interesting physicists who ever lived.
Ernest Shackleton, the great explorer of the early twentieth century.
Nelson Mandela, who really changed my home country for the better.

What would you say if you were invited to give a College commencement speech?
I think everyone's life should be balanced. Throughout my life, I always balanced sports, academics, friends, and family and worked on myself on a deeper level. Set big goals, but don't get attached to them either. I think this holistic approach to life is very important.

What's one specific thing you'd advise people to do to improve their quality of life?
Meditation, without a doubt. When I did my bicycle adventure from China to India, I stumbled upon a book that talked about meditation and spirituality. I thought to myself: "Wow, this sounds incredible, I want to learn this." Shortly after, I got sick for a couple of weeks and the doctor in Cape Town wanted to describe antibiotics. But I said to him that I wanted to try out a holistic, natural method and talked to him about my ideas about meditation. The doctor answered that an Indian healer had just moved into High Street. So without hesitation, I went searching for him. When I met him, I frankly asked: "Can you teach me how to meditate?" He answered "No," but he did invite me to come back. So for five days in a row, I came back and talked with the Indian doctor, until he finally taught me a meditation technique.

I remember the first time I tried to meditate at home. Diving really into my head for the first time in my life was very scary. I noticed that my mind was full of ugly thoughts. There was so much ego in there. When I was done after 20 minutes, I felt happy for the first time in my life. Meditation was the catalyst in doing sports from a destructive, ego-centered place to doing it from an ethical place. It helped me become a better person and contribute to the world. And that's really good because if you do these extremely long swims, you can't act out of the ego. If you're running a marathon or even doing feats that last eight hours or so, your ego can push you through the pain. When you undertake a 50-hour long swim, your ego isn't strong enough to be the driving force. I've experienced it myself. The first time I planned to swim around Barbados, I wanted to show how good I was. I started off really fast with the result that just past halfway I was completely done and gave up. The second time, I came back much more humble. I let go of the ego and tried to enjoy every single moment.

I still meditate on a daily basis. Meditation brings me to a state of transcendence. It's in this state that I feel connected, that I feel aware, present. The result is a nice, happy life.

What would you put on a massive billboard in San Francisco?
Know yourself.

Find out more about Cameron:
www.ubunyechallenge.com
facebook.com/CamUbunye
instagram.com/cam_ubunye

The Combination Surf-Adventure Appeals to a Lot of People

EWEN LE GOFF travels the world with his buddies, Ronan Gladu and Aurel Jacob, in search of fun, adventure, and above all, good waves. Each time, they use ecological ways of transportation, whether that's a trimaran, donkeys, or fat bikes.

"We tried to get our adventures on television, but no TV station was interested. So we put our videos online for free, and by word-of-mouth, we gained a big and loyal audience pretty quickly."

How did *"Lost in the Swell"* get born?

In 2008, Aurel and I went surfing in Morocco. We lived really off-grid in a house without tap water and electricity for one month. Ronan joined us for ten days as well. For us, this was a real test of whether or not we would be able to live this kind of simple lifestyle. And in fact, we liked it so much that we made a plan for a follow-up adventure. We spent hours on *Google Earth* to find the right spot and eventually came up with uninhabited Indonesian islands. The coasts of these islands (as far as we could figure out on the internet) had never been surfed before. We called this project 'Des Iles Usions' (a French word game with the words 'island' and 'illusion') because it was a real catastrophe, actually. We had to come back to France earlier than anticipated, and we tried to convince television channels to broadcast our adventure, but no one was interested. Anyhow, Ronan (who was a hobby-cameraman at the time) made wonderful shots of the trip, edited them, and posted a series of short videos on *Vimeo*. On social media, we did a little bit of marketing but it mostly spread word-of-mouth. Before we knew it, we had almost one million views.

A Loyal Audience

Next, we left for the Solomon Islands with an ecologically constructed trimaran. We got in touch with the famous French sailor Roland Jourdain. Thanks to his help, as well as the help of the French region Bretagne, we managed to construct a trimaran almost entirely built out of natural materials, following the example of our surfboards. It took a tremendous amount of research, time, and effort to get the trimaran constructed, but we managed. We baptized the boat *Gwalaz*. We learned the necessary navigational skills while testing *Gwalaz* at the coastline of Bretagne and thereafter set off to the Solomon Islands. We made another web series of our 3-month-long adventure, as well as a film which got projected in movie theaters. This way, our audience grew even more. Meanwhile, we had started selling books, movies, and t-shirts on our webshop. For our next big adventure, we organized a big crowdfunding action in which we gave away our products in reward to people supporting us. We are really lucky that we have a following and an audience that turns out to be very loyal and continues to watch every new series we put on the internet. Apparently, the combination of surf and adventure appeals to a lot of people. Luckily, since it's thanks to those people that we can afford this amazing lifestyle!

What is the best part of your lifestyle?

It's a combination of a whole lot of things. First of all, sur ing is our passion. To be able to do it less or more as a living is extraordinary. But there are so many interesting aspects to our projects: The discovery of new spots. The encounters with the locals. The search process of making the adventure as eco-friendly as possible. The connection with nature. The satisfaction and pride after each completed adventure. Having the ability to in luence and inspire young people. The felicitations of people appreciating your movies ... And of course, the fact that we're doing this with three close friends together. I have known Ronan since the age of 12 and Aurel since age 20, we really know each other very well. I guess that's why it works out so well.

Real Work

You know, in the early days, inding the budget was a hassle. But as I said, we quickly had a big online following. This makes it easier to approach sponsors as well. Besides, our adventures have always been low-budget. Today, we can live less or more from our passions and adventures. Ronan is a full-time cameraman now, who's also ilming for other companies. Aurel and I are both surf instructors. And I also work for an association called *Water Family* which develops educational projects for youngsters and enterprises about the oceans and the environment. I would say that today, the only unpleasant part of being an adventurer is the time we spend preparing for the next adventure. We spend a lot more hours than we would like to before a screen, looking up travel regulations, contacting local authorities, arranging visas and permits, things like that. It's real work.

Dealing With Danger

After our trip to the Solomon Islands, we decided to go to what we called 'the lost paradise', which is the coast of Gabon, a country in West Africa. It was a spot that had not been surfed before. We went there on fat bikes constructed from bamboo, which we borrowed from the guys of *Solidream* (Read the interview with Brian Mathé from Solidream on page 300) and put all our gear and our boards in a carrier. Boy, did we suffer pulling that much weight across the sand! Anyhow, this was a trip that involved a lot of danger, not at least because of the wild animals living there. The coastline where we wanted to surf is well-known for its high intensity of sharks. Luckily, we didn't see any of them. Although, that might be thanks to the very murky water.

We did stand eye-to-eye with hippopotamuses, crocodiles, and other wild animals though. How did we deal with the danger? We tried to prepare as best as possible ... We had shark-resistant wetsuits and we were accompanied by and thoroughly instructed on how to deal with wild animals by Anicet, a Gabonese ranger, before we were left alone in autonomy. But despite the precautions, we still got a lucky star, for sure.

What's the advice you give to youngsters who want to build a life full of adventure?

Don't waste your life doing something you don't like. Do what you feel like, follow your heart. Things will figure themselves out from there ...

What's your biggest dream left?

When it comes to adventure, one of the things on top of my list is surfing in Antarctica. And actually, if COVID-19 allows us to travel to South America, that dream is about to come true this winter. We'll board the famous boat *Maewan (Read the interview with Erwan and Marion from Maewan on page 176)*, which is a boat that has been traveling around the world since 2014, thereby hosting top-level athletes and executing educational and environmental programs along the way. We are looking forward to it a lot!

(Note: by the time this book got published, the collaboration between *Maewan* and *Lost In The Swell* already took place – watch the video here: www.youtube.com/watch?v=xxnuIGfzrus)

Find out more about Ewen and Lost in the Swell

www.lostintheswell.com
instagram.com/lostintheswell
facebook.com/lostintheswell

Most People Struggle to Walk the Talk, But I Struggle to Talk the Walk

FIANN PAUL holds 34 Guinness World Records. He is the only person on earth to have rowed every ocean and is also known as the fastest one. Fiann does not only strive for excellence as an explorer but also as an artist and Jungian Psychoanalyst, thereby following the example of the ancient Greek Arete: using strength, bravery, and wit to achieve real results.

"70% of a rowing expedition is hell. That's why, when I'm searching for expedition partners, I'm looking for true warriors."

A Person of Excellence

I grew up in the coldest, least developed, and least populated area of Poland. There was an unemployment rate of 40%. As a result, criminality and violence rates were very high. Most of my friends were very athletic and saw the Foreign League as their only viable option. I wanted to take my life to a brighter place. I wanted to move to a cold country (I really do hate heat) so Iceland got in the picture because of its unique landscapes and skyscapes. 3 years later, at the age of 29, I presented myself to the government requesting citizenship in order to be able to represent the country internationally as an athlete. The official response of the government was actually very cool; it stated that I was accepted because I was a person of excellence and that's what the country needed.

I did art as a major source of income for a while. I earned €500 a month, which was sufficient for shelter and food, and it took me to some of the most amazing places in the world. Apart from my upbringing, traveling contributed a lot to my understanding of extreme lifestyles. For most of my adult life, Iceland has been my base. But I've also lived 3 years in Asia, 2 years in South America, one year in Africa, one in Australia and New Zealand, and one in the US as well. Living in third-world countries made me encounter a lot of normal people living like explorers on an expedition, nearly on a daily basis. With the difference that these people never considered it as something difficult and never complained about it. I read a lot of stories about explorers and adventurers. And very often, the ones from the West try to decorate their life story with a childhood of poverty, because a story like that makes their achievements look more remarkable. I've experienced that those who really lived in poverty will try to hide their upbringing because they are really scared by it and they don't want it to be remembered.

Did you ever have a 'real' job?

I have a degree in architecture but it didn't become my main occupation . . . Today I define myself mostly as a Jungian Psychoanalyst and a speaker. Speaking is something I definitely want to take to another level. What's a 'real' job anyway? A friend of David Bowie once said to him on his 57th anniversary: "It's about time to get a real job." Bowie's answer: "I have a real job: Rock God."

The Hard Things About Being an Explorer

Being an explorer is completely different than being an athlete. As an athlete, all you have to take care of is your body. The rest is done by the team staff or managers. If you want to be a good explorer, a lot of different factors are just as important as physical strength. You also need extreme stamina, you need to be a manager, a designer, an entrepreneur, you need to attract sponsors, you need to be a good communicator . . . In some of these aspects I'm very good, in others I'm not so good. For example, I suck at marketing and PR . . .

Before every single expedition, it's a very hard and painful process to get the money. Sometimes you have to sell a part of your soul. I always try to organize the expeditions as economically as possible, so I can pick the best instead of the wealthiest team members, with minor exceptions. There are other expedition leaders who let people pay to get involved, but then they have crappy expeditions because they don't have a good enough team to ensure an amazing outcome. As a result I earn from the opportunities that a successful expedition brings.

A skill I do excel in, on the other hand, is understanding my body. I know how to perform ultra-endurance on a high level without getting injured. I know how to deal with sleep deprivation. I know how to eat on an expedition and how to combine power and endurance performance. Some rowers lose up to 15kg during an ocean crossing, I lose 2,5kg maximum. I have even completed expeditions where I lost no weight at all.

Overall, getting to the start line of every expedition is extremely complex. The expedition that people get to see is only the tip of the iceberg. There's a proverb that says: "In every joke, there's a little bit of joke." I apply it to expeditions as well: in every expedition, there's a little bit of expedition . . . There's so much happening behind the curtain that nobody will ever know about.

Which achievement made you the proudest?

I understand human psychology very well, so I understand that there is an enormous amount of self-gratification in achieving goals as an explorer, that's the reason why we do it. Yet, my answer might surprise you. The project that makes me the proudest is not an expedition, but an artistic project. In 2011, I photographed countless breastfeeding women in the remote areas of Iceland (in their local outdoor environment, often next to remarkable natural landmarks) and got my pictures exposed as a large-scale outdoor art installation in the heart of Reykjavik. Iceland is one of the leading countries in breastfeeding and with my photography I wanted to underline this fact. I believe that breastfeeding is important because it's our true nature. We're mammals, and we need to be in a good relationship with the mammal within. Breastfeeding is healthy for the baby and it's good for the vitality of the child's potential, including athletic potential . . . This artistic project went beyond self-gratification. It gave me something extra, it made me connect with and contribute to the community, which made me feel very good.

Lover and Warrior

When I look at the archetypes of the human psyche, two of them are nearly contradictory: the lover (mostly credited to art and creativity) and the warrior (known for achievement and withstanding difficulties). The two archetypes are presented equally strongly in my life. I had expected to become a successful artist, but the art world didn't embrace me as an artist, but as an adventurer. However, in the adventure world, I'm seen as a weirdo athlete; I'm a little bit artsy, a little bit hippy. On the other hand, among artists (which is definitely another playground where I belong) I'm macho, the control freak. On top of these two personalities, there's also a spiritual identity of mine that's hard to define. During my expeditions, I had several mystical experiences, as other explorers do. These experiences felt like a rite of passage. Deep and profound layers of me came to the surface . . . and at these moments I felt bright and dark at the same time.

When it comes to rowing, I do only select team members that are warriors. Lover-archetypes like the fun of adventure, but they don't like the hell of it. At least 70% of the time during rowing expeditions is hell. Only warriors want to go through the discomfort and pain in order to achieve a goal.

Still, amongst the warriors I rowed with, I notice that I have a different threshold for danger. Maybe it's due to my rower's experience, maybe it's due to my wiring of neural pathways or maybe I'm just crazy and stupid, I don't know. There have been moments where I hadn't perceived dangers while I heard crewmembers calling home with the satellite phone to tell their partners: "I just wanted to let you know that I love you . . . " I also learned that when I talk to American magazines and tell them there were no dangerous moments during the expedition, they won't be interested in me and will talk to another team member who will tell them about some dangerous moments.

In order to be an explorer, what did you have to say 'no' to?
I had to say no to pursuing a business path. I have a lot of skills, I'm very talented, I can take a lot of things to completion, and I'm aware of all of this. But I have the curse that I can't do something I don't feel like doing, not even for one single day. If I would focus on money, I would very rapidly lose the drive for what I'm doing as an explorer. I know a lot of people that were much less talented than me but achieved much more success because they did the things I don't want to do. I admit that sometimes I feel bad because I haven't yet translated all my talents, skills, and achievements into money.

I also feel like it's more of a natural order instead of a sacrifice or compromise. I can still complete things I haven't done yet. I have to tell you that I am not afraid of dying, because I'm fulfilled by the experiences I had. But I haven't built up a family yet, and it would feel like a major loss if I would disappear without it.

About Laughter
My personal website is called *www.rowlaughexplore.com*. I am often defined by a very prevailing and sophisticated sense of humor. Laughter is one of my highest values. If Youtube would have been big when I was young, I would probably have been a famous prankster. I did pranks on most of my expeditions, and one of them I still remember very well. It was in 2014 before the crossing of the Indian Ocean. The whole crew was sitting at the table after dinner chatting about natural medicines. Suddenly, my teammate, Tim pulled the opener of the

well-thought-through prank. In quite complex-sounding medical gibberish, he properly introduced the diversity of methods by which to support yourself in extreme settings such as our row. Most importantly, he alluded to everyone at the table that we might have some stuff worth looking at. Then I chipped in with some motivational talk, mentioning how intense of a challenge we are about to undertake and how every extreme achievement goes along with sacrifices. As we are going to achieve something superhuman, we need to perform superhuman, and the most superhuman that a person can become is through the application of Human Growth Hormone (HGH). Thereafter, Tim and I kept on adding more and more advantages of HGH, not all of them being true. We said that we could save money by importing cheap hormones from Thailand, that cleansing our bodies would improve HGH's efficiency by a factor of five, that we could gain 20kg of muscle mass each and that we would have to rest less often during the ocean crossing. At last, we concluded that messing around with needles on a rocky boat that swings left and right might be too risky, and we'd better opt for the intrarectal version of HGH. By this time, everyone except for the captain had understood that Tim and I had set up a prank. The captain thereby started a moralizing speech about the fact that we really couldn't cheat . . . we all burst out in laughter and disclosed the prank.

People and Happiness
The women in my life have been extremely important in my achievements as an explorer. My mother, my sister, my girlfriends, and my lovers all gave me tremendous amounts of emotional support along the way. I think partners have been important for every explorer in history.

I wish I had some kind of guidance, mentorship, or support in building up a passionate career from a very young age. I found my passion quite late. I first had to sort out a range of psychological issues. I didn't start at zero, I had to start from below sea level before I could get to zero and start climbing the mountain. I would like to know if a mentor could have steeped the learning curve, made me climb the mountain faster. Whether it's possible, I don't know. Maybe you first have to encounter hardship or be unsatisfied in other areas of life, before the drive to follow your passion really emerges.

I cannot be happy in my unit alone . . . as in me and my partner and a house and a less or more successful life . . . I have a deep craving for socializing. I told you I'm about 30% hippie, and my wish is to live in a community. But I'm quite picky about people as well . . . it's difficult for me to find people with whom I can entirely and properly connect. My best friends are all around the world, and that's really difficult. My dream is to live with about 5 well-befriended families together, like a modern Epicurean community. I believe that Epicurus is one of the rare people who cracked the code of happiness. I would like to be wealthy enough to make it happen financially. Otherwise, it's difficult to manifest the concept.

What's the impact you want to have in the world?
One of the biggest problems in my life is that I don't feel like I have a mission to preach anything. And that's a problem because you need to at least believe that you have something to preach about in order to write books and so on. I don't like people who tell others what they should do and how to live their life. Since my childhood, I looked up to people who do a lot and speak little. I genuinely believe that people already know what they need to know. As a psychoanalyst, I help people to ask themselves the right questions. I never tell them what they

should do . . . When I was younger I believed I understood the world, that I had everything sorted out, but the longer I live, the less I know.

When it comes to adventure: we do it for ourselves. We either have the courage to admit it or we have not. We make the excuse that we do it for others, to deliver a message to the world. If it's just a part of the excuse, it's forgivable. If it's the entire story of the person and the self-gratification isn't recognized, then it's basically BS.

I see a lot of postnominal letters after your name: CGeog, EUR ING, FRSA...., several titles and awards. What do these mean to you?

According to Aristotle, an award says nothing about the recipient, and only testifies as to how he is perceived by society. When a society or system changes, a source of pride can become a source of disgrace. I have achieved many trophies such as the Ocean Explorers Grand Slam, which are achievements and not social perceptions. These particular postnominals are also a result of certain achievements, even though they do have an award status of some sort. I think that the greatest award is building yourself in a way that allows for true self-expression without borrowing from ready-made cultural templates, especially from pop culture.

What do I have to do if I (having been a triathlete for over 10 years) want to become an ocean rower?

You've got enough light endurance. Light endurance is like being an antelope that has to keep running to survive. In ocean rowing, light is counterproductive. You need to awaken the gorilla within you. But don't go vegan like all the gorillas, just pump up. What you need is rowing technique and power. Your 1.83m height is a really low limit for an ocean rower and you need to gain at least 10 kg of muscle mass, bringing you to 85kg, and learn to perform power combined with endurance. Once you'll have done that, you'd be actually a really good team member, because you already have the endurance mindset. If you're not going to be the captain of the boat, you don't even have to learn to row in the ocean before the expedition, just train the technique on flat water, and the endurance on the ergometer, and you'll quickly adapt when you'll be out on the ocean with the team. You may like to go on the water with your team to get to know them and the boat prior to the expedition. On the other hand, if you want to be the captain, you have to learn a lot about the ocean. A lot!

The World Would Be More Beautiful With Fewer Wankers

If you want to become an adventurer or explorer and live from it, I would give you the advice to always aim high. Always do things that nobody has done before. Go where everyone fears to go, that's where you can win the most. Also, be creative. Imagine you're building an extremely paradigm-breaking enterprise. And you have to be absolutely sure you're going to make it happen. That's the only way to break through with achievements.

Unfortunately, the world of explorers is divided into the wankers and the achievers. The wankers are really good at getting media coverage, but don't necessarily achieve big things. The achievers generate less noise around them, and nevertheless accomplish unbelievable things. I compare it with Tesla versus Edison. Tesla, I consider an achiever. Edison, I consider a wanker. If you want to be an achiever, you have to aim for the highest goals.

The Haiku That Describes Fiann the Most
GIFTS OF WOUNDS

Life's blade, deep cuts

Many to burden and dust

Some into diamonds

Find out more about Fiann:
www.rowlaughexplore.com

Be Positive and Kind

JUSTINE CURGENVEN kayaked on the coastlines of some of the most remote places on earth: Patagonia, Alaska, Siberia, Greenland, and Antarctica. She also kayaked around Ireland, Wales, and Sardinia, cycled across the Pyrenees, hiked in Nepal, and climbed Mount Aconcagua. But most of all, she's known as an adventure filmmaker and kayak expedition leader.

"I have a problem with following rules, I like to do my own thing."

The Taste of Adventure

I grew up in Jersey, an island between Britain and France. As a child, I loved being outdoors. At school, I liked a lot of sports: hockey, netball, volleyball, everything. I spent my high school career at a boarding school in England, where I played hockey at a high level. It wasn't until after University that I got in touch with adventure and kayaking. My best friend at the time, Cheryl, persuaded me to join her at the kayak club. Over there I had the bad luck to bump into a teacher that only let us kayak on still waters. I found this quite boring. Luckily, after a while, I discovered that I had the chance to join team members on open sea kayaking trips on Sunday. The first trip I took changed my entire feeling towards kayaking: being taken away by the waves, going into caves, spotting wonderful birds. This was *discovery*, this was *adventure!*

Together with Cheryl, I did some other adventures as well. We cycled across the Pyrenees on an ordinary mountain bike. The next year, Cheryl found a job as a travel guide in the Himalayas and asked me if I wanted to come and explore the area with her. Of course, I said yes. Meanwhile, I had also moved to Wales. There I could learn under the wings of Fiona Whitehead, a very experienced sea kayaker. Together, we did the first circumnavigation of Wales. Up until that point, I had always gone out with experienced kayakers. On one hand, that's a good thing because you learn a lot and they make you push your limits. On the other hand, as soon as things got a bit tricky, they were the ones making the crucial decisions. Because I wanted to become more confident and autonomous, I decided to do a solo trip in the Westfjords of Iceland. On that trip, I made so many mistakes! For example, I had borrowed a cooking stove, and I didn't know how to fix it when it didn't work. It took me two hours before I figured out how to make a fire. I guess these mistakes were what I needed to learn and grow. I came back from this trip as a much more mature kayaker.

Filmmaker

After University, I worked for two years as a video journalist. This was followed by a multi-skilled media job, which also involved video editing and production. Pretty soon, I got bored with the job, so I bought a camera and went out to become an adventure filmmaker. I wanted to do my own thing. Despite being very ambitious, driven, and full of energy, it would turn out to take a while until my passion projects really took off. At first, I combined my own work with promotional videos for companies and shooting documentaries for a *National Geographic* series. This way I even had the chance to climb the highest mountain in South

216

America: Mount Aconcagua. The first project of my own that was a success was a series of DVDs called *"This is the Sea."* I filmed beautiful kayak spots and followed well-known kayakers. I set up a one-page website with a PayPal button and sold the DVDs. This was the early 2000s when Youtube wasn't big yet. My videos were one of the very rare sources where people could learn about and discover more about sea kayaking. I also started making instructional DVDs, which these days sell better. People seem to be willing to pay more to learn than they are willing to do for their enjoyment. Over the last few years, a lot has changed. There's so much free content to find online nowadays, young people are no longer willing to pay for an online film or DVD. The competition has become very big. That's why nowadays, I'm focusing much more on real-life teaching and guided tours, together with my partner Jean-François. I'm also working on a project to teach people how to make adventure movies.

Aleutian Islands

In 2014, I kayaked together with Sarah Outen from the Aleutian Islands to Alaska. This was part of Sarah's human-powered trip around the world. This was probably the most difficult expedition I've ever done. The Aleutian chain consists of many small and bigger volcanic islands. It's a very rough place to be with a lot of wind and high waves. The goal was to kayak from one island to another. Sarah had a lot less experience than I did and had to go way beyond her comfort zone. The most difficult for me was to be concentrated on navigating and making the right decisions, while at the same time having to push Sarah beyond what she actually wanted to do, all without losing gentleness and patience towards her. We would eventually spend 101 days together, kayaking 2500 km. It was not always easy dealing with each other in challenging conditions. I encouraged Sarah to learn as much as possible and not to rely solely on me. Very soon she became a much stronger paddler, her stamina improved as well and we managed to have a great adventure. Today we're still good friends.

On one of the islands, we also had a tricky encounter with a bear. Before our trip, we were told that most bears are scared of people and will flee if they see you. One day, Sarah told me she would take a dip in a stream on one of the islands. Suddenly, I heard her screaming: "Justine, there's a bear!" So I took my camera and walked to Sarah. It was clear that this bear wasn't afraid of us. Actually, because the Aleutian Islands are so remote, we might have been the first humans the bear had ever seen in his life. He was walking in our direction and came as close as 30m from us. I started swearing out loud in the hope to scare him. In the meantime, Sarah had hidden behind me, grabbed some rocks, and threw them at the bear. Luckily this made him turn around and leave us alone. Or maybe it was my swearing that scared him?!

Freedom

I've always had problems following rules. I can follow rules if they make sense, but not otherwise. I'm a big believer in freedom of choice. When I was working for a boss, it was really difficult for me to follow instructions if I thought I could do something better, differently. The great thing about my lifestyle today is that I'm my own boss, I can do what I want. However, it's a double-edged sword. I constantly have to motivate myself to be productive. It can be very hard work as well. In the run-up to a film release, I work up to 18 hours a day.

I called my company *Cackle TV*. I have a very particular laugh, as if I'm cackling. When I was playing hockey, 'Cackle' was my nickname on the team. When I was brainstorming about a name for my kayak film company, I didn't want something mainstream (adventure-this or adventure-that). I looked for something unique and evocative. There was a small voice in my head telling me: "Call it *Cackle TV*". At first, I ignored the whispering because I thought it was ridiculous. But after a while, I said "why not?" After all, it was my company, so I should give it my own identity.

The most beautiful moments are when you're kayaking in remote places, as in Patagonia or Antarctica. The worries and constraints we have at home vanish; paying bills, sending emails, filling out papers . . . We tend to wind ourselves up because of these things, while they aren't important at all for our survival. The irony is that on an expedition the few things you have to take care of are actually important for survival: making sure to stay healthy, happy, warm, and fed. At the same time, the expedition life is pure simplicity. It's liberating.

I met my partner Jean-François 4 years ago. He has decades of experience as a kayak teacher. We're a really good team. We balance each other; he's more risk-averse and more rule-oriented than I. We learn from each other, I took him skiing and he taught me hunting. You know, we try to live as self-sufficient as possible. We live on the west coast of Canada and we fish from our kayaks a lot. We've made the choice not to have kids. I do have a niece and nephew. I adore them and like to spend time with them, but having kids yourself is a lot of work and hard to combine with the adventurous lifestyle we have.

Thinking about future projects, I'd love to enjoy myself a bit more. The big expeditions I did in the past were great experiences, but they're also very hard work. Especially if you go to areas where the political situation is difficult. Then you need to arrange permits, do a lot of paperwork, pay authorization fees . . . I feel like taking it a bit easier, taking the time to be really present and enjoy the landscapes even more than before, without having to hurry.

What are your most important values in life?
Freedom, honesty, loyalty, friends, and family.

What personality traits does an adventurer need?
Resilience, curiosity, and optimism come in handy. You also need to be organized. A lot of people dream about an adventurous lifestyle, but they never make a concrete plan. The most important trait might be to believe in yourself, to be confident that you'll make it happen. You can grow confidence by starting small. The first time I saw a kayaker doing a roll in rough water, it looked very scary and I said to myself: "Why would I want to do that?" Today, it's a reflex that usually comes easily. It also helps if you can find guidance from someone who's more experienced in the thing you want to do.

What does a life well-lived mean to you?
A life well lived means being true to yourself. Don't live your life because it's comfortable, or because of what others expect you to do, but follow your dreams. Also, be kind to others. Kindness doesn't cost you anything. And be optimistic. All the people I like to hang around are optimistic and kind, so if you reflect this yourself people will love to be around you.

Find out more about Justine:
www.cackletv.com
facebook.com/cackletv
instagram.com/justinecurgenven

I Want to See How Far I Can Push My Body

*Since 2017, **SARAH THOMAS** holds the World Record for the longest non-stop unassisted swim – 167 km in 67 hours – which she completed in Lake Champlain (USA). She is the only person on earth to have swum the English Channel four times non-stop, good for 209 km in 54 hours. In between the two feats, Sarah had to go through a 10-month-long breast cancer treatment.*

"While the doctors were worried about my life, I was worried about my swimming career."

Epiphany

I started swimming at ten years old and loved it right away. During my childhood and teens, my coaches said that I had a lot of potential. I astonished them with my work ethic; I always was the first one in and the last one out of the pool. I went through a traditional path of competition in the swimming pool. My results got better and better but at the age of 16-17, I reached a plateau. This left me unmotivated. Around the period of going from high school to college, I thought that my swimming career was over. Nevertheless, I hadn't really ended it the way I wanted to. After a lot of reflection, I committed to giving it another chance until the end of my studies. I think that this choice of sticking to swimming for four more years has been one of the most important decisions in my life. If I would have quit at age 18, I probably wouldn't have become an accomplished marathon swimmer.

It wasn't until age 25 that I discovered open water swimming. I enrolled in a 10km swim with one of my main motivations that training for it would keep me in shape for my upcoming marriage. During the swim, I had two college friends in a kayak, guiding me and cheering out loud. This swim was almost an epiphany for me. It felt so right, it felt as if this was what I was born to do. I was so happy that it almost made me cry. A new passion was born, one I never turned my back towards since that day.

The Doctors Were Worried About My Life, I Was Worried About My Swimming Career

In November 2017, I got diagnosed with breast cancer. I was only 35 years old and at the top of my game. That same year I had swum the length of Lake Champlain, good for 104.6 miles (167,3 km). This was the longest non-stop, non-wetsuit, open water swim someone had ever done. I was also already planning to swim the English Channel four times in a row. Then, while being ready to conquer the world, I got to hear that my existence was in danger. I had to go through radiotherapy, chemo, and breast surgery. When the doctors proposed a breast reconstruction to increase my chances of survival, all I could think about was how that would affect my physiology and as a result my swimming capacities. It was terrifying to make a decision that could mean the end of my passion. To me, a life without swimming doesn't look like much of a good life.

Luckily, it turned out that this whole period did not affect my swimming that much. During the ten months of chemotherapy, I was in the pool 3-4 times a week most weeks. This being said, it was an extremely difficult time emotionally. To the people around me, it looked as if I took cancer with grace, humor, and a positive attitude. But on the inside, I was suffering. I spent entire nights crying.

I think that my history as a marathon swimmer helped me through it. I am a Type-A personality; always driven, always have clear goals, and have a well-structured schedule. This definitely helped me to deal with the challenge. When you go through chemo, you feel exhausted. But because I'm a marathon swimmer, I was already used to feeling tired and being uncomfortable. Actually, I looked at the treatment as one giant training session. I didn't let fatigue stop me from going to the pool, because I knew it was good for me.

During this period I always had the goal of swimming the English Channel four times non-stop in my mind. Having something to look forward to in the future definitely helped me to push through. People often ask me whether having survived cancer gave me the mental strength to be able to swim the Channel 4 times. I have to answer no; quite the opposite. Cancer made me weaker, not stronger. I did this challenge only one year after the end of my treatment and that meant that I was not yet at 100% of my capacities. The reason I had the mental strength to accomplish it is simply because I had the physical and mental strength as a result of many years of marathon swimming.

You are the Roger Federer of marathon swimming, yet you have very little recognition and no financial rewards for your accomplishments. Is that something that frustrates you?
If you grow up as a swimmer, you know that it will never make you rich, unless you're at the level of Michael Phelps. It would be very nice if I just had to focus on swimming. I'm still working full-time. Although I can arrange my working hours as I want, it still takes up a lot of energy I would rather use for swimming. Also, every swimming challenge is a financial investment. I can't do every project I want to, only my top choices. I even have to pay for my swimming suits! I sent out a sponsorship request to Speedo three times and never even got a reply.

The good thing about having no prize money involved in the sport is that it keeps it pure. Everything I do is for myself; because I want to. Not to please sponsors or earn money. Most often, the only other person who cares about what I'm doing is my mum, I guess.

How difficult is it to combine a full-time job and 20-30 hours of swimming per week with a social life?
I can make it work, it's all about finding the right balance. My husband is very understanding, patient, and supportive. He has his own hobby's, so when I'm swimming he's concentrating on those. We make sure to have dinner together every day. Most of my family lives eight hours drive or more away, so it's really about focusing on quality rather than quantity. The same holds true when it comes to friends. If there is fun stuff to do, I make sure not to miss it and adapt my training plan.

What goes through your mind when you're spending 20 to 50 hours at a time in the water for a challenge or record attempt?
Everything, really. I think about work, family, what I'm going to do when it's finished. Before the English Channel swim, a lot of people told me I wouldn't be able to do it. Wanting to prove them wrong was something that motivated me too. The best swims are the ones where you're in a calm, peaceful mind for the majority of the time. Where you're soaking in the environment, feel zen, and don't think that much at all.

Why?
My main reason for doing incredible long swims is the desire to see how far I can push my body. The drive comes from within, I want to show myself something. If by doing so I can inspire others, that's great. The biggest compliment someone can give me is that I inspired them, that I gave them hope. Especially if it is someone who's going through cancer treatment themself.

What is something you believe most people think is insane?
Swimming for 12 hours straight is something most people think is insane. For me, it's just part of the training schedule for a big challenge.

If you were forced to live on a desert island and could take only two people and five objects with you, who and what would you choose?
I would only want one person; my husband. Other people would drive me crazy. Can I exchange the second person for my three dogs?

When it comes to the five objects; things that would help us survive, I guess. A water purification system, a tent, a cooking stove maybe . . . actually I should ask my husband, he has a better understanding of which tools could come in useful.

What is the maximum distance the mainland should be in order for you to try to escape from the island and swim to the mainland?
If it would be 100 miles I would try to swim it, for sure.

What is the biggest gift someone can give you?
Their time. I spend so much time in the pool that it makes me so incredibly grateful to have people swimming with me, or even just hanging out at the side of the pool and encouraging me.

What advice would you give to the 18-year-old Sarah?
To the swimmer Sarah I would say: "Start open water swimming now!" My general life advice would be to not be afraid to fail. We, humans, are capable of much more than we think. I think it's our obligation in life to do the big things that appeal to us, even though we will fail many times along the way. You just have to find a way to follow your dreams, because that makes you such a happier and better person.

What is your definition of a life well-lived?
Doing good in the world, having a positive impact on other people.

Find out more about Sarah:

www.sarahthomasswim.com
instagram.com/sarahswims04
facebook.com/SarahThomasMarathonSwimmer

What if Money Was No Object?

ALEX ALLEY has been a professional sailor since the age of 19. In his 30-year long career, he has broken several World Records. In 2019, he intended to put the icing on the cake by attempting to become the fastest person to sail around the world solo. A damaged mast shattered his dreams.

"Initially, it felt like a failure. I felt like I had let down everyone around me. But then I became aware that this could not have been prevented and I could be quite proud of what I had achieved."

That's Where I Belong

I grew up in a conventional family on the Southeast coast of Britain. My parents weren't really adventurous, but when I was eight years old my dad wanted to start sailing. He bought a small boat. We went sailing together and I fell in love. Soon I was sailing all by myself and it was like magic. I absolutely loved the sense of freedom it gave me. I built my life around being on the sea as much as possible. Eventually, I went to University to study *Yacht Design*. That way, I could at least be around yachts a lot. After graduating, I worked for three months in a design of ice. Every day, I would look out the window and see all the yachts sailing in and out. I thought: "That's where I belong." So I resigned, left the of ice, and found a way to become a professional sailor.

Meeting Paula

In 2004, I participated in *The Global Challenge*, a yacht race around the world. That's where I met my now-wife Paula *(Read the interview with Paula Reid on page 322)*. I was a watch leader on the boat; this meant that I had to lead half of the team. Paula and I were at the two extremes of the crew. For me, it was all about competition, about winning. Paula had never sailed before, she was just an adventurous woman who made it a goal to sail around the world. As the race progressed, all of the team members found each other somewhere in the middle of us two. I had to temper my expectations down. Less competitive people like Paula got enthusiastic by being in a race and pushed themselves to the best of their capabilities. Actually, *The Global Challenge* was conceived by a British military Sergeant whose ethos was that everyone with the right attitude can be taught the technical aspects of sailing in a very short time and, subsequently, sail around the world.

Paula definitely had the right attitude. She was very hungry to make her dream of sailing around the world happen. That's why she got her chance. Today, this is typical advice we give when we train business leaders: "Recruit for attitude and not for skills. It's better to train a highly motivated person who's eager to learn than to give the job to someone who already knows how to do it, but doesn't really care about it."

I often joke that Paula is more like me than I am. We both have an enormous lust for life, we enjoy life to the fullest, we have tremendous fun, and both of us like to stretch ourselves. If Paula leaves for a couple of months on an expedition, I don't make an issue of it because I understand that adventure is something she needs to be happy, to learn, and to grow. Paula feels the same when I leave on a big sailing trip.

PixelBoat

In 2019, I tried to break a speed record for sailing solo and non-stop around the world. We calculated that the whole expedition would cost somewhere between €300,000 and €500,000. It's very hard to find a company that wants to sponsor such a large sum of money. That's how Paula and I came up with an original crowdfunding campaign. We offered everyone the chance to pay €30 and in turn, we would put a picture of each and every supporter on the side of the boat. We named the yacht 'PixelBoat' because of this. I set off on New Year's Eve 2018 from northern France. About 2-3 weeks in, I had a lot of problems with one of my two autopilots. Carrying on with only one autopilot is very risky, so I tried to repair the broken one. I called the French manufacturer, and they said I should return it by post. Of course, I told them I couldn't because I was in the middle of the ocean on a non-stop World Record attempt. Then, they asked me if I could go ashore and search for a post office. Again, I told them I was on a non-stop World Record attempt, meaning I couldn't stop . . . but they didn't get the picture. Anyway, I got in touch with people online who gave me the right advice. This way I managed to solve the problem and continue the record attempt.

When I was struggling with the autopilots and getting frustrated about the loss of time, I was glad to have written two of my favorite quotes on the boat: "Pain is temporary, pride is forever" and "Choose your attitude". These quotes reminded me to stay cool and just do the work that had to be done. Halfway through the record attempt, bad luck struck again. A piece of my mast broke. as a consequence, I could no longer pull down my mainsail. This would definitely have gotten me into trouble during storms and around icebergs. I discussed with Paula whether I would take the risk and we decided to abandon the record attempt. I sailed *PixelBoat* 1500 km to Adelaide. At first, I considered myself to have failed. I felt I had let down so many people who had supported me. But pretty soon, I realized that this could not have been prevented. I could not have taken a spare mast with me, that would just have taken too much space and weight. I hadn't made any mistakes. I had prepared every aspect of this expedition in great detail for nine years. I had taken all the right precautions needed to pick the right pieces. I had done my daily check-up of all equipment and ropes. This was just bad luck. I had never broken that piece of the mast before, and I had never heard of another yachtsman who had broken this particular piece either.

So little by little, the disappointment made room for pride. I had made one of the longest solo sailing trips in history for this class of boat and I had broken several speed World Records on the way: from the start to the cape of South Africa, from the equator to South Africa, and from South Africa to Australia. Today, the boat is still in Adelaide. Bringing it back to the UK would cost €30,000. Doing a second solo nonstop around-the-world record attempt would cost just as much as the first one; it would be incredibly difficult to fundraise this a second time. As a result, I'm focusing on other projects now.

Adventure Psychology

Paula has a Master's Degree in Positive Psychology. When I was at sea alone in 2019, I got the chance to call her once a week for 30 minutes. This time was really valuable. She coached me with the same models we had developed and continue to use in our *Adventure Psychology* training. She made me think through every problem and find a solution for it. In times of trouble, she encouraged me to think one day at a time, or even one hour at a time. I had to forget about the whole project, just focus on the task at hand. It's a trick Paula had used when she skied to the South Pole by herself. It's also one of the many lessons we give when we work with businesses. The world today is VUCA: Volatile, Uncertain, Complex, and Ambiguous. We believe that in today's business world, it's no longer '*survival of the fittest*', but '*survival of the most adaptable*'. Being flexible, versatile, and adaptable is a skill that can be learned. One easy way to do so is by changing the language you use. If a problem arises, don't call it a problem but a challenge. Nobody likes problems, but a lot of people like challenges. It's also about pushing your boundaries, adventure is a perfect way to do so. If you train for hardship and practice resilience through adventure, you'll have a better coping strategy when life throws real difficulties at you. I remember one of the clients we worked with was a lady in her 70's. She asked for our help because she had had a panic attack while driving her car and suddenly arrived in a thick cloud of mist. So we encouraged her to swim with us in the sea on the first of January. She was terrified but agreed. Afterward, she called us up and said: "That was the most incredible thing I've ever done. I feel like superwoman now!"

What if money was no object?
I am very grateful that I can do what I love as a profession. I think I mostly made my own luck, by having the right attitude and being willing to sacrifice. Often people tell me they would like to have the kind of life Paula and I have. I ask them: "what's stopping you?" Then, they come up with excuses: "I don't have the money." "Easy," I answer, "sell your BMW"; or "my girlfriend doesn't want me to go away for so long." "Easy: get another girlfriend . . ." If adventure is really what you want to do, then you'll find a way to do so. I've had to make huge sacrifices. I sold my car, I sold costly possessions, I was homeless for a while and lived on the floors of friends houses . . . I advise people to listen very carefully to the speech by Alan Watts 'What if money was no object?'. Watts says that if you do what you love, and you do it over and over, you'll eventually become a master in it and someone, somewhere, will pay you for it. According to me, Watts is very much right.

Find out more about Alex:
www.alexalley.com
instagram.com/thealexalley

PART SIX:
Snow (Hey oh)

When We Let Go Of the Ego,
We Can Accomplish More

KIT DESLAURIERS is the first person to have skied down the Seven Summits (the highest mountain on every continent) and a two-time freeride ski World Champion, climate advocate, writer, public speaker, and mother of two girls in their early teens.

"I raised a wolf named Alta throughout my twenties, it was the most spiritual relationship I ever had. Alta taught me to always be true to myself."

Mountain Girl

I was born in New England into a family of five, with a sister two years older and a brother two years younger. During my early childhood, our family moved around the country quite a bit. My parents were in search of better jobs and, especially, a better lifestyle. I'm very thankful to them for that because this way I learned to be flexible, and their quest led us to settle down in the supreme natural beauty of Arizona when I was 10 years old.

Already as a child, I was highly driven in sports and academics. My parents always valued me doing my best, but only for the things I was genuinely interested in. They never forced me into a certain direction. I enjoyed every type of sport that came in front of me, from soccer to nordic skiing. But when I went alpine skiing for the first time at age 14, that's when I felt something really special. I felt a joy far beyond what other sports could offer me. I decided to immerse myself in this newly discovered passion.

The discovery of downhill skiing coincided with my first international travels without adults, at age 15. Although I was still a teenager, I spent entire weekends working as much as I could, in order to save up money to travel to Europe in the summer. I'm very grateful that my parents gave me the freedom to do this. Their only requirement was for me to pay my own way and study my chosen foreign language, French, while being there.

Because I loved the outdoors and traveling so much, I decided to study Environmental Political Science and French at the University of Arizona. When I was 19, I studied for one semester in Marseille, France. Over there I fell in love with rock climbing and deepened my passion for skiing. I eventually dropped out of University and moved to Verbier, where I spent all of my days in the Alps. I remember coming back to the US and going on a ski foray with my dad. Noticing my improved level, Dad said: "I'm pretty sure they don't teach you to ski like that in school. So where the hell have you been?!" . . . I had no choice but to confess.

After that one semester, I returned to the University of Arizona. I highly valued completing my education and I still wanted to save the world. Nevertheless, one year before graduation, the weight of reality had become too big. I got discouraged by the size of the world's environmental problems and the roadblocks of the political system I would encounter if I wanted to make a valuable change. I thought a moment about narrowing my focus and shifting to a degree in Ecology, but that would mean two more years sitting in school; a sacrifice I didn't want to make. So instead, I finished my studies, graduating with academic honors. I adopted a newborn wolf, moved to the mountains in Colorado, and became a stonemason.

Spiritual Animal

If I wouldn't be able to save the world, then I would at least contribute to uplifting its energy by doing what I loved most, being in the mountains and raising a wolf. As irrational as it may sound, this has been one of the best decisions I ever made. I learned so much from my wolf, Alta. Lessons I've translated into my own life. For instance, wolves have an incredible, deep, and loving commitment for the other wolves in the pack. Yet, they are very comfortable being alone. The relationship I had with Alta has been the most spiritual one in my life. He lived true to himself. If he ever veered from that it was from a place of love, which was also true to his life. Let me tell you a story to illustrate. One day, I went hiking with Alta and we encountered a herd of elk. His instincts were urging him to chase the elk, I was asking him to stay. I saw him looking back and forth between me and the elk a dozen times, as if he was saying "What do you want me to do Kit? I'm born to run after them?!" Alta was too strong, fast, and independent for me to stop him, other than by asking with love. I'd made a commitment to him to help him live his life without being killed for being a wolf in the human world. Alta understood that my demand for him to stay came out of a place of love. He obeyed and thus let love win over his instincts.

How did you go from stonemason to professional skier?

While I was a stonemason, I kept on skiing a lot and also enrolled in ski patrolling and helicopter rescue training programs. In 1999, a friend and I asked *The North Face* for funding to climb and ski Mount Belukha, the highest mountain in Siberia. To our fortune, *The North Face* agreed to support the expedition as long as we included some of their professional athlete team. They also had my now-husband Rob as cinematographer. We met on this trip and fell in love immediately. Spending time in the company of those professional ski-mountaineers, and hearing their stories about the lifestyle they were leading, made me understand that's what I wanted to do with my life too. I started dreaming about becoming a member of *The North Face* athlete team. I decided that the next step was to work on my skiing to the point where I was good enough to win competitions. In 2004, my first year on the Freeride World Tour, I won the Women's Champion title. This competition was sandwiched between ski expeditions with Rob. Annually, from 2000 to 2004, I sent my resume to *The North Face* and asked for a spot on the team. I was finally accepted in 2005 when I was on my way to my second Women's Championship title and had several ski descents already completed on my *Seven Summits* project.

Letting Go Of the Ego

After skiing from the summit of Mount Everest in 2006, I was fortunate to meet Phakchok Rinpoche. He is a Tibetan Buddhist teacher based in Nepal. Although he is a many-time re-incarnated soul, he's also a husband and father, very humorous, and speaks perfect English. Many of us westerners find him highly relatable. By good fortune, Rinpoche often comes to my home village of Jackson Hole, Wyoming to share his teachings. Whenever he makes the journey, I spend as much time with him as possible and attend his events. I've even asked him for personal advice on many occasions. I vividly recall one of our interactions several years ago when I was telling him about someone who was bothering me. When my story was over, Rinpoche said to me: "Kit, there is way too much 'I' in your story." "That might be true", I replied, "but what am I going to do about it?" He said: "Next time you see this person, think 'love'. Repeat in your head over and over the word 'love'." So I tried that and, as hard as it was, it worked. I literally had to repeat love in my mind constantly as I listened to this woman talk. I watched all of my negativities dissolve.

Rinpoche's lesson is something I remind myself of all the time. I've experienced that when you let go of the ego and replace the negative thoughts with love, then life flows more effortlessly and it's actually far easier to accomplish what you want in life. Not only do you suffer less when you let go of the ego, but it's also more possible to have your actions and accomplishments become a type of service to others. If you live the life you really want, it being soul- and not ego-driven, you can become an uplifting example.

Live Like a Pro Even Before You are One
Thinking back about my journey, I can definitely say that I had to pay my dues. For the past 20 years, I've continued to improve my skill sets, both personally and professionally. I tried for years to earn a living in the outdoor industry. Although I was turned away for a while, I never gave up on my dream. I do what I do because I truly love it, regardless of the compensation. And now that I have it, I still work at it. When people who dream of living the life of an athlete or adventurer ask me what they should do, I tell them to train like they are a professional already. And to always do what they love.

What other advice would you give to people who want to become professional adventurers or outdoor athletes?
Craft useful skills. By the time I got a spot on *The North Face* team, I had gained mountaineering, skiing, medical and rescue skills. All of this made me a valuable team member and someone people could trust in the mountains. Trust is very important in general; if you want to become and stay a professional athlete, you have to have good expedition behavior. This means being a team player, as well as having valuable skills. And always, always, keep a beginner's mind!

More than ever before, marketing and social media have become a very important aspect of our job. While this reality holds the potential to spread kindness and inspiration, it is also inherently easy to get pushed in the opposite direction of chasing the ego . . . When I notice I get too caught up by the 'likes' and 'shares' of my posts, I go on a 'social media fast'. Sometimes I let it go entirely for several months. This allows me to focus on what really fills my cup: being a mother and spending a maximum amount of time in the mountains.

Health Game-Changers
Health is one of my top values and I'm always in search of ways to improve it. The beginner's mind here, mixed with consistent effort, appears to be working. I'm now 51 and feel as if my mental and physical condition is as good as it's ever been.

Throughout the years I've discovered some game-changers:
- Prioritizing sleep. I'm an early bird, I get up at 5.30 a.m. and go to bed around 9 p.m. I use a ring on my finger that helps me learn about sleep and recovery patterns.
- Meditation. It's the first thing I do in the morning. It gets me ready to approach the day with fewer distracting thoughts and greater calm.
- Evening rituals. I turn off all distractions – laptop, smartphone, television – and focus on quality time. For example, taking a hot bath or reading a story to my children.
- Nutrition. I eat mostly whole foods; a whole lot of vegetables, nuts, seeds, and quality wild-sourced animal protein. I even hunt elk, thanks to Alta! I eat as close to nature as possible, but I do enjoy a bag of chips every now and then.

Do you think the world would be a better place if adventure would be a mandatory part of the school curriculum?

Absolutely! Being outdoors, we realize that the world doesn't revolve around us. We are quite vulnerable as we relate to the natural world. Understanding that we're actually rather insignificant on our own, is a special lesson that nature can teach us. Adventure also makes us flexible. It makes us learn to do more with less and to grow our capacity for grit and resilience. When we come back from an expedition into our normal, comfy lives, we gain a new perspective. We realize that our everyday problems are rarely insurmountable, or even that big of a deal. On top of this, when we go on an adventure with others, we're forced to work together. We get a chance to uplift each other, something of enormous value in society.

What is your definition of a life well-lived?

A life full of kindness, compassion, authenticity, and love.

Find out more about Kit:
www.kitdeslauriers.com
instagram.com/kitdski
facebook.com/KitDSki

When You Set the Bar Very High, That's When You Learn the Most

HILAREE NELSON is a Professional Ski Mountaineer. Amongst many impressive defeats, Hilaree has climbed two 8000 meter peaks in less than 24 hours. She and her life partner, Jim Morrison, were the first people to ski down Lhotse. She is also an Athlete Captain at 'The North Face' and mother of two boys.

"Gratitude is one of the main values I try to transfer to my kids because it's so closely related to sanity and happiness."

Hilaree's Defining Factors of Success:

Setting Big Goals

I like to set goals beyond my skill set. I am not afraid to fail. If I make a plan for an adventure, I want bang for my buck; an esthetic line, a beautiful location, great people to work with. I've experienced that when you set the bar very high, that's when you learn the most. When you're out in the wilderness for several weeks and extreme tiredness kicks in close to the summit of your chosen mountain, that's the moment when your mental resilience becomes key. That's when you get stronger.

Curiosity

Curiosity is a huge part of success. As I am getting older, I get more and more afraid of getting too comfortable. That's why I make sure to continue to push the envelope. I want to maintain this childlike curiosity. I'm convinced that curiosity is what keeps us young, mentally and physically.

Courage

Courage is a difficult construct. Because you can never have courage without fear. Courage can only result from putting yourself out there and overcoming something. For me, courage translates to finding tools to deal with fear. Tools such as focusing on the here and now, breathwork, journaling . . .

Discipline

It's something I struggle with, quite honestly. Discipline is very important in order to start an expedition very fit and well-organized. Although discipline is very important, there's a flip side to it. Namely, becoming too regimented and too rigid. In the mountains, things can change very quickly so you have to be able to adapt easily. That's why ski mountaineers have to find a balance between discipline on one hand, and agility and adaptability on the other hand.

Gratitude

It is everything. What's the point of success if you can't appreciate things along the way? For several years in my career, I had difficulties being grateful. This reflected in my behavior on the mountain. I would feel anger and bitterness all the time. Thankfully traveling made me relearn gratitude. It's a cliché, but I noticed so often that the poorest people I met were the happiest. It made me reassess my own ideas about happiness. Happiness is not about achieving the goal, it's about being present and being grateful for the people around you. Nowadays, gratitude is one of the main values I try to transfer to my kids because it's so closely related to sanity and happiness.

Kindness

This ties in with gratitude. Being kind is not something you have to do to achieve success, but I see it as a moral obligation of being a human being. Unfortunately, for the last couple of years, the political system in the U.S. has been lacking morality and kindness. It's awful to see how that's been passed on in society. If we want to be decent human beings, we truly have to pull out more kindness and gratitude again.

Community

The community of ski mountaineers is a very special one. The people in it are very passionate. They can be really tough and abstinent. In my personal life, they have given me support which helped me out so much in the achievement of big goals. When I'm at the end of my forces on an expedition, a message or phone call from one of my closest mountaineering friends immediately cheers me up and gives me the energy for an extra push. The community has also backed me up when I have faced criticism. For example; when my eldest son was only 10 months old, I left for an expedition to Alaska. For the general public, this was not understandable. I got to hear that I was an irresponsible mother. My friends reacted to those comments; they understood how much I need adventures in order to be me.

Communication

That has been a really difficult one for me. My good friend Conrad Anker defines a successful expedition as 1. Coming back alive, 2. Coming back as friends, 3. Having achieved the goal the team had set. Luckily, I've managed to stay true to the first rule. However, poor communication has definitely caused the downfall of expedition success and friendships. The expeditions to Gasherbrum II in 2008 and Myanmar in 2014 come to mind right away. When things get raw on an expedition, my nature is to go into my own little bubble. I stop talking and just do the necessary work. Often that attitude doesn't work well in groups. Communication is something I had to work on very hard, and continue working on today.

The irony is that one of my main tasks as the Athlete Captain for *The North Face* is to assure good, positive communication with the athletes. Despite the difficult times resulting from COVID-19, I have the impression that most of our athletes have kept their spirits high. An important contributor to that has been the global Zoom calls on Thursdays. Each week, about 60 of our athletes met each other in the virtual space to talk about ongoing projects and future plans, but also about doubts and setbacks. I have the impression that this has bonded the Athlete Alliance tighter than ever before.

Optimism

Hmmm, difficult one. I am surely not optimistic all of the time. I think that's a good thing. In the mountains, it's better to be a realist than to be a blind optimist. I prefer a combination of humility and humor over just being positive all the time. One thing is for sure, the opposite – negativity – is poison. I've been on expeditions with pessimistic people. It's the worst thing you can imagine.

Social Media

I've seen the rapid evolution of social media and its increasing value in the sport. The number of Instagram followers that an athlete has is a crucial element in sponsorship and contract negotiations. Your social media value has also become important in having a chance of expedition grants.

I think it's a double-edged sword. There sure is a very positive side to social media. Firstly, it gives athletes the opportunity to share incredible stories with a lot of people. By these stories, followers might get attached to some things they would otherwise not be interested in or exposed to. Climate change is the most obvious example. In turn, this attachment might motivate them to take a stance.

For me personally, the biggest advantage of social media is that it allows me to stay in touch with my kids during week-long expeditions. I don't even know if I would be able to leave them alone for that long without social media.

The negative side of it is that it's a crazy time suck. It's also a way in which you can put out a false reality to the world. Seeing how amazing other people's lives seem to be can cause issues with self-worth and depression. Besides, social media can be a very dehumanizing way of communication. I hear stories of kids being bullied online. And, of course, there's Trump who even fires staff people through Twitter . . .

What are the biggest life lessons you teach your children (besides gratitude)?

Work ethic. I want them to understand that there's a linear equation between the work put in and the success. I define success not by money or by summiting a mountain, but by feeling satisfied and proud of yourself. I also foster them in being curious and developing a passion.

Jim

I have been in a relationship with fellow ski mountaineer Jim Morrison for five years now. It has been amazing in so many ways. When I was together with my first husband, I kept my crazy mountaineering ideas to myself. With Jim, I can just share them and be sure he'll give great feedback. Jim is very much a "Yes, let's do it!" person. This way we're often capable of starting off from an insane, seemingly impossible idea and anyway create a plan to realize it.

Jim is also very good at communication. He forced me to become better at it myself.

On top of this it's just tremendously assuring to be out in very remote, dangerous places with someone you feel 100% secure with. I know I can fully trust Jim's skill set, his decision-making, and him taking care of me.

What is your definition of a life well-lived?
Learning all the time.
Taking risks.
Smiling and laughing.
Having a positive impact on the people around you.

Find out more about Hilaree:
www.hilareenelson.com
instagram.com/hilareenelson
facebook.com/HilareeNelsonOfficial

Progress is Better Than Perfection

LORRAINE HUBER is a Professional Freeride Skier, Freeride World Champion, and Mental Coach. She's also the protagonist in award-winning ski films, a fully certified Ski Instructor and Ski Mountain Guide, and the organizer of the 'Women Progression Days': freeride and ski touring camps for women. In the summer, Lorraine loves surfing and rock climbing.

"I live to learn new things and progress in them. Having a lot of new and different experiences is my definition of a life well-lived."

Different Influences

I grew up in Lech, a tiny village in Austria. Both my mom and my dad were quite adventurous for their time period. My mom is Australian and sailed from her home country to the U.S.A. when she was only 22 years old. Later on, she worked in global cities such as New York and Geneva. My dad left Lech to work as a chef in London and later Southern France. For someone coming out of his small, conservative village this was a very big step. My parents met in Lech.

Lech counts only 1,500 inhabitants, yet the village is situated in the biggest and best ski area in Austria. The house I grew up in was 100 meters away from the closest ski lift. I sometimes went to ski school instead of kindergarten. My dad was a ski instructor and I wanted to become like him when I grew up. Throughout my childhood, I witnessed both of my parents, especially my father, work extremely hard. If I would not have learned the value of hard work back then, I probably would never have become a World Champion many years later.

When I was eight years old, we moved to Australia. We lived there for ten years and that period definitely broadened my horizons. Luckily most of our summers we were able to return to Lech to ski for a couple of weeks. We didn't ski in Australia because it's very expensive and not very accessible. My main passions at that time were ballet dancing and horseback riding. Looking back, I can say that living in Australia has been very important in my development as a person. Australians are very outgoing and open and that shaped me for sure. My sister and I are able to adapt easily to different cultures and people.

From Business School to Becoming a Pro Skier

In Australia, I went to a Catholic girl's school with 1,200 students. The message we were often given was to get into the marketplace early and build a successful career. That's what society expects in the Western world. I decided to study business administration in Vienna. The Austrian University system allows students to pace their own rhythm in their studies. This allowed me to spend a lot of time skiing. So in parallel with my studies at University, I managed to get my education as a ski instructor. By the time I was 23, I had obtained my Level III Ski and Snowboard Instructor Certificate as well as the Ski Mountain Guiding Certificate.

During my studies, I started seeing the possibility of creating a different life for myself from what society usually expects. My boyfriend at that time, who was a fully certified Mountain Guide, was a big influence on me in this regard. He lived a life he had created for himself, climbing and skiing all year round. He asked me if I wanted to help him establish what would be Austria's first freeride school. At first, I saw this as an opportunity to gain practical work experience in the business field and was happy to accept the challenge. Little did I know that the Freeride Center Sölden would be an important stepping stone for me in becoming a Professional Freeride Skier.

At the end of my studies, I had to make a conscious decision about my future: a conventional career or putting all my energy into skiing. I chose the latter, with the main motivation being my curiosity about how far my abilities as a skier could reach. Yes, I was already 23 and I had been skiing quite a lot over the past years, but that was mostly as a guide or instructor. I felt that I had not at all reached my potential as a freeride skier and wanted to see how far I could get.

This decision came with a lot of resistance from my father. He felt I was wasting my degree by choosing to focus on skiing. I understand where his point of view comes from. When he grew up, Lech was a very poor village. His upbringing was tough. My father told me stories about having to milk cows from the age of eight and not wearing shoes in summer simply because there was not enough money to buy them. At age 15, he had only two options: becoming a chef or a ski instructor. He worked very hard to give his daughters a better life, more options than he had had. Security and certainty are very important values to him. So, I can understand his reaction when I ignored a secure, well-paid career to chase the seemingly impossible dream of becoming a Professional Freeride Skier. My father simply couldn't see how that would work out, and honestly, I didn't either. At that time freeride skiing was a new sport. There were no role models. No Austrian woman had ever made a living out of it . . . yet, deep inside I knew that was what I had to do.

My mother had a completely opposite perspective. When my sister and I were kids, she used to tell us that we could do whatever we set our minds to. The world was our oyster. After college, she even encouraged me to take a gap year and travel. She believed that money wasn't the most important thing. Having inherited my mom's risk-taking behavior has helped me a lot in building a career as a pro skier. If I would have been concerned about the money, I would never have built a successful career. I think that my own values and life philosophy lay somewhere on the middle path between my mother's and father's vision on life and I'm glad about that.

Lorraine's Superpower
Because I had lived in Australia for ten years and freeride skiing still hadn't been my main focus in my early twenties, I entered the freeride competition with much less experience than most of my competitors. I think I have been able to compensate for the lack of sport-specific training hours because learning fast is my superpower. The reason why I learn fast is that, once I decide to put my mind to something, I get totally involved in it. If something sparks my interest, I am able to become very passionate about it very rapidly. I even dare to say that I live

for learning new things and progressing in them. Having a lot of new and different experiences is my definition of a life well-lived.

Another important thing is that I'm not afraid to look stupid, maybe this skill can be described as courage. I'm not afraid of failing, I'm not worried about what other people think about me. I notice that so many women are afraid to make mistakes, to look like a fool, or embarrass themselves. They want to do everything perfectly. I noticed this when I'm teaching or training skiers, as well as during my career. Some riders I knew would compete for one or two seasons, and when that didn't work out as they wanted it to, they simply quit. They were just in it to get good results, so when that didn't work out, they lost motivation. For me, one of the main drivers was to learn and progress and become the best skier I could be.

It took me ten years to figure out how to compete on the Freeride World Tour venues under intense pressure. One of the things I struggled with the most was putting too much pressure on myself. As a result, I didn't ski to my full potential during the competition. My training runs were better than my competition runs. I was too stiff and distracted by negative thoughts. After doing a lot of mental strength work and working with a coach, my skiing finally became more relaxed and dynamic even in a high-stress competition situation. The year I became World Champion (2017), my primary goal was to find flow in my competition runs. I focused on the process rather than the outcome. If you're thinking too much about the opponents, points, and judges, you don't concentrate on what is really important: your skiing.

How can people get into a flow state?
An important factor to start with is that you need to have the intention to find flow. Therefore, you have to focus on yourself and not on your ranking, winning, or your competitors. It's about being *your* best instead of wanting to be *the* best. This goes hand in hand with the desire to grow and learn as an athlete. When you focus on the process of learning instead of fixed outcomes, you'll not only be more able to tap into a flow state. You'll experience more fun, more motivation, and more mental strength to push back after setbacks.

Another skill that is essential to finding flow, especially in freeriding, is visualization. In our sport, we can't do any practice runs at the competition venue. Instead, we visualize the run in our minds' eyes from our own perspective. Effective visualization involves using all of your senses to make it as real as possible; the physical sensations, sounds, feelings . . . Then you rehearse your run until you can visualize it smoothly from start to finish. This way, by the time you're at the starting gate, it will be as if you've done the run several times already. Now all you have to do is push off your skis and let your body take over and do what it knows to do.

Do you write a journal?
I have two journals: a ski journal and a relationship journal. Yet journaling is not a regular practice. I write in my journals when I feel I have to work something out in my mind. Recently, I also started working with a planning diary. It's a notebook in which you work out the different steps you have to take in order to achieve your goal. By the way, an interesting side note: there is a whole lot of power in putting your goals onto paper. Especially in combination with visualization. I realize almost every goal I put on paper and visualize myself achieving them.

The Need to Chill Out

I am a very ambitious person, a goal chaser, and a hard worker, but I do really need downtime too. At certain times of the year, I'm just mellow, calm, and relaxed. It's important to not always push myself, to chill out sometimes. For me, the ocean is a great place to do so. I always relate the mountains to challenges and danger. The ocean feels much more welcoming and friendly to me.

Besides technical skills and mental strength, what do girls need to make it in your sport?

They most of all need confidence. I see a lot of girls lacking the confidence to really go for it, although they are technically proficient skiers. Building confidence has a lot to do with setting yourself manageable and realistic challenges. The fastest way to progress is step-by-step.

Secondly, I highly recommend connecting with a group of motivated, skilled, and reliable skiers. It's maybe the most important thing of all not only for reducing the risk out in the backcountry but for pushing yourself and progressing.

What advice would you give the 18-year old Lorraine?

"Don't believe the lies you tell yourself."

The 18-year old Lorraine struggled a lot with self-doubt. I would teach her that our brain is going to try to trick us our entire life into believing thoughts that aren't true. An important part of mental strength is to be aware of when negative, self-limiting thoughts pop up and not to attach to them or engage with them. Instead, let these negative thoughts pass by and refocus your attention on the task at hand. That takes practice of course, but it's a skill you can develop just like any other physical skill.

In your opinion, how should outdoor athletes and adventurers use social media?

A couple of months ago, I posted anti-racism messages on my Instagram account after George Floyd's murder by a white police officer. I did this because the event had moved me and I wanted to take a stance. I see this kind of use of social media as taking leadership. If you look at 95% of the content that gets posted on Facebook or Instagram, it is just about people presenting themselves in the best way possible. I argue that as role models we have to do more. It is our obligation to create value for others.

In my posts, I also want to be relatable to others. I wasn't the most talented skier. I had to work very hard in order to build a successful career. As a result, I don't want to present myself as a superhuman. Instead, I want to show people that they can achieve big things too, and even help them out in doing so. Personally, I'm much more suited for education than entertainment.

Outdoor athletes and adventurers also need to take leadership when it comes to climate change and global warming. On social media but also in their practice. I think that every individual has to ask themself how they can get involved in a way that fits their own personality, talents, and interests. One thing a lot of us struggle with is travel. Whether we travel because we love visiting new places or we feel an obligation to compete abroad, we also want to protect our environment. It's important to reflect upon that dilemma and to find the right path for yourself. In this regard there's one trend I notice which makes me optimistic: heli-skiing is pretty old school and has been replaced with human-powered skiing adventures.

What are your ingredients of happiness?

It's important to understand that happiness doesn't come after you've achieved something, such as meeting your soulmate or becoming a World Champion. Happiness is a state within. Happiness can also be incredibly elusive. I prefer to focus on enjoyment. According to Mihaly Csikszentmihalyi, we're at our happiest when we're challenging ourselves doing an activity we're totally absorbed in, and I would have to agree.

Find what is truly fulfilling to you, what you love to do just for the sake of the activity itself, and find lots of moments in your life to do this. You might just find that it makes you happy.

Find out more about Lorraine:
www.lorrainehuber.com
instagram.com/lorrainehuber
facebook.com/lorraine.huber

Nature, Friends, Health. If You Have Those Three, You Can Do Everything and Be Happy

VICTOR GALUCHOT is a professional backcountry skier, coach and YouTube hit thanks to the series 'Bon Appétit Ski', in which Victor and his friends Fabien Maierhofer and Nico Favre remind us that the ultimate goal of life is to have fun.

"We are told that what we are supposed to do is go working from Monday to Friday and save fun for our weekends. With this dominant narrative, it is extremely hard to stay mentally and physically healthy in society."

A Life Full of Skiing

My parents are two people who very much value adventure and time in the outdoors. When they were young, they alternated seasonal jobs at the coast and in the mountains. Luckily for me, they decided to settle in the French Alps before having kids. As a result, as soon as I was born I got in touch with the mountains. I hardly knew how to walk and I was already skiing. What followed was a classical itinerary followed by many top-level freeride skiers: enrolling as a kid in the local ski club, starting off with alpine competitions, going to a college for skiers, getting fed up with alpine skiing, and shifting towards a focus on freeriding. In my late teens, I competed in freeride competitions. I didn't like it, but I needed good results to get the attention of sponsors. I was lucky to do very well in my first races and as a result, I found some companies interested in supporting me. I was honest right away with them: "I don't want to continue competing. I want to go backcountry and make movies about my adventures. Can you give me the confidence to make this work?" They did, and so the ball started rolling . . .

For a lot of youngsters in this region, skiing becomes too present in their lives. They don't enjoy it anymore and quit. My sister is the perfect example. As a kid, she was actually more talented than me. But, she got sick of skiing, focused on studying, and followed a traditional career path. For me, losing passion has been a risk for a long while too. When skiing becomes your major source of income, it comes with a lot of pressure. There is almost an unhealthy aspect about it because selling yourself becomes very important. This way, skiing can start feeling like a job instead of a passion. Luckily, as soon as that feeling arose in me some years ago, I got aware of it and knew I had to change some things. I asked myself what it was that I really wanted? I listed where I wanted to go skiing and the kind of films I wanted to make and focused on the projects that excited me. This way, I've been able to keep skiing fun throughout my entire career.

I Will Never Get Rich, But I Won't Have Missed Many Snowmageddons In My Life

Thanks to sponsorship and the income from my movies, I'm able to pay for my costs of living for six to nine months of the year. Mostly in autumn, I find myself a seasonal job. Yet, saving up still isn't my biggest talent. There's a video from early 2019 on YouTube where I have only €26 left on my bank account. Still, I decided to travel to Austria because there was a snowmageddon which provided extremely good skiing conditions. At the end of the video, I say: "I will never get rich, but I won't have missed a lot of snowmageddon in my life." I admit that this was an extremely stressful period for me financially, but the video was important in the sense that it reminded me and people watching that it's more important to live good moments than to have money.

Besides sponsorship, filmmaking, and seasonal jobs, I also earn an income as a coach for young skiers in our valley. That is something I really love. Transferring my knowledge and skills gives me even more fulfillment than skiing for myself. I don't explicitly teach those youngsters life lessons – they'd say I'm an old idiot – but I try to understand how each individual's mind works. Some of them like to be very free, others need more guidance and encouragement. Some of them are real thrill-seekers, others more careful and rational about the risks. By trying to understand their personality, I can change my coaching approach to every individual and navigate through the challenges in what is the best way for them.

A Lot Of Drops Form an Entire River

The organization of our society is quite insane, in my opinion. We are told that we are supposed to go working from Monday to Friday and save fun for our weekends. Saturday and Sunday are when we can enjoy ourselves in the mountains (unless there's a corona lockdown and they even forbid us to go in nature). With this dominant narrative, it is extremely hard to stay mentally and physically healthy.

The organization of our contemporary society is also detrimental to our planet. People say that 2020 has been a shitty year, but actually, we've just paid the price for the mistakes people have made over the last three generations. COVID-19 has an animal origin. The reason it could spread is that people have infiltrated the biosphere of wild animals, whether it's for hunting, deforestation, wildlife farming . . . in order to make a profit. COVID-19 is here to remind us that we have to change our relationship with the natural environment urgently. The way society is organized nowadays is very harmful to our planet. Yet, even in this organization, each individual can take a couple of small steps to reduce his or her environmental impact. If 68 million people in France or 7 billion people in the world take small steps, that will be a huge improvement. A lot of drops form an entire river.

A lot of adventurers and outdoor athletes from my generation are really aware of and worried about climate change. You can see this in the powerful dynamic of *Protect Our Winters (POW)*, where hundreds of athletes, scientists, creative storytellers, and companies work together to develop programs to protect nature. *POW*-founder and pro snowboarder Jeremy Jones has even been invited to talk with people from the US Senate about the topic. I guess adventurers and outdoor athletes are so passionate about making a change because we are a frontline subculture impacted by climate change. We are out in nature so often that we can actually see the change happen with our own eyes. This year (2020) I made a short movie called *Projet*

Zéro about a four-day trip where I skied on the biggest glacier of the Belleville-valley. I went there by bike and made use only of non-motorized means of transport during those four days: cycling, hiking, skiing. I wanted to show that if we want to continue enjoying our winter sports, we have to take another approach to experiencing them. I got very good feedback from people who watched the movie. I hope it inspired most of them to make environmental-friendly decisions more often too.

How would you describe yourself in three words?
Curious. Joyful. Contemplative. With the latter, I mean that I try to be conscious about what it is I really want and also to be very grateful for what I have already, especially for the last couple of years. For example, when I go out into the mountains, I try to appreciate the moment, enjoy the beautiful surroundings with full attention, and put myself into perspective.

What have been the biggest setbacks in your career and what did you learn from them?
I'm sorry, I can't give you a tragedy. I didn't really have big setbacks, actually. Maybe that's because I never had very big dreams I absolutely had to realize. Amusement has always been more important than accomplishment. As opposed to the typical hyper-ambitious goal-chaser, I've been more like a feather in the wind, guided by opportunities that come along the way.

How do you train physically?
The best training for skiing is skiing. I maintain a good physical shape by going outdoors for the activities I like. For example, I hike or ski up 1000 meters of elevation gain to ind a spot where I can set off with my paraglider. Some days when I have little time – when I'm editing a movie for example – I do some strength exercises at home.

If you'd be able to turn back time and relive one moment of your life, what would you choose?
The moment I saw a whale for the first time. I was sailing from Spain to Madeira. There were only two people on the boat and I was still learning how to navigate. We had a very rough night which got me totally exhausted. My mental state was really low. Then, at 6 a.m., the wind calmed down, the waves vanished and a whale made its appearance just next to our boat. It was magical.

What is the importance of humor in your life?
It is super important. As I said, I'm a joyful person. When I'm outside, I'm happy, and when I'm happy I say stupid, funny things. I think that's what explains the success of the YouTube series *Bon Appétit Ski,* which I make with my friends Fabien Maierhofer and Nico Favre. People can see we don't take ourselves too seriously, we don't even take life too seriously. Everything is quite futile after all, nobody knows what life really is and what we're really supposed to do here. As a result, people don't see us as idols but just as cool, funny dudes. When we meet people who watch *Bon Appétit Ski,* they most often come to us and start talking as if we've known each other for years.

What is your favorite quote?

"It's close to death that man feels most alive." It doesn't mean that I'm a thrill-seeker, it comes back to understanding that you aren't eternal. I think that if you are aware that life is temporary, you appreciate it more.

What are the ingredients of Victor Galuchot's happiness?

Nature, friends, health. If you have those three, you can do everything and be happy.

Find out more about Victor:

youtube.com/Bonappetitski
instagram.com/victorgaluchot
facebook.com/VictorCavalierLibre

There Are No Failures, Only Lessons

ALBAN MICHON has dived all over the world, with scientific expeditions at the North Pole and the East Coast of Greenland as highlights. By means of his books, documentaries, and services as a diving instructor, Alban motivates the public to take care of the planet, follow their dreams and break the rules every now and then.

"Luckily, there are people who don't follow the rules. If not, nothing would happen. Those who make history are the ones with the perseverance, patience, and courage to follow their dreams."

Childhood Dream

I knew from a very young age that I wanted to become an explorer. As a boy, I was fascinated by the expeditions of the legendary *Commandant* Jacques-Yves Cousteau, broadcasted on national television. Having fixed my mind on my own destiny as an adventurer, I started diving at the age of 11. I was a very bad student. I quit school before obtaining my secondary school graduation certificate. From that moment on, the only way left was to pursue my childhood dream. It was 100% up to me to realize it. I got more and more skilled as a diver and at age 22, I bought the *Ice Diving School* in Tignes, in the heart of the Alps. This way, I became more and more specialized in ice diving. This passion would eventually lead to joining an expedition to the North Pole in 2010. With a team of eight explorers, we spent 45 days on and below the arctic ice cap. Our goal was to bring home evidence of its rapidly decreasing volume and to make a documentary about this to sensibilise the audience about climate change.

So you never followed a 'normal' career path?

What is normal? What is considered normal is what people make us believe it is. I always did something I loved to do. In my opinion, that is normal. The life choices I made may raise the eyebrows of some people, but that's because of their subjective opinion. I'm on this planet to be happy, to feel alive. That's all that counts.

"If You Think That Adventure Is Dangerous, Try Routine: It's Lethal"

This quote by Paolo Coelho adorns the homepage of my website. I love the theme of Coelho's books: listen to your heart, follow your dreams, live your legend. It's a message I like to disperse by my own work as well. Every single person on this planet is extraordinary. We all have a treasure inside, but you have to explore. The good thing is: once you make the decision to follow your dreams, you've put yourself in a position where you will have to be audacious. Where you will have to be creative and develop skills that otherwise, might never have developed. This way, confidence increases. When I decided that I wanted to become an explorer as a kid, I started off with no confidence at all. But, by leaving school, I had burned my boats. This way I quickly grew into the right direction. I learned new competencies very quickly, and confidence followed by itself.

Our society becomes more and more risk-averse. Recently, I was in a company building and dirt from my shoes had smirched the floor. I proposed to quickly vacuum the floor. But they said I couldn't vacuum just like that; a whole prevention procedure had to be activated first! I couldn't believe my ears.

Sometimes, people come to me, they say I'm doing crazy things they'd never be able to do, they tell me they don't even dare to sleep in a tent in the wilderness. Then I reply; start by sleeping in your tent in your garden. You'll see it's not that bad. Really, there's only one best way to get over your anxiety and gain confidence: you have to face your fears and feel the apprehension, but do it anyway.

Has the building-up of your life as an adventurer been difficult?

No. I simply have to answer: no. Life is difficult and complicated anyhow. There's no escape from that. The process of realizing dreams isn't different. Because it's the realization of a dream, it never felt difficult to me. It has been a long process though. I guess that's the problem with society today. People have very little perseverance and patience in this day and age, and I can understand why. Today, if we have an appetite, we take out our phone and 15 minutes later there's a pizza at our front door. If we feel sick, we order painkillers online and in no time you can swallow them and get rid of the discomfort. If we want to get laid tonight, we open our dating application and start messaging people.

I see it with my nieces and nephews as well. I ask them to sit still on a chair for ten minutes and they simply can't do it! Twenty or thirty years ago, we were used to waiting. Patience was normal. Things have become too easy, maybe. I like it when it's hard; when there's a challenge and I need to persevere. This being said, I don't want to tar everyone with the same brush. There are some youngsters doing incredibly impressive stuff as well.

Besides patience and perseverance, what other characteristics does a good explorer need?

First of all, if you have one out of two, that's already not bad. If you're patient but not perseverant, or if you're perseverant but not patient, you're already ahead of most people and you can get somewhere. (laughs)

Next, as I repeated a couple of times yet, you have to be a dreamer and be confident enough to chase your dreams. I'm really moving through life in my bubble full of dreams. What's more beautiful than that?

Thirdly, don't listen too much to what other people say. People want to protect you, they're afraid something will hurt you. They advise you to stay away from risks. As a result of this risk-aversion, we have a society with endless rules and regimentations. I tell you the opposite of most people: the greatest risk in life is to take no risk at all. History has been written by people who've taken risks. Take the example of Franky Zapata. Franky is a former jet ski World Champion who dreamed of being able to fly. He started to construct his so-called 'Flyboard Air' in his garage. In 2017, he got summoned by the French police and forced to stop doing tests with the *Flyboard* because it wasn't a homologated means of transport.

Luckily, Franky didn't throw in the towel, he took the risk to continue and didn't follow the rules. The result? One year later he got inanced by the French Army to further develop the *Flyboard*. On the 14th of July 2020, at the festivities of the National Holiday in France, he was doing an act on his lying hoverboard under the approving eye of the president and his ministers.

Talking about presidents, if you'd be 'President of the World', what would be the irst thing you'd change?
President of the World, what a nightmare! Oh my God, that's the biggest horror imaginable. (Laughing)

To answer your question, let's say I'd have a magic stick, then I would evoke more goodwill in people. If all of us would show some more goodwill, be kind, help each other out, and be trustworthy, then the planet would be a better place to live.

What is your 'Why?' as an explorer?
First of all, I just love it. It's my passion and my pleasure. It makes me feel free, happy, and alive. A second motivation surely is because I want to show other people that it is possible to realize your dreams. I didn't finish secondary school. For many people, that's a failure. For me, the word 'failure' doesn't exist. There are no failures, only lessons. The lesson I got out of that was that I was in charge of my own future. There would be no more school teachers to hold my hand. As I told you, this made me develop skills and gain con idence faster than I would have done if I'd have completed school. The third reason for my exploration is to serve, to be useful to something or someone. Doctors, nurses, architects, engineers, postmen . . . they all have their own contribution to the community. Well, my contribution to the community is scienti ic research. I collect data that can be used to better understand the world. If we better understand the world, we are better able to protect it. Lastly, as we talked about goodwill, I like to share my knowledge with young explorers. I had to igure everything out myself. I think it could have saved me some time if I would have had someone guiding me. That's my little act of goodwill as an explorer.

What's your opinion about purely achievement-oriented adventurers?
The early adventurers, the pioneers, were very useful. Think about people like Edmund Hillary or Ernest Shackleton. In their pursuit of accomplishment and fame (without a scienti ic goal) they were explorers at the same time since they discovered new places which led to growing knowledge about our planet. Nowadays, there's a whole bunch of adventurers who mainly have an athletic pursuit; they want to do the fastest or longest feat or be the youngest person to accomplish something. I have a double feeling about that. On the one hand, I'm a fan. They often show that the impossible is possible, they inspire people to follow their dreams, they show the value of rising above yourself. The igurehead is, of course, Mike Horn. Luckily Mike Horn exists and other adventurers like him exist too because they inspire so many folks to get the best out of themselves.

On the other hand, this type of adventurer makes me think: "What's the point of it?" For example, there's a young French adventurer – who I like a lot – named Matthieu Tordeur (read the interview with Matthieu on page 313). In 2019 he got a lot of merits because he became the   youngest person to ski solo to the South Pole. It was a wonderful accomplishment, but I don't totally agree with the merits he got because of the fact that he's the youngest person ever who did it. Tomorrow, I can put on a green pullover and run around the block and be the youngest person who ever ran around the block in a green pullover, you see what I mean? The cool thing about Matthieu is that he was completely honest about the fact that he was doing it just for himself. He was really genuine about the fact that it was a selfish pursuit. Anyhow, my dream is that every adventurer would undertake feats for a pursuit beyond themself; as by testing new equipment, setting out signposts, things like that.

Put Your Whole Heart in It
I have several streams of income as an adventurer/diver. I sold my ice diving school in Tignes a couple of years ago, but I'm still a diving instructor in many different places in the world. I have books and movies which I sell, but that's only giving me a small income, most of my revenues come from speaking engagements and sponsorship.

I have some good advice to give when it comes to finding sponsorship. You know, when you go on an adventure, you always think you're the best. There's no adventure that sounds cooler than the one you're about to do. But imagine; the big companies get 10, 30, 50 sponsorship requests each day. The bulk of these proposals are great projects. Why would they choose yours? Here's the secret: approach the sponsors not because you want the money out of their pockets, but because you're wholehearted and want to partner up with that company. If they notice that your entire soul is in the proposal, if they notice the passion you're showing, they'll be much more likely to support you.

What advice would you give to the 18-year old Alban Michon?
Ne t'inquiètes pas!   [don't worry]

What does a perfect day look like for you?
It depends whether it's an expedition day, a workday, or a leisure day. I really separate my personal life and my professional life as much as possible. A perfect day at work would be if I feel like another domino stone is put in line. What I mean by that is that every expedition is a succession of small successes, it's a row of domino stones. A day in which I get optimistic e-mails, do phone calls with people who help me out, inish a sponsorship deal . . . these days feel meaningful.

Of course, a perfect leisure day is completely different. It would be navigating with my boat on the ocean, diving on beautiful territory, having a delicious meal, enjoying the sunset . . .

What is your de inition of happiness?
Happiness is freedom. Freedom in itself includes many things. It means not having to justify what I'm doing. When you asked me my 'Why?' for adventure, I could have answered: 'Why not?', you see. Freedom also involves being able to do what you love to do but also making a living out of doing what you love to do.

I am lucky, I feel free, I'm actually seen as the pirate of freedom. I am one of the rare people who's living his dream. I had the luck to be born in a country with amazing natural beauty. I'm living on an island in the Côte d'Azur [French Riviera], I take the apero [apéritif; drinks and appetizers before dinner] while looking out over the sea, I get to travel the world . . . I'm a happy man. While we're doing this interview I'm in Paris. If I look out the window, there's tristesse [sadness] everywhere, people are depressed, there's traffic all over the place. It's hell to me.

Find out more about Alban:
www.albanmichon.com
facebook.com/alban.michon
instagram.com/albanmichon

If You Want to Make This Your Job,
Be Prepared for a Hard Time

Inspired by Mike Horn, as well as Scrooge McDuck, the young French adventurer **DYLAN AUGUSTE** *bought the cheapest equipment on the market and hiked across Iceland, less or more unprepared, and found himself in situations where he could have died. Thereafter, Auguste found a mentor, got solid equipment, and hiked solo for 3000km in the Canadian wilderness during winter.*

"By less or more putting your life on the line, you really get to know a new side of yourself. Surpassing the difficulties of an expedition also leads to an incredible improvement in confidence, which makes it easier to deal with the obstacles of daily life."

Inspiration

I grew up in the countryside around Bordeaux, in the Southwest of France. My father was very much into wildlife. He taught me which plants are edible, how to make a fire, build a cabin, etc . . . At the same time, I read a lot of comic books. The tales of Scrooge McDuck (*Picsou* in French) ure did inspire me to travel from a very young age. Later on, I started reading books from famous adventurers, it was mostly Mike Horn who gave me the desire to become an explorer. He's still a huge example for me today. Horn is really the paragon of showing how far we can push our limits.

In 2015, I left on my irst real adventure. I bought myself an inexpensive sleeping bag, tent, and backpack and lew off to Iceland. The cheap equipment would soon turn out not to be fitted to the harsh weather conditions I encountered on the island. Also, I wasn't very well-prepared. I hiked almost the entire length of the island on glaciers, snow fields, and volcanoes . . . without knowing how to help myself if something would go wrong. Honestly, I could have died a couple of times on this first adventure. It taught me that I had to approach things differently next time.

Girlfriend as the Logistics Manager

When I was preparing for my next adventure, hiking across the Canadian wilderness during winter, I reached out to Alban Michon. He's a very accomplished French explorer, and one of the best polar freedivers in the world (Read the interview with Alban Michon on page 248). Alban took me under his wings, he spent a tremendous amount of time and energy giving me advice and helping me out. I'm proud to have had a champion like Alban as my mentor, and happy to call him my friend today.

I am really lucky with my entourage. My parents and my sister have always supported me in my life choices, even though they weren't the most evident ones. And I have a wonderful girlfriend who not only supports me emotionally but also takes care of most of the logistics in the preparation of and during the actual adventures. The fact that she takes so much load on her shoulders makes sure I have fewer worries. That helps a lot.

What did your solo trek across Canada do to you?
In January 2019, I started off in Montréal with the goal to walk to Vancouver. In the midst of the winter, I found myself sleeping in -50°C temperatures, and even during the day the temperatures dropped to minus 20-30. For me, the most beautiful aspect of this kind of expedition is not only the connection with nature but also the connection with yourself. Surmounting yourself in harsh conditions leads to a unique form of self-knowledge. By less or more putting your life on the line (I got to deal with hypothermia symptoms on this expedition) you really get to know a new side of yourself. Surpassing the difficulties also leads to an incredible improvement in confidence, which makes it easier to deal with the obstacles of daily life.

I also had some profound experiences in relation to nature. I've experienced a magical sunset I just can't describe in words and I had an encounter with a pack of wolves. At first, this scared me. I saw them at three o'clock at night after I had been walking non-stop for 70 km. Although humans normally aren't considered prey for wolves, I was afraid they would notice that I was limping and looked fatigued and their instincts would lead them to attack me. Luckily, they didn't make any attempt to do so. In the end, it was just a gift to witness these wild beasts in their natural habitat.

Of course, another beautiful aspect of each adventure is the encounters with people who have a completely different lifestyle than the people at home.

How do you physically and mentally train?
When it comes to the mental side, I did a lot of martial arts as a young boy. Meditation and visualizations are a part of that and have stayed important tools in my preparation. I do also write a journal, as almost all adventurers do. In most of my physical training, there's also a big mental challenge. Recently I started experiencing apnea-exercises and freediving. I do a lot of strength training and pull tires in a rugged and hilly forest near my home. I can assure you that when the tires get stuck in between trees, bushes, and rocks for the fifteenth time in ten minutes, all you want to do is freak out. So this is definitely an exercise in patience. Besides, I've worked as an ambulance driver before. This got me into a lot of difficult, heated moments. That's where I learned to stay cold-blooded at all times. This helps me a lot during my expeditions. I never panic.

The Most Difficult Aspect of Being an Adventurer
Creating the budget is always difficult. If you want to make this your job, you have to be ready for a hard time. I know some very good explorers – who achieved incredible things – who had to struggle for ten years before they could earn a living out of adventure. If you dig into Mike Horn's early travel journeys, you find out that even he had to struggle enormously to get the budget for his first expeditions.

That's why, to people starting out, I would advise taking a part-time job in an environment where you can develop your skills and physical abilities needed for big adventures. Get yourself a seasonal job in the mountains, even though it's a job you don't care about. As you gain more experience and confidence, at a certain point, you'll have to do something very big in order to get recognition and credibility in the world of explorers. It's also a good idea to reach out to people who are further down the line than you are, as I did by contacting Alban Michon. Ask for advice and learn from them.

When it comes to sponsorship, you have to send out millions of emails to potential sponsors in the hopes of getting one positive response. You have to approach them with a very clear proposition, know every detail of your expedition. Before sponsors will support you, you need to have done at least one very big adventure to gain credibility. They have to be assured that you have the ability to do it. Social media is important, but sponsors are also very interested in traditional media exposure; local newspapers, radio, and television. Don't expect your first adventure to get exposed on national television.

Books, films, conferences . . . There are so many of them out there, you risk getting drowned in the mass very easily. Actually, it's all about commitment and perseverance. At some point, you're most likely going to find a company who's interested in partnering up with you. Then, you have to really cling to this company, follow through on every step of your project, spoil them with attention during and after the expedition. Organize a banquet where you put them in the picture, things like that . . .

It's really about patience, about keeping on going until you find that first believer. Try to remind yourself that if you can't keep on going in the preparation, you sure won't be able to do it during the actual adventure. Once you get your first sponsorship and your first big accomplishment, a lot of doors can open.

Nowadays, I can live less or more from being an adventurer. I do this by differentiating my income streams. I earn a bit of money by monitoring adventure camps, a bit of money by selling films, some more thanks to my YouTube channel. I'm giving survival courses and have a couple of solid sponsorship deals . . . a lot of adventurers have five, six, or more different, rather small streams of income.

Characteristics and Personality Traits
[I asked Dylan to rank himself from 0 (not like this trait at all) to 10 (very much like that)]

Optimism: 8
Discipline: 6
Courage: 9
Resilience: 7
Stubbornness: 9. I can be very stubborn. When I have an idea in my head, often I'm not able to listen to the advice of others. Luckily, I've learned to listen to people who have a lot more experience than me. That's why I don't score a 10.
Social Skills: 9-10
Creativity: 7-8. I always try to come up with new ideas if I can't realize a planned expedition.

Find out more about Dylan
instagram.com/dylan_trekking
facebook.com/5000kmbyfoot
youtube.com/c/DylanTrekking

We Have to Work Together And Include Everyone in Order to Uplift the Entire Community

VASU SOJITRA is a professional skier who also loves trail running, hiking, and skateboarding. Vasu does all of those sports relying on nothing but his left leg and his two crutches, better known as 'ninja sticks'. Besides being an outdoor athlete, Vasu is also one of the world's leading voices in the advocacy for the inclusion of people of color and people with a disability.

"A mass-cultured ecosystem is still something very difficult to grasp for many people. What delights me is to see that more and more people are combating racism and discrimination. That gives me confidence that there will be light at the end of the tunnel."

'Aha' Moments

I was born in Connecticut as a child of Indian parents. When I was nine months old a viral infection affected my right leg. This caused septicemia and eventually, my entire leg had to be amputated. Shortly after the operation, our family moved back to India where I lived for the first six years of my life. Because I was growing fast and being an active kid, my prosthetic leg had to be adapted and repaired constantly. To do so, the leg had to be sent back and forth to the U.S. each time, a process that caused a lot of trouble. So after a while, my parents decided it would be more convenient to move back to Connecticut. Growing up as an Indian kid with a disability in a predominantly white community was extremely challenging. I couldn't fit in. I didn't have any real friends and I got bullied. My older brother was the only one of my peers I could rely on. Luckily, he always took me under his wings, empowered me to be autonomous, and encouraged me to do a lot of activities with him. This way, when I was ten years old, I joined him and a friend of his to go skiing on a small slope near our home. That day there happened to be another skier with one leg there who came greeting me. Seeing that guy being a decent skier made something click in my head. When I came home I started searching the internet to see if there were other skiers with disabilities – more commonly known as adaptive skiers. I discovered that there are paralympic skiers doing incredible things! A dream was born. From that point on, I continued to challenge myself on the ski slopes, my brother as an ally. This way not only did my confidence get a boost, but I also started making friends in the skiing community.

When I was 20-21 years old and studying engineering in Vermont, I was helping out in a ski class with an organization called *Vermont Adaptive*. One day, one of the kids of the group was going completely wild on an easy run on the way back to the lodge. He was laughing, dancing, enjoying it to the fullest. That moment put things in perspective. For me, it was just an easy run. In my head, the ski day was already over. Yet I recognized the same excitement in that kid as I have when I'm out with my friends doing something challenging in the mountains. His enjoyment showed me how important these kinds of programs are, how much good feelings they can give to people. In the end, what matters in our life are the feelings of joy, freedom, and connection we experience. What better place to find those feelings than in the outdoors? This specific epiphany, or 'aha' moment, has been very monumental. It made me step away from the engineering path and focus on working with people of marginalized groups instead.

Another important moment has been the release of my first film *Out on a Limb*. It really kick-started my career as an athlete. Thanks to this film I got in touch with Conrad Anker. This encounter led to becoming a *The North Face* athlete.

Words of Wisdom
I do have only one leg and I'm a person of color living in the United States. Yet, I like to focus on my privileges instead of my limitations. I'm benefiting from being a male in a patriarchal society. Having Indian origins causes me to have to deal with less oppression than Black and Indigenous people do. Even my disability is a privileged one, because I have access to places that many people with other disabilities view as inaccessible.

I try to be as self-reliant as possible. At the same time, I recognize there's no way I can live without other human beings around me, and no way I can live without the natural world. The main message of the different projects I'm working on is exactly this interdependence. We have to work together and include everyone in order to uplift the entire community.

In the capitalist- and consumer-centered society we live in, it's almost impossible not to have a negative impact on our planet. Nevertheless, I take care of her as much as is in my ability, because nature relies on human beings and human beings rely on nature. People have to understand that we not only have to take care of other human beings but also non-human beings because we all depend on each other.

My parents and my brother have always held me accountable. They never did something for me if I could do it by myself. I'm very grateful for that. Although, it can be hard and frustrating when I have to put a lot of energy into something they could do for me without effort. But I know they let me do it because they want to empower me. It's coming from a place of love.

Role Models
James Baldwin
Audre Lorde
Malcolm X
Kimberlé Crenshaw
Mia Mingus
Octavia Butler
Judith Heumann

Throughout the years, have you seen matters changing for the better?
As in many cases in history, things first need to get worse before they get better. The discriminational political climate under Trump's mandate has been reflected in society. On top of this, I have the impression that the fear-response as a result of COVID-19 only resulted in

more egocentrism and intolerance. Honestly, in the U.S. I don't notice much positive evolution. A mass-cultured ecosystem is still something very difficult to grasp for many people. What delights me to see though, is that more and more people are combating racism and discrimination. That gives me confidence that there will be light at the end of the tunnel.

You're very engaged in improving diversity, equity, and inclusion in society. You do this by engagements on different levels and in different organizations. Is it hard for you to maintain a balance between taking care of yourself and taking care of the community?
That's often a tricky balancing act, indeed. The average time before people burn-out in this professional field is only five years. I've been walking the tightrope for a while myself, but throughout the years I've become better aware of my own needs. I understand that I have to prioritize my own well-being if I want to have the maximum impact on others. I like to use the airplane metaphor: put on your own face mask before taking care of the people next to you.

Vasu's Training
I work out every day. I'm out on the skis about 120 days per year, and next to that I do skateboarding, hiking, and trail running. Unfortunately, my professional demands as an athlete, my engagement with the *Inclusive Outdoors Project,* and my forerunner's role as a DEI-strategist (diversity, equity, and inclusion) cause me to spend a lot of time behind the screen. When those projects fill the majority of my daily schedule, I most often do my workout in the gym. But that isn't too bad either, because strength training is very important for me. Since I do only have one leg, there are a couple of muscle groups taking up massive loads; my work-outs in the gym help me to work on otherwise neglected muscle areas. These muscles can then support the ones that are most relied upon while skiing, hiking, or running.

What is the best gift someone can offer you?
Quality time; the genuine energy of a relationship. There is a great book called *The 5 Love Languages*, written by Gary Chapman. It says that people can feel most loved, heard, and appreciated by either one of 5 different things: Words of Affirmation, Acts of Service, Receiving Gifts, Physical Touch, or Quality Time. The latter is definitely my personal favorite.

What is the best compliment someone ever gave you?
There have been so many. I prefer the ones that don't refer to my disability, but to my personality. For example: "Your smile makes me smile", "You lighten up the room" or "You bring brightness to my day".

Don't Call Me Inspirational
Don't call me inspirational only because I am a skier with only one leg. My goal is just to not be regarded or treated as different. It shouldn't matter. If you just want to compliment me on being inspirational without actually helping me to break down the barriers of injustice and discrimination (and without making me feel like a full human being) then your compliment doesn't really mean much to me.

Of course, this doesn't hold true for other disabled people calling me inspirational. I love to hear that compliment from them because I love to be a positive representation of what's possible for people with a disability when provided access to support and resources.

What would you put on a massive billboard in New York?
Access is love

What would you put on top of the political agenda if you were to become the first president of the world?
Give indigenous people their land back.

One book people should read?
So You Want to Talk About Race, by Ijeoma Oluo.

If Warren Buffet would write you a 10 million dollar check, how would you spend the money?
I would focus on improving the recreation system for people of minority groups and making all public spaces accessible for people with disabilities.

Which advice would you give to the 12-year old Vasu?
You'll always run into people who don't like your message, even though you're empathetic with them. Don't let yourself be discouraged by them. Just keep failing forward, keep moving step by step. Also: hold yourself accountable if you want to become a better person.

What does a perfect day in your life look like?
It's what I do with the *Inclusive Outdoors Project*. Enjoying our natural world with people of color, people with disabilities, the LGBTQ community, and others that have been historically excluded; to share great experiences and stories.

What is your definition of a life well-lived?
I compare life to climbing; you have to progress bit by bit, always going higher. A life well lived means you never cease to do this. It also means supporting people as best as we can with the resources we have and centering the needs of communities over our own needs. Lift as we climb.

find out more about Vasu:
www.vasusojitra.com
instagram.com/vasu_sojitra
facebook.com/vasu.sojitra.athlete

There's Real Pleasure to be Found in Going Out of Your Comfort Zone

XAVIER DE LE RUE is a professional snowboarder, entrepreneur, climate activist, and father of two. He's a former double World Champion boardercross (2003, 2007) and triple winner of the Freeride World Tour (2008, 2009, 2010). Films shot about his ventures have been watched by thousands of viewers in movie theaters, as well as on YouTube.

"I'm someone who needs to feel as if I'm evolving constantly, I get bored if I don't regularly shake things up."

The Need for Change

Throughout my career, I focused on different disciplines of snowboarding. In the early 2000s it was in boardercross. Next, it was freeride. Next, I shifted to backcountry snowboarding, often related to big film projects. Along the way, I also became a better mountaineer. As a result, a couple of years ago, I decided to shift away from heli-snowboarding and big film projects. Instead, I made the *XV DIY series*, which are short YouTube videos of adventures I went on with my wife or with friends. I filmed everything with a simple *GoPro*.

I'm someone who needs to feel as if I'm evolving constantly. I'm very curious and get easily bored if I don't shake things up regularly. Thankfully my sponsors have always supported me in my need for change. They even enjoyed me trying out new things because often I did something which nobody had done before, which was commercially interesting for them.

The downside of this urge to be in constant evolution is that for many years I had a hard time appreciating the present moment. Nowadays, I'm much better at being happy in the moment. I don't have much choice actually. I've got two daughters aged 15 and 2 and they force me not to only think about myself. I'm really conscious about enjoying my time with them in a qualitative way.

Besides being curious, what other personality traits do you have which have contributed to your success?

I'm very good at dealing with risk and controlling my emotions. I'm also a hard worker and very stubborn. Once I have something in my head, I won't give up before accomplishing it.

The Best Lesson Of My Life

In 2008 I got caught in an avalanche while snowboarding in Switzerland. That day I escaped death. After the accident, I said to myself: "What the fuck am I doing? Why do I take these risks if they can cost me my life? I have to stop fooling around." I was convinced that I would draw a line under my professional career. But when I looked outside the window from my hospital room, I could see the mountains. I could see the powder. I caught myself imagining the lines I could snowboard and realized I was not yet ready to quit.

This being said, the accident has been a very defining moment in my career. I would even argue that it has been the best lesson of my life. It changed my approach to safety and risks. After the accident, I continued riding similarly difficult lines, but less often. Only when all the conditions were in the right order. I got better at renouncing when I had to. In the end, that meant that I got confronted less often with dangerous situations and large fears. This way my confidence actually increased.

On the homepage of your website is written "After 22 years of amazing snowboard opportunities, my goal is now to pass on my knowledge and inspire others." How did this shift from focusing on your own accomplishments towards helping others happen? It was a gradual process. It comes back to what I said earlier on; I found myself doing the same kind of adventures, telling the same stories over and over. I got bored of that and looked for the next step in my evolution.

I also often found myself asking out in the mountains: "Why am I here?" Especially in moments when a film crew was involved. I no longer saw the interest of riding down a difficult line, getting it filmed, and putting it on the internet . . . This feeling got further nurtured by noticing my daughter's generation consuming content on social media, content that is just made to entertain or impress, nothing truly meaningful. I wanted to be part of the solution, not part of the problem.

Raising Cool Girls

When it comes to social media, I feel a bit like a hypocrite because I'm telling everyone I hate it, while at the same time I make a big part of my income thanks to my social media value. In my opinion, social media can be a good tool for outdoor athletes because we are the master of what we publish. This means we can choose to publish meaningful things. But as a consumer, I hate it. As a parent, I hate it even more. My wife and I made a deal with my eldest daughter, Mila. We proposed to give her a tiny amount of money for every week she would not be on Instagram and Facebook. It was up to her to take or refuse the offer. After some hesitation, she decided to give it a try. She stuck to it and feels perfectly fine. She has WhatsApp, but not Instagram, Facebook, TikTok, or other rubbish. I'm very proud of her for that. I'm proud she has the balls to stay away from it while she notices that all her friends are online all the time. I can clearly see that her decision is helping her in her process of self-discovery as a teenager. I notice that her friends are very much influenced by what happens on their screen, while Mila is just a strong, cool, independent girl.

From a young age, I've taken Mila into the mountains. I've never withheld her from taking risks, though I always encouraged her to think thoroughly and take responsibility for the risks she's willing to take. Today, I know that I can fully trust her in making the right decisions in the mountains. In my opinion, way too many parents nowadays limit their kids too much: "Don't do this, don't do that, it's too dangerous . . . " But risks, falling, and failing are extremely important for personal growth and development. The mountains are the perfect canvas to have our children learning to deal with difficulties and setbacks. By taking them out into the mountains, they inevitably learn to crash and get up again. It is also an environment where they become very good at making the right decisions because the consequences of wrong decisions can be very bad. I'm convinced that the development of decision-making skills in the mountains transfers to other areas in life.

From what you're saying, I can imagine that you agree with me that the world would be a better place if Adventure would be a course in school?
Absolutely! Adventure opens our eyes to the world. It makes us bond with nature and helps us forget about all the worries in our head which are mostly just futile things. There are countries where adventure and nature are much more part of the culture, New Zealand for example. The result is that there's an amazing vibe around those people.

How Xavier Puts Meaningful Content Into the World
I am very concerned about climate change. This year (2020), I've been hosting a podcast called 'The Sustainability Dialogues'. In this podcast, I talk about climate change with Professor Johan Rockström, director of *the Potsdam Institute for Climate Impact Research*. During our conversations, a lot of light bulbs were switched on in my head thanks to Johan's great ability to translate very complex scientific subjects in a way that is very understandable to the general public.

The biggest message I got out of my chats with Johan was that you don't have to be perfect, but you always have to try to improve your way of living. I've been moving the needle towards a more sustainable, ecological lifestyle in different ways: I take fewer flights, in supermarkets I've become very conscious about what I buy, I sort my waste the proper way and I purchased an electric car.

You have a lot of different projects going on in your life, as well in the world of snowboarding as in business as in climate advocacy. How do you juggle your different pursuits?
And I'm also renovating my house! (laughs) It's true that often I'm too enthusiastic and I say yes too often. For the last couple of years, I've really tried to structure my life around my family and my own well-being. This means slowly dropping less important things. It's not an easy thing to do, but life is like that. I try to remind myself that being forced to cut ties means that I'm in a privileged position, it's a luxury problem.

If you could go and grab a beer with three people dead or alive, who would you choose?
Neil Armstrong, the Dalai Lama, and Johan Rockström.

Recommended Book
Economix, by Michael Goodwill. It's a comic book that explains how society has evolved over the course of history according to the economic situation.

What does a perfect day in your life look like?
A day in nature, in which I do something out of my comfort zone. There's a real pleasure to find in going out of your comfort zone, more people should try it. A perfect day would also

involve having my friends, wife, and daughters with me, preferably in the Pyrenees where I grew up. Last but not least, a perfect day has to go hand in hand with delicious food!

Find out more about Xavier:
www.xavierdelerue.com
instagram.com/xavierdelerue
facebook.com/xvdelerue

You Always Carry Your Home With You

DANI REYES-ACOSTA *is a splitboarder, surfer, rock climber, mountaineer, and trail runner. She's also a climate activist, brand strategist, artist, storyteller, and community builder.*

"In 2013, I left behind everything I had – my relationship, my apartment, and a secure job at a Fortune-500 company – to travel in South America for the entire year. It was a slow, sometimes painful process of discovering my own wildness, but it allowed me to start living the life I truly wanted."

From Olympic Dreams to the First Roadtrip

I spent the first years of my life in a small beach village called Playa del Rey, close to Los Angeles. Later we moved closer to the mountains. Yet, it took a long time before I would discover rock climbing. The main reason is that my parents didn't want me to fuck up my fingers because I played classical piano (laughs). I spent much of my summer holidays surfing, staying with my grandparents who were living at the coast. My parents would also take me and my sister skiing once a year and camping every once in a while. I remember that during one of those camping trips, when I was eight or nine years old, I rowed an inflatable raft for the first time in my life and loved it right away. I rowed so much that I had calluses on my hands. It hurt but I didn't care because I was enjoying it. I even announced that when I grew up, I would become a rower at the Olympics.

My Olympic ambitions did not become reality, on the contrary. My teenage years were really tough because both of my parents were very ill and eventually my father passed away when I was only 19 years old. At the same time, I had entered University with the idea to become a marine biologist. I wanted to save dolphins! Pretty soon though, I figured out that I hated being in a laboratory. I shifted to Geopolitical Movement And Sustainable Development In Global Societies, this time with the idea to become a diplomat for the *United Nations*.

Processing my father's death in combination with a challenging University program was very hard. During those years, the mountains were the place where I could take a breath and reclaim the joyfulness that I had lost during my adolescence. By the time I graduated, I was burned out as a result of all the emotional and mental tensions of the preceding years. I wanted to feel fully alive and decided to take a gap year, mainly to surf as much as possible.

I fell in love with a surf guy who treated me badly, unfortunately. He spent his days doing nothing but surfing and belittling me. His behavior motivated me to create my own identity, so I started working for a publishing agency as a marketeer. It was a job I found enjoyable and that gave me fulfillment. After a couple of years working for the agency, I got the chance to sign a contract at *Nike*. I worked at *Nike* for one year but felt inside me that it wasn't the right job for me. I gathered my courage together and not only quit the job but also ended my toxic relationship, canceled my rental contract, and decided to reset my life in South America.

When I was packing for South America, I noticed that I had way too much stuff to carry with me all the time. Back then, I didn't know yet that it is perfectly doable to travel for several months with only a small backpack. Instead, I had two giant suitcases filled with way too many dresses (laughs). I looked at my bank account and decided that I could invest all the earned corporate money into buying a car. So as soon as I arrived in Chile, I bought myself a vehicle that I would eventually drive across the continent for 13 months.

When I announced my plan to quit my job and leave for South America to my friends, a lot of them said they would join me for a part of the trip. But in the end, no one came over. Those false promises taught me that people don't like change, people need safety. Unfortunately, that often leads to complacency. Complacency to what I call 'the squared life'; having a job, a partner, a house, and nice objects. The typical consumer path in which we are supposed to have certain things and hit certain milestones at specific time points in our lives.

During those 13 months on the road, did you have a 'guilt voice' in your head, a voice that questioned why you had left 'the squared life' and whether that was the right choice?
Honestly, I did not. But there sure was an external guilt voice coming from friends and family. They thought I was crazy for leaving *Nike*, one of the biggest companies in the world. I can understand them. Working for *Nike* is cool, but – for me anyway – by far not as cool as standing on the summit of a mountain in a foreign country.

This being said, the whole trip has not always been fun. It was a slow and painful process of discovering my wildness. There was a lot of difficult processing about my past relationship, the passing away of my father, family problems . . . But it has been absolutely worth it. Not only did I discover so much about myself, I also got to know my life partner up until today; Johnny.

I ended the South American road trip financially broke and with a broken knee. Luckily, I could count on Johnny who 'imported' me in Colorado (laughs). The question that became upfront at that moment was: "What am I going to do career-wise now?" I thought a moment about soliciting *Nike* again, but that would have felt like going three steps backward. So instead I worked in bagel shops and bars while side hustling on my own brand, remotely. I worked very hard for a couple of months, then took a couple of months out to go play in the mountains. And of course, the good thing about Colorado is that there's very easy access to the mountains. So even at times when I would sell bagels eight hours a day, I could still benefit from time outdoors.

Today I'm fully self-employed and my job consists of four major branches. In order of importance: 1. brand strategy and consultancy, 2. public speaking, coaching, and education, 3. freelance writing, and 4. being a professional athlete. The overarching themes in all of my work are adventure, climate and sustainability, and community building.

What is the secret to building strong communities?

The foundation is to know and love ourselves irst. If we don't love ourselves, we can never give wholeheartedly. Self-knowledge and self-love can only arise by doing uncomfortable things. These can be very small things, I don't think that selling everything and going on a road trip to South America is the answer for everyone. To most people, I would advise just doing one small thing differently each day. Shut the internet down earlier, put a time limit on your Instagram usage, don't drink that second cup of coffee, take a different road to work . . . This way, we grow and learn little by little. We get emotional resilience and become better people. We can then share our insights with others and help them in their own journey towards understanding and loving themselves.

Would the world be a better place if Adventure would be a course at school?

Absolutely, because life is an adventure! At least, we can choose to make it an adventure. We can also choose to surrender to routine and complacency. But, in my opinion, that's not more than submitting to a slow and painful death. You might as well be a robot.

PS: I'm being very negative about routine, but there is one important footnote I have to be clear about: routine is necessary to move safely through the mountains. Know your rope techniques, people!

Imagine it's the year 2050, all human beings have a microchip planted in their head which is connected to a supercomputer. If you'd be given the power over that supercomputer, which idea or belief would you plant into people's brains?

I wouldn't be able to handle all that power, I don't want to be Donald Trump (laughs). By the way, morally I'm 100% against the idea of planting microchips in people's brains! Nevertheless, if there's one thing I would like to have people remember, then it is to be kind to ourselves and others.

What advice would you give to outdoor athletes and adventurers who are starting out, when it comes to creating and marketing a brand?

The most important aspect of any kind of business is relationships. You really have to nurture them and make use of them. It's also important to find a way to make a living without sacrificing what you stand for and what you believe in

.

When it comes to social media, you have to pick the ones that are most in line with your interests and with the people you want to reach out to. Personally, I'm a fan of Instagram because you can create good content quite easily. Making decent YouTube videos requires a bigger investment in time, energy, and/or money.

Favorite Quote

It comes from Toni Cade Bambara: "The role of the artist is to make the revolution irresistible." This quote de ines the 'why?' of all the projects I work on.

If you could choose three people dead or alive to drink a cup of tea with, who would you choose?

Maya Angelou, Sandra Cineros, and Audre Lorde. They have turned very interesting and often painful life experiences into a powerful narrative that is actionable.

There lies enormous power in storytelling. People have gathered around the fire for many thousands of years of history. By my own storytelling – whether it's in educational programs, public speaking, or writing – I try to uplift people to make a revolution happen. A revolution that leads to more understanding, happiness, and care for our planet.

What advice would you give to the 18-year old Dani?

You don't need a man (laughs). No, seriously: you always carry your own home with you. *(While speaking these words, Dani puts her hand on her heart.)*

What is your definition of a life well-lived?

Embracing who we are and what we experience. Living from our hearts. Experiencing all the different identities that we carry in us.

Find out more about Dani:

www.danireyesacosta.com

instagram.com/notlostjustdiscovering

Every Person Makes a Difference

MATTY MCNAIR led the first-ever guided expedition to the North Pole in 1997. In 2005, she completed the fastest expedition to the North Pole in 36 days, traveling by ski and dog sled. She has also led four expeditions to the South Pole and was part of the first team that circumnavigated Baffin Island. She's the founder of the family company North Wind Expeditions, where her son Eric, daughter Sarah, and son-in-law Eric Boomer have taken over the torch as leading guides.

"It's wonderful to see my children sharing the same passion for Polar Expeditions. But it's also scary, because their boundaries are far beyond what I've ever done."

Freedom as a Normality

Outdoor adventures have never been foreign to me. I grew up in the great Philadelphia area, spending weekends paddling whitewater, downhill skiing, sailing, and backpacking with my parents, sister, and twin brothers.

Finding my own adventures was how I grew up. For me, freedom has always been a normality. It strikes me how most parents today have become very protective and consider the outdoors as a dangerous space for their children. My family culture was different. As long as we said where we were going and promised to be back before dark, we could do whatever we wanted in the wilderness. I always wanted to prove myself to my dad. He believed that girls were somehow less capable when it came to sports and adventures, so I did everything to show him that I had a lot in me.

With my outdoorsy upbringing, it is not a surprise that I completed a B.A. in *Outdoor Experiential Education*. This led to a job for *Outward Bound*, an international organization that takes folks outdoors with the goal to improve their competence, confidence, and cooperation skills. The job didn't pay well, but I had lots of fun, worked with amazing people, and fell in love with Paul Landry, the program director of *Outward Bound*. While living at *Outward Bound*, North of Thunder Bay, on Black Sturgeon Lake, we started our family. Eric was born in 1984 and Sarah in 1986. In 1990, Paul, me, and two other *Outward Bound* staff members (Jeff and Rosemary Murrey) went on a 4-month long circumnavigation of Baffin Island. It was an epic dog-sledding adventure and the beginning of a career as a polar explorer and polar guide.

Racing *Top Gear*

There are not a lot of people in the world training sled dogs and skiing to the Poles. As a result, once I became an established polar guide, all kinds of contracts were proposed to me, some of them quite unusual. For example, in 2014 I was the leader of an expedition for Massy Ferguson with a Dutch woman called Manon Ossevoort, who had driven a tractor from The Netherlands to Cape Town. My job was to get Manon and her tractor to the South Pole and back. I also got broadcasted in *Sesame Street*, *Popular Mechanics for Kids,* and *Wilderness Walk*. But the most remarkable experience was in collaboration with the television production *Top*

Gear in 2006. With my team of dogs, Richard Hammond and I raced against Jeremy Clarkson and James May who were driving a *Toyota Hilux Arctic Truck*. We started off from Resolute Bay, North of Baffin Island, and raced to the Magnetic North Pole. Dog sled versus 4x4. It was a very fun expedition. The dogs were better at navigating through rough pack ice and the trucks were faster over hard-packed, flat snow and ice. The 24 hours of daylight allowed us to film and race very intensely, up to 23 hours a day.

Every Person Does Make a Difference

I've been going on polar expeditions since 1990. Throughout the decades, I've witnessed the results of climate change. The ice in the Arctic has become a lot more unpredictable. Nowadays, expeditions to the North Pole have to finish by the end of April, because of the thinning ice pack. Compare this with my first expedition to the North Pole in 1997 where we arrived on May 26, and finally, after our food ran out, were picked up on June 2nd.

I hope that COVID-19 has ignited some environmental awareness in people. With the sky clearing up above big cities, I hope there's a longing evoked in people to keep the air clean and the natural beauty of the planet protected. Nevertheless, my hope is small, because we're slow learners. We've been making a mess out of Earth for many decades. As long as success is being evaluated by the stuff we have, not much is going to change I'm afraid. Another problem is that all too often people say they can't make a difference as an individual. I don't agree with that, every person makes a difference. If you use plastic bags in the supermarket, you support a polluting system. If you buy things on Amazon, you support a monopolistic and polluting system.

What makes for a great polar guide?

Go to the school of learning from your own adventures and miss-adventures. Lead yourself before you lead others. Take a look at what the *International Polar Guide Association* requires to become a polar guide, it's impressive. You will need: solid skills in winter camping, skiing, glacier travel, crevasse rescue, navigating over the shifting polar pack ice, wilderness first aid, personal expedition experience, plus solid group leadership skills.

In my opinion, soft skills are just as important as hard skills. You have to know when to encourage people and tell them, to quote my daughter Sarah, "to toughen the fuck up."

What did you personally add to that equation?

On my expeditions, we have always traveled in style. The most important thing was that we were enjoying ourselves. We took proper time to eat and drink, sleep and laugh. My golden rule was to stop skiing when the weakest team members had emptied 80% of their energy. It's essential to reserve energy to set up a safe camp, melt enough snow to rehydrate, and sleep warm.

Having fun has always been an integral part of polar travel. Often I've been criticized for not being serious enough. But if you're not enjoying what you're doing then what's the point? On expeditions, I've come to notice that on the days we had the most fun, we made the most mileage. The same held true when I was cross-country skiing racing in my college years. I had my best performance when I didn't take myself seriously.

If your dogs could talk, what would they say about you?

"Watch out, here comes the boss!" No, I'm joking. I'm quite confident they genuinely love and respect me. They love me because I love them and take care of them. And they respect me because I am clear on my expectations and I don't let them get away with anything.

How is it to see that your children, Sarah and Eric, have followed in your footsteps as polar explorers and guides?

It's wonderful to see them share the same passion for the outdoors. But at the same time, it's scary as a mother. What Sarah and Eric are able to do is way beyond what I have ever been capable of. They really redefine boundaries. In addition to polar expeditions, Sarah does a lot of wild water kayaking. When I see pictures of her paddling down a 20 ft. waterfall, my heart stands still . . .

Taking Baby Steps

Most people's jobs belong to one of two categories: a job that's enjoyable and purposeful but doesn't pay well, or a job that pays well but isn't giving them satisfaction. Depending on what you value most in life – status or pleasure – you should pick one or the other. A third option is to carve your own way; do something you're really passionate about and which, over time, can become a fruitful career. This option is for the people who put the highest value on inner growth. It's a pathway that takes a lot of courage. A lot of people would like to take this path, but the fear of failing is too big. I encourage those people to take baby steps. Go one step beyond what you did yesterday. Move one small step closer towards your big goal every day and inevitably, you'll get there.

What is your definition of happiness?

Having a sense of flow. Being grateful for living on this beautiful planet. Shining through life.

Find out more about Matty:

www.northwindsexpeditions.com

Often Silence Is All We Need

In 1994, LIV ARNESEN became the first woman to ski to the South Pole. Seven years later, she joined forces with American explorer Ann Bancroft to become the first female team to cross Antarctica by skis and kites. It was the start of a cooperation between two soul sisters, who are putting their stamp on improving the world up until today.

"At the bookshelf of Ann's parental home, there were the same books that had inspired me as a kid. I guess it was written in the stars that someday we would team up."

Inspired by Amundsen

As a child, my father used to tell me stories of big explorers. I adored those stories and soon found myself taking up books from the shelf at home and reading through them. The one that inspired me the most is the story of Norwegian explorer Roald Amundsen, who was the first man to ski to the South Pole in the Antarctic summer of 1911-1912. I was deeply inspired. I remember one day on a trip with my school brass band. We were about six girls exchanging dreams. My friends dreamed about having a fancy car, living in a beautiful house, getting married, and having children . . . In my childhood naivety, I thought these were things that would automatically come with adulthood. So I disclosed my dream: skiing to the South Pole. Up until today, I still remember my peers' reaction of big laughter and making a fool out of me. They said that skiing to the South Pole is a boy's dream, something that wasn't possible for me.

I was only 3 years old when I got my first pair of skis under my feet. Soon enough the sport grew into a big passion. As an adolescent, I dreamed about going to the Olympics, until a severe accident injured my back and I had to put this dream in the closet. Nevertheless, I kept on skiing and after a while found myself guiding small expeditions in Svalbard. Not much later, a friend and I became the first female team that crossed the Greenland Ice Cap unsupported. This way, my childhood dream of skiing to the South Pole found rebirth and I started the most difficult aspect of every expedition: fundraising. Despite the fact that Norway was a pioneer in the emancipation of women – we even had a female prime minister at the time – it was hard to find credibility in the male-dominant world of explorers. So I ended up with an Italian sponsor instead of Norwegian. On the 24th of December 1994, after 50 days on the ice, I followed in the footsteps of Amundsen by reaching the South Pole. I was the first woman ever, 82 years after my compatriot had finished his feat.

In 2001, you achieved a second 'world's first' together with Ann Bancroft. How did you get to meet each other?

When I skied to the South Pole in 1994, I was working as a school teacher. Coming back from the expedition, I wanted to teach my pupils how they could translate the lessons I had learned throughout my adventure into the management of their own life. The importance of clear goals, defining a vision, defining what kind of competence is needed, what types of people do they want on their team, communication, how to cope with resistance . . . are all valuable lessons if you're looking to find success and happiness in any area of life. That's how I decided to write a management book for children. The problem was that the children who needed these lessons the most were the least likely to pick up a book . . . Then, one day (this was the era before Gmail and Facebook) an old-fashioned letter from Ann Bancroft came falling out of the sky. Ann had tried to cross Antarctica the year before but had failed, she was now looking for a strong partner to team up and give it a second go. Ann had heard about me being a teacher and, just like me, she had the desire to influence young people and empower women. But instead of writing a book, she had the idea to reach out to youngsters via the internet and television. I recognized that these would be better media than a book, so I responded by showing my interest. Little later, I flew to the United States to meet Ann. We just wanted to see if the chemistry between us would feel right. Actually, during this first meeting, we didn't talk about the expedition at all. Instead, we chatted about our daily life and our family. When I got invited to Ann's parental home, I discovered the same books my father had on his bookshelf, the books that had inspired me to become an explorer myself. I guess it was written in the stars that Ann and I would one day become soul sisters.

When Ann and I were doing our actual expedition – crossing Antarctica on skis (on which we covered 2,747 km in 94 days) – , we got broadcasted on CNN twice a week. We reached out to kids every day. Three million youngsters from 116 different countries followed us on television and the internet. I remember one of my students telling me: "Thank you for teaching me that I don't have to become a lawyer, just like my dad, granddad, and great-granddad." Getting these kinds of messages is truly heartwarming and fulfilling. When we noticed that we were influencing so many youngsters so deeply, Ann and I said to each other that we had to continue our journey of empowering young people, especially women.

Access Water

A couple of years later, we came up with the Bancroft-Arnesen Explore (BAE) Access Water Project. The mission of BAE Access Water is – shortly stated – to get from hope to action, to empower young people to follow their dreams, and make the world a better place. Our main action field is improving the access to freshwater all over the planet. For this, we searched for one strong female ambassador on every continent. Women who would be a valid representative for their continent. Women that dreamed of making the world a better place and that have the courage, creativity, and discipline to do so.

The team's functioning today goes way beyond the access of clean water, it's much broader. We're involved in educational programs, the democratization of adventure, cultural and economic empowerment of women. For example, one of the ambassadors is Olfat Haider, a woman who is both Palestinian and Israeli. She's working on improving the dialogue between the 2 population groups.

Ann and I have been privileged to grow up in two wealthy countries – the U.S. for Ann and Norway for me – which gave us a lot of opportunities. In a lot of countries all over the world, this isn't the case. Often women are not even allowed to do sports or go on an adventure. Even the women we selected for BAE Access Water are privileged. Each one of them was raised in a supportive household and is very well educated. Today, these ladies act as role models in their own communities.

Today I must say that the sense of fulfillment and happiness I feel working on these sustainable and empowering projects is much bigger than what I felt by my personal accomplishments as a young athlete or adventurer. It even tops reaching the South Pole.

Hiccups

I'm most famous for my two big achievements on the Antarctic ice. But I also experienced some hiccups in my career as an adventurer. Together with Ann, I tried to reach the North Pole twice on an expedition called the *Arctic Ocean*. During our expedition, we wanted to teach children about climate change. On our first attempt in 2015, we were picked up out of the ice by the Russians. Due to a political conflict, we were no longer allowed to continue our journey. Two years later, a plane landing close to us hit our gear. My snowshoe got damaged and as a result, I ended up having frostbite in three of my toes and we had to retreat. Another failed expedition was my attempt to climb Mount Everest in 1996. Due to high altitude cerebral edema, I had to cease the climb. Nevertheless, this expedition did lead to a management book I wrote with my climbing partner Jon Gangdal, titled *"Can I Do It? From Dream to Reality."*

What are the first steps to take if you want to turn a dream into reality?

First, you have to identify whether your dream is the right one. Does it make your heart beat harder? Does it make your blood run faster? If the answer is 'Yes', then you should pursue it, even if your friends and family don't like it. Nurture your dream, get engaged. Investigate what you need to do to make it a reality. Look for the right people.

Today, I coach a lot of people who are looking for direction in their life. This can be people who lost a lot of money, who lost their job, or who simply don't have any idea about their purpose in life. I always make use of what I call 'walk-and-talk'. I go into nature with these people, because that's where insights and good ideas are often found. Scientific studies have shown that walks in nature decrease stress and improve creativity. And there's another advantage; when you're walking, a moment of silence feels natural. You can go on for several minutes without talking. When you're sitting in front of someone at a desk, silence feels awkward. There's always an urge to say something. But often, silence is just what we need to come up with an idea, an insight, or a breakthrough.

Actually, during these coaching sessions, I don't do a lot. I mostly listen. I try to ask the right questions. Sometimes I make suggestions, but I never offer solutions. The people that come to me do already get a lot of advice from their parents, their friends, their colleagues . . . but that's not necessarily what they need. I believe that a solution for their problem is already in them. They are the ones that have to come up with it. Walking, silence, and empathetic listening can help them with that.

Mental Tools

When I was going to the South Pole in 1994, during the first days I had to face endless miles of sastrugi, which are parallel wave-like ridges caused by winds on the surface of hard snow. These sastrugi were strenuous. I had to pull very hard going up and run very fast down to prevent the sled from bumping into my calves and heels. I got frustrated, found myself swearing and tearing. When I hit the cushion at night, I felt exhausted. Not the kind of exhaustion you feel after a good workout, but rather tiredness as a result of the mental challenge. I said to myself: "If you keep spending this much energy on being angry and frustrated, you might not make it." I decided to change tactics and the following day I visualized myself skiing in a modern art gallery. It changed everything, it drew me back into a positive mindset. It made me wonder about the beauty of the landscape again. The closer I got to the South Pole, the better I felt.

I think that as adventurers, we should never forget that we're privileged. When things get hard, we have to remember that it has been our choice to take up the challenge. We also have to remind ourselves the 'why' of our feat. What has been the motivation for us to take up the challenge that makes us suffer at this moment?

Recommended Books
Man's Search for Meaning, by Viktor Frankl
Scott and Amundsen, by Roland Huntford
Endurance: Shackleton's Incredible Voyage, by Alfred Lansing

How would you like to be remembered?
As an educator and adventurer. Educator first.

What are your biggest dreams left?
I have 6 grandchildren. I want to be of a positive contribution to their upbringing, get them motivated to read valuable books. And of course, there's the work with BAE Access Water, which still has a lot of fulfilling adventures in store.

What's your definition of a life well-lived?
For me, it's about purpose. Creating something, setting goals, and achieving them. Or at least failing while doing your very best. Knowing that you've made a difference in some people's lives. In the end, that is what truly makes you feel good.

Find out more about Liv:
www.livarnesen.com
www.bancroftarnesen.eco
facebook.com/BancroftArnesen
instagram.com/bancroftarnesenexplore

In Making the Most Out of Your Life, Grit is More Important Than Talent

BEN SAUNDERS is a record-breaking polar explorer. He was the leader of the longest polar expedition in history, a 105-day round-trip from Ross Island on the coast of Antarctica to the South Pole and back again. Ben has skied more than 7000km in the polar regions, including a solo expedition to the North and South Pole. Ben is also an author and public speaker, named 'a master storyteller' by TED.

"Although I'm a rational rather than spiritual person, I do believe that if you pursue what you really want to the best of your ability, then the Universe will help you."

In Search of Heroes

I was born in the southwest of England. When I was three years old, my Mum and Dad separated. After the divorce, it was essentially my Mum who raised me and my younger brother. Because I grew up without really knowing my father, I had to look for male role models elsewhere. I found them in books and magazines, and they tended to be adventurers and explorers.

Our upbringing was a rural one, so – from as early as I can remember – my brother and I were outdoors whenever we could be. The only thing that matched my love of nature was my dread of going to school! 'Sit still, be quiet, listen to the teacher' is a framework in which I couldn't thrive. Nonetheless, I finished secondary school thinking I would go to University. But I decided to take a year out first, to make sure that it was really what I wanted. I worked in a local shop for six months and with the money I earned, I left on the first real trip of my life. The destination I chose was Nepal. We were still in the nineties and the internet was not yet a mainstream thing. I had no laptop and no smartphone, so I was completely disconnected from the world I was familiar with. I carried not much more than a walkman, a paper travel diary, and some clothes with me. What I discovered was that I was perfectly content with just that.

During this first adventure, I hiked to Everest Base Camp and traveled around India. The entire experience was so thrilling that I concluded that University wasn't for me. When I came back to the UK, I moved to Scotland to work for a guy called John Ridgway. John had sailed around the world and rowed across the Atlantic Ocean in a simple, open, wooden boat. I looked up to him. He was a real-life superhero in my eyes. I worked as an instructor in his 'adventure school for business people'. We guided CEOs of big companies through harsh challenges in the outdoors. Such was the experience, I regularly saw transformational processes going on in these people. It was amazing. I look back at my year with John as probably the most decisive of my life. It is when it clicked in my head that going on amazing adventures and expeditions was what I wanted to do, and hopefully by doing so that it would be a means to inspire others and create positive changes in their lives.

After my job at the adventure school, I decided to join the army. The army had been a phase in the life of many of my heroes (John Ridgway, Borge Ousland and Ranulph Fiennes for example) so I thought joining the military was what I had to do if I wanted to become like them. Despite not having a higher education – which is a prerequisite for Sandhurst – I set my sights on joining the officer training at the Royal Military Academy. Somewhat against the odds, I achieved this. Shortly into my tenure a car accident – which injured my leg significantly – put a stop to my training. This enforced pause gave me further time to reflect, and I asked myself the question of whether the army really was where I belonged. The answer my soul gave me was 'no'. I hung my boots on the hook and went to work once again in the same shop from when I was a 17-year-old boy dreaming of hiking in Nepal. From the outside, it looked as if my life had gone backward. But in my head, a powerful seed was planted about my next destination; the Arctic Ocean.

There Is No Secret; You Just Have to Keep Trying
Chasing my dream, I pretty soon got in touch with Pen Hadow, an experienced arctic explorer. He agreed to team up and try to ski from the Russian mainland all the way to the North Pole; projected as a 1000km journey over two months. I had run marathons, trained with the army, climbed in the Himalayas, learned from John Ridgway and ski toured in Norway; I was sure I was ready. I was confident of success. But the Arctic humbled me immediately. On our first day on the ice, temperatures dropped to -46°C, far below what I had ever known before. I was shocked at how hard it was. Our progress was slower than anticipated, and two-thirds of the way to the North Pole – nearing the ends of our rations and our physical limits – we had to be rescued from the ice.

Back in the UK, I looked at the expedition as a huge failure. Not only hadn't we reached our objective of reaching the pole, but the rescue operation had also left me with a £35,000 bill to pick up. I was only 23 years old and had no savings at all. To make matters worse, I could no longer live with my Mum because the house she was in was too small for the two of us.

I couldn't return to the shop again – it would take ten years of shifts there to clear the debt. I had to find another way. I was in deep already, so decided to go deeper and seek to raise the money through another polar expedition. At that time, I heard that more and more celebrities and wealthy businessmen were searching for personal trainers. So I moved in with a friend in London and started working with private clients in a local gym. This way, I soon built relationships with clients who were both interesting and influential. This was a network that could potentially help me find the sponsorship needed for the next expedition I had in mind: skiing solo to the South Pole and the North Pole as well as climbing Everest, all within the next year. I also looked beyond this network, sending a handwritten letter to Sir Ranulph Fiennes asking for his advice in the quest for sponsorship. The synopsis of his reply (hand-written across two pages and still cherished to this day): "There is no secret to it, Ben. You just have to keep trying!"

The Hidden Adventure
Nowadays, I get a lot of young aspiring explorers sending me questions; just as I did to Sir Ranulph Fiennes two decades ago. They ask me for advice on nutrition, training, equipment,

and other logistical elements. However, all those aspects are the easy part, you could Google most of it. What is really hard is getting the finances for your expedition together. It's actually an expedition in itself which took me a long and hard apprenticeship. I have had to deal with years of struggling through financial worries.

I remember that for my first North Pole expedition, Pen and I had agreed to divide and conquer on the fundraising. Each of us had to pay for their own part of the expedition, a cost of £40,000-£50,000. Pen found a personal sponsor in less than a week. I, on the other hand, sent out letters and emails to hundreds of companies; with a spot for their logo on my expedition kit as the return-on-investment. My first meeting was with the CEO of the company my Mum worked for. I assumed he invited me out of politeness rather than genuine interest. I sold him the vision; an expedition that was harder than climbing Everest, had never been done before, and traversed across an environment that was so harsh it was uninhabitable. I finished by telling him his logo would be across all the kits for this maiden voyage. His reply? "Who the hell is going to see our logo in the middle of nowhere?" (laughs)

We Think You Should Fly Business Class

When I started thinking about my second big expedition, I wanted to do a smaller one in preparation. This required less funding and was a price met by the company of one of my clients from the gym. After returning from the expedition, I got invited to speak at a conference organized by *the Duke of Edinburgh's Award*. After my speech, a man came up to me and presented himself as the CEO of a company and wanted to support my next expedition – skiing solo from the Russian mainland to the North Pole. He was excited, motivated, and insistent about meeting to discuss it further. At first, I was reluctant. I had never heard of the company and was skeptical of whether they could supply the level of funds required. I remained suitably non-committal that day.

When I got home, I searched for him and discovered that he was the CEO of a global company with 30,000 employees! A couple of days later we met. He remained just as engaged, something I hadn't known from prospective sponsors before. I had always been forced to put a tremendous amount of effort into fundraising; insisting over and over about the value in meeting me. And yet, here was a situation the opposite of that. It felt too good to be true.

He put me in front of the financial manager of his company to outline my needs. Wherever possible I looked to minimize costs. For instance, I selected the cheapest flight to Russia and a second-hand *Land Rover* to travel around to schools to give talks after the expedition. While I was presenting my expedition, the financial manager didn't say a single word but was constantly taking notes. I didn't quite know what to think about it. I was afraid I was being too demanding. When I was done talking, it was his turn to speak. He said: "We think you should fly business class, Ben, so you'll be sure to start your expedition totally rested." He added a zero at the end of my projected flying costs. "Don't worry about buying an old *Land Rover*, our company is going to offer you a *BMW*." As if that wasn't enough, they raised the budget so that I could pay myself a salary. During this one meeting, I was transformed from an unknown outsider – with huge debts to his name – into a professional polar explorer!

Earning a Year's Salary in a One-Hour Speech

The North Pole expedition in 2004 was a success and led to being invited to give a *TED talk*. At the time there was only one *TED event* per year in California, USA (before the franchise went global). After achieving a first in the polar exploration world, I felt invincible! Yet, when I arrived there and started speaking with the other guests – people creating a cure for malaria or integrating the internet in Africa's health centers – I understood that skiing 1000 km on a frozen sea was rather less significant! It was a humbling experience, which nonetheless opened the door to another speaking engagement in the USA. My eyes were opened to the value associated with effective and engaging motivational speaking. In one hour of rambling about my expedition, I would earn as much as I did in a year as a shop assistant!

I've never been a religious or overly spiritual man. I'm a rational human, a logical thinker. Yet, I do believe that if you pursue what you really want, to the best of your ability, then the Universe will (in some way or another) conspire to help you. I have taken enormous risks in my life, accepting the failures that inevitably come with that. I've been deeply in debt and riddled with doubt – both of myself and from others – but I have always found a way through. Today I'm in a privileged position, I'm financially secure, have led and shared in some incredible adventures, and had the chance to meet some remarkable people. Some of whom I feel honored to call friends to this day.

As well as – and in balance with – perseverance, I encourage people to ask for help. Too many people have big dreams but are afraid to reach out to people who are further down the line. If in my early twenties I hadn't written that letter to Sir Ranulph Fiennes, sent emails to Borge Ousland, or canvassed my clients in the gym for sponsorship, I would not be where I am today.

If Warren Buffet would write you a 50-million dollar check with a note "to be used to do good," how would you spend/invest the money?

I'd use it to make some of the things I'm working on now happen a little faster. This means everything from investing in start-ups that are trying to help humanity and the planet, to establishing an annual grant for young field scientists that want to work in the polar regions.

Do you have a favorite quote or a quote you live your life by?

I started learning Chinese in 2019 and there's a term that I love: 劲草, pronounced as *jìng cǎo*, which means literally 'tough upright grass' and figuratively 'a staunch character able to withstand a tough test.'

As you've probably guessed already, I think grit – and the ability to endure, to work hard, and to stay positive when things are difficult – is way more important than talent when it comes to making the most of your life!

Grit = Self-Belief

Your ability to persevere is ultimately a measure of how much you believe in yourself. By self-belief, I don't mean self-importance or ego, but the belief in your own sense of agency, your own ability to act and make things happen, and your own ability to cope with whatever might happen as a result of your actions. Self-belief comes from a combination of courage and confidence. It is important to note, however, that confidence only ever follows courage. Only if you have the courage to act, do you then gain confidence. However important research is – and it is certainly valuable – you still can't get the confidence for polar expeditions from reading a book; you need to get out there and experience it.

How do you prepare physically for an expedition?
My training involves a combination of strength and endurance, and I believe that is what every human being would benefit from. In training for North Pole expeditions (where the conditions on pack ice tend to be pretty crazy) I realized that weight training in the gym with perfect form (my feet absolutely level on a flat floor) didn't translate to the challenges of getting a sledge through smashed up ice. Instead, I started doing deadlift-type movements in all sorts of different positions. Often with one foot randomly up on a bench or step, with some sort of twist involved, and sometimes using a rope rather than lifting the weight directly.

How do you break big expeditions down into concrete action points?
I use elements of David Allen's *Getting Things Done* methodology every day. I have done so for every big goal I've accomplished in the last 15 years. The trick is to break big goals down into subsidiary projects. For example 'organize and book flights to Antarctica', 'create expedition website', 'raise £xxxxx sponsorship', etc. I create a list of all of these elements - using an app called 'Things' - and then identify 'next actions' for each project. For example, Google good website designers, brainstorm potential sponsors, email for a logistics quote, etc. From there, you have to keep doing the next actions of course, along with reviewing your lists every week.

If you could go and grab a beer with three people dead or alive, who would you pick?
Fridtjof Nansen, Sir Ernest Shackleton, and either Marcus Aurelius or Seneca.

Recommended Books
Getting Things Done, by David Allen
Anything You Want, by Derek Sivers
The War of Art, by Steven Pressfield
So Good They Can't Ignore You, by Cal Newport
The Guide to the Good Life, by Rolf Dobelli

What is your definition of a life well-lived?
The attainment of self-knowledge and self-awareness, and to have left people, places, and things better than when you found them.

Find out more about Ben:
www.bensaunders.com
instagram.com/polarben

PART SEVEN:
AROUND THE WORLD

Sometimes We Think That We Are Still Little, Naive Children Who Don't Understand How the World Works

MAXIME PAVIE and DELPHINE POCINCHO are travel bloggers, photographers, and videographers. They travel all over the world under the banner 'Entre2pôles' (translated: In Between 2 Poles) with the goal to spread positivity into the world and collect money to fund Amyotrophic Lateral Sclerosis (ALS) research.

"We could get paid to travel as so-called 'Instagram influencers', but that's not our goal. Our purpose is to put ALS in the picture and to stay true to the journeys and creative projects we really want to do. It's idealistic, but it's the only way to flourish authentically. "

The Distance That Brought Maxime and Delphine Together

Delphine: The mountains have been part of my identity for all my life. I was born and raised in the French Pyrenees. I was only two years old when my dad guided me to hiking up my first summit at 2,870 meters altitude! Since then, I never stopped climbing and hiking in the mountains. Up until today, the Pyrenean mountains are the only place on earth where I feel at home. Meanwhile, my natural curiosity has led me to visit many more beautiful spots in the world.

Maxime: My thirst for adventure started with sports. When I was a kid, I enjoyed watching all kinds of competitions on television - World Cups, World Championships, the Olympics - all of which made me dream of "the other side." During my studies I started traveling. Discovering another culture, learning a new language, adopting new habits . . . it gave birth to a big desire to explore more of the world. I completed my studies at a University located in the Pyrenees. I found a student job at sports retailer *Decathlon* and when I got presented to my colleagues, I saw a beautiful girl who would later become my girlfriend.

Delphine: That didn't happen right away, though. Maxime and I were friends for four years before getting into a relationship. As soon as Maxime finished his studies, he went working in New Zealand for nine months. Surprisingly, the increased distance between us brought us closer together. When he came back, he had very clear plans in his head and as it turned out I was part of those plans (laughs). Right away when we started our relationship, we felt very complimentary, very fusional. Pretty soon, we went traveling together in Iceland. We rented a car, road-tripped across the highlands while sleeping in the back trunk of the car. We absolutely loved it! That trip only nurtured our desire to maintain this lifestyle, so we decided to leave France and go on a big adventure.

#SLAchallenges

Delphine: We decided to travel for an unlimited period of time, with not much more than a backpack and two brains full of ideas of where we wanted to go. We also wanted our trip to have a positive impact and thus started thinking about a platform that would allow us to share a meaningful message with the world. My mom had died two years earlier from the consequences of ALS *(Amyotrophic Lateral Sclerosis - Sclérose Latérale Amyotrophique (SLA) in French)*. ALS is a progressive nervous system disease that affects nerve cells in the brain and spinal cord, causing loss of muscle control. The disease isn't very well-known and there's too little financing for the research of its causes and potential treatments. Maxime and I decided that we wanted to put this disease in the picture – quite literally – on Instagram. We came up with the idea of *#SLAchallenges*: athletic feats we did along the road in order to raise awareness for the disease. For example, the 'Bring Sally Up' Challenge. We met the president of the French ALS League and created an online page where people could make donations in order to support ALS research.

Becoming Popular on Instagram . . . By Hazard

Today, we have almost 70,000 followers on Instagram and that's far beyond our expectations. We created our Instagram page without any big ambitions. The only goal was to give attention to ALS. We really liked the process of creating an Instagram post; modifying pictures, writing an interesting comment, making everything look aesthetically pleasing . . . This way, Instagram soon became a sort of travel diary for us. We never had any tactics to make our following grow, it just happened organically. In the beginning, the only people following us were our friends and family. It got picked up here and there by their friends and by people we met along the road. After a while, some of our pictures got shared by people who have millions of followers. This caused a snowball effect. I remember waking up one morning and seeing that 5,000 people had started following us overnight! In less than one year we had 50,000 followers. We actually still can't believe this happened.

In fact, today's Instagram 'strategy' is the opposite of what all experts tell us to do. We don't post a lot, sometimes we spend weeks without putting out new content. For our own mental wellbeing, it feels good to disconnect regularly. I think that our 'secret' simply is that we focus on creating good content. We approach every single post with care and try to make every single post tell an interesting story.

Learning Videography

Every time someone tells us they like our photos and YouTube videos, we feel flattered. That's because we learned everything ourselves. We've spent many, many, many hours watching tutorials and many, many, many more hours finetuning our art.

Today, photography and cinematography have become our 'normal' job and provide 80% of our income. We work as freelancers for different individuals and larger brands. Most of the projects that come to us are in the outdoor and travel industry, but not always. We're aware that, thanks to our large Instagram following, we could get paid for traveling as so-called 'influencers'. We could get paid by certain travel agencies, hotels, or cities if we'd make a video about the destination in return and promote it on Instagram. It's something we occasionally do, but only if it feels right to us. As we said, *Entre2Pôles* has been created with the goal to share an important message, not to make money. Sometimes we feel a bit naive, as if we're still little children who do not understand how the world works. But we believe it's important to stay true to ourselves instead of trying to cash out as much as possible. We live a very simple lifestyle and we are supported by a handful of sponsors who provide us travel assurance and gear for free. We are very content this way. Our freelance jobs, the simple lifestyle, and the sponsorship support give us the freedom to do the travels and creative projects we really want. It's idealistic, but it's the only way to flourish authentically.

Give a sales pitch for yourself. Why should people follow you?

Oh, not our favorite question! We don't like to sell ourselves, but let's give it a try. People should follow us to get a big dose of evasion in simplicity and good humor. To discover pleasant, human adventures. To discover our next *#SLAchallenges* and, last but not least, for Maxime's imitations of Mike Horn.

How would you describe your partner in 3 words?

Delphine: Maxim is altruistic, funny, and . . . a battery! (laughs) I mean he's full of energy. Oh, can I give a fourth one? Easy-going. Everything is ok for him, he's always optimistic.

Maxim: Delphine is very altruistic, I've never seen someone care so much for other people's happiness. She's also real, passionate, and fascinating. Oops, that's four too.

What does a perfect day in your life look like?

It starts with the sound of a zipper, opening the entry gate of our tent at dawn in an unknown, magnificent place, thereby giving us the view of a beautiful sunrise above a sea of clouds. Around us are the tents of people we care for, they're enjoying the natural spectacle with us. We put on our caps, make a fire, and have breakfast all together. Next, we leave for a day-long hike in a wild, grandiose landscape. The air is fresh, but the sun is radiating. During the hike, we tell stories, bring up memories, and get the giggles. At noon, we eat artisan cheese and drink local beer, or the opposite, it doesn't really matter. We witness impressive wild animals, get the giggles once again, and before we notice we get totally lost. By hazard, the people of an ancient tribe find us, we don't speak their language but we understand they're inviting us to regain warmth in their village. Once there, we discover their small wooden cabins. We help them gather their herds and prepare dinner together with them. After dinner we gather around the campfire, a cup of tea in our hands, warm-hearted exchanges take place, everyone appreciates the presence of the others. We go to bed all together, covered cozily by a giant blanket.

Would the world be a better place if Adventure were a mandatory course at school?

Adventure to us means going beyond yourself, pushing your limits, having the courage to step outside your comfort zone, staying curious about the unknown, perseverance, having the audacity to take an unknown direction in life, having the courage to open up to others, learning to have confidence in strangers . . . So of course we think that if those values would be instilled in school, the world would be a better place! And in order to not overload the curriculum, we vote for it to replace learning to play the flute. Who is with us?

Imagine you are 90 years old, sitting in your rocking chair and making a reflection about the life you've lived. What needs to happen for you to be 100% satisfied and happy at that moment?

If we've lived every moment to the fullest. If we've collected (hundreds of) thousands of euros to help fund ALS research, if we've had the courage to overcome our fears. If thanks to our life-long journey we've encountered plenty of nice people who have become friends. If we have accomplished a couple of athletic feats. If we have written at least one book and produced at least one movie. If we've been to a World Cup rugby game. If we've constructed a small café just next to our wooden house in the mountains. If we've at least tried to brew our own beer. If we've done our very best to take care of the people we love and if we've taken up the challenges that have faced us. And of course, all of this without ever losing the goodwill towards and love for our partner.

Happiness =

Happiness depends on our capacity to be content with simple things, but also on our capacity to be open to others and to the present moment.

Find out more about Delphine and Maxime:

www.entredeuxpoles.com
instagram.com/entre2poles
facebook.com/entredeuxpoles

I Am Very Persistent

*In 2005, after a 14-year-long career at Microsoft, **DIMITRI KIEFFER** decided it was time to leave the company and follow his dreams. He began volunteering with international relief organizations as well as completing races and adventures waiting on his bucket list. He started with the famous 'Iditarod Trail Invitational' footrace in Alaska. From there, together with Karl Bushby, he became the first man to cross the Bering Strait westbound, after which he decided to continue circumnavigating the world human-powered.*

"We're 17 years later now and I'm still in the execution of my endeavor. And I continue to love it."

Becoming an Adventurer

I grew up in Normandy, in northwestern France, as part of a family that enjoys adventures and sports. My father was a general practitioner who loved sailing and flying small aircraft in his spare time. My mother worked various jobs throughout her life. She was successively a school teacher, an elected official, a prison counselor, and assisted my father with his practice throughout his career. I can say that most of my family has an adventurous spirit. I have some family members who worked for the organization *Médecins Sans Frontières (Doctors Without Borders)*, responding to medical crises in different parts of the world.

One of my cousins was one of the first professional female sailboat racers and her sister has been a pilot for many years, while her brother flies gliders or sails catamarans.

Since there were no very good schools in my hometown, I was sent to boarding school when I was only nine years old. I learned then at an early age to become very independent. I progressively went home to visit my parents more and more sporadically. When I was ten years old, I started calling my parents by their first names instead of by the traditional 'Maman' and 'Papa'. Maybe this was an early sign of my search for independence. I also took on small jobs as early as I could. When I was 17 years old, I came to the United States as an exchange student in an American high school. I had planned to come to the U.S. only for one year. But I fell in love with a woman who eventually became my first wife. Consequently, I continued my University education in Seattle.

During my University years, I tried to limit asking my parents in France for financial support. Instead, I worked as a waiter in Swiss, French, and Italian restaurants as well as in a private club. I did not have any spare time to travel, except once a year, when I visited my family in France to celebrate Christmas. At the *Columbia Tower Club* (an establishment where local notables used to frequent) I often waited on Bill Gates and his family, not knowing that I would eventually end up working just a few years later for his company, Microsoft.

After finishing my University studies, I worked in marketing planning for one year in Hong Kong before coming back to Seattle and joining *Microsoft*. I started in the company as a 'French Localizer' on software applications. This meant adapting U.S. software applications to the linguistic, cultural, and technical requirements specific to the French market. As a result of *Microsoft*'s rapid expansion, the company needed to outsource a large amount of its localization work. I was then offered a position where, with the help of my team, I was sourcing the appropriate localization partners mostly in Asia, the Middle East, and Brazil. As a result of my business travels, I had the opportunity to visit some fascinating parts of the world. Although, I was mostly spending time in meetings, airports, hotels, and restaurants. My knowledge of these countries was quite limited, and it did not allow me to gain an extensive understanding of their local cultures. With my current *Nexus Expedition*, I am pleased that I now have the opportunity to correct this, taking the time to gain a good in-depth comprehension of the cultures I am crossing.

Adventure Racing

While at *Microsoft*, I spent my weekends partaking in sports activities and races. At first, I started running short races. Then I stepped up to full marathons and eventually moved on to completing longer ultra-running races. At the company, we had to work a large number of hours per week. I did not have the time, nor the desire to train. As a result, I became a 'weekend warrior'; running long races on weekends and letting my body recover at my work desk during the weekdays. Progressively, one race led to another. I gradually started adventure racing; a multidisciplinary sport involving navigation, trekking, mountain biking, kayaking, cross-country skiing, etc. This became somewhat addictive. I started thinking of partaking in longer and more extreme races, such as 333 to 555 kilometer non-stop running races through the scorching Sahara desert. Or equally long foot races through the frozen Alaskan tundra. One of the races on top of my bucket list was the *Iditarod Trail Invitational race*, a self-supported 1,800-kilometer footrace throughout Alaska, from Anchorage to Nome, which follows the same route as the infamous 'Iditarod' dog-sledding race.

I wanted very much to take part in this long race but I needed to be able to take the time off. In order to do so, after fourteen years at *Microsoft*, I requested for my first time, a three months unpaid leave of absence. This was not the easiest request to fulfill. For one thing, I was then managing a team of 55 employees spread throughout the world. Above all, this type of request was not very much in line with the company's demanding work ethics at the time. One of *Microsoft*'s presidents supposedly stated once: "If the company can survive without you for more than three weeks in a row, you are obviously not very much needed here."

A few weeks prior to my departure for Alaska, while running in a short local footrace, I broke my ankle. Regrettably, I had to cancel my plans. I noticed then that my manager was to some extent pleased by my misfortune. He was delighted to see me be able to stay in town and work. This is when I realized it was time for me to completely leave the company in order to live my dreams. Looking back, I must say that I enjoyed my career at *Microsoft*. But I am pleased and thankful I was able to leave when I did.

A Crawl Through a Giant Slurpee Drink

The following year, in 2005, fully recovered from the injury, I was able to go to Alaska and complete the Iditarod. In a remote cabin along the trail, I fortuitously met Karl Bushby, a British adventurer who had been walking since 1998. He was in the midst of his *Goliath Expedition*, which he had started in Punta Arenas, Chile. He walked all the way through South,

Central, and then North America. By the time I met him in Alaska, he had already walked 25,000 kilometers. His ongoing goal was to trek across the Bering Strait (between Alaska and Russia) and continue by foot all the way back to his native United Kingdom.

We quickly started discussing how we could cross the Bering Strait together. Father Dmitry and son Matvey Shparo, a team of Russian adventurers, had by then been the only men who had walked across the Bering Strait. They succeeded in 1998 on their third attempt, going eastbound. If we were to succeed, we would then become the first men to have crossed the Bering Strait going westbound, from Alaska, U.S.A. to Chukotka, Russia. We discussed our trip with a team of adventurers who had failed to complete the crossing. After spending time meticulously testing our selected equipment during a one-year preparation period, Karl and I set off. Even though the Bering Strait is only 82 kilometers wide at its narrowest point, we covered 322 kilometers in 14 days. The ice floes we were progressing on were pushed in all directions by the strong local currents. During 5 of these 14 crossing days, we had to swim in our dry suits across open leads, while pulling our floating sleds from one ice floe to the next, progressively going westward. The swim sometimes felt like a crawl through a giant *Slurpee* drink, where it was both difficult to swim freely and impossible to stand. We would then use ice axes to extract ourselves from the frigid water, and climb on top of the ice floes. We also made use of the ice axes to carve our ways through steep ice surges.

During the night, while camping on ice floes, we had to be especially attentive. We listened carefully to the ice floes potentially cracking wide open, near or underneath our tent. Twice, we had to move our tent and gear within minutes, when the ice started breaking up right below us. After our challenging but successful crossing, we landed in Uelen, Chukotka Autonomous Okrug, Russian Far East where our situation became quite complex. We had proper Russian visas but were not aware that the entire region was a closed military zone, therefore requiring a specific travel permit. As a result, we were detained for 55 days and had to go to trial to fight potential jail time and/or deportation. We also had to appear on the main state-owned Russian television channel to apologize officially to the Russian Federation and specifically to Russian president Vladimir Putin for the potential embarrassment we had caused to anyone. We were also asked to officially state on camera that we were not spies.

17 Years Later

After having crossed the Bering Strait, and while being detained in the barracks of the Russian border guards in the village of Uelen where I could stare at an old world map hanging above my bed, I started pondering: "Why should I not continue going westward?". The following winter, when we returned to Chukotka, Karl Bushby and I started out walking and skiing together through the tundra. However, we eventually split, since we both wanted to explore different routes. Karl chose a northern route through Chukotka while I chose a more southern route. Since then, our paths have not crossed again yet, but we keep in touch and remain good friends.

For 17 years now, I have been moving forward in this human-powered circumnavigation of the globe, progressing intermittently according to local visa restrictions and weather conditions. Taking into consideration the length of this expedition, I very much consider it a lifetime commitment. This means that it is crucial for me to be able to balance my overall time between the time spent on the the expedition, time spent with the family, and time spent exploring/experiencing as much as I can along my way. Sometimes, I am forced to stop the expedition for a certain amount of time to return home in order to obtain a specific visa, permit, or something else. For example, when I walked across the Russian Far East, I was only allowed to step into the country for three months at a time, and then I had to wait another three months before I could enter the country again, following the "3 months in, 3 months out" visa rule. As a result, it took me five winters to cross this remote part of the world.

In 2009, while being back at home, I foolishly fell off the roof of my house while cleaning it. I fractured the L1 vertebrae in my spine. Consequently, I was not allowed to return to the expedition to pull a sled for the following year. After crucial back surgery, several months of having to wear a clamshell brace at my chest level, and intense physical therapy, I had partially recovered my mobility. However, I was not allowed to return to the expedition and pull my sled until the following year. Somewhat restless, I gladly accepted when a friend in Seattle offered me to borrow his motorcycle which was parked in Germany. I rode this motorcycle through Europe, visiting my family and long-lost European friends. At one point, I decided to fly to Morocco to go and visit a longtime friend. Together, we went to a music festival in Essaouira where I met my now-wife, Gulnara, a Russian Tatar. She was, at that time, a guide for Russian artists traveling through Morocco.

At the beginning of our relationship, Gulnara asked me how much longer my expedition would take to complete. I answered then: "5 years." After dating for one year, she decided to join me on the expedition because she was interested in participating, and did not want to wait for me at home for the following years. Obviously, much more than 5 years have passed and I'm still on the road, not able to tell when I will finish this long expedition. I estimate about 5 more years . . . (laughs)

Dealing With Danger
When I am facing a dangerous or challenging situation, I try to very much zone in and not panic. If possible, I try to sleep on it. Then I can make the right decision about what needs to be done, with more clarity, the next morning. As we say in French: *"La nuit porte conseil"*.

One spring, while crossing a remote region north of the Arctic Circle in Russia, I was dealing with 24-hour periods of sunlight. As a result, the frozen rivers were melting very quickly. Much faster than I had anticipated. Because of this rapid melting, I had to trudge through what had become a cold and dangerous raging river instead of a frozen calm one. I improvised and started using my sled as a kayak and my snow shovel as a paddle.

A few days later, as I was walking and pulling my sled along the riverbank, the current took my sled and pulled it under dangerous protruding ice surges. Being still physically attached to my sled, I was also immediately sucked underneath the ice surges. Unable to see anything, looking for an opening to breathe, I searched with my hands for a way out from under the ice surges. Thankfully, I was able to extract myself from that frightening situation.

I once had a bad experience in sparsely populated Mongolia. When coming out of a village at dusk, I noticed that a group of young men was following me. Not sure what this was all about and not wanting to take any risks, I decided to hide by burying myself, my bicycle, and gear in the sand and under a tarp. It worked. I had a similar experience after leaving a village at dusk, in what is usually peaceful Sudan. I will never know if these groups of men intended to rob or even potentially kill me, but the fear in me got quite real, sadly taking me to a paranoiac level.

In Ethiopia, I got into a ight with a drunk man. He attacked me with a frying pan because he had noticed a regional flag on my bike. Unbeknownst to me, the region I was crossing had two different regional flags from two different political parties. The drunk man didn't like the flag I was carrying with me and it almost cost me an eye. Since then, I no longer display flags on my bicycle and try my best to stay away from any person under the influence.

While crossing tumultuous and crowded parts of the world, I also now tend to keep a fully grown white beard. This, at least in my head, may command more respect. For example, I believe that children are less inclined to throw rocks at someone who looks like a grandfather.

Connection

The root of the word *Nexus* is the Latin verb *nectere* which means *to connect*. The goal of my expedition is to circumnavigate the world through human power while *connecting* different societies, civilizations, and landscapes.

By now, having experienced along the way potential dangers while connecting with some of the more challenging humans, I have learned to be vigilant while meeting new people on the road. Having said that, I want to keep trying my hardest to still trust almost everyone I meet and therefore stay true to my mission of connecting. Accordingly, when locals I meet on my route ask me why I'm doing this expedition, I often answer: "So I can meet you."

I also think that we, adventurers and travelers, need to be fully aware of how privileged we are to be able to do what we do. We truly have quite a unique and luxurious position that most people around the planet will most likely never have the chance to experience. Consequently, from time to time, this can lead some to envy. Sadly perceived by some as just a money bag, I receive from time to time random requests for funds, or for help to acquire visas or to ind a European wife. This is quite understandable since my financial position is better than that of most of the people I come across along my way. Some travelers are bragging about how little money they can spend per country and per diem, blind to the fact that they are taking advantage of the kindness of poor strangers by systematically trying to stay with families along their way. In some parts of the world, it is quite customary for people to welcome a traveler with open arms into their home. Some people even go through the expenses of preparing and offering a lavish meal that they can sometimes barely afford. Gulnara and I always try to return the favor, especially with the most destitute ones, by offering to either buy food for the family or leave some cash for the parents so that they could buy a small gift for their children.

Generally speaking, I usually try not to rush through a country. I like taking the opportunity to maximize my time, absorbing as much of the local culture as I can, in a similar fashion to a sponge absorbing water. I once met Jonas Deichmann in Ethiopia (read the interview with Jonas Deichmann on page 163) while he was on his way to breaking a world speed record. I have tremendous respect for what Jonas does, but it's not the way I like to travel. I enjoy the fact that I have the time to truly immerse myself in the local cultures, at the cost of a much longer journey.

In order for this expedition to be truly a human-powered circumnavigation of the planet, it is necessary for me to cover every single meter of my route by human power. I travel by foot, bicycle, kayak, row, ski, swim, or any other form of human-powered mode of transportation. In this perspective, I am very persistent, some call it stubborn. I deliberately chose a complex route for Nexus Expedition through the Middle East. In some of these countries, it has been extremely difficult to obtain the proper visas and permissions to allow me to come through via human power. For example, I spent 17 months trying to secure permissions from the Egyptian ministries in order to be allowed to kayak a mere 17 kilometers across the northern tip of the Red Sea. These are situations that challenge my patience, but I never give up. I always find a way.

How do you finance your trips?
I had a good career at *Microsoft*. It was quite demanding but it allowed me to save some money.
In addition to that, my wife and I have been able to rent our home when we are gone. Over the years, a few generous companies have also sponsored us with mostly gear and clothes, and friends have supported us logistically. Finally, we try to have a frugal lifestyle to make it all last longer.

In the 'industry' of adventurers, from what I have seen, the only way to make a profitable lifestyle out of it is to have a good honest story to sell, well packaged, and become a professional guest speaker. Of course, not everyone is capable of doing this successfully. Will I follow this path after I have completed the expedition, and will I have the proper skills to do so? I am not quite sure yet. For the time being, I am focusing on completing this long expedition, while collecting experiences and amassing data by means of photos, films, audios, and personal notes. In the future, if I am not able to become a successful guest speaker, I will probably have to look for a more traditional type of work, more in line with my previous managerial career at *Microsoft*. Or Gulnara and I may also choose to move to a more affordable country.

Which books and movies have inspired you?
Le Tour de la France par Ddeux Eenfants, by Augustine Fouillée. This book recounts the journey of two young brothers who, after the death of their father, searched for family members throughout France. The diversity of the people they met along the way led them to want to learn more about local food, dialects, and customs.

La Terre N'est Qu'un Seul Pays, by André Brugiroux. It is about the author's first journey around the world. A journey that lasted 18 years (1955-1973) before he returned home. He hitchhiked 400,000 kilometers through 135 countries. I read the book as a teenager, dreaming about following Brugiroux's footsteps . . .

Conquering the Impossible, by Mike Horn. This book is about Mike Horn's *Arktos Expedition* when he took more than two years to go solo, by non-motorized transport, around the Arctic Circle, covering 20,000 kilometers. This book definitely inspired me while crossing the Bering Strait and beyond.

Man's Search for Meaning, by Viktor Frankl. It chronicles the Austrian author's experiences as a prisoner in Nazi concentration camps during WWII. It follows his journey of identifying a purpose in life to feel positive about, and then immersively imagining that outcome. I used this book to learn about different positive ways to face adversity.

Agnostic: A Spirited Manifesto, by Lesley Hazleton. A great book to learn to appreciate what ambiguity entails.

Silence: in the Age Of Noise, by Erling Kagge. Written in 2017, the Norwegian adventurer explores the power of silence and the importance of shutting out the world.

The Motorcycle Diaries, 2004, directed by Walter Salles. It is a biopic about the journey of the 23-year old Ernesto (Che) Guevara when in 1952, he rode a motorcycle throughout South America with his friend Alberto Granado. Through the characters they encounter during their continental trek, Guevara and Granado witness first-hand the injustice that the destitute face. They are exposed to people and social classes they would have never encountered otherwise.

What advice would you give to someone who's stuck in a job they don't like and dreams about being an adventurer?
Do not care what people think, the haters, the naysayers, etc . . . Surround yourself with like-minded, experienced adventurers from whom you can learn and get mental support when facing adversities.
From there, plan the adventures you're dreaming of and gain the needed skills. And, once you get there, be honest about your accomplishments.

What advice would you give to your 18-year-old self?
Actually, it's what I did: "Study hard, try to get a well-paid job, save some money early."
While working at *Microsoft,* I used to compare myself to a miner, digging in the mine and planning to save for later. Thankfully, this is what I was able to do.

What's your definition of happiness?
I think that for a lot of people happiness means safety. Now, for myself, I am not quite sure what to answer. I actually feel happy, incredibly lucky, and grateful to have my current life. I believe that these 'expedition years' are the happiest years of my life. So far, anyway, because I cannot know what the future entails . . . I have a wife, family, and friends who support what I do and I have the flexibility to go at the speed I want, making progress on my *Nexus Expedition* while experiencing cultures and landscapes on my way. Being surrounded by these incredible people and experiencing freedom are, in any case, two major sources of happiness for me.

Find out more about Dimitri:

www.nexusexpedition.com
facebook.com/nexusexpedition
instagram.com/nexusexpedition

In 34 Years of Traveling, I Can Count the Bad People on One Hand

MIKAEL STRANDBERG traveled around the world on a bicycle, rode through Patagonia on horseback, traveled through Yemen with camels, and through Siberia with reindeers and sleds. Despite this impressive list of achievements, Michael considers his biggest adventure to be raising his daughters Dana and Eva.

"Everything fades in their comparison, they're the best of the best"

How did you come to make adventure a major part of your life?
First of all, I think that some people have the urge to explore the millions-year-old 'adventure-gene' while others don't. There's not much to change about that. My adventure-gene has always been very active and it still is today. I was brought up in the countryside by a working-class family where everything that counted was hard labor and valuing the family. Traveling didn't exist. Fortunately, this was during the sixties and life for most Swedes was getting better by the day. My older sister went as an au pair to the UK, stayed, and got married to a guy who likes traveling. So Mum and I went to visit them each time we could afford it, which was once every 2-3 years. These holidays were always camping trips in Wales and Scotland. That's where my sense of adventure got triggered. The joy I experienced during these times opened my eyes. I realized there's a life outside the garden face of our house.

Another catalyst for my adventurous spirit was books. In my early teens, I got a nasty disease and was forced to spend a couple of months at home, and obviously, I got bored. Our family had three books that my dad had stolen from the library. Amongst them, I remember Jack London's *Call of the Wild,* and another was *The Last Of The Mohicans,* an adventurous story about the French and Indian war of the 18th century. These books opened a new, exciting world to me, and they got me hooked on reading. For the following years, books would change my life completely. I preferred the library to school. I got shitty grades but knew Kafka before my agemates. I read a lot of books about explorers, adventures, animal catchers, and foreign countries and cultures.

As quickly as I turned 14, I started traveling Europe by train every summer. At age 17, I went to South America as a backpacker for a few months, to hike the Inca Trail amongst other things. At age 18, I went to India and South-East Asia for a year as a backpacker, trying to figure out life. I came back home having lost 22 kilograms. On this trip, I met an Irish guy who had cycled from Ireland to Nepal. He impressed me and gave me a new calling. At age 24, I set off on my first bicycle trip. Altogether it would be 6.5 years on a bicycle. During the last part of it, I was given a Hi-8 camera to document my journey from New Zealand to Cairo for a Swedish Travel Program. At that time, I had already made myself a name within the adventure world, mainly as a motivational speaker and entertainer. The travel episodes for the Swedish television show became an instant success and set me up for doing my first self-made documentary about a one-year-long horse ride through Patagonia. This way, travel, adventure, and storytelling have been my sole job since 1986. Today I get mainly financed by broadcasters, film institutes, and one big sponsor, *Kensington Tours.* On and off, I do motivational speaking, write articles, and so on. But right now, film does the job.

What have been the most difficult moments in the building-up of a lifestyle based on adventure and travel?
I have to say there haven't been that many obstacles or difficult moments. Right from the beginning, I have followed my heart. Of course, at times, people have been jealous or discouraging, but such is life. My life has been full of ups and downs, a constant back-and-forth between tragedy and joy. I see this as part of being a human being.

I don't consider the choices I have made as sacrifices. I wanted this life from very early on. For me, it is the best life possible. This life made me meet so many wonderful people. In 34 years, I can count the bad people on one hand.

What personality traits do you have that are crucial to your success? What sets you apart from others?
You don't ask a Swede a question like that, we cannot say anything good about ourselves! But I will give it a try and this is only based on what I think, I might be totally wrong. I'm someone who sees very few obstacles. I honestly believe I can do whatever I put my mind to, but at the same time, I am very realistic and rational. I love people, and I love living. I like being by myself and this means that most of the time I am in a very good, positive mood. I am also a bit creative, artistic and humorous, and I guess quite ambitious and focused. But most of all, I am good at dealing with my failings and failures, which are many. And I am brave in not pretending to be anything but the failure I am as a human.

What have been your biggest weaknesses you had to work on?
I hate tax papers! Such a complete waste of time! Today I outsource 80% of my work to accountants, editors, color graders, and so on. I concentrate on the creative work.

About Being a Father and Adventurer
Every single expedition or adventure made me grow and gave me a new perspective on life. I learn something new every day. Even at age 58, I feel I know nothing. But if I look at life in general, the best that has happened is my daughters. Everything fades in their comparison, they're the best of the best. I have made two films which include my daughters. One walk with my youngest daughter in a pram through the UK, and one about living as a family together on Greenland. The best is to see how wonderful human beings they have become through these journeys!

Being an adventurer involves risks. In the 34 years I've been doing this, I could have been dead so many times. Since I enjoy being with my daughters and see it as my job to provide them with opportunities, love, and a decent life, I don´t wanna die yet. I reduce risks as much as possible. Good planning, good reasoning, and experience make a difference. When it comes to longevity, I take care of myself. I train, sleep, eat, and love the right way.

How do you stay in shape?

I work with a Polish dietist who is herself a well-known ultra runner. For the last 6 months, she has monitored my eating to suit my upcoming expedition. It works wonderfully! The diet is mainly vegan, to which I add small amounts of cured parma ham, fish, eggs, and yogurt or kefir.

As an ultra runner and explorer, I'm not a big fan of today's popular ketogenic diet. It empties your engine when it needs to be fed regularly. I do a weekly sauna alternated with cold baths. I practice yoga 4-5 times a week. I carry an Oura Ring to measure my sleep. I run 3 times in a 9-day period, averaging 21.1 kilometers per run, mainly on trails. Nowadays, I go to the gym 4 times a week, but I also like bouldering, kayaking, skiing, and cycling. I have one or two rest days per week.

What advice would you give to an 18-year-old who has no idea what to do with their life?

Start reading. Believe in yourself. Surround yourself with positive people, avoid the negative ones. If you want to go on an adventure, you have to be convinced that's the life you really want, because it ain't easy. And if you do so, don't become a self-absorbed asshole!

Find out more about Mikael:
www.mikaelstrandberg.com
facebook.com/explorermikaelstrandberg
instagram.com/explorerglobal

Travel is a School in Living Together

*In 2010, **BRIAN MATHÉ** went on a bicycle trip around the world together with his friends, Siphay Vera and Morgan Monchaud. They didn't stick to 'ordinary' cycling, but along the way sailed to Antarctica, kite-cycled the Australian outbacks, climbed mountains, and cruised the river Yukon on a self-made raft. After coming home, the friends kept on exploring the world, writing books, and making films about their adventures.*

"I recommend young people to not do what is possible or logic, but to pursue what you really love."

Brian, the Adventurer

As opposed to the archetypical temperamental and fearless adventurer, I'm a rather introverted and reflective person. I very much like reading and journaling, especially on expeditions. I'm rather easy to live with, which is a good thing in collective adventures. I like to propose original ideas, which sometimes turn out very well. My biggest flaw is that I can be too much 'head in the air' and thus lose or forget things.

Alone We Go Faster, Together We Go Further

In 2011, I joined my childhood friends, Siphay and Morgan, in Chile for a trip around the world. This trip would eventually last three years. Although the three of us knew each other for over a decade, we discovered new sides of the other – and ourselves – we hadn't seen before. These discoveries were the result of living on each others' lips in moments of extreme beauty, as well as cruel hardship. Sometimes, these were dark sides. The hardest thing about collective adventures is probably learning how to live together. Effective and positive communication is not something present and well-understood in our culture. We don't get taught specific techniques for this in our educational system. Our adventures have schooled us in this. They've taught us a lot about dealing with other people; accepting that nobody is perfect and also putting yourself in question. Sometimes, for long periods of time, someone had the feeling of not being listened to by the others. At these times, we started feeling useless, or even counterproductive, to the collective. This way, self-doubt, and fear arose. We had to learn to surmount these moments by means of non-violent communication: not keeping things for ourselves too long, being honest about our feelings, sending out messages without hurting others, setting the ego aside, and thinking in terms of the collective.

Of course, traveling with your best friends also has a lot of advantages. I joined Morgan and Siphay for our around-the-world tour when they were already traveling for a couple of months. If they wouldn't have come up with the idea of cycling around the world, I might never have gotten into big adventures. I've also experienced that having friends alongside you eases physical suffering. When you know the guys next to you are having a hard time as well, but don't crack, you're able to push your own limits further. Encouraging each other helps with this as well.

One experience of what a well-coordinated and motivated group can obtain stays with me forever: going down the river Yukon on a self-made raft. At first, I wasn't into the idea. But, I said to myself that if this is what the group wants, I should give them confidence. I let go of my doubt and joined my friends in their quest for enjoyment. The 700 km on the Yukon turned out to be one of the best experiences of my life. It has been one of the many examples supporting the proverb: "Alone we go faster, together we go further."

Trust In the Road
In 2011, Siphay, Morgan, and I rode the 2,500-kilometer-long Transamazonian, a terrible dirt road in a tropic climate. Right from the start, we found ourselves with a broken hub on one of the bikes. In a region where you can't find bike shops, this normally means big trouble. Thanks to teamwork and people along the way helping us out, we managed to go to the end anyway. In moments of uncertainty like this, I like to keep the mindset of 'having trust in the road'. You never know who you'll meet, who will help you out, or even which opportunities will come out of the difficulties.

When traveling by bike, the generosity of people is unbelievable. As the French author Pablo Servigne underlines: *"L'être humain est prédisposé à l'entraide"* (English: people are predisposed for mutual support). On the road, this statement is so often confirmed. I especially remember the hospitality of people in Central Asia. Certain ethnic groups consider the possibility of receiving a traveler as God's gift. I'm not religious, but I have indeed had the pleasure of feeling sacred. For example, in Tajikistan's Mountains of Heaven. Often, these people had very little means, but they received us with a big heart. I'm very thankful for them because without them our road would not only have been more difficult but also less fun.

The Rule of Three
Unfortunately, we aren't champions in physical training. In our opinion, you don't have to be a trained cyclist in order to cycle around the world. You just have to start off easy, applying the 'rule of three'. When you're not specifically trained, you'll suffer a bit during the first three days of your trip. The idea is not to abuse your forces so you stay injury-free. After three weeks, you start to feel really good but – because your body needs a lot of nutrients to build muscle – you find yourself eating a lot. After three months, you're in excellent shape, ready to conquer the world.

Less is More
When we left for our around-the-world trip 10 years ago, we knew this involved renouncing comfort. We had to learn to be satisfied with the essentials of life. The more you travel, the easier it gets. The simplicity of life on the bike serves us up until today. However, we have to admit that it's very easy to adapt to comfort when coming back home again. Man easily adapts to everything, scarcity as well as opulence. It helps to remind ourselves why we're living a simple life; because it means freedom to us. Less is more. We don't have unnecessary subscriptions running and don't buy bulky and useless gadgets. Stuff we don't use anymore gets sold or donated. Our wardrobe is the equivalent of 2-3 full washing machines. We're happy with that.

How do you deal with the danger of adventures?

During our adventures, we've escaped death a couple of times. The majority of these cases were cars and trucks taking us over leaving no space in between. Being hit by a car is a very frequent cause of death amongst bicycle travelers. We have very little control over this risk, though it happened – when we observed drivers acting too crazy – that we chose to take another road or jump into a truck instead of cycling.

While doing adventures, we feel very much alive. The downside of the coin is that some disciplines (alpine climbing, for example) always involve a risk of dying. Recently, we started parasailing, a sport with a high number of accidents. I think it's important to be humble in the face of risk. In advance, you have to define where your limits are and don't go beyond them on the terrain. When you're hesitating, it's important to not let pride get you from renouncing. If possible, share your doubts and fears with the leader of the group and your team members. This creates constructive discussions preventing us from making mistakes or taking too much of a risk.

What advice would you give to an 18-year-old who aspires to a life full of adventure?

Instead of doing what is possible and seems logical, go towards what you love. Accept that to arrive at remarkable results, you need effort over a prolonged period of time. No big results are easy to achieve. And actually, when you're doing what you love, no effort does really feel like one. Along the road, it's normal to get discouraged. Although I have difficulties applying it in reality, I like the idea of 'discipline equals freedom'.

The most difficult thing about adventure is getting paid for it. You need to figure out intelligent strategies to feed yourself. Working part time might be a good idea. For our trip around the world in 2010, we had to rely on our savings. The deal was: working two years to travel three. Thanks to the books and movies that resulted from this trip, we've been able to continue exploring, but it's still not 100% sufficient. We still have to exercise a 'normal' job every now and then. With the experience of writing, filming, and composing stories, we've recently created an audiovisual company that further helps us meet ends. Anyhow, if you're just starting out, don't bother approaching big companies for your upcoming project. Mostly, that's just a waste of time. Act first.

Love Matters

When kicking off our world trip ten years ago, each one of us was single. Having no stable relationship for three years felt like a big absence, but we knew it was the price to pay. Nowadays, we aspire for more of a normal couple or family life. We're now aiming to do shorter projects which don't interfere with this aspect of life too much. We don't have kids yet, so that makes things easier. We now made a deal with our girlfriends: two months on an expedition (most often with *Solidream*) followed by two months of living as a couple together. When I'm adventuring with my friends, my girlfriend keeps busy with her own projects. So far the deal seems to work out very well.

Find out more about Brian:
www.solidream.net
facebook.com/solidream
instagram.com/solidream_team

Good is good enough

As a teenager, JELLE VEYT was homeless, living in squats and eating out of dumpsters for 3 years. But Jelle got out of the misery, became a physiotherapist, and took up a big challenge that turned out to be a life-work: going to each of the Seven Summits starting off from his front door, fully human-powered.

"Human-powered doesn't only mean I'm not using motorized vehicles, it's also a realization of hundreds of people working together."

Life's Work

When I started off *'The 7 Summits Of Happiness',* as I call my project, I was quite naive. I thought the project would take me 5 years to complete. I had the idea I would rush through it. The reality turned out to be different, with a lot of obstacles along the way. The thing I had underestimated the most is the administration and practical difficulties that come with it: obtaining visas, getting permits, mapping out routes, finding the finances . . . We're 9 years later now, and with 4 summits under my belt I'm only just over halfway. When I'm talking to the public, I often joke that adventurers with little time don't live long, you truly need to have patience. If I would have to give advice to my 16-year-old self, I'd tell him: "Jelle, it's ok to be driven, it's ok to go for something hard, but that doesn't mean you have to want to get it quick. Be patient." Nowadays, I really consider *'The 7 Summits Of Happiness'* as a life's work. I've accepted that it will take me very long and I've made the vow that I will complete it unless something really bad happens, an external factor by which I end up in a wheelchair or something like that. That's the only thing that can make me quit. Actually, today I welcome every obstacle and look at it as another challenge, every difficulty shapes and strengthens me in some way. Although, I admit this demands a huge sense of perspective. But I still find the project pleasant.

What's your definition of happiness?

Good is good enough. If you want to be happy, you have to be able to accept that things are going just well. Not constantly aiming to go higher, faster, better . . . Not comparing as well. Don't compare with previous situations in which you had more or felt better, and don't compare with others that have more. That's advice I heard from the Dalai Lama by the way.

A Human-Powered Adventure

When I came up with the idea to go human-powered to *the Seven Summits,* I admit there was a big egocentric component in my motivation. I wanted to show the world what I was capable of. Pretty soon, I realized that it was not at all about me. And it's not all about climbing *the Seven Summits* either. There's much more behind it. It's about the journey, about the connection with people and nature. About learning about myself and the world. About really 'feeling' the world; feeling rain, heat, cold, fatigue, hunger . . .

304

Nowadays, human-powered reflects the power of humans working together. It's me standing in the spotlight, but literally, hundreds or maybe even thousands of people already played their role in the success of it. For example, I've raised over €40,000 for a good cause – a foster home in Nepal called 'Shangri La Home' – now. But often, it's actually not me raising the money. Sometimes, school children would sell waffles to collect money for the foster home after I gave a talk in their classroom, or sponsors would organize a party and fund the profits . . . In these cases, my role is very small.

There are also a lot of people helping me out from 'basecamp' at home, as well as people on the road. One example, when I was rowing to Papua New Guinea to climb Carstensz Pyramid. I was the first man rowing on certain parts of the ocean. Because of the lack of information about this section, I had to rely mostly on the knowledge and advice of the local islands' inhabitants. Despite their help, I was surprised by strong currents. At a certain moment, I started hallucinating (I had been rowing for 35 hours non-stop and was very dehydrated) so I called my girlfriend on the satellite phone and asked if she could try to contact local fishermen. A few moments later, a fisherboat came and dragged me to the safe shores of an island.

Risk
Despite hallucinating on an ocean and being caught in an earthquake on Everest, I consider climbing my first mountain as potentially being the most dangerous thing I've ever done. In the early 2000s, I cycled from Belgium to the Pyrenees with my older brother. With our youthful enthusiasm, we decided to climb the highest peak of the Pyrenees: the Pico de Aneto. We were both wearing running shoes and had never put on crampons or used an ice axe, but there we were crossing a slippery glacier in our runners. At a certain moment, big clouds appeared in the sky. My brother wanted to continue but I decided we'd better go back to the refuge halfway up the mountain. We had no experience at all, so my proposal to turn back came out of pure intuition. It turned out to be the right decision because a big storm hit. The following day, we made it to the summit and thereafter safely back down. It's only afterwards – by following mountaineering courses – that I realized how stupid we had been that day. We didn't have the right shoes, nor the right equipment, nor technical knowledge about the equipment we did have with us. For me, using an ice axe seemed evident: "If I slip, I just stretch out my arm and try to plant its point into the ground, like serving a tennis ball . . . " Not the right way of course.

The more experience I gain, the more conscious I become of the risks. By preparing myself as best as I can, I try to limit the risk almost solely to external factors. The avalanche on Everest was much more detrimental to my life than the situation on Pico de Aneto, but I had nothing to blame myself for. In the row to Papua, I might have gone too far physically. But because I had prepared well, I knew that my hallucinations about entering a bay couldn't be real. And because no one had ever rowed over there, the strong current couldn't be foreseen. The fact that I made it out there alive, is also because I had an emergency plan . . .
Nowadays, in face of every dangerous situation, I make a risk/reward analysis: is the gain I'll get out of this worth the risk? I think that's something very few people in society do. So many people are driving too fast in their car only to win a couple of minutes, while at the same time putting the lives of themselves and others on the line. I lost one of my best friends this way, involved in a hit-and-run . . .

My family deals quite well with me being in risky environments. My mom always tells me: "I know you will make the right decision, Jelle." My older brother gives me confidence as well, referring to the storm situation on the Aneto where I was the one deciding to not take any risk. They're also used to me doing crazy stuff from a young age. For my girlfriend it's much more difficult. She's more concerned, and she tries to hide her fear because she wants me to fulfill my dreams and not feel bad . . .

Do you train your mind and spirit?
Yes, quite recently I started meditating. I have a scientific background as a physiotherapist, so when things get too wooly I tend to opt them out . . . that's why spirituality and meditation weren't really my cup of tea. Until I read a book called *Siddhartha's Brain,* which talks about the science behind meditation. It describes all the proven benefits of meditation on health and well-being. This book got me into it and now I do really believe that meditation can help adventurers. Because on an expedition, you not only have to be good in the action, but also in resting and recovery. For example, before a summit push, you're always very excited. It's definitely useful if you have tools to calm down. Meditation is probably one of the best tools, but you have to practice it in advance . . .

I'm also doing a sort of mental training at home by pushing myself. For example, I would go out for 4 hours on the bike on a snow-rainy day, come home, eat something and have a warm beverage. At that moment, every brain cell and every muscle vessel is screaming to take a bath and spend the rest of the day on the couch. So what do I do? Get back on the bike and ride another 2 hours. This way, I mimic the conditions of an expedition, where you often have to push through on moments you feel like giving up.

Humility
When I'm not on my adventures, I work as a physiotherapist in Belgium. It happens that I meet other adventurers who're able to make a living out of what they do. One of the best ways to do so is by speaking engagements. I think, as is typical for Belgian people, that I'm too humble to sell myself. My parents weren't salespeople. They didn't have a commercial mindset, so it just wasn't a part of my upbringing.

At the time my parents were about to break up (I was 17 at the time) there were a lot of fights at home. My brother and I no longer wanted to live in this ambiance and went living in a squat. Down there, I experienced real poverty. I learned to get through the day with very little. I guess that's why today I'm still living as a minimalist and I'm giving most of the money I earn away to the non-profit organization 'Shangri La Home'. The 'Shangri La Home' is a foster home in Kathmandu, founded by 2 Belgians: Inge Bracke and Paul Jacobs. For most of my speaking engagements, I ask €500. Nearly all of the profit goes to the home. Actually, it's only recently that I've started asking for an expense allowance to pay for my transport. At least now I no longer lose money by telling my story. I'm glad that I've managed to find sponsors who help me to fulfill my dreams. Thanks to them, *The 7 Summits of Happiness* is a zero-sum game. It wouldn't feel right to me to earn a lot of money on top of this. Especially not on the pretext of doing the project for a good cause. It bothers me that there are more than a few misleading adventurers who use the money they collect from the public to finance expensive expeditions. For example, they sell a story of climbing Mount Everest to raise money for a good cause, but they don't tell people that the first €40,000 raised goes into the expedition costs.

Everest

When I was studying physiotherapy at Ghent University, I had a friend called Tenzing who has a Nepalese father and a Belgian mother. He lived in Kathmandu and had come to Belgium to go to University. After graduation, he created a private practice in Kathmandu and I decided to join him. But I didn't want to take the airplane, I wanted to go there by bike. So I did. Along the way, I also climbed Mount Elbrus, the highest mountain in Europe. During this trip from Belgium to Nepal, some people talked to me about a Swedish adventurer called Goran Kropp who had cycled from Sweden to Nepal in 1996, followed by climbing Everest. Hearing Kropp's story made me dream even bigger. I came up with the idea to travel to each of *the Seven Summits* human-powered and climb all of them.

Once I settled in Nepal, I soon became part of Tenzing's family and had the good luck that his brother Dawa owns an expedition company (read the interview with Dawa Steven Sherpa on page 90). Dawa wanted to help me out in fulfilling my dream project, but not in vain. I had to work for it. I was of icially registered as a sherpa and was handed the tasks of communication manager between basecamp and Kathmandu. I also volunteered as a so-called 'icefall doctor', this meant I had to prepare the summit route together with more experienced sherpa's. We had to make a trace in the snow and install ladders over crevasses.

I needed three attempts on Everest. The first time, in 2014, I had to cease my climb because of a strike of sherpa's after 16 of them had died because of an icefall. The year after I escaped death during the massive earthquake. I might have been lucky to have the right connections in Nepal, and I acknowledge that not having to pay for climbing Everest has been of huge importance in the realization of my project. But it has also been a massive test of resilience and patience, and I had to work for it.

Dreaming

Little by little, gates are starting to open to make money in a way that feels right to me. I've been contacted by a publishing agency that wants to help me to write a book about my adventure and life story. I also started thinking about life after *'The 7 Summits of Happiness'* and would like to create a project to help people follow their passion and ful ill their dreams. I think there will always be people with a lot of money inspired by my story. It'd be great if I could be the catalyst that makes them invest in a project that realizes the dream of less fortunate people; street children, or drug junkies for example.

I notice that very few people have a true passion or a big dream. Or at least not the kind of dreams I have. One of my brothers started a family, his dream was: cottage-garden-child. If that's what you want, that's great. But I think there are a lot of people who might have big, adventurous dreams but let fear stop them.

I receive very few negative comments on what I do, but the ones that come through are almost always about me being so lucky and wealthy enough to do this. I think those comments aren't valid. I see it simply as a matter of choice. I choose to not have a car, not to have a home. When I'm on an adventure, I hardly have any fixed costs left in Belgium. The funny thing is that it's almost always young people giving me criticism. The elderly find it amazing what I do. They tell me I'm making the right choice to follow my heart and do what I want to do. I guess retirees are more aware of how short and vulnerable our life actually is, and we better enjoy it. This being said, I am very aware that my life is very insignificant in the history of the Universe, so neither do I take it too seriously.

Favorite Quote
This one comes from Seasick Steve, a homeless man who turned into a popular singer-songwriter: "I was born with nothing, and I still have most of it left."

Find out more about Jelle:
www.jelleveyt.be
facebook.com/Jelleveyt.veyt
instagram.com/jelleveyt

Very Rarely, Things That Are Worthwhile Are Just Given To Us

*When **GEORDIE STEWART** turned 17, his father gave him a book about Everest. It was the start of a dream that would lead Geordie to become the youngest British person to have climbed the Seven Summits, by the age of 22. After a five-year military career, he left on a 22,500-mile long solo bike trip around the world. Geordie wrote two books about his adventures and is currently training for ultrarunning.*

"Maturity ties in with identity. Once you understand who you are, you no longer feel the urge to do what the others are doing."

Drained and Hungry on the Streets of Nairobi

I spent half of my childhood in the countryside of Hampshire and half of it in Scotland. I've always been active. I was constantly running around in the fields and climbing trees. I enjoyed a lot of different sports such as football and cricket. In some way or another, I naturally looked up to sportsmen and adventurers. I remember giving a lecture at school about Ernest Shackleton when I was only 11 years old.

When I turned 17, my dad gave me a book about Everest. I was captivated by it. Not much later, I made it my goal to not only scale the tallest mountain on the planet but to climb the highest mountain on every continent. As a result, while plenty of my peers were taking traditional gap years, I went on my first expeditions to Aconcagua, Kilimanjaro, and Elbrus. Of *the Seven Summits*, these were the 3 least expensive expeditions to organize. For many months, I worked seven days a week in order to save money. Nevertheless, after my second expedition to Kilimanjaro, I was completely broke. The night before catching my flight home, I spent on the streets in Nairobi, drained and hungry. I couldn't pay for food or accommodation and my bank card was declined when I put it in the ATM. You might think, at that moment I would ask myself what the hell I was doing with my life, pursuing this seemingly unreasonable dream. Yet, those thoughts never came to mind. I had a clear goal, so for me, that lonely, hungry night in Nairobi felt like a normal sacrifice.

After hiking Kilimanjaro, I went back to work again in order to save money for a guided expedition on Mount Elbrus, Russia. When I came back from scaling my third summit, I enrolled in University. I put my *Seven Summits* ambitions on the shelf for a while. I tried to embrace student life for the first few months and everything that entailed, but after one semester, my mindset shifted back to the *Seven Summits*. I then tried to balance being a student and socializing, while running in sand dunes and dragging a sled on the beach to train for my expedition to Denali.

The expeditions to Denali, Mount Vinson, Carstensz Pyramid, and Everest are very costly. There was no way I could just take a student job and save up enough money for those. I sent out hundreds of sponsor requests and received hundreds of negative replies. For a guy in his early twenties that was a tough pill to swallow. On top of this, I failed on my first attempt on Everest. A series of dangerous events forced me to turn back just 150 meters from the summit. I remember being really discouraged after it. Not only because I had not reached the summit, but also because I would need to put in many hours of knocking on company's doors once more if I wanted to go back.

The Legs Underneath Us

When I announced my plan to climb *the Seven Summits* at age 17, my parents were supportive and worried at the same time. My dad understood my mentality and grasped why setting myself a big goal like that could be rewarding. My mum, on the other hand, struggled to understand it as much. For her, it makes no sense to completely exhaust yourself by doing hill sprints, or to collapse on the floor after a long bike ride . . . only in the pursuit of climbing a mountain. Nonetheless, she's extremely loving and supportive in her own way. As an athlete or adventurer, your lifestyle is inherently selfish. It demands that you make sacrifices that are often to the detriment of those who you love. Not every parent or girlfriend understands that. But it is so important, almost necessary, to have mental support from the people around you. It gives you stability. The people close to you are the legs underneath you.

Free Soldier

After the success of my second attempt on Mount Everest, I had realized my dream of climbing *the Seven Summits*. The question arose about what I was going to do next. Continuing the path as an adventurer and trying to make it a living was attractive, but I didn't want to be identified solely as an adventurer. Many people I've admired in life have been polymaths. In this regard, I didn't want to be labeled as 'an Adventurer'. So instead I chose to enter an environment where it wouldn't matter that I had climbed *the Seven Summits*. An environment where I could start as a nobody. One that would put new challenges on me and where I could be of service. I chose to become an army officer and entered the Royal Military Academy Sandhurst.

After 5 years, I felt a greater constraint with army life. Perhaps it came to labeling again and not wanting to be identified solely as an Army officer. Identification is what happens when you're in the army. You get a military ID and a uniform, but I wanted to be free.

With this spirit, I decided to leave on a bicycle trip around the world. I calculated that my savings would be enough for two years of cycling on a shoestring budget. I made the conscious choice not to have sponsors involved in order to feel completely free.

The same day I handed in my military ID, I left on my trip around the world. It was a crazy, hectic period with not much time for planning beyond the overall aims of where I wanted to go. I remember my mum crying just before I stepped out of the front door, saying "It's odd saying goodbye to someone and not knowing when you'll see him again." I didn't really know how to react. I climbed onto my bike. But on the inside, I felt bad, almost guilty.

After a couple of days cycling, I luckily managed to let go of the guilty feeling and get the headspace I wanted. My first goal was to reach the South of France, where I would meet up with Ben Saunders and his wife (read the interview with Ben Saunders on page 276). From there on, I just kept on focusing from checkpoint to checkpoint. A checkpoint could be a certain country I was really looking forward to, entering a new continent, or a meet-up with friends living somewhere on my route.

What are the biggest lessons that adventure has taught you?
Accepting uncertainty. In the West, we want to control everything. But when you're traveling, that approach doesn't work. You have to be flexible, able to adapt to the circumstances. This being said, for every situation, I try to have a contingency plan, a valuable lesson I picked up in the military.

Another thing I've learned is that there's amazing value in setting big goals and pursuing them step by step. Although it demands a whole lot of sacrifices, patience, and hard work, there's a real joy to be found in the process. In life, very rarely things that are worthwhile are just given to us. A lot of people who see pictures of people standing on the top of Mount Everest or at the finish line of an ultra marathon imagine it must be an incredible feeling to accomplish such a feat, not realizing that that picture is just the tip of the iceberg. Underneath are years of dedication and hard work.

Another valuable thing I learned through traveling and adventure is the importance of communication and the realization of how wonderful human interaction can be. Thanks to my *Seven Summits* project, I learned to understand and communicate with sponsors, sherpas, and teammates from across the world. Thanks to my bicycle trip, I learned to be vulnerable and let my life depend on the goodwill of strangers.

Maturity is Identity
I've written 2 books: *In Search Of Sisu* about my *Seven Summits* project, and *A Rolling Stone* about my bicycle trip around the world. *In Search of Sisu* is quite a vulnerable, in-depth narration about my transition from teenage life to adulthood.

I think my *Seven Summits* pursuit taught me to deal with the highs and lows that come with realizing a dream. Partly this was because I was always the youngest team member, so I could learn from amazing people with far more life experience. When I entered Sandhurst afterward, I noticed my *Seven Summits* project had fast-tracked my process of maturity. I felt less of a need to compare myself with others. I didn't feel as if I had to do the same things. I had my own identity and acted according to what I felt was the right thing to do, not to impress someone or to be part of the herd. For me, maturity ties in with identity. Once you understand who you are, you no longer feel the urge to do what others are doing.

What do you hope people take away from reading your books?
Having the belief that it's worthwhile to set big goals and pursue your dreams, and that anyone is capable of doing so. I hope reading my books can inspire people to diverge from the "normal", well-recognized path and instead dare to go on the journey they really want. Have faith in who you are and what you're capable of. I also want to show that people achieving big

things aren't superhuman. They have weaknesses too. It's often the case that people achieving the most are the ones with the most mental issues and use these challenges as a coping strategy. In this perspective, I think it's important for adventurers like me to share our weaknesses openly, as I do in my books. One; because sharing it helps us to accept our weaknesses. Two; it makes us own the narrative: yes, we have flaws and insecurities, but we're aware of them and are taking action to deal with them the best way possible.

How do you deal with fear?

I instinctively try to manage fear in a rational way. When I feel fear emerging, I try to understand the situation and make a plan to deal with it. Probably yoga – something I have done since my teenage years – helps me to stay grounded. The one fear that stands out to me still is the fear of heights. Walking on a ridge makes me experience the most genuine form of fear I know. The only way I've found to cope with it is to focus on every single step I take because I know that every new step will provide a sense of security.

If you could go and grab a beer with 3 people, dead or alive, who would you choose?

Ricky Gervais, Bob Dylan, and Barack Obama

What's your definition of happiness?

That's a really tough one. I don't think I'll ever find the right answer to it. 'Being content with who you are, being loved and loving others' is the closest definition I can get to.

Find out more about Geordie:

www.geordiestewart.co.uk
instagram.com/geordie_stewart

I Want to Feel Intensely Alive!

MATTHIEU TORDEUR sailed across the Atlantic Ocean, did a world tour in a Renault 4L, competed in the transcontinental bicycle race, hitchhiked the length of Argentina, cycled across Eastern Europe as well as on the Karakoram highway and across the Sahara Desert, motorcycled on the highest mountain pass in the world, ran the Marathon des Sables as well as a marathon in North Korea and skied solo to the South Pole. Though, Matthieu is only 28 years old [at the time of writing in 2020].

"As a child, I was inspired by the comic books of 'Tintin'. Tintin inspired me to become an adventurer too, so I decided that I better start early."

Tintin

As a child, even before I could read, I loved to flip through the comic books of *Tintin*. I got fascinated by the pictures of *Tintin* doing heroic actions all over the world and as soon as I was able to read, he almost became an obsession. I wore *Tintin* t-shirts, I had *Tintin* posters hanging up in my room, I slept on *Tintin* bedsheets . . . When I say to people today that I got inspired by the adventures of *Tintin*, that's not just to create an interesting story. It's the absolute truth. I didn't want to become a hero like him, but I was very much attracted by the idea of adventures and globetrotting.

As I grew older, I got inspired by other adventurers as well, though I never had real "heroes." One of the most influential people in my life has been Jean-Louis Etienne, the first man to go to the North Pole solo in 1986. Many years later, I was honored to have Jean-Louis as the Peter of my South Pole expedition. Another inspiring person was my mom. Both my parents are doctors. For the last 20 years, my mom has left home to go on humanitarian missions all over the world as a doctor. My dad started doing the same a couple of years ago now. So as a kid, I very soon got used to seeing my mom closing the front door to go to Asia or Africa or so on, and hearing amazing stories when she came back. This definitely increased my own thirst for adventure even more.

From Student to Adventurer

At age 19, I went on my first real adventure: cycling solo from Budapest to Istanbul. At that time, I sure didn't have the idea to become a professional adventurer. But I knew I wanted to travel a lot in my life, see deserted places, and go on expeditions. So I said to myself: "I better start early on because if I want to get good at this, there is a lot of experience to be gained and a lot of skills to be learned." But since I was at University, my adventures were limited to summer holidays. I worked as a waiter to finance them. Little by little, I learned how to approach sponsors, how to get visibility on social media, and how to be an interesting storyteller. In 2013, my childhood friend Nicolas Auber and I left for a tour around the world in a Renault 4L to promote entrepreneurship by micro-financing. This has been my first adventure that was less or more professionally organized. We managed to get great sponsors

313

on board. We made a movie about it, wrote a book . . . This adventure was a huge learning experience that prepared me well for everything that followed.

I've always been interested in geography and international politics. It wasn't by chance that I went to study European Studies at King's College London, followed by a Master's degree in International Security in Sciences Po Paris. These studies evoked my interest to discover rare destinations such as Sudan, Iraqi Kurdistan, Kirghizistan, and North Korea. I wanted to see and feel by myself what it's like to live in these remote areas. Besides, my higher education helps me in my life as a public speaker and adventurer today. It made me feel at ease in an international company. My English got fine tuned, I learned useful communication skills, I built a network . . .

After my studies, I worked sporadically for *Doctors Without Borders*. This was awesome because I was surrounded by nothing but adventurous spirits. I got inspired by their courage, their commitment, and their drive. On the other hand, *Doctors Without Borders* is a big NGO. This involves a hierarchy, strict rules, and a clear task description. I don't fit in very well in these organizations. I like to have my freedom and make my own choices.

Skiing to the South Pole

On the 13th of January 2019, I became the youngest person in the world and the first Frenchman to have skied to the South Pole, solo and unsupported. This was the adventure that gave me the biggest visibility in the media. I think partly because I was the youngest and the first French person, but also because people are fascinated by the solitary aspect of it. Solitude is something most of us don't consciously search for in our life. So, for most people, it's hard to imagine what it would be like to be all by themselves for two months, without other people, without roads and buildings, even without animals. When I am asked the question of how this solitary experience felt, I answer that I felt very small, but at the same time very privileged. I also felt very intensely alive.

In total, I spent 51 days on the Antarctic ice. But in fact, this was a five-year-long expedition. I prepared extremely well. I went on expeditions in Norway, Svalbard, and Greenland. This way, I was used to the cold beforehand. All the needed skills were automated and I knew I could fully trust my equipment. As a result, I never felt scared in Antarctica. Then, after coming back to France, the work wasn't done yet. I got invited for interviews, I had speaking engagements, released a film . . . We're almost two years later now, and I've just finished my book about the expedition.

Do you prefer solo or team expeditions?

Hmmm, I like both of them. They are very different. The cool thing about team expeditions is that you have a lot of fun. There's also a real sense of brotherhood. On the other hand, I love the freedom of solo expeditions. You don't have to take into account the preferences of others. You get to make your own choices; when to eat, where to sleep, when to rest, which trajectory to follow, when to push a bit harder . . . The downside is that you don't have a backup, and you can make the wrong decision, with big consequences. But I guess, to answer your question, I have a slight preference for solo adventures anyhow. That's where you really get to dig deep. As a result, you discover who you really are.

Who are the most important people in your life?

First of all, my parents of course. When I announced to them as a 19-year-old that I would cycle across Eastern Europe, they were surprised. But, they didn't push back and even helped me with the preparation of the trip. Since both of them are adventurous spirits, they understand my need for the outdoors. They also noticed that from very early on I was preparing every expedition thoroughly. This comforted them in my safety and also in the fact that I wasn't just a wild dreamer but instead put in the essential work to organize my adventures as professionally as possible.

I also have a very tight-bounded group of friends I know from secondary school. They are really solid, we go on quite a lot of micro-adventures together. And then, at last, there's a growing ecosystem of adventurers in France and beyond who really support each other. You probably notice it by writing your book, but adventurers seem to be a race of people who have the willingness – even desire – to share their knowledge and inspire other people. This way, we really pull each other upwards.

What makes you a great adventurer and public speaker?

It's always difficult to judge yourself, but I think that I have a good capacity to adapt. As an adventurer, you have to be able to adapt. Conditions change all the time. I manage to stay less or more at ease under all circumstances.

Secondly, I'm a good communicator. That's really essential in this business. There are mediocre adventurers who know how to tell a story, who have a lot more visibility and merits than some amazing adventurers who do incredible things but don't know how to sell themselves. Communication is such an important skill, you need it to find sponsors, to tell a story by means of a book or a movie, and to speak in public. I'm also convinced that you always have to be honest in your communication. For instance, when I wanted to ski to the South Pole, I wanted to do this just for myself, to fulfill a childhood dream. I could have disguised my real intention by promoting a good cause or spreading a message about climate change . . . but I chose not to do so because it would not have been sincere. I had the impression that sponsors appreciated this. The story of a 26-year old guy who wanted to fulfill his childhood dream appealed to them more than enough to support me.

A Pregnant Woman in Antarctica

As a public speaker, I mostly work with companies. From all my streams of income, this is the most profitable one. But sometimes I also go to schools and speak in classrooms. This can be really fun to do. Over there I get to deal with very different, sometimes really amusing questions. Recently, a boy asked me: "If a pregnant woman skis to the South Pole and she's having a baby on the way, is that baby then called Antarctican?" (laughs)

The Easy Way to Be an Adventurer

Often people look at my life from a distance and think it must be amazing. They suppose I spend my time crossing oceans surrounded by dolphins, kite skiing on endless ice fields, and witnessing the Northern Lights. But what is visible in documentaries, on my website, and in the media is only a very small fraction of my life. Most of the time, I'm at home, at a desk, doing research on the computer, talking to someone on Zoom or on the phone . . . That way, being a 'professional adventurer' isn't that different from most other jobs. It's really hard work, actually.

When people who don't like their job ask me how to become an adventurer, I advise them to search for a job they like and go on adventures during the holidays and on micro-adventures during the weekends. And then, every couple of years, do a sabbatical in which you go on a big trip for several months. That's a formula that is actually easier than doing it my way.

What's your definition of happiness?
Being able to live the life you really want, having the freedom to do so. And also, experiencing a lot of moments where you feel intensely alive. Life is short, you know. I want to delight in being alive as much as possible!

If you were obligated to live on a deserted, uninhabited island, and you're only allowed to take 5 objects and 2 people with you, what and who would you choose?
I would take my childhood friend Nicolas. I already drove around the world with him. We went cycling together in the Sahara desert and motorcycled in the Himalayas. I know I can tolerate him and rely on him for a long period of time. Instead of a second person, I'd rather take a dog actually. All my life, I've been surrounded by dogs. I think their company would come in handy in that situation.

When it comes to the objects; probably a knife, a diary, and a pencil. And an inflatable buoy or something like that; anything that could help us to escape from the fucking island! (laughs)

Find out more about Matthieu:
www.matthieutordeur.com
facebook.com/MatthieuTordeurAventure
instagram.com/matthieutordeur

As Soon as We Had Our Son, I Felt an Urge to Try to Impress Him

SEAN CONWAY *ran, swam, sailed, and cycled the length of Britain, climbed Mount Kilimanjaro in a Penguin suit, and completed a 4,200-mile long triathlon. Along the way, he broke World Records, as well as his spine. Now, he's thinking about building his own rowing boat and crossing an ocean with it.*

"I am normal, I've been tested, there's nothing superhuman about me. What probably sets me apart is that I can endure the pain more than others."

How a 30-Year-Old Got Back to Living With His Mom

As a kid, I dreamed about traveling the world as a National Geographic photographer. So, eager to pursue my childhood dream, I became a photographer. But soon, I found myself stuck in London shooting school portraits. I was far away from that daring, traveling photographer I thought I was going to be. When I turned 30 I felt miserable and sold my share of the photography business for 1£ to my business partner. At that point, I asked myself what I really wanted to do. I wanted to travel, but I had fallen out of love with the camera. So, I had to think about something different. I didn't have enough resources to take a gap year and enjoy life abroad, so I reflected upon a way to find sponsorship. Trying to break a World Record would lead me there, I thought. I immediately aimed big and tried to break the 'around the world cycle record'. In order to do so, I had to go all in. So, I sold pretty much everything I had. I left my apartment and moved back in with my mother, in a one-bedroom flat. That first year when I was training for the world cycle tour, I was grinding with enormous determination. No social life, 40 hours a week on the bike . . . It was a hard year in every aspect, but mentally I was really strong.

From Zero to Hero

I always looked at record-breaking adventurers as if they were astronauts . . . like something that just couldn't be done by a normal person like me. In 2012, after this one year of extremely hard training, I set off with the goal of breaking the World Record of cycling around the world. Three weeks in, I was ahead of schedule with a daily average of 180 miles. But then I got run over by a car in America. I suffered severe whiplash, a concussion, torn ligaments, and a compression fracture to my spine. This ruined my dream of breaking the World Record, but I still wanted to continue in order to follow my dream and raise money for the charity *Solar Aid*. My average speed dropped down to 140 miles per day. I didn't break the World Record, but riding 12,000 miles with a broken spine changed my perception of what was possible. In my whole adventure career, cycling around the globe is probably the project that has made me grow the most as a person.

After this project, I tried to go back to "the real world." I worked as a photographer again for a little while, but I felt that the only thing that would fulfill me was another challenge. So, I decided to try to swim the length of Britain, about 900 miles. This was such a hard expedition to get off the ground because nobody believed it would be possible. Sponsors turned me down, telling me I would die trying it. I used social media to find a three-headed crew and a small boat and set off from Land's End. The physical challenge was grueling. I had to grow my beard to protect me against jellyfish. I got frostbite-like injuries to my toes because of the cold. All four of us got seasick and I almost got crushed against the rocks at Cape Wrath, surprised by a sudden storm. That could have been the end . . . Despite all this suffering, I experienced some wonderful moments as well: I swam with dolphins and seals, I had a unique view of the British coast, discovered tiny hidden coves and explored shipwrecks, and had a lot of nice evenings with the crew in pubs along the coastline. From everything I did, this is definitely the adventure I'm the proudest of. This project also involved a financial shift. At the beginning of my journey as an adventurer, I focused on spending less instead of earning more. It was my only option. No hotels, no restaurants, no pubs, no vacation . . . After swimming around Britain in 2013, I kind of started to do adventure full-time. I got sponsorship deals and earned money by writing books and speaking engagements. Nevertheless, the income was very insecure and fluctuated quite a lot. I would eventually stay at my mothers' flat until age 33 and would then move into a small boat.

Training 70 Hours per Week and Other Keys to Success

Because I don't have A-levels and I didn't go to University, it's difficult for me to get a job. So, when I gave up photography, adventure became less or more my only option.

Believing that it's going to be a one-off helps. If you believe you're going to do this crazy amount of training only for one year, it's easier to not see your mates that much . . . because in your head it's like "I'll be doing this kind of thing just once, thereafter I'll have a life again."

I don't let failure be an option.

Everything that I do has to be unique and interesting.

I am normal, I've been tested, there's nothing superhuman about me. What probably sets me apart is that I can endure the pain more than others.

I'm also good at bouncing back from setbacks. That's a skill you can learn actually. You can learn to change your thinking of the past and convert it into positive thoughts about the future.

In hindsight, carrying on after the accident in the U.S. was the best thing I could have ever done.

I'm pretty practical. I always ask the question 'What can I control, what can't I control?' Then I focus on what I can control.

Keep putting yourself into stressful situations. The more stressful situations you go through, the stronger your mind becomes.

Run without music, take ice baths, practice sleep deprivation.

Finding sponsorship is mainly just networking. Meeting people, contacting people online, going to events, and making friends . . . Most of my sponsors came out of friendships. Of course, the better you get, the easier it becomes.

My wife and I eat plant-based food most of the time. Fridays we eat fish, Saturdays can be anything, Sundays we like a roast.

I don't set an alarm clock. I let my body tell me when I got enough sleep.

I never go to the gym. I don't follow proper training programs. Now and then, I use the treadmill and stationary bike, but I prefer going outside. Training goes from 10 hours a week up to 70 hours a week. I try to do a big training block of three or four weeks of 70 hours in preparation for a big goal. During these phases, I go out from sunrise until dark, each day.

Being Unique and Interesting
[Sean grew up in Zimbabwe and South Africa]
I had an adventurous upbringing in the Mana Pools National Park together with my conservationist game ranger father, Tony. I spent my early years climbing trees and chasing elephants out of his garden. I suppose that this unique childhood has been the fuel for my adventurous ambitions. It also got me involved in charities and wildlife foundations.

[Sean climbed Kilimanjaro dressed in a penguin suit]
I raised money for an environmental charity by walking up the highest mountain of Africa dressed as a penguin. It was a great experience with friends. My one continuous problem was the giant yellow feet covering my shoes. These soon got wet and muddy which meant they kept getting caught on rocks which would make me lose balance on some pretty steep climbs. They soon looked all tattered. This would have been a great excuse to take them off but I had committed to wearing them the whole way and wasn't going to back out. No matter how hard it got.

[Sean has his own bicycle brand]
Basically, I was looking for the perfect touring bike for me. The perfect touring bike for me is steel-framed, lightweight, and suited for fast touring. A fast and comfortable bike that would allow me to ride 200 miles a day. I noticed very few options on the market. So, I contacted the amazing bike designer Simon Stanforth and we created my dream bike, called *the Stanforth Conway*. With this bike I can tour with less than 15kg of weight, camping gear included.

[Sean wants to build his own rowing boat]
I love woodwork, and a future project in the back of my head is to build my own rowing boat and row a big ocean.

[One day, Sean will live on an island]

Of course, I do already live on an island (Great Britain), but It's a dream my wife and I have to live on a remote island and be self-sufficient. Our son is now one year old, I guess we'll have to do it before he starts school. So, that'll be pretty soon.

Who are you thankful for?

First of all, I want to thank Martin and Missy Carry, the doctor and nurse who were on duty when I got run over in America on my cycling-around-the-earth project. They took me in and looked after me for a month while I recovered. I owe them so much, because of them I could carry on my bike ride . . . and I wouldn't be a full-time adventurer today without them.

Of course, I owe a lot of thanks to family and friends as well. In the early days, family and friends thought I was weird. They thought it was a stupid idea that I was pursuing this adventure dream . . . but now they see I'm a better, happier person when I do these big things.

I work with some amazing partners that have been supporting me for a long time. I really believe that sports sponsorship is such a good platform for businesses to reach a wide audience. Putting money on someone who's doing a great challenge is a much better idea than paying for advertising in a magazine.

About Being a Father

I don't do any longer, dangerous things just for the sake of them being dangerous. There has to be a bigger goal. When you're young and you don't have a family, you kind of accept that your adventure comes with risks. Since I'm a father, the idea of longevity is a lot more present in my mind. On the other hand, I have to take some risks. I want to teach my son that taking calculated risks is important.

As soon as I got my son, I felt an urge to try to impress him. I became this hungry hunter that wants to get out and do stuff my son can look up to. I had expected that I would want to become more of a home-dad. But, weirdly enough his birth made me want to do even bigger projects, projects that will inspire him and lots of other kids . . . I don't have a big ambition for the world, I never think about a legacy. All I want is to have my children and grandchildren look back and say: "Wow, that granddad Sean sure was a bit crazy."

What advice would you give to an 18-year-old who doesn't know what to do with their life?

You still have another 12 years to find it out (laughter). I've wasted my time chasing the wrong dreams and that was a shame. The fact that an 18-year-old should know what he's going to do for the rest of his life is simply crazy. So, my advice would be: "Don't worry about that. Relax, go traveling." Traveling broadens your mind. It's a social development tool, you learn to understand other cultures, you learn about yourself.

I once heard a quote, I think it came from a Chinese businessman, that went something like this: "In your twenties: try different things, learn a lot. In your thirties: start focusing on a single thing and learn from a mentor. In your forties: you should have a good understanding of what you're doing. Focus on that thing and become successful. In your fifties: you can start looking at giving back and mentoring others. In your sixties: start thinking of slowing down and focusing on giving back."

How do you make adventure your profession?

Basically, you must be a storyteller. If you want to make a living of it, people have to pay for your stories. I sell my stories in book format, in TV documentary format, and in talk format. There are other ways as well: by being a YouTuber, by being a blogger or a vlogger, by being a journalist. Accept that it will take a lot of time and patience. In the beginning, you have to do lots and lots of work before you'll see any results. But if you do the legwork, you'll eventually find a way to sell the stories.

Find out more about Sean:
www.seanconway.com
instagram.com/seanconwayadventure
facebook.com/MrSeanConway

I Am Nemo

PAULA REID sailed around the world, skied to the South Pole with two frostbitten thighs, obtained a Masters' Degree in Positive Psychology, and is currently cycling across 50 countries, executing 'one good deed' in every one of them.

"The more I'm challenging myself with these hard adventures, the more I get the idea that the human potential is nearly limitless."

Live Life to the Full

I have a bucket list full of challenges on my website. I call it my 'live life to the full' list. From the age of 18, I started looking back at the calendar of every past year, taking notes of the moments that had made me feel the most alive. After a while, I thought: "Why don't I plan these kinds of highlight moments in advance?" I hoped that this proactive approach would set me up to have more of them. In the beginning, the challenges were rather small, but executing them made me gain confidence. So I started dreaming about big expeditions. This is how I eventually sailed around the world and skied to the South Pole. Today, I have completed 118 of the items on my list. There are still 56 left. Skiing to the North Pole and rowing the Atlantic Ocean are two other big projects I'm thinking about.

Often, the simplest adventures are the most beautiful; wild camping, swimming in a winter lake, hiking in unknown terrain. It's easy to have fun. It's easy to be a child again. One of the silliest things I've done was zorbing – rolling down a hill in a plastic ball – you can't imagine how much fun it was. Also, just sitting still in nature, watching a river, feet in the grass, looking at the beauty of the landscape, noticing the butterflies around you . . . these kinds of moments in nature bring us fully into presence. They strip away the noise, the clutter in our head and make us realize how beautiful this world is.

I would encourage everyone to create a 'live to the full' list. You can make a list alone, or with your partner or family. Life is such a precious gift; we should make the most use of it. A 'live-to the full' list definitely encourages us to do so.

The Big Adventures

When I was 16 years old, I went to India with seven other students and two teachers. We went to very remote places, where they had never seen white people before. This has been my first spark for traveling. At age 18, I took a gap year. I went to some of the typical backpacking places; Nepal, Thailand, Australia. But I also spent a lot of time in Indonesia, away from tourist spots. After my gap year, I started working in a travel agency. It wasn't that special. Mostly I was organizing trips to Spain and Greece. At the same time, I did some more adventurous trips by myself until I came up with the idea to sail around the world. I registered for *The Global Challenge* in 2004-2005. *The Global Challenge* is the toughest yacht race in the world. It's very dangerous: you encounter tornadoes, icebergs, 22 meter high waves. And there's the social challenge; you have to live 24/7 with 18 people on a 25-meter-long boat.

Skiing to the South Pole in 2015 was a completely different challenge. It demanded 100% of my energy, 100% of my focus. I had to pull an 80-meter sled in -40°C temperatures for 46 days. Every mistake I could make would be detrimental. For example, if you take off a glove, you can lose your fingers because of frostbite. I actually got a non-freezing cold injury (NFCI) on both of my thighs. While everyone was recommending that I quit, I knew that I absolutely wanted to continue. So I did. This definitely increased my resilience. Sailing around the world and skiing to the South Pole had totally different dynamics. Nevertheless, I consider them as having been equally hard and difficult. Both of them taught me that I can do anything I put my mind to.

How much of your full physical and mental potential did you use during these expeditions?

Hmmm, difficult question. The more I do, the more I know I can do. Humans are really amazing . . . I would say, maybe 80% . . . However, it might be that our potential is more like a bottomless well . . . like we can never get to the edge of it because every hard experience increases our potential . . . I've read Victor Frankl's *Man's Search for Meaning*, about surviving in concentration camps. The psychological and physical pain and deprivation those victims had to endure probably comes close to 100% of what is possible for the human race . . .

The Hero's Journey

Another book that has influenced me is *The Hero's Journey*, written by Joseph Campbell. If you look at human evolution, we're designed to challenge ourselves, to progress. In almost any ancient tradition, there have been rites of passage from the youth's world to the adult's world. The hero's journey is also the red line in a lot of fairy tales and Disney movies. Think about Nemo; a small fish going out on a huge adventure with courage and determination. According to me, it's very important to go on your own hero's journey.

I divide human experience into three zones: the comfort zone, the stretch zone, and the panic zone. The zones come with a scale of challenges. When you're in your comfort zone, you're living 'Zero to Two challenges'. Think about activities such as watching TV, answering emails, loading the dishwasher. You might feel quite pleasant and relaxed in your comfort zone, but there's not much growth in it. Spend too much time in the center of your comfort zone, and you languish. The panic zone is the other end of the spectrum. They're the 'Nine or Ten challenges'. In this zone you're worried, stressed, in fear, out of control . . . it's not a place where you want to be. In between the comfort zone and the panic zone, there's the stretch zone. This is where the growth happens. In the stretch zone, we learn, we're excited, we feel the buzz. You can stretch a little bit, searching for 'Three or Four challenges'. Or you can stretch a lot, like a Seven or Eight.

I'm convinced that it's very important for everyone to go out of their comfort zone and stretch. First of all, doing things out of your comfort zone will make you grow. It will expand your comfort zone and it will make you proud. Secondly, the world gives us surprises. We can't escape difficulties such as epidemics, natural disasters, and illnesses. If you've never gone out of your comfort zone, when these bad things happen, how can you ever expect to be able to cope with them? We need to keep stretching, like an elastic band, to keep supple and not go brittle with lack of use.

Personally, I like the Seven to Eight stretch. It's where I have to dig deep, to show grit and mental toughness. These are the moments where I feel most alive, where I feel the proudest. I love to search for these peak experiences. Having the courage to go out into the world on a big adventure is my realization of 'the hero's journey'. Actually, I am like Nemo. (laughs)

Positive Psychology

During my adventures, I noticed the impact of my mindset during times of hardship. I felt as if my attitude affected 99% of my performance. This made me curious to learn the science underneath it; so I started a Master's degree in Positive Psychology. In 2018, I graduated. For my dissertation, I researched the benefits of adventure. I've discovered that the three phases of expeditions – before, during, after – all have positive effects. In the preparation phase, you get to go knowingly into the unknown. You're slowly building up knowledge which turns the original anxiety more and more into excitement. In the second phase, during the adventure, you can be who you really are. You experience a sense of liberation, self-reliance, and flow. One of the participants of my dissertation told me: "I once had to sleep in a ditch. I had no money, no food, but it was the happiest moment of my life, because I felt completely free." In the third phase, when you come home, you've got this sense of pride and wisdom, but there's also the danger of falling victim to the 'post-adventure blues'. Our adventure has been like a drug. We became hooked, and now it's over and we have to adapt to the 'normal' world again. To prevent the post-adventure blues from striking too hard, it's best to slowly start planning the next one.

Tips and Tricks

People can live in one of three different mental states at each moment, during adventures, or in life in general. The one we want to avoid as much as possible is the survival mode, where we feel anxious and tight. The best thing to do in this phase is to forget about long-term plans and to focus on the next best step. A second phase is a coping phase. Here we feel in control, we're managing the situation. The third mode is thriving. When we're thriving we feel fully alive. We're growing and learning, and we're more able to help people. However, it's hard to influence which state you are in. You can make use of the 'think-do-feel-triangle'. What we think, how we act, and how we feel are interrelated, they influence each other. So if you want to feel better, more confident, more energetic, it helps to think constructively or do something that energizes you, like listening to pumped-up music.

Look at fear as your friend. It's a sign of our body to be careful, so be curious about what it wants to tell you.

I wrote down two mantras on my skis when going to the South Pole: "Choose your attitude" and "Pain is temporary, pride is forever."

I make use of anticipatory thinking. I visualize the whole adventure and especially things going wrong. If you have a scenario for when things go wrong, and you run this through in your head in advance, you won't freak out when this really happens. You'll have spare mental capacity and you've rehearsed what to do.

I also talk with people who have already done the things I want to do. For example, before going to the South Pole, I asked other explorers detailed questions about what was going on in their bodies and minds the moment they arrived on the ice, how they went to the bathroom, how to set up the tent, etc. I gather as much detailed information to improve my anticipatory visualizations.

I don't have explicit meditative practices, but being present has become a lifestyle for me. I'm trying to be really mindful and aware, in nature as well as in daily life.

Favorite Books
Man's Search for Meaning, by Viktor Frankl
A New Earth, by Eckhart Tolle
The Hero's Journey, by Joseph Campbell
Becoming a Person, by Carl Rogers

If You Want to Do What Paula Does
When people approach me and say something like "I would really like to do adventure X or Y, but unfortunately I don't have the money, I have to take care of my kids, I can't take those risks, I can't leave my job, etc.", I used to be very sensitive. I used to think through a solution with them. But honestly, these are all just excuses. When I wanted to sail around the world, I had to quit my job for a year, the project cost £30,000, I would miss my friends and family for one year, I knew it would be dangerous and my mother wanted to kill me. On top of this, I had never sailed before. Despite all of the reasons not to do it, I went. Because I knew it would be the biggest, best, most enriching experience of my life. So really, just bloody go for it and stop making excuses!

Find out more about Paula:
www.paulareid.com
instagram.com/ThePaulaReid

I Wasted Many Years When I Was Young and Lazy, Which I Regret

JAMES KETCHELL rowed solo across the Atlantic Ocean, summited Mount Everest, cycled around the world, and flew around the world in a gyrocopter. His secret to a life full of passion:

"I'm not sure if something sets me apart from others. I think you need to want something badly. When you want something badly enough, you will always find a way to get the funding, learn the skills required, and find the time to do it."

How did you come to the point of making adventure a major part of your life? Was this a one-moment decision or a gradual process?

It was a gradual process, I never woke up one day and thought: "I'm going to be a professional adventurer." I have always wanted to row across the Atlantic Ocean ever since I was young. The prognosis that I might not walk again after a motorcycle accident in 2008 was the push I needed to do it. I then met like-minded people in my preparations and one thing led to another.

What were the most difficult moments in the building-up of a lifestyle based on adventure and travel?

It was certainly financially difficult, and also mentally. It took me a long time to get my head around pushing myself as my own brand. Even now I don't always feel comfortable with it. Socially it was tricky as well. When people asked me what I did for a living, I'd often tell them I worked in sales as sometimes it was just a pain to tell my whole story.

Over the years, I had to sell many things, including motorbikes and cars. Over time, I've learned that these material possessions are not that important. On the other hand, I have found relationships particularly difficult. Long periods of time away and putting 100% of my energy into expeditions can make it hard on a partner. They may be left feeling undervalued and not important.

What are the most dangerous moments you've encountered during all of your adventures? How did you deal with the danger?

In 2015, I was rescued while rowing the Indian Ocean. Climbing onto a rope ladder on the side of a 100,000-ton crude oil tanker in storm-force winds was extremely dangerous. It was something I could have not really prepared for or replicated in training. It was the adrenaline and I believe a higher power that guided me and my rowing partner through the experiences, without any harm.

Another dangerous moment was descending Mount Everest with pneumonia. Without my Sherpa, it's unlikely I would have made it back down again. I was quite unwell but somehow managed to keep moving. Also, the second time I had to be rescued while rowing, in the Atlantic Ocean, was particularly frightening because I knew what was coming.

The _____ Expedition

Most beautiful: Cycling around the world. The people I met and places I experienced were truly amazing. But actually, all expeditions have been beautiful. I'll never forget some of the sunsets I have experienced at sea on a calm, beautiful evening. The views whilst climbing Everest were also stunning.

One that made you grow the most: The expedition that made me grow the most would be flying a gyroplane around the world. There was no room for any errors and it was tiring and stressful at times.

One that made you the proudest: Rowing solo across the Atlantic.

Most memorable: The memories that will stick with me forever are the different people I have met on my travels.

What were the biggest setbacks you've had in your adventure career?

I have had three large-scale adventures not go my way. I have been rescued in the Indian and Atlantic Oceans. I had a failed attempt to row around the coast of Great Britain. It was extremely demoralizing, but I simply didn't give up and decided to work on a project to gyroplane around the world. Thankfully that worked out. I completed the project in 175 days, having flown 24,000 nautical miles.

How do you stay in shape, mentally and physically?

Physically, I train every day and I log my food intake into a diary. It's only over the last few years that I have taken nutrition more seriously. I wish I had done so years ago. On average, I try to sleep for 7 or 8 hours. I find that too much sleep makes me feel tired, lethargic, and unmotivated.

When it comes to my mental health, I try to read as much as possible. At an absolute minimum, I read for half an hour every day. This helps give me clarity to carry out the various tasks of my day and leaves me with a calmness of mind.

What personality traits do you have that are crucial in your success? What sets you apart from others?

I'm not really sure what sets me apart, to be honest. I tend not to spend too much time looking at what other people are doing. I think you need to want something badly. When you want something badly enough, you will always find a way to get the funding, learn the skills required, and find the time to do it.

Who have been the most important people in your journey?

People have come in and out of my life with different projects. So it's hard to pick out one person. My parents and mentors have properly made the biggest contribution. There will always be one person out there that will believe in you. That's all you need.

How do you get your projects financed?

I do not have a "real" job. I make a living through speaking at events. All of my projects are funded through sponsorship. I am asked a lot about how I go about gaining funding. Here's the answer: I approach companies with a business project plan, outlining what I call the four 'W's'. 1: What am I doing? 2: Why am I doing it? 3: What can I offer a sponsor? 4: What do I want? This is the basis of all my sponsorship proposals. I then simply play a numbers game and contact thousands of different companies. If this process is followed, you will get funding. It will only fail if you become disheartened when you don't get the interest you hoped for and give up.

Inspiring Young People

I want to inspire as many young people as possible to go out and achieve their own goals and dreams, whatever they may be. I tell them not to worry, to focus on doing something they enjoy. It's not sustainable to do something because an older person or someone else told you to do something because they think it's the right thing for you to do. Above all: maximize your time. No matter what happens, you'll never get that time back. I wasted many years when I was young and lazy, which I regret.

If people want to make a career in adventure, it's totally possible. There is so much opportunity out there. It's unlikely to happen overnight. But, if you put a plan together and execute that plan with a strong work ethic, you will be able to build a dream life of adventure and travel. However, it will not always be easy. You will need to develop the ability to do things when you do not feel like doing them.

Find out more about James:
www.jamesketchell.net
facebook.com/james.ketchell.7
instagram.com/ketchelljames

Iraq Is Less Dangerous
Than McDonald's

Mike Spencer Bown is the most traveled man on earth. After several years living in the wild, Mike decided one day that he wanted to see every ecosystem on earth. He took the bull by its horns and backpacked for 30 years, thereby visiting every country on this planet.

"I mostly prefer going to war zones and living with ancient tribes."

Losing Identity

I grew up in an ordinary Canadian family. As a kid, I spent most of my free time outdoors with friends, playing games, having fights. In high school, I had very good grades and my teachers told me I didn't have to come to school. So I just went when I had a test and did what I wanted to do for the rest of the time. After high school, I went to University, but pretty soon I got bored and decided to live in the wilderness. For a couple of years, I would live up to six months in the woods and then go back to civilization for a couple of months.

In the wild, I've experienced very impressive things happening with the human psyche. I can tell you that there are two ways to be human: the human as a wild animal, and the human in the camp. The latter is the only version most people in western civilizations get to know. There's a very clear timeline for the transition process from camp-man into wildman. After 24 days alone in the wild, you lose the habit of compressing words into thoughts, you stop using language in your head. After 40 days, you're actually dreaming the reality around you, you know which movements the animals around you are going to make. For example, when a bear is approaching you at night, you'll dream about that. During the daytime, the subconscious and the conscious mind melt together and you're in a constant state of daydreaming. During this daydreaming, you're sometimes having visions about the future. They're actually warnings that something is seriously wrong. For example, once I had a vision of a skeletal arm coming out of mud. What this was telling me is that I had to pay more attention to my water supplies. After 65 days, all sense of self disappears. You only need a self when there are other people around you. After 65 days, you lose your identity and become truly one with nature.

Coming back to civilization after months in the wilderness is very difficult. It's like learning a foreign language. You have to study how to become normal again. It takes the same amount of time to adjust as the time you spent in the wild; if you've been three months in the wilderness alone, it takes three months to feel normal in society again. If you've been six months in the wilderness, it takes six months to re-adapt. The biggest problem is that when you come back you can read people's minds. You get a deep insight into the person in front of you. You can read their thoughts just from their facial expression. That's really interesting, but also very exhausting and it makes people feel uneasy. I've lived with several tribes in the Congo and other places, and I've seen they have the same capacity to read people's intentions. In those tribes, quite often, people get banished. I assume that through evolutionary history this must have been the case as well. My speculation is that being able to understand the intentions of others is a fixed skill in our DNA, because when you're banished from a tribe and you come into contact with civilization again, it's useful to know other people's intentions. If you would come back to your original tribe, it's best if you can sense whether they're ready to welcome you again. If you bump into another tribe, you have to be able to judge very quickly if they would be willing to accept you or instead intend to kill you . . .

$100,000 in a Backpack

I've found it easy to make money. I spend about 5% of my time making money, and 95% of my time traveling. Every three to five years, I look for a product in some country, ship it to another country and make massive gains. This way, I make a couple of tens of thousands of dollars in just one or two months of work. For example, in Japan I found out that some people were selling wood from coffee trees. They almost gave them away for free. I brought the wood to a furniture manufacturing place in Bali and told them I wanted low-to-the-ground tables made of this wood. I continued my travels, came back after a couple of months, and bought the tables from the manufacturer for ten dollars each. I sent them to Seattle and went to some furniture selling companies and asked for $40 per piece. The companies said to me "We don't know if we want to spend $40 per table." I answered that these weren't ordinary coffee tables, they were coffee coffee tables, because they were made out of coffee wood. Saying this one funny thing was enough to make the companies buy 500 tables. Another time, I made a lot of money by selling statues of chickens made in Indonesia. Due to an economical crisis, the value of the Indonesian currency had dropped by 90%, so I flew there to make use of the economic opportunity. I found a wood carver who had statues of chickens that looked high quality. I asked him if he could make thousands of them. Sure enough, a couple of weeks later I came back, paid one-and-a-half dollars per chicken, shipped them to Vancouver, and sold them in shopping centers for six dollars. This way, I made $120,000 in 20 days.

In the 90s, there weren't ATMs in most countries. Traveler's checks or bank cards were useless. Often, I left for two to three years of traveling. My only option was to stuff all the money I needed for that time period in a bag and carry it with me, and then some in case I saw a business opportunity. This way, I often carried $50,000 to $100,000 with me in a bag. Once I was stopped at the airport, the police said: "Mr. Bown, we found a big amount of cash in your bag." I said: "It better be, I put it there." (laughs) Next, I had to explain all of my travel plans to the police officers. . .

What are you afraid of?

Not really anything, actually. For example, the COVID-19 lockdown we're experiencing at this moment [I interviewed Mike in spring 2020], I find it completely unnecessary. There's a 3/1000 risk of dying. The risk of dying from malaria is three times higher. Do you think African people stay confined under a mosquito net?! I think the governments should have distinguished amongst people, along with the Swedish model where only the vulnerable people got confined. For example, I have a friend who's a DJ. All summer long, he won't have any income because there will be no festivals, while the risk of dying for young people is probably something like 1 out of 10,000 . . . That's a risk a lot of people would be willing to take in order to enjoy themselves at a music festival . . . I've got the impression that people have forgotten that you don't get through life alive.

In 30 years' time, this obligated lockdown is the first thing that has stopped me from backpacking. I don't agree with it. I'd rather take a small risk of dying, continue traveling, and have interesting experiences. I've been in Afghanistan during the war. There was a road they called 'the death road'. Locals told me there was a 30% chance of dying if you took that road. I think they were exaggerating, it must have been about a 5% risk. I was willing to take that big a risk because I wanted to see the mountain range where the death road headed to. Actually, I often seek out civil war zones because they're cheap places to hang out. But you have to find the right kind of conflict areas. If it's too severe or there is too much media attention, prices skyrocket.

Humans are not as dangerous as people think. If you use common sense, you can move around quite safely everywhere, even in conflict zones. I've found my time in the wilderness much more dangerous, because of wild animals and the risk of starvation.

I've been arrested quite a lot, but I always managed to find a way out by making jokes and being friendly. The worst was in Somalia, where they thought I was a terrorist. People from the government even came to threaten me. Eventually, I managed to make friends with them and got out. At the same time, there was an American guy who was held much longer because he couldn't talk his way out. Once I had managed to convince the people of the government that I wasn't a terrorist, they made me a guest of the country and protected me with soldiers while I was visiting interesting places. This kind of 'armed tourism' where I got protected by armed police officers or the military has happened to me several times.

Real Risks

I read a lot during my travels; mostly it's about history or science. I've found the journals of early explorers such as Henry Morton Stanley and Richard Francis Burton very interesting and useful. Traveling by myself also helped me understand what they were talking about. Stanley, for instance, talked about how difficult it was to stay well-nourished in Africa. When I was traveling through the African wilderness, I experienced the same.

Living with tribes has delivered me some of the best moments of my travels. It educated me about human nature. I think people in the West have become weak, mentally and physically. We can no longer deal with hardship. Most ancient tribes have rites of passage from boyhood to manhood. Some of them we shouldn't have given up. For example, I would like to see modern societies bring back the torc. The torc is a Gallic tradition. It's a metal ring that's a little bit open, worn around the waist. The rule would be that if you couldn't wear your torc, you couldn't appear in public and participate in social or political gatherings. People who had become too lazy and fat to wear their torc were considered to be dishonorable because they were no longer able to defend the tribe. Today, we're facing an obesity epidemic that's much more serious than COVID-19. If we would have the old barbarian tradition of the torc, it would deal with it. it would prevent us from becoming too relaxed and growing a beer belly.

Often people tell me I take a lot of risks. But when I look back at some of the people telling me this, I'm thinking "You're taking even more risks." In the U.S., about 40% of people are obese. They carry 20, 30, or 40 kilograms too much weight with them. That's an extreme risk. You can die at any moment because of a heart attack or stroke. I've been in Iraq, Afghanistan, and Somalia during wartime, but I think it's much riskier to go to McDonald's every day. At least, my risks are interesting, they are fun. Eating a burger and drinking coca-cola every day is a boring and much more severe risk.

A Life Well-Lived

Most people today want a very soft life. But I find that life to be very boring. For me, the definition of a life well-lived is to do things that are interesting and repeat them over and over, it's about taking risks that come with adventure and challenges. I wouldn't like to live in a utopia, that would be like hell to me. There's a quote that says something like this: "In a world where all adventure is removed, the last adventure is to destroy society."

Find out more about Mike:
www.mikespencerbown.com
facebook.com/mike.s.bown

I Am Happy For No Longer Being a Full-Time Adventurer

TIM MOSS is a British adventurer. He conducted challenging expeditions in deserts, polar environments, and high mountain ranges. At the antipode of these extreme athletic feats, Tim's creativity led him to original challenges such as hitchhiking on a 100-pound budget, breaking a Guinness World Record for 'the Longest Distance Cycled on a Rickshaw', and traveling around the world using 80 different methods of transportation. Despite these accomplishments, Tim decided to return to a "normal" job and kept adventuring as a hobby.

"Nowadays, I no longer feel guilty about indulging in adventure activities"

(No) Interest in Adventure

At school, I was given the opportunity to go on an expedition to Africa but I declined. I just had no interest in the idea at all. But, I did enjoy some outdoor activities. I spent my summer holidays walking across the UK's National Parks and wild camping with friends. By the time I got to University, something had obviously changed because my imagination was captured by a poster which read: 'Expedition grants available for students'. I applied, won, and went on a climbing trip to Kyrgyzstan. It opened my mind to the big world that exists. I have never looked back since.

Staying Away From Danger

On that first expedition, mountaineering in Kyrgyzstan, I got into lots of scary situations. Falling down snow slopes at 5,000 meters and dangling on a rope when my ice axes lost their grip, for example. Although I loved the trip as a whole, I did not like those dangerous moments at all. I swore never to put myself at risk like that again. I have been mountaineering since – in Russia and Bolivia – but have always been more controlled and avoided anything I considered to be too dangerous. I like the thrill of exploration and trying new things, but I have no interest in danger.

Who have been, and currently are, the most important people in your life?

My wife Laura has easily been the biggest influence on my life, both personal and professional. The early days of our relationship involved lots of adventures. Our first date involved a wild winter swim. Not long after, we started our attempt to run the length of every London Underground train line. We had a second honeymoon trying to walk across Patagonia. We later quit our jobs to spend a year and a half cycling around the world.

We now have a son, so our adventures need to accommodate him and the way in which our lives have changed, now that we have more than just ourselves to think about. Our biggest trip with him so far was a month spent cycling around the Baltic states and on to the Åland Islands.

Around the World in 80 Ways

In the summer of 2005, my friend Thom and I completed a journey around the world using eighty modes of transport. It was the result of a brainstorming session in a remote wooden hut in Bolivia, high on expedition-related endorphins and low on blood sugar. This was my third and final consecutive summer holiday at University. Thom and I set ourselves the goal of getting all the way around the world without using the same method of transport more than once. That didn't include buses around town and that sort of thing. But we did stretch the rules a bit by including an electric train, a steam train, and a diesel train . . . Nonetheless, in time for the very definite deadline of my brother's wedding, the two of us stormed our way across the globe at speed. We racked up our 80 modes of transportation and had some wonderfully odd encounters en route. We raised a few thousand pounds for the TreeHouse School on our way and, as a result, I was given a Year of the Volunteer Innovation Award.

These were our 80 different ways of transportation:
    Steam Boat Willy, human-powered hovercraft
    Mobility Scooter
    Red London Bus
    Pogo Sticks
    Shoe Skates
    Toy Car
    London Underground
    Car Hitchhike
    Catamaran Ferry
    4×4 Jeep
    Catamaran Sailing Boat
    Jet Ski
    Cessna Light Aircraft
    Sinclair C5
    Tractor
    Fire Truck
    Dumper Truck
    Hovercraft
    Unicycle
    Ferry-Port Shuttle Bus
    Cross-Channel Ferry
    Big Green Hippy Van
    Lorry
    Human Wheelbarrow (in the Louvre)
    Novelty Bike
    Watering Machine
    Dotto Train
    Diesel Train
    Conference Bike
    Free Running
    Velo Taxi
    Forward Rolls (in front of the Reichstag)

S-Bahn
Tram
Coach
Digger
Trolley Bus
Piggy Back
Trans-Mongolian Railway
Horse
Camel
Climbing
Hopping (past a Ger hut)
Steam Train
3-Wheeled Pickup Truck
Cable Car
Pigeon Steps (inside the Forbidden City)
Rickshaw
Tuk-Tuk
Battery-Powered Bus
1st Class Train
Evil Henchmen Shuttle Pod
Elevator (to Cloud 9, Shanghai)
Domestic Flight
Minivan
Hydrofoil
Funicular Railway
Pedestrian-Powered Rickshaw
Escalator (World's Longest)
Double Decker Tram
Leap-Frog (in front of the Hong Kong skyline)
Swimming
Coast Guard Caterpillar Rescue Vehicle
Star Ferry
Airport Golf Buggy
Mobile Floor Polisher
Boeing 747
Bicycle Sidecar
Jeepney
Horse & Cart
Cartwheels (in Paco Park, Manila)
Airbus
Hire Car
Freight Ship
Moon Walking
Channel Tunnel Train
Army Crawling (past the House of Parliament)
Black Cab

Mobile Dustbin
Walking (back into the Quad)

The Next Challenge Grant

I received many expedition grants when I was younger. They helped me undertake some fantastic adventures, which have helped shape the person I am today. This led to me wanting to give something back. In 2015, the 'Next Challenge Grant' was born. Each year, over £1,000 is collected by crowdfunding, gifts from other adventurers, and by my own contribution. Applications are open to anyone, anywhere in the world. The focus is on people who have not done many adventures or expeditions before. I typically choose around ten winners each year.

Getting Back a "Normal" Job

Being an adventurer was a struggle financially because I was naive and never gave any thought to money. I had no business plan and, indeed, a real aversion to charging money. A bigger issue was a mental one though. Working at home alone all the time was much more isolating than I realized, even at the time. I am an introvert but having no colleagues and no regular interactions was not good for my head. This lack of contact with other people, combined with the impact that not making any money was having on my already low self-esteem, finally led me to depression. Today, I'm no longer a full-time adventurer and I am much happier for that. Although being an adventurer theoretically meant I had more free time, I never had any money to do anything, such as going out for lunch or buying a drink at the pub. I would feel guilty if I did go away because I felt like I should be earning money instead.

Now I have a normal job, four days a week, and do the adventure stuff in my spare time. Despite having reduced time for adventure, I have still managed to cross a frozen lake in Siberia during my two weeks' annual leave, spent a month cycling through the Baltics and Scandinavia thanks to paternity leave, and completed a round-the-world bike trip in between jobs. I also get a monthly paycheck, which is much better for me than trying to chase money. I no longer feel guilty about "indulging" in adventure activities.

Find out more about Tim:
www.thenextchallenge.org
facebook.com/thenextchallenge
instagram.com/nextchallenge

Life Lives Itself

*When **Don Read** decided to retire, he and his wife **Alison Armstrong** knew they wanted to travel the world. The only question was how to pay for it. To find a solution, Don started writing morning pages:*

"For a couple of days, all that came out of my pen was garbage. But then, all of a sudden, I came up with the idea to sell all of our belongings. The answer was so obvious. When I told Alison about it, she was immediately enthusiastic."

Falling in Love

Don: I met Alison in 1994 when I was giving a workshop for therapists in Vancouver. From that point on, we developed a relationship as friends for 4-5 years. We did a lot of activities together; watching movies, walks in the park, having a drink together. However, there wasn't any physical attraction. All we felt for each other was friendship. We were a listening ear for each other. We were both single and our most recent previous relationships had been terrible. We both vowed never to get into another relationship again. But then, suddenly, one evening everything changed. We were in a restaurant after having seen a movie together. Alison went to the bathroom, and when she got back I had this feeling of electricity in my body. I knew that I was in love. Later, Alison told me that she'd had the same experience at exactly the same moment.

Jumping Off a Cliff

Alison: I've traveled a lot throughout my life. I grew up in a traveling family in Australia. Throughout my twenties and thirties, I traveled to Western Europe, the US, and Canada, and also traveled overland for four months in Africa and four months in South America.

Don: I was born and raised in the UK, in a conventional family. In my early 20's, I intuitively felt that I had to make a big change. I decided that I would move abroad, and was left with the choice between Canada and Australia. In Australia, I knew nobody, but I had a friend living in Canada so I chose to go there.

Alison: On the surface, it might look as if I am more adventurous than Don. I never had a conventional career. I traveled a lot and always let myself be guided by life. At one point, in my mid-thirties, I was left with only 19 cents in my pockets. That's all I had, but I knew I would figure a way out. However, what I was trying to say is I think Don is just as adventurous as me. He has never been willing to be categorized in a certain box and stay in that box for the rest of his life.

Don: It's true. When I was 29 years old, I left my corporate job and for the first time went to University. It felt like that was the thing I just had to do. I had no idea how I would pay for it, but I trusted that that would take care of itself . . . And it did. Nine years later, I graduated with a Ph.D. in neuropsychology. I retired in 2011 because my job was starting to burn me out. It was time to jump off the cliff again. We knew we wanted to travel a lot, the only obstacle was how to find the money for that. A friend of mine suggested that I write 'morning pages', an activity in which you let your subconscious mind speak by writing three pages of everything that comes up in your mind. You do it first thing every morning. On the first two days, all that came out was garbage: practical concerns and financial worries about this idea of traveling. But then, on the 3rd day, I wrote down "We could sell the apartment." All of a sudden the solution was clear.

Alison: I agreed immediately. Our friends were more concerned about the outcome than we were. We sold our house and most of our possessions. What was left – winter clothing, photo albums, camping gear, file boxes – went into a small storage locker. Only four months after making the decision to leave, we got on a plane to Italy.

Don: Actually, for me, it was only a couple of years before I retired that I got the travel bug. We had planned to go on a 6-week trip to Oceania; visiting the Cook Islands, traveling to New Zealand, and spending time with Alison's family in Australia. And then, intuitively, I had a strong feeling that we should also go to Vietnam to visit a good friend who was living in Hanoi. For me, Vietnam was by far the most exotic place I had ever traveled to. Seeing the people of the hill tribes in their traditional clothing made me realize what traveling was really about. I can't exactly explain why, but in Vietnam, something shifted. From then on, I understood why people like Alison were fascinated by traveling.

Alison: When we took to the open road in 2011, our first destination was Italy. I wanted to see the Temples of Humankind at Damanhur, and Don dreamed about Tuscany.

Don: Since then it has been an amazing journey. We traveled as nomads for almost six years. We saw so many beautiful places and did so many fun things. For me, the best memories are the moments when I felt most alive. Where I stepped way out of my comfort zone: going in a boat under Iguazu waterfalls in South America, parasailing in Mexico, climbing a volcano at night in Bali, ice trekking in Patagonia, zip lining in the Amazon jungle. I felt more alive in those six years than I did in all the 68 years before.

We Don't Need All That Stuff
Alison: One of the biggest lessons that travel has taught me, is that we really don't need all the stuff we're collecting. Last year we visited the holy city of Rishikesh, in India. It was our third visit to India. The first time was a real shock. There are beggars everywhere. It gave me a very bad feeling inside, a contraction as if something was wrong. But then, it made me think that we're all born in certain circumstances. These circumstances determine the choices we have in life. For a lot of these beggars, this is the best choice they have. When I understood this, I started looking at these people differently. I started seeing them as people whose job was to beg for money and food. My feeling of discomfort disappeared. When I go out on the street in Rishikesh now, I make sure to have a pocket full of small change with me to hand out.

Don: I remember this one disabled woman in particular, she had a deformed body and couldn't stand up. Every time we saw her, we asked how she was doing. Each time she answered – with a big smile – that she was doing great. Another phenomenon in India are the *Sadhus*, the ascetic men who isolate themselves from society and try to reach enlightenment through meditation. They are homeless and most are living in makeshift shelters or out in the open. I cannot even imagine living like this, but they seem to have the equanimity to do so.

Alison: We don't need much stuff. I think this simplicity is really a lesson westerners can learn from third-world countries. All over the world, we've seen that people are essentially just making sure they have a roof above their head, enough food, and are taking care of their family. That's all we really need. Once during our travels, my suitcase didn't arrive on time at the airport. I had to wait for it for five days to arrive. I bought myself a t-shirt, a pair of pants and some face cream and shared underwear with Don. This experience made me realize once more how little we need.

Trust

Alison: We are both spiritual people. We follow the *Advaita* tradition. *Advaita* refers to the idea that the true self (Atman) is the same as the highest metaphysical reality of the Universe (Brahman). We're really trying to live in the moment. We let life lead us. During our travels, we had many experiences where we were reminded of this. Sometimes, as people, we try to control our destiny. But actually, we have nothing to say about it. We just have to surrender . . . Surrender involves trust: trust in yourself, trust in strangers, trust in the fact that everything will be alright.

Don: We've experienced that 95% of people are friendly and helpful, all over the world.

Alison: I would even say 99%

Don: You're right, it's probably closer to 99%. Only taxi drivers will rip you off sometimes. (laughs)

Alison: They rip you off sometimes, but at least we've experienced that we can trust them. I remember situations in Fiji and in Jordan. In each case, a taxi driver was taking us away from town, in very strange directions. We got suspicious and thought they might take us to a place where we would be robbed, or worse. But in the end, they just dropped us off in front of our hotel.

Don: We take very few risks during our travels. We don't wear jewelry, we rarely go out at night, and if we do, we take a cab home. We've never encountered really dangerous moments. But I admit that we've also just had dumb luck, and we've been protected by angels.

Alison: One of these angels was an old woman in Argentina. We were wandering around in the La Boca quarter of Buenos Aires because we were interested to see the brightly painted houses. We drifted away from the tourist path until we were stopped by this woman. She made a sign with her index finger, telling us "don't continue this way." She guided us back to the tourist route. Later on, we found out that tourists had been held up at exactly that same place a couple of days before we got there.

Nature

Don: One of the most beautiful and profound experiences of our six years of traveling was in the Galapagos Islands. Our cruise ship dropped us off on the shore, and there we were, a bunch of tourists in the middle of wild birds. The birds didn't show any sign of fear. It made me appreciate the thousands of tourists that have come before us and have respected the tranquility of these birds.

Alison: Unfortunately, as humans, we have come to set ourselves above nature. But we're an integral part of it. We have to keep this connection. Nature will speak to us if we let it.

Don: I'd like to encourage people to reconnect with nature. Go into a forest, sit down and listen to the sounds around you. Or go to a beach and just watch the movement of the waves. Or walk along the shore barefoot.

What's your main reason for traveling?

Alison: For me, it's about curiosity. About noticing how every culture, every individual, tries to answer the question of how to live a good life.

Don: For me, it's because Alison wants me to come with her. (both laughing)

What are the 3 best qualities of your partner?

Alison: 1. Steadiness. 2. Kindness (Don interrupts: "and sense of humor" – both laughing) ... and 3. I would say his wisdom.

Don: Courage, fortitude, and curiosity.

What's one negative personality trait of your partner?

Alison: Don can be too cautious.

Don: She sticks her nose into everything, it's the flip side of her curiosity.

What advice do you have to keep a relationship healthy while traveling?

In unison: "Communicate continuously, be an open listener, give compliments."

Are you afraid of dying?

Alison: It depends. If tomorrow I get diagnosed with a terminal disease, I won't be afraid of dying. But if all of a sudden I'd have to face an angry bear, damn sure I would be afraid!

Don: I'm not consciously aware of fearing death, but I've no idea how I'll feel when the time comes.

Which books or movies have influenced you?

Don: We both love the *Harry Potter* series. We read the books out loud to each other, all seven of them. One movie that impacted me is *Shawshank Redemption*. It made me think about patience and redemption.

Alison: I have read an enormous number of spiritual books throughout my life. I remember reading Jane Roberts' *Seth Speaks: The Eternal Validity Of The Soul* in 1984, and it turned me around. Eckhart Tolle's *The Power Of Now* has been another important one.

How do you stay in shape?

Alison: We hike every day. We try to eat as healthy as possible. We try to eat vegetables every day, but in some countries, especially in South America, they're hard to find.

Don: I do some strength exercises every morning. I'm no longer a *Rolls Royce*, I'm an old *Chevy* now, so I need to do regular maintenance.

What's your meditation practice?

Alison: It has changed a lot over the years. It always comes back to being present in the moment, feeling the body, and sinking in. I've done three 10-day Vipassana retreats over the course of my life. They are boring, brutal, powerful, and necessary. The body is the most present place where you can be.

Don: I'm mostly following courses online. I watch videos from spiritual teachers like Mooji. I'm also doing a daily gratitude practice. Every night, before going to bed, I think about three things that made me grateful that day. Alison is always one of the three, so I only have to come up with two more. (both laughing)

Alison: I think gratitude is extremely important. I think we should never forget that we've won the lottery just by being born in a Western country, which gives us so many choices in life.

Do you watch the news?

Alison: I have better things to do than watching the news. I don't trust it anyway. If you believe the news, nowhere is safe.

Don: We wanted to see the orangutans in Borneo. The travel advice was: "Don't go there, it's dangerous, you could be kidnapped by pirates." A friend of ours was there and said: "Come over, it's safe, it's wonderful." We went. Our friend was right, it was magical.

Alison: The human mind loves drama, it loves catastrophizing. The news adds to this. I think it's smarter to focus on the positive. Anyway, I try to add to the positive energy of the world.

What are the most important messages you want to send out?

Don: I would like to set an example of how to live a life of fulfillment at any age.
Alison: Trust and gratitude. Let life guide you. Just follow your heart and put one foot in front of the other. If you want to live an adventurous life, don't let the fear stop you. Commit to it 100%. It gets easier with practice.

Find out more about Alison and Don:

www.alisonanddon.com

PART EIGHT:
I would walk 500 miles

344

My Advice Is: Go Out There, Do Some Work and Learn From Life!

When **ALICE MORRISON** was forced to shut down her company, she made an important life decision: following her heart and pursuing her adventurous dreams. Participation in the Marathon des Sables led her to definitively move to Morocco.

"If the desire is big enough, everyone can become an adventurer. But you have to be an optimist. If you're not an optimist, you're not going to succeed in this world . . . "

How did you start your adventurous lifestyle?

Actually, it started immediately. When I was only 6 weeks old my parents took me to Africa. I lived in Uganda and Ghana until the age of 11. Then we went back to Scotland. I followed the British educational system grade by grade and finally went studying Arabic and Turkish languages at Edinburgh University. After graduation, I started a career in journalism and quickly found myself working for the BBC. In 2002, I became CEO of a media development quango called *Vision+Media*, a company partially funded by the government, partially by private money. Probably the biggest turning point of my life was when David Cameron came into power in 2010 and shut down all quangos. This meant the end of the company. Having to shut down the company, after nearly a decade of putting my heart and soul in it, was very painful. Seeing my employees left without a job was definitely the hardest part. I decided to turn the negative into a positive. I had a reasonable amount of savings and properties that supplied me with a little basic income. So at that moment, I decided to do something that looked very exciting and wonderful: I registered for the Tour d'Afrique, the longest bike race in the world. It includes biking from Cairo to Cape Town, 12,500 kilometers, through 10 countries in 100 days. My first book, called *Dodging Elephants,* came out of the experience.

A second landmark was when I signed up for the Marathon des Sables in 2014. I wanted to prepare properly since I'm a terrible runner. So I moved to Morocco in order to be able to train in the sand and heat. It turned out that I would stay there until today. Imagine; I was 50 and got from being a successful CEO to living like a student in a small flat in Marrakech! I dreaded doing it because it was so far from my comfort zone . . . The good thing, however, is that I could survive with very reasonable expenses, in a country full of options for tremendous adventure. I think, after having grown up in Africa, that Morocco was the place where my soul was calling me.

After completing the Marathon des Sables, I slowly started doing more adventures and writing books. Eventually, in 2016, BBC approached me for a television program called *From Morocco to Timbuktu: An Arabian Adventure*. It was a dream come true for me! My quest for the 'furthest place on earth' was an epic journey along the ancient salt roads, over the snow-covered Atlas mountains, and across the Saharan sands. I mined for gold, risked death in a donkey cart, and spent hours up to my thighs in pigeon shit. All in a day's work. This television project was a lot of fun! I learned a lot of new skills from it and it was very well accepted by the public. As a result of the public visibility, I got a publisher for my third book *Adventures in Morocco*. This book, in its turn, led to sponsorships and a less or more secure income. In 2019, I finally started the 'real' expeditions, by walking the Draa River in Morocco. I was very lucky to find Jean-Pierre Datcharry of *Désert et Montagne Maroc* who helped me organize the expedition. Jean-Pierre had 40 years of experience in the region, so he knew all the possible pitfalls. Finding good people to work with is a must for adventures. I call this my first 'real' expedition because there wasn't a race organization. There wasn't a track to follow. I had to put everything in place myself and walk the entire 1500 kilometers myself, with a couple of local guides and camels to carry the luggage. Less than one year after the Draa Expedition, I crossed the Sahara Desert, a 3-month journey over 1000 kilometers of dunes and desert.

Finding a Place in the World

When I was CEO of my media company, I had a clear identity: I had a nice house, a beautiful car, a decent income, and a wide group of friends. Life was challenging due to work. But, at the same time, it was easy in a lot of ways: I knew who I was. When you want to be an adventurer, the situation is completely different. There is no safe and cozy place in the world. You have to make a place yourself. I was lucky to find a wonderful roommate in my flat in Marrakech, Alex. She was half my age. As a result, many people understood her for my daughter, which I always considered as a huge compliment because she was so intelligent. She had a totally different look at life. I found her refreshing and stimulating, and she taught me so much. It was also a great learning experience to have to cooperate, stop being selfish, and negotiate.

I'm not married and I don't have children, so that makes my adventurous lifestyle easier. On the other hand, I do have a lot of friends and close family members living mostly in Europe. After every adventure, I always come over to see them and spend time with them. I value these relationships very deeply and make sure to take time to nourish them.

What It Takes to Become an Adventurer

The only trait you really need is wanting to do it. You have to make the absolute commitment to pursuing this as a professional career. That's the only way you'll be able to get past the many, many rejections you'll get. You have to build an audience that really wants to hear from you. That's very difficult, people are so busy nowadays . . .

It's very hard to get the money. You constantly have to sell your ideas, sell what you're doing, sell the excitement, sell the achievements. I was lucky to find 3 amazing partners: *Craghoppers* (outdoor clothing), *Epic Travel* (Moroccan travel company), and *NTT Data* (IT innovation). I believe the people behind these companies do an amazing job by sponsoring dreams.

In order to become a successful adventurer, you need to be extremely resilient. Don't take 'no' for an answer, not from others and not from yourself. Never say "I can't do it". Patience is another important skill you'll need to develop. When I'm walking in the desert, the conditions are harsh, there's nothing to see around you, it's boring, it's hot, there are sandstorms, there are daylong headwinds, your body hurts . . . it's all uncomfortable, but you can't stop it. The only way out is patience.

Next, I would say that you have to be able to connect with other people, genuinely. When you're on an adventure, you're far away from friends and family, so you better make new friends along the road.

Having a short term memory is useful as well, you have to be able to forget the harshness of an expedition in order to be willing to take up the next challenge. If you would be honest about how hard your previous expedition was, you probably wouldn't start a new one.

Last, but not least; you have to be an optimist. If you're not an optimist, you're not going to succeed in this world . . . but remember what I started with: everyone can be an adventurer, all you really need is the desire to become one!

100 Times Worse Than Hollywood Movie Stars

I'm a rather lazy person and finding the courage to train is really difficult for me. I am really bad at it. It's very hard for me to stay motivated unless I'm really frightened that I'm going to be bad at a certain adventure, as was the case when I prepared for the Marathon des Sables. However, once I manage to force myself to start exercising, I often really enjoy it. I live at 1,700 meters altitude and I am surrounded by mountains that go up to 4,000 meters. I go running or hiking in the mountains a couple of times a week. Unfortunately, where I live, there are no women at all interested in adventure. Sometimes I hire a mountain guide and go out for a very long hike, but the big majority of my training sessions are executed on my own. I do quite a lot of weight training and pilates, which is great for core stability.

In between adventures, I tend to let myself go. I'm like those Hollywood film stars. If you see some of them when they're not working on a film they are like these big fat slobs. But, you know what, I'm like 100 times worse than that! The moment I stop my adventure, I stop exercising. I sit on my butt all day long and gain 6kg in two days . . . I feel like I need this time to recuperate my mind. When I have had to focus on a tough adventure, often for months in a row, it feels like my bank of mental energy is completely empty. And for me, the best way to compound again is by eating chocolate and watching Netflix.

What advice would you give to an 18-year-old who has no clue what to do with his/her life?

My advice definitely is: "Go out there, do some work and learn from life. Don't go straight away to University, or straight into a career path or even an apprenticeship." For example, if you think about becoming a plumber but you love the mountains: just go out and work in a bar, or a hotel, or a tourist firm in a mountain range for one year . . . Don't even worry about what you're going to do with your life . . . It's the path I followed myself: I went living one year in Dubai, learned Arabic, and worked on a magazine. A crucial part of my advice is 'work'! What you shouldn't do is take a lazy gap year. In Islam they say: "Hard work is worship," learning how to work is such a joy. Working hard gives you a big sense of satisfaction, purpose, and contribution. Before my job for the magazine in Dubai, I was a chambermaid and I rubbed the men's toilets on Sunday mornings. There was nothing romantic about it, but I loved it when I got my cash! That salary enabled me to buy things and to travel. Maybe you'll be lucky and find a job you really like and then you can follow this path . . .

So, to recapitulate, my advice to an 18-year-old is: go out, do the things you love, work and learn, learn, learn, learn! . . . And equally important: be a good member of your community, be good to your friends, good to your family, and kind to the people you meet.

How to Start an Adventurous Career

If you are really young, I think you can go all-in. There's time to recover from mistakes. But if you're a bit older already, then don't all of a sudden put your life on hold to become an adventurer. Build it up slowly. Make sure you have some security, some savings. Choosing the adventure pathway is very probably never going to give you much security. Nowadays, I can make enough money to do my adventures and fulfill my basic needs for now, but I can't put anything aside for the future . . . But yep, again, if you want it: just get started!

What impact do you want to have in the world?

I would like to help people understand that we're all the same. I'm British and Christian and was educated in Western culture. Today, I'm living in Eastern culture, I'm surrounded by Muslims, and yet I've been able to build profound friendships. I've found love, warmth, and acceptance. So often in the media, the word Islam is linked to terrorism, but that's not reality. True Muslims believe exactly the same as Christians and Jews: life is sacred and must not be taken. The opposite is true as well: a lot of Muslims believe that Western women don't have morals, that we are too loose, that we don't respect marriage, that we don't love our parents because we put them in nursing homes . . . and these beliefs are equally wrong.

I would also love to bring out the things I find out while doing adventures to a broader public, to cooperate more with scientists, environmentalists, the National Geographic Society . . . that's a big ambition for the future.

The best way for humans to survive and to be happy is by being together. And the best way for others to enjoy my company, is to become a better person myself. So, I hope people will remember me as a kind, good, warm person, someone who made them laugh. It would be great if they remember me as a great communicator, a good writer, a good tv broadcaster, a good podcaster . . . Shortly put: someone whose stories took people away to an exciting and beautiful place, informed, entertained, and touched them.

Find out more about Alice:

www.alicemorrison.co.uk
instagram.com/aliceoutthere1
facebook.com/alicehuntermorrisonadventure

I Am More Interested in Others Than I Am in Myself

For every adventurer dreaming about Mongolia, there's one address: MARC ALAUX. At age 25, this French traveler, writer and adventure books publisher got fascinated by the East-Asian country, its geography and its inhabitants. Since then, he has come back countless times.

"By far the most beautiful aspect -and the most enlightening- of traveling in Mongolia is to be accepted by a community. This mongolian sense of belonging is beyond comparison."

Falling in Love With Mongolia

Thanks to my parents, who moved seventeen times, I got the privilege to live in a lot of different regions. Everywhere I had to adapt. Everywhere I met people of value. Already as a child I was very interested in archeology, and this even increased my interest for the other, the traces people had left before me, the respect for previous generations. From adolescence on, the practice of martial arts and the discovery of hiking gave me the feast for traveling and a taste of what big efforts involve. This only grew after my first 2,5 years in Mongolia: hiking 7000 km across the steppe and the Gobi desert, followed by living as a shepherd in a yurt a whole winter long, and several months in the capital Oulan-Bator. Ever since, I exclusively traveled to the country I fell in love with as a young guy.

Sense of Belonging

The exhilarating feeling of freedom and the sense of pride and contentment after overcoming obstacles are two of the main reasons I love adventures so much. But by far the most beautiful aspect – and the most enlightening – of traveling in Mongolia is to be accepted by a community. I think that westerners have just as much to learn from the Mongolians as they can learn from us; and this sense of belonging is definitely one of those things. Valuing silence and selflessness are other ones.

The best example demonstrating this sense of belonging and the mongolian selflessness is something that happened to me in 2001. A poor family in the East of the country saved me from a snowstorm and offered me the only alimentation they had: a small bowl of soup. This simple bowl of soup will forever stay in my memory as an illustration of humanity. It was more than a life lesson, especially for the 25-year young man I was back then. It was an excellent introduction to the courage and humility you have to demonstrate while traveling.

What's the most difficult aspect of being an adventurer?

Choosing is accepting to keep quiet. I don't think that any obstacle you've chosen is insurmountable. Time is the most consequential problem: having enough time for traveling involves declining other temptations. But in my philosophy it's the sacrifice that gives value to the action.

When it comes to the finances, I work as a publisher for adventure- and travel books. In my opinion, a job is the way adventures have to be financed, not sponsoring. I have an average salary, but it's sufficient to travel the way I prefer: by foot, sober and in full immersion.

Tell us about *Transboréal*, your publishing company?
Transboréal was founded by my colleague Émeric Fisset, in the mid-nineties. Émeric had traveled for ten years all over the world, followed by a 2,5-year long raid by foot, kayak, ski and dog sled from Seattle to the entry gate of the Bering Strait in Alaska. Émeric wanted to give the floor to authors who had completed feats that made proof of a real connivance with the human environment or natural world. Together, Émeric and I continue this œuvre by searching courageous, honest and modest authors.

Essential Writing
I'm always traveling as pure as possible. No sponsor, no logistics, no GPS, no cell phone, no music. With me, I carry only a writing block and a camera. This, on the other hand, is essential. I'm constantly taking notes of every thought and reflection I have about the geography and the society in Mongolia. Writing is at once a research and a conclusion; it is the confluence of a state of mind, a glance, a knowledge and a physical energy. This way, writing is a concentration of my existence, which carries in itself the capacity to lengthen the travel, to deepen it and to give it a supplementary scope. In fact, nowadays, I'm no longer interested in traveling without the act of writing.

Characteristics and Personality Traits
[I asked Marc to rank himself from 0 (not like this trait at all) to 10 (very much like that)]

Optimism: 5
Discipline: 5
Courage: 5
Resilience: 5
Stubbornness: 5
Social skills: 5
Intelligence: 5
Five, because there is always better and worse than me. Five, because I already did improve a lot, but I still desire to become better. Five, because I prefer to be interested in others instead of me.

What's the advice you would give to someone who's stuck in a job they don't really like and wants to become an adventurer or digital nomad?
Don't procrastinate. The first step is the most difficult one, jump!

What advice would you give to your 18-year-old self?
Walk and build yourself, or shut up and starve!

Find out more about Marc and Transboréal publishing:
www.transboreal.fr
facebook.com/transboreal.editions
instagram.com/editionstransboreal

Shelter, Warmth, Food, Drink, and Friends

*When it comes to adventurers, **STEVEN PAYNE** is a breed of his own. He walked a 200-mile-long pilgrimage from Southampton to Canterbury in medieval clothing, traveled through Wales in a coracle, crossed the Alps on a spacehopper, and is currently planning to ride from London to Paris on a penny-farthing bicycle.*

"Being offered a meal by a homeless man on my first pilgrimage was the epiphany."

A Medieval Passion

Ask a kid, my family moved around a lot. My father was in the *Royal Air Force*. We lived on the Forces' bases in the UK, West Germany, and Cyprus. I went to 13 different schools during my childhood. I guess I got the medieval 'bug' when I was 6 years old. At that time, we lived in a small village in Northumberland, a wild and bleak area in the UK, close to the Scottish borders. Whilst playing out on the moors, a friend of mine found what looked like a rusty old sword buried close to a riverbank. Because there were several large castles very close to the village, we knew that it was likely to have come from one of these. The sword was excavated and turned out to be a Viking sword. It was probably dropped by a raider on one of the many attacks on the Holy Island of Lindisfarne, about a mile away. The restored sword was brought back and exhibited at our school about six months later. We then studied the legends of Beowulf in class, made Viking helmets from paper maché, and re-enacted the story in a school play.

Many years later, in my early twenties, I started reenacting medieval life and warfare again. In those days, you had to make all your own equipment by yourself. So, the standard was pretty poor. But, by the late 1990s, I was often somewhere in a castle at the weekend, kitted out in full armor, re-enacting a battle, playing medieval musical instruments, or telling castle stories to children. My various interests and jobs as a teacher, a musician, and a martial arts instructor could all be combined in the one hobby as a medieval reenactor. In 2015, I did my first medieval adventure, the pilgrimage from Southampton to Canterbury. Today, I still occasionally teach medieval swordplay and I still enjoy playing medieval music. Additionally, I have spent the last five years doing a Ph.D. in Medieval History. So, now I am not only a 'gentleman adventurer' – attempting eccentric challenges and recreating hazardous historical journeys – but I'm also Doctor Payne.

The Flip Side of a Depressing Coin

About five years ago, in the course of only a couple of months, I was forced to deal with a bunch of severe setbacks. My father had died, I was made redundant from my job, my fiance had left, I had to sell the house, and I had been given a diagnosis of a potentially life-threatening illness. After several simultaneous disasters, I needed to clear my head and re-examine my direction in life. The flip side of this depressing coin, however, was that I suddenly had no ties or responsibilities. No job, no relationship, no house, no need to even consider the risks of anything I might decide to do . . . I was suddenly freer than at any time since the age of five when I first went to school. From my studies, I knew that medieval pilgrims often undertake pilgrimages in order to re-evaluate the spiritual aspects of their lives. I thought that this would give me time away from my present worries. Time to concentrate on the simple essentials of life; Shelter, Warmth, Food, Drink, and Friends. I had always enjoyed walking and had often been camping without a tent, just sleeping wherever I found myself. So, I decided to recreate a pilgrimage from Southampton to Canterbury for the celebration of the life of Thomas Becket. This was the route that foreign pilgrims would have taken in the 14th Century. After six months of research, planning, and clothing manufacture, I set off to become the first person to do the authentic Canterbury pilgrimage in period clothes, sleeping rough along the way and relying only on the help of others for food and drinks.

I simply walked as far as I could each day, visiting as many of the medieval towns and sites along the way as I could. As it was the middle of January, it was often cold and wet. Many times I had to take shelter from the weather in church porchways, under trees, and even on one occasion, I slept in the burial chamber of a neolithic burial mound. Many times I thought of giving up, especially as the route, at one point, took me close to home. But, I settled into a routine and the walk became almost like a meditation. I posted a Facebook blog every day about the journey. My iPad and an emergency credit card were the only non-medieval things I took with me. In the beginning, I had 18 followers on Facebook. But, by the end, I had received more than 180,000 comments from people all over the world. It took me six months to answer all the questions.

In the entire journey, I bought no food at all. I had made some to take with me from various medieval recipes. I was prepared to go as far as I could on that, but as people found out about what I was doing from radio and TV, I began to experience strangers coming up to me with bread, apples, milk, and freely giving them. A pub landlord in Westerham would not accept any money when I spoke to him about the medieval history of his pub. Another in Charing, on my last day, even let me sleep on the floor of his public bar, giving me the pub keys and telling me to let myself out in the morning and post the keys back through the letterbox.

The Pope and the Archbishop of Canterbury had written to me before the Pilgrimage and given me permission to sleep in the shelter of any Catholic or Anglican churches along the way. Many others helped me out with directions, food, meals, or advice as I went.

Satori

On my first pilgrimage, I met a homeless man in Winchester. After having seen me in the newspapers, he bought me a pasty – a takeaway meal – with virtually the only money he had. As he approached me with the meal in his hand and a smile on his face, I had what some people would call an epiphany, or perhaps Satori *(Satori is a Zen Buddhist notion, referring to the experience of kenshō: "seeing into one's true nature")*. Here was a man with nothing more than three pounds in his pocket, who had spent much of what he had on a gift for me, a man he didn't even know. I couldn't process it. For a full five minutes, I could barely speak.

We sat on the street within sight of Winchester Cathedral, suffering the disapproving looks of many of the passers-by in their smart clothes and expensive raincoats and we shared the pasty, talking about what I was doing and why. He gave me some hints and tips about keeping warm on the road in winter, and where to find shelter. He had recently lost all his warm overnight clothing and his sleeping bag, as someone had set fire to it one night. So, with my emergency money, I bought him some replacements. I never saw him again. I did try afterward, but the homeless often move around a lot, so I never got to tell him that I had made it all the way. But, the encounter did start me thinking that I could use what I was doing to help homeless people more generally. I started talking about their plight in my blogs, not asking for money, but encouraging people to go out into their local communities and help their own local homeless people. I think that has worked to some extent. I have certainly been able to raise several thousand pounds since then, by other activities such as running events, awareness campaigns, etc. I have also been able to sell many of my former possessions to aid homeless people.

After having a very well-paid job and living in a large five-bedroom house, I had suffered a series of disasters which had led to my discovery that in fact, we can survive very handily on very little. Much of the stuff I had collected over the years was sold. It paid for tents, sleeping bags, food, clothing, boots, haircuts, etc. for a wide variety of people who were down on their luck. All because of a man in Winchester who one day spent the last of his money on food for a man he didn't know.

Walk a Mile in Someone Else's Shoes Before You Judge Them

One year after this adventure, I went on a second pilgrimage. Again in the month of January, following the route of St. Brendan across Wales in a homemade coracle, a traditional Welsh wooden, lightweight, rounded boat. This trip was notable for its isolation. Mid-Wales is largely empty of people. I spent many nights looking up at the stars and getting the feeling that this was the closest I was ever likely to get to a real feeling of solitude. One day, a very rough-looking group of local lads pulled up in a car as I was carrying my boat across a road. They wanted to know what was going on, why I was dressed as a monk, and why I was walking across the mountain with a boat on my back. Theirs was not the kind of language usually heard in polite society and I thought there might be trouble. But, once I explained what I was doing and they explained that they thought I was an idiot, they drove off. Twenty minutes later, they caught up with me at a bend in the river and gave me the burger, fries, and coffee they had bought for me at a *Mcdonald's* in the nearest town. Now, I try not to judge people by how they look or how they speak.

On all of my trips, without exception, I had literally no negative comments from the people I met. People brought me food, clapped as I went by, hooted car horns, cooked me meals, introduced me to their children, and generally made me welcome wherever I went. Everyone, whether English, Welsh, French, Italian or German, always responded with a never-failing enthusiasm for what I was doing. Now, I try not to judge people by their nationalities. People are the same everywhere, some good, some bad, but if you make an effort it usually pays off. Walk a mile in someone else's shoes before you judge them.

Crossing the Alps on a Spacehopper

After coming home from my second adventure, I conducted several programs with homeless people in the UK. One time, I was talking with a man who told me: "It's virtually impossible to find a job without a permanent address, it's like crossing the Alps with a spacehopper." My next adventure was born.

The Alps are serious mountains, the largest on the continent, and not to be attempted lightly even for experienced walkers. Crossing them from Bardonecchia in Italy to Grenoble in France on a spacehopper is an idea so ridiculous that no-one in their right mind should even attempt it. So, it needed serious preparation. It took eight months of practice and many, many hours of pouring over maps, seeking out different routes. At the time when I left, in June 2018, Europe was experiencing its biggest ever heatwave. Along the way, I suffered heat exhaustion, heat stroke, altitude sickness, and physical injury. The fact that I chose to do it again by sleeping rough, and wearing a tweed suit and an old British Army pith helmet of the late 1800s, probably didn't help. I experienced rock falls, lost two of the four spacehoppers to punctures or accidents along the way, and twisted my knee near the finish which made bouncing extremely painful. Two years later my knee still often aches on cold mornings.

After I came back, it got a little scary. I was interviewed on TV in three countries and articles appeared in just about every major newspaper in Europe. I appeared on the BBC, current affairs programs, radio . . . in fact, everywhere. I had calls at 6 a.m. asking me to go on New Zealand radio and at midnight asking if I wanted to fly to Germany to appear on a chat show the next day. I was interviewed for the National Catholic Press, I was voted 'Pilgrim of the Year' by the newly formed British Pilgrimage Society. For months after every trip, I hardly dared open my emails. I was dubbed 'Britain's Greatest Eccentric' and was enrolled in the *Eccentric Society*, a London Gentlemen's club based in Mayfair and formed in the late 1700s. In short, I was exhausted. I now have had a very brief and minor glimpse of what celebrities must go through every day. To be honest, I could have done without that aspect of it all. The only disappointing thing was that so many media outlets wanted me to talk about the various trips, and almost none of them asked about the reasons for doing them or the situation with the homeless.

Take-Away Messages

Mentally, I experienced something odd as a result of doing adventures. As a Project Manager, I had been used to planning everything down to the last detail. But, as time went on and the adventures came along one after the other, I worried less and less about what tomorrow might bring and learned to live in the moment. If it rained, I got wet. If the sun came out, I dried off. If I was tired, I slept. If I had no food, I went hungry. If I had food, I shared it if there was anyone about, and if there wasn't I ate it myself. Today I live in a very small house. Most of my possessions are gone, although I have kept the things that really matter to me. I live more simply and have rid myself of a lot of the ambition associated with wealth and prosperity. I am happier because of it.

The world is a big place. Try to learn something about it before you go, but go out into it anyway, and take a look around. Different doesn't mean wrong, different can be exciting and rewarding. Even if it all goes wrong, you will make memories that one day you will realize mean more than the things you collect along the way. Time is precious . . . nobody on their deathbed ever wishes they spent more time in the office, or more time making more money.

If you're 18 years old, and you don't know what direction to choose for your life, don't worry about it. Work hard at what you enjoy, whatever that is. Cultivate relationships. The most important thing is not to confuse standard of living with quality of life. Be happy.

Find out more about Steve:
facebook.com/14thcenturypilgrimsprogress
instagram.com/historicpeddler

Experiences are Made Unforgettable, Thanks to the People With Whom You Pass Them

ALESSIA CAPRARO is Italian and loves dancing, coffee, and eating delicious food. JENTE JACOBS is Belgian and loves sports, Belgian beers, and reading a good book. They met each other during an AFS exchange program in the Dominican Republic, and have since then never stopped traveling together. Their preferred means of transportation: hitchhiking.

"We are both open-minded and easy-going. That's necessary for hitchhiking."

Travel Bugs and Love Butterflies

Jente: When I was a child, we often traveled to France and Switzerland. My father is also interested in traveling low-budget and backpacking. Once, I was with him in a hostel in the Algarve in Portugal. We got in touch with backpackers from all over the world. At the time, I was still very young. The adventurous stories I heard from these backpackers seemed so unreal. While hanging on their lips, I realized this was what I wanted to do one day.

More than a year later, I did a summer job in a restaurant on the Belgian coast side. One of the waiters had traveled a lot. He had spent several months in South-East Asia, had walked the Camino de Santiago, and so on. He told me that life is happening now, that we shouldn't wait for 'the perfect moment' to follow our dreams. I was 17 at the time. After this summer two young guys came talking in our school about the 'AFS Exchange Programs'. These programs allow you to go abroad, study, and live for one year together with a local family. I immediately knew: "This is it!" I applied and a couple of months later I left for the Dominican Republic.

Alessia: At the same time, some guys came to my school in Italy to present the AFS project. I also knew immediately that this was what I wanted to do. So, I passed my exams and got accepted to join a Dominican Republic host family. During this exchange program, I met a lot of amazing people, amongst them Jente, and we fell in love.

Jente: After our year in the Dominican Republic, Alessia and I had a long-distance relationship for 3 years. A couple of times a year, we visited each other and sometimes we did a trip together to another country. As we were both students, we had to get by on a small budget. I suggested to Alessia that we'd try hitchhiking as a way of travel, and so we did.

Alessia: After the exchange program in the Dominican Republic, my desire to travel became bigger and bigger, especially under the influence of Jente. I wanted to discover the world and meet people from different cultures. Traveling was also the only way to stay together as a couple. The first and second hitchhiking-trip we did was in Spain, and the year we graduated we did a big trip across Europe. We really love traveling together. I couldn't imagine myself doing the same thing with another travel companion. Now we try to turn our passion into a job, and our brand is called 'The Art of Hitchhiking'.

What makes you good hitchhikers?

Jente: I am a very open-minded and easy-going person, I like to go with the flow. Hitchhiking is not for everyone. A control freak would never be able to hitchhike, as you need to let go of everything. We never have any clue about what will happen during the day, where we will end up, where we will sleep . . . My patience is also a very big advantage, as is being a social person. You have to be willing to meet new people every day, talk about your story and be interested in their story as well.

Alessia: I am a very extroverted and open-minded person. I'm very flexible and understanding. When I start to do something, I want to do it to the best of my abilities. And of course, staying positive also helps a lot!

Guardian Angel

Jente: Three people have been very important in my journey: my dad, the waiter of the restaurant who told me I should go for it, and Alessia of course.

Alessia: I have to thank my family a lot. It's thanks to my parents that I am the person I am today.

Jente: And then there are all the amazing people we meet on the road. We've experienced so much hospitality and kindness, everywhere. Experiences are made unforgettable, thanks to the people with whom you pass them. We've met so many kind and beautiful people, but one person deserves a special mention.

Alessia: It's a German man who gave us our first lift in Croatia. Croatia was a very difficult place to hitchhike. I remember one afternoon when we were on the verge of accepting that nobody would take us with them. Nevertheless, without real belief behind his gesture, Jente tried one last time to put out his thumb. A car with a German license plate stopped. The driver let us in, drove us in the desired direction, invited us for dinner, and eventually even paid for a hotel room for us. The following day he took us to a big farm which was property of one of his friends.

Jente: A couple of days later, we were in the city of Split. We had planned to take a bus from the city center to the highway, and start hitchhiking from there. At that moment, our German friend called us, said that he was in Split, and asked if we needed a lift. We started calling him our guardian angel. Later that week, we arrived in Zagreb, Croatia's capital and by hazard, our guardian angel was there as well. He invited us to sleep in the same hotel as he did. He again paid for dinner and we spent all night long talking with him. He was such an interesting and inspirational person, and one of the people that helped me most in my personal growth.

What it Takes to Live a Life Full of Adventure

Explaining our mindset and desires to the people surrounding us is difficult. The social pressure a person feels is far too often underestimated. Even if no one ever told us literally that we can't do this or that, we feel that what we're doing is seen as 'not normal'. Many of the people around us don't understand us. We are supposed to fit into a society where we get a job, find a place to live, start a family . . . We think the main reason for this structure is because those social rules put us in a sort of comfort zone. Everything in this comfort zone is easy and okay. When you want to do something totally different, it's very difficult for others to accept it. For 90% of people, stability is a very important aspect of life, and that's just the biggest thing you have to deny if you want to live an adventurous life.

For now, we're alternating our travels with a normal job. But, we're building up a lifestyle in which we can earn our living with our passion for travel.

The advice we would give to all adolescents is to pack your stuff in a backpack and go explore new places and cultures . . . and above all, explore yourself. When youngsters become 18, they leave high school and are supposed to convert into 'responsible adults' who know what to do with their lives. But we can guarantee you, nobody knows his life purpose from going to school for 12 years. It's impossible to know what you want in your life as long as you stay in your comfort zone. You need to have life experience and put yourself into difficult situations to discover who you really are. Spend time alone and get confronted with your limits. That's how you'll start to understand your goals in life. You'll recognize what you're missing, what's truly important in life. Maybe you'll notice that you don't miss anything at all. If so, then you are a born traveler. Welcome to the club!

There will always be excuses, things that will hold you back. There will never be a perfect moment. But, who needs a perfect moment if perfect can't bring you happiness? If you experience setbacks – and you will – then you are doing great. Because these setbacks will teach you something and will help you grow. And when you grow, you take another step on the mountain you have to climb to build a life full of adventure and traveling. Every trip we made until now, made us grow. It doesn't matter if we spend just one week or two months away from home. But, for sure, what really changes us for the better, is the kindness of strangers we meet on the road . . .

Find out more about Jente and Alessia:
youtube.com/theartofhitchhiking
facebook.com/theartofhitchhiking
instagram.com/theartofhitchhiking

Don't Be Afraid to Make Your Own Choices, Instead of Doing What Seems Logical Because of Your Education, Societal or Family Expectations

From February 2018 to February 2020, **MARIE COUDERC** *and her boyfriend* **NIL HOPPENOT** *hiked from Portugal to Turkey. They crossed 16 countries and more than 120 natural parks, walked 10,000 kilometers, invited 36 people to join them, cleaned up 1000 kilograms of waste, and made 70 YouTube videos. Marie and Nil called their project 'Deux Pas Vers l'Autre' (2PVA) (Translated: Two Steps Towards the Other).*

"If I was to be the President of Europe, I would try to develop a European identity, show people that we have a shared history, that we are very similar to each other."

The Road Leading Up to *2PVA*
Both Nil and I grew up in Paris, but that didn't keep us from getting in touch with nature and adventure from a very young age on. My grandparents lived in Aveyron, a region with amazing natural beauty. I spent a lot of my holidays over there and that's how I got connected to nature. From the age of 18 on, I traveled quite a lot with my friends, mostly in South America. Nil, on his side, lived with his father and brother. They did a lot of typical boys' stuff: tinkering, construction, fishing . . . When he grew older, he went on several solo speed-hiking trips; hikes in which he left home very minimalistically, only carrying a tiny backpack and running part of the trajectory.

Nil and I met in a climbing gym and soon became friends for several years before we got into a relationship. The moment that happened, both of us were in a transitional period in our professional lives and looking for something adventurous to do. So, pretty soon we decided to make a plan together. Nil had long since had the dream to hike a very long route and that sounded cool to me. Next, we had to decide on our destination. We realized there were a lot of countries that at least one of us had already visited – Nil knew big parts of Asia very well, I had seen a lot of places in South America – but that we didn't know our own backyard: Europe. We tried to put all of the continent's countries on a map and when we didn't manage to do so, we realized it would be absurd to go elsewhere . . .

Leaving on a two-year-long trip as a freshly formed couple definitely came with its challenges; we got to know each other very well, very quickly. Today it feels as if we've been together for 15 years, just because it has been so intense! During the trip, the fact that Nil is someone who is very perseverant and optimistic confirmed what I knew already. In Nil's head, everything is possible. He can go very far in order to make things work out. I'm much more realistic. I investigate much more the pros and cons of an idea before deciding to give my best for it. I think that this blend of Nil's ambition and my realism serves us very well.

You have linked the hike to different projects: building a community, cleaning waste along the way, and a YouTube series. What was the main message you wanted to spread this way?
We wanted to show that adventure isn't only reserved for the Mike Horns of this world. Adventure is very accessible to everyone, as well in terms of skill level, travel distance, and budget. On a big part of our route, we felt like true explorers. We crossed areas where we met nobody and where it seemed as if nobody had ever been there before.

Doing Things Professionally
We didn't look at our trip as a sabbatical period. Our goal was to do things professionally. We almost considered *2PVA* as starting a company. Before we left, Nil was a freelance photographer, mostly in the model world. I was a Human Resources manager in a big enterprise. Both of us didn't feel 100% fulfilled in our positions. Thus we approached *2PVA* with one of the goals in mind that it might open new doors for our careers. As a matter of fact, for ten months we worked full-time to prepare for the actual trip. We went on micro-adventures in the Pyrenees and the Alps to test our equipment and to make footage we could show to potential sponsors. These micro-adventures worked out quite well. We managed to get sponsors on board and they also gave us a sound social media following.

Honestly, I have to admit that we might have tried to do a bit too much. Writing articles, making videos, communicating with many different sponsors, keeping the website up-to-date, cleaning waste along the way . . . there were times we worked more than we had ever done before in our jobs! The most energy-consuming task was video editing. We had made a big deal out of making one video for every different country we visited. On top of this, we had a video logbook: videos about our gear and videos of special encounters. Each one of these montages forced us to stay 5 or 6 days in one place. This being said, I don't have regrets that we did so much because in the end it all turned out well . . . but next time we might take it just a little bit easier.

Nine months after finishing our endeavor [at the time of interviewing Marie in November 2020], can I say that we succeeded in opening new doors for our careers? I have to say yes and no. The *2PVA* project led to a lot of collaborations, but we're not yet earning any money from it. Nevertheless, it gave Nil a couple of opportunities to work as a filmmaker and photographer in the world of travel and adventure. On my side, I've decided to keep a secure job in parallel with the following adventures. If I would pursue making a career in this world, it would come with a whole lot of pressure and stress. I'd rather work in a conventional job which I find amusing part of the year, so I can fully enjoy the adventure in my free time.

[Note: Marie and Nil rebranded in 2021 and are now known under the banner 'Further Stories']

What advice would you give to people who want to go on an adventure and are looking for sponsors?
They have to understand that sponsorship demands a big investment in time. A lot of companies receive several requests a day. So, you need to have a special project with a strong record. You can't just turn up and say: "Hey, I want to hike or bike or run this route, can you sponsor me?". Instead, you have to show what you've accomplished in the past. You have to prove to them that you are planning your trip very meticulously and make them understand what will be in it for them. Which exposure are you able to give that company?

In our choice of sponsors, we were very picky. We only wanted durable, light, and eco-friendly gear. Often, we would contact companies and ask for just one article. If, for example, we asked a brand if they wanted to sponsor us by offering jackets and they proposed to also give sleeping bags, we bluntly said no to that. The result was that we ended up with about 50 different sponsors. This gave us quite a lot of work because often we would receive a message from one of these sponsors with the question if we could make a YouTube video about the product they gave us. The filming and editing of that video would then cost us 2-3 days . . . Of course, that is not really time lost, because that video then got spread out by the company and gave 2PVA more exposure.

What are the biggest similarities and differences amongst people in different countries across Europe?
The biggest similarity surely is that everybody thinks they are different from the others. No matter where we were when we talked to people about where we planned to go next, the response was: "Watch out, the people over there are not that kind, not that hospitable." Of course, when we entered that village, we were welcomed just as warmly. This polarization could be found amongst different villages, regions, or countries. Everywhere we got warned for 'the other'.

What we also discovered is that people are more alike in the geographical area where they live than they are alike in the country. For example, a person living in the mountains in Croatia is much more similar to a person living in the mountains in Spain than a Croatian living on the Croatian coast or in a Croatian city.

If you'd be elected as the 'President Of Europe', what would your politics be about?
When the European Union got shaped, it was emphasized that European countries would form an economic and political union. What has been forgotten, is to create a European identity. If I was to be the President of Europe, I would try to develop a European identity. I would show people that we have a shared history, that we are very similar to each other. As I said, people feel too different from each other. This way, they don't feel like sharing with and helping each other.

Another point on my agenda would be to tackle the migration crisis. On our trip, we've heard a lot of racist comments about immigrants, even against us. Some people thought we were immigrants. I even had a guy asking me if I was in the Taliban. We've found it very difficult to open discussions with people looking down on immigrants.

Personally, I don't get what the so-called 'national pride' is about. In my opinion, your pride for your country shouldn't cause you not to want immigrants to come in. You can only be happy that you got damn lucky you were born in a country where things go better than theirs!

What is your de inition of a life well-lived?
Listening to your heart. This involves not being afraid to make your own choices, instead of doing what seems logical because of your education, societal or family expectations. It also involves that you have to renounce certain things. But, that comes in favor of embracing more beautiful ones.

Find out more about Marie and Nil:
www.deuxpasverslautre.com
youtube.com/furtherstories
instagram.com/further.stories
facebook.com/furtherstories

When I'm In Nature, I Feel Free

BRIEG JAFFRÈS is the host of the French blog 'Besoin d' Aventure' (translated: Need for Adventure). He teaches navigation skills for marines, coaches people leaving on their first big adventure, and made a guidebook for hikers in the Annapurna-region (Nepal). But foremost he's an adventurer himself.

"Traveling made me realize that in the West, we complain about futilities."

Discovering the World

When I was 9 years old, I already imagined myself going on an adventure every day. I had to hike one kilometer to school, with a heavy backpack. And at the end of the day, I was welcomed with great hospitality by my mother at home. When I was 17, I left for my first real adventure. I cycled the length of Ireland together with two friends. Four years later, I went hitchhiking in Australia, a surfboard beneath my arm. I had dreamed about going *down under* for many years. I remember myself sitting on a bench one day, looking at the shore, being speechless because I realized that I was living my dream.

When I was about 25 years old, my wife and I left on a two-year-long bike trip around the world. We started off at home in Bretagne, cycled to Moscow, then took the trans-Siberian railway to Lake Baikal. From there, we continued on our bicycles through Mongolia, South-East Asia, and New Zealand. We flew to South America and crossed the continent on our bikes. Then we took a plane to Dakar and cycled back home from there.

The main goal of our trip was to have as many beautiful encounters with people as possible. We often asked if we could set up our tent in people's gardens. It was quite interesting to see how people from different countries reacted differently to our presence, even amongst neighboring countries. For example, in Bolivia and Peru, it was difficult to connect with people. The population was very discrete. But as soon as we crossed the border into Argentina, people came towards us. They were curious and wanted to chat. In Russia, people seemed very cold and distant at first, but once the ice was broken, they were really welcoming. In Mongolia, people hardly looked up when we came around – as if two European cyclists were the most normal thing to see. Maybe that was because they're nomads themselves. In China, we faced the most problems. Chinese people never say no. If you're asking someone; "Is Peking to the right?", the person will say yes. If you ask the person next to him: "Is Peking to the left?", he will say yes too. Sometimes, we asked if we could put up our tents somewhere and of course the answer was yes. Moments later we would see several people discussing and find out that having our tent planted on that spot actually was a problem, they just hadn't dared to tell us no.

Stop Complaining

Despite the differences amongst nations and cultures, we do all have commonalities as well. All over the world, people put a high value on family. Everyone wants a good education for their children. Everyone wants to enjoy good moments with other people. Everyone is longing to interchange with others. I've also experienced that 90% of people are good at their core. 90% of people are kind, caring, and willing to help. When my wife and I cycled around the world, people would always warn us about their neighbors. In Belarus, they would say that the Russians are dangerous. In Russia, they would tell us to watch out for Mongolian people. In Mongolia, they would warn us for the Chinese . . . And every time we would realize that their warnings weren't legitimate. In reality, there are very few bad-hearted or dangerous people.

Another realization I had after this big trip around the world is that, as westerners, we shouldn't complain. In France, we're the world champions of strikes. No matter what the government decides, the population moans. I can no longer withstand it. When you travel to poor countries, you see true suffering. You realize that all these things we worry and complain about at home are nothing but futilities. We're living in an enormous comfort. We really don't have the right to complain.

Je m'en Fous [I Don't Care]

I have a different lifestyle compared to most people. I do a lot of sports. I try to be ecological. I'm quite minimalistic. Before, it was sometimes hard to go against social norms. A couple of years ago, I went to Greenland on a kayak expedition. Some acquaintances of mine told me I was crazy. But I knew what I was doing, I'm an experienced kayaker, and so were my two expedition buddies. Nowadays, I do no longer care about what other people think about me, *je m'en fous [I don't care].* I have a small group of friends whom I know are true friends because they accept and love me as I am.

Being One With Nature

When I'm in nature, I feel free. My wife and I are toying with the idea of living off-grid (in a yurt or so) and being as self-sufficient as possible. Personally, I feel very connected to nature. I don't see myself as standing above animals and plants, being 'better' or 'more' than them. Each year, I try to do a ten-day-long hike in the mountains all by myself. I hitchhike from my home in Bretagne to the Alps or the Vosges, and then I follow a hiking trail. This period gives me time to reflect on life, to think about future projects, but also to empty my mind. On one of these trips I had taken Eckhart Tolle's *The Power of Now* with me and was reading it every night in my tent. Tolle talks about being present, being fully aware in the now. I tried to apply his lessons during my walks. Then, two very bizarre and magical things happened. At one moment, I had the idea that I was walking on a treadmill, and the environment surrounding me was moving, like in a movie. The second surreal experience was when there was sunlight coming in between the branches and I saw this light differently, in a surreal and powerful way.

Besoin d'Aventure [Need for Adventure]

In my early twenties, I was a marine. I decided to cycle around the world. But, afterward, I could easily find work again in the industry. I worked on a big sailing boat and was always away for one to two months. When I was 30 years old, my wife got pregnant and I decided I no longer wanted to be away from home for that long. For one year, I worked on a cruise ship and had missions that lasted a week or two. Then I got the chance to become a teacher for future marines. I took the opportunity, not at least because this job allows me to have a lot of holidays. This way, I've always been able to continue my adventures. In 2016, I started a platform online where people could buy or rent adventure movies. I did this for one year, but the profits I got out of it weren't worth the effort. After some reflection, I decided to write a blog. It's mostly a work of passion in which I share my knowledge and experiences to help people organize their own adventures by foot, bicycle, or kayak. People desiring to have more detailed and personal guidance for their next trip can also contact me for an online training. During this coaching program I take them from picking the right destination according to their capacities and preferences, to choosing the right gear and learning all the necessary navigation skills.

On top of this, I sell a French guidebook of hikes in the Annapurna region in Nepal. A couple of years ago, I wanted to walk up there but I couldn't find a topo-guide in my own language, so I decided to make one. There are still a lot of regions in this world that don't have a French guidebook. However, I don't know if this is a real market opportunity. I sell a couple of tens of guidebooks a year, despite being one of the first search results on Google. A third stream of income I have is from a movie I made about my kayak expedition in Greenland. All the projects of *Besoin d'Aventure* together yield me a couple of hundred euros a month. I'm working on another coaching program at the moment, and really want to expand the projects I'm conducting with *Besoin d'Aventure.*

I have some aspirations to become a mountain or kayak guide, but I'm aware it's not "la vie en rose" [life seen through rose-tinted glasses]. Although guiding is a nice job, it's not idyllic. It's still hard work. You're also repeating the same route over and over, while an important reason we like adventure so much is to discover something new, isn't it?

If You Want it Enough, You'll Find a Way

I believe that if you want to become an adventurer, you can find a way. Some people complain about their job, their 'superficial' life and say they'd love to have more adventures. But they don't undertake any action. I think that's because their desire isn't big enough. When I came back from my two-year-long trip around the world, I didn't want to do the work I did before anymore. However, I gave in anyway because I didn't see other options. Only when my wife got pregnant, did the desire to do something different become big enough, because I didn't want to be a father away from home for so long. That moment, I searched and found a way out. I think this holds true for every project you want to undertake. If you want it enough, you'll find a way.

There are 3 questions I ask myself every time I'm planning a big project. 1) Does it give me good vibrations? Do I feel in my gut that it's really something I want to do? 2) Will it deliver a beautiful story? In 30 years' time, will I still remember it and think about how great the experience was? 3) If I go and it fails, what will it cost me and how can I recover from it? Asking myself these 3 questions determines whether I plunge into the project or not.

Find out more about Brieg:
www.besoindaventure.fr
facebook.com/besoindaventure
instagram.com/besoindaventure

Deep Inside, Every Individual Is Only Looking for Happiness and Love

*In 2011, **CAROLINE MOIREAUX** quit her job to walk around the world, an adventure she called 'Pieds Libres' (translation: 'Free feet'). Her daily budget: €4. She arrived back in France 8 years, 52,000 kilometers, and a whole lot of experiences later.*

"I think I'm still the same Caroline, just a little bit more awakened."

The Notebook

I can't really remember when the travel bug hit me, whether it's something that started in childhood, or during adolescence. What I do remember is that I really started longing to go abroad in my early twenties. I wanted to travel and learn English. But at the time, I was together with a boyfriend that didn't like traveling and who didn't want me to leave alone. I was quite frustrated about this. When we broke up, after 8 years, I decided to follow my desire and I went to Australia for one year. I enjoyed my time *down under* a lot. Over there I also read about people who were planning to travel around the world on foot. I was amazed by that! A little while after, I watched a documentary about these people. It triggered me to follow the same path. When coming back to France, I went to a traveling festival and got in a conversation with a guy who advised me to read two books: *The Small Prince* by Antoine de Saint-Exupéry and *The Alchemist* by Paulo Coelho. At the time, I hated reading books. But he convinced me and so it happened that I got struck by a specific sentence from *The Alchemist:* *"It's normal to have fear to exchange everything we managed to obtain only for a dream. So, why do I have to listen to my heart? Because you'll never manage to keep your heart silent, and even if you pretend not to hear what he says, he'll be there in your chest and won't stop repeating what he thinks about life and the world."*

This quote resonated so much with what I felt. So often in life, we're frustrated because we don't act on what we feel we should do. You know what's really crazy, just before I left for my world travel, I found a stack of old notebooks from my childhood. There were about 10 of them. I took one and opened it to a random page and read a short text, written when I was 9 years old, titled "Air hostess." It said: "When I will be grown-up, I'll be an air hostess. I will serve the old people, the young and the children. I dream of going to Germany, but – exclamation mark – in life we go where we go. Maybe, we'll see, I'll travel the world without seeing Germany.

The Hard Thing About Leaving

Once I had decided to go around the world, leaving my job as an aerospace engineer was actually easy. I simply knew it was the right thing to do. Convincing my mother was a whole otter ball of wax. I remember sitting on my computer in the kitchen when my mother came in and asked me what I was doing. Off the cuff, I said: "I'm preparing my trip around the world by foot." Then: silence. I rolled my eyes back and forth from my screen to my mother's face. She was frozen. I went to my room and it took her a full hour to come up to me and ask what it was all about. She was never supportive in the months before I set off. Our interactions were quite tense. She kept on asking me annoying questions: "Why are you doing this? Where are you going to sleep? How are you going to take showers?" She just wanted me to change my thoughts. Even after I left, she said to one journalist: "I hope something bad will happen to her, so she has to come back."

Despite the friction, I did a video call with my parents every week during my 8 years on the road. And now, being 40 years old, I'm living with them again. But we still don't talk about what has happened. My mother isn't ready to put herself in question. As with so many people, she's not willing to "do the work". I understand, though. Going inside your soul is a difficult process. It's much easier to keep up the illusion that everything's fine.

Let the Magic Happen

There's a French author who once wrote down something about travel I like a lot: *"Traveling goes without motives. Traveling doesn't hesitate to prove that it suffices on itself. We think we are making the trip, but soon it's the trip that makes us, or unpacks us. We travel to have things happening and changing; if not we would stay at home."* I think that's really true. I think I am still the same person as I was 11 years ago, I think we are already what we're meant to be at any time. But for sure traveling made me become more conscious about the world, it made me more awake.

I do really love life. I think life is magnificent and magical, literally and metaphorically. I'm a big believer in metaphysics. I've seen so many things happen in life I can't logically explain, so there must be a magical force acting. I'll give you an example from my trip. Although I did most of my trip on foot, I completed some sections by boat or by bike. For instance, I crossed the Russian steppe by bike together with another cyclist. At a certain moment, I had problems with my bike seat, I needed some extra foam to fill up the coating so I'd be comfortably sitting on the bike. We were in a village and searched for this kind of foam everywhere, but couldn't find it. My bike partner was freaking out: "What are we gonna do? You're gonna have terrible buttocks pain, you won't be able to ride." I answered him: "Calm down, we're going to find it." He shouted: "How do you possibly think we're going to find it? We're seeing one car a day if we're lucky, and the next town is 4000 kilometers from here!" I responded: "Yeah, but we looked everywhere in this village and didn't find the foam, so we have to accept that there's no solution to be found in this place. And the definition of a problem is that there's a solution. So without a solution, there's no problem. Let's just continue cycling and we will find the foam."

So we hit off the endless road. Every night, we would put up our tent hundreds of meters away from the road, out of sight in the steppe. Because, if people see you over there, there are pretty fair chances you'll get robbed or even killed. One morning, I think it was the 6th or 7th day after we had left the last village, I was walking with my bike at hand from the steppe onto the main road to start a new cycling day. In the corner of my eye, I see a big white ball. I came close and noticed that it was a ball made of exactly the foam I needed for my seat. And while it had been pouring rain all night long, the foam was dry and clean. Can you imagine that?! I showed it to my mate; he couldn't believe his eyes, he thought I had tricked him. I hadn't, I had just been right: I knew that if I needed it, I would find it. Sometimes in life we just need to let the magic happen.

Traveling Alone

I set off for my trip around the world in June 2011. During the first 4 years, there were people with me all the time. Mostly Frenchmen who wanted to support me. But in fact, I didn't really like being on the road with them. Those people didn't really feel like travel partners. They had just come to follow me on my trip, they didn't make choices on their own. I often found myself guiding them. One exception was Cédrik, another traveler I met, with whom I would eventually spend two years on the road. Anyway, about halfway through my trip, I decided that I wanted to continue alone and from that point on refused all requests from people who wanted to join me. The result was pure happiness. Spontaneously I met other travelers and spent a couple of weeks together with them. Then the dynamics were different, we were just a bunch of travelers having a good time together; each individual making choices and taking responsibility.

One major insight I had while traveling is that every individual, regardless of their culture and nationality, is longing for the same two things: love and happiness. We may have different layers, different masks and different preferences, but our deepest selves all just want to feel connected and be happy.

I'm a very tactile, very affectionate person. I love touching and cuddling. But, when I was outdoors, I just felt connected with nature and I didn't need anything else. I felt like a 2-year-old on this trip again. There was always something to discover, always something fun to do. I just didn't have the time to feel lonely.

Never Bored

I can't understand people who are bored. Life is so amazing! There are so many nice things to do, my days are always too short! I've got stacks of books I want to finish, mostly about well-being, metaphysics, alchemy, human communication . . . Nowadays, I'm learning about business; making a website, marketing, legislation . . . My plan is to coach people that want to make the leap to a more passionate life, that want to throw themselves into an adventure.

Although I see myself as a social person, I can be anti-social as well. I like silence and solitude. When I was starting my spiritual journey, I was a bit afraid to discover myself. It's something we don't learn at school: understanding emotions, understanding yourself. I think that this internal work has helped me to better deal with anger. Today, when I feel anger coming up, I calmly observe it and analyze whether it's justified and what actions I can undertake.

I've done some silent retreats during my travels. The longest was a 40-day-long retreat in Guatemala. I also attended a retreat in which I was locked down in a dark room for 48 hours, that was heavy. When I'm home, I'm not disciplined enough to sit down and meditate for 20 minutes or so. I always have too many other things to do. But I do sometimes take time to do nothing, like just lying in my bed and observing the surroundings.

Thought experiment: If for the following 8 years you'd have to spend your time in one single spot, and you could only take 5 objects with you, where would you go and what would you take?

I would live in a log cabin in Alaska. Since it's cold up there, I would take my sleeping bag, which can keep me warm even at -30°C. I would take a box full of books, paper, pencils, and a man for hunting. You know, that's actually something I'd really love to do: live with a family in the woods, off-grid, in connection with nature.

Find out more about Caroline:
www.piedslibres.com
facebook.com/Piedslibres
instagram.com/piedslibres

372

PART NINE:
GO YOUR OWN WAY

I'd Tell My Younger Self Not To Worry. Everything Works Out. You Can Do Anything You Want To

LINDSEY COLE is an adventurer who deserves her own category. She has been rollerskating in a nude suit, ran with the Kenyans, cycled to South Africa to attend the FIFA World Cup, swam the Thames dressed as a mermaid, and walked the length of the Rabbit-Proof Fence in Australia.

"Although I don't earn much at all, I do have freedom, which is undeniably wonderful. I can create dream journeys and chase them when I want and venture into nature and not be rushed to leave."

Rabbit-Proof Fence

As soon as I left University, I wanted to go and see the world. I gave myself five years to do whatever I wanted to do. I worked in France, Austria, Canada, Turkey and built homes in Sri Lanka after the tsunami. Then, I went to Australia. My plan was to circumnavigate the entire country, work on farms and earn my second-year visa, and live there forever. I broke my leg whilst drunk at a festival and had to recline for three months. That's when I came across the film and book *Follow the Rabbit-Proof Fence*. It's a moving tale about three young aboriginal girls who were forcibly removed from their families and placed in a settlement in 1931. Children taken during this time became known as *The Stolen Generation*. Molly, the eldest of the girls, didn't like the settlement and engineered a plan to escape. Molly, her half-sister Daisy, and her cousin Gracie escaped and walked all the way home. They crossed some of Australia's most inhospitable environments, following the Rabbit-Proof Fence. They had no maps, no provisions, no shoes. Nothing but each other. Along the way, Gracie got recaptured but Molly and Daisy made it back home.

Shortly after being acquainted with their story, my dad suddenly passed away. Back home in England, I was totally lost and depressed and began self-harming to help process it all. One accident that led to the emergency unit of the hospital made me realize I had to channel the negative energy another way. I decided to take part in the London triathlon. Having not ridden a bike since I was 12 years old, I struggled and wondered how on earth I was going to complete it. I then remembered how those 3 young girls traversed 1,000 miles across Australia's desert. That put it all into perspective. After the London triathlon, I cycled the length of Britain, followed by the length of the African continent. Then I did whatever idea came into my mind: rollerskating to Bude in a nude suit (only because 'nude' and 'Bude' rhyme and I thought that was funny), running from London to Manchester while busking with a ukulele, and training with Kenyans to see how fast I could run a marathon when I turned 30. I always wanted to return to Australia to retrace Molly and Daisy's journey and, in 2016, I finally did.

It was the most beautiful journey I've ever made. I was alone for 1,000 miles by foot in the heat of the Australian outback, but anyone who heard about me wanted to help . . . The girls' story helped spur me on when I was at my lowest moments. I was taken in by Molly's family when I made it to Jigalong. Molly sadly passed away in 2004, and Gracie never made it back to Jigalong, but Daisy was still alive. She lived in a retirement home on the Northwest Australian coast and it was the most incredible ending to my journey to meet her. She died two years after I met her. It was such an incredible journey that I didn't want to go home, so I circumnavigated Australia with truck drivers.

Lindsey's Adventures
Cycling From Lands End to John O'Groats (2010)
Cycling From Cairo to Cape Town (2010): "I wanted to see the Soccer World Cup in South Africa"
Roller Skating 250 Miles in France (2012)
Running From London to Manchester With a Ukulele (2012)
Roller Skating Nude to Bude (2013): "Just because it rhymed"
Running With Kenyans (2013): I turned 30 and wanted to see if I could run a marathon in less than 3 hours. As if that idea wasn't ridiculous enough, I decided to train with the fastest runners in the world. They gave me the nickname 'Fatty Mzungu'.
Circumnavigating Australia With Truck Drivers (2017)
Swimming the River Thames in a Mermaid Tail (2018): "Along the way, I fished out all the plastic."

About Being an Adventurer
Finances are an obvious pressure. I am often struggling to make ends meet. Sometimes I feel even more pressure when I'm meeting up with friends with bigger incomes.

My lifestyle can have an impact on my mental health too, sometimes. Not knowing how much my next paycheck will be, will I ever own a home, what will I do when I have a family, etc . . . But, I think everyone has all those doubts, regardless of what your job is.

I don't earn much, but I don't spend much either and I do have freedom, which is undeniably wonderful. I can create dream journeys and chase them when I want and venture into nature and not be rushed to leave. I also like creating different ways to make income. Although it can be very stressful hustling all the time, it can also feel liberating to spend less.

How do you deal with danger? What have been the most dangerous moments in your career? Have you faced death? If so, what did that do with you?
I've gotten seriously lost a couple of times. I was understandably scared, worried, and yelled. But then I remembered my survival expert friend, Bob Cooper, saying the number one tip for survival in the outback/desert is to not panic.

Who have been and currently are the most important people in your life? Both on a personal and professional level?

My mum. No matter how much she has not wanted me to do an adventure at times, she has always been there rooting for me, and quietly worrying to her friends.

Books and Movie Recommendations
Follow the Rabbit-Proof Fence, by Doris Pilkington.
Tracks, by Robyn Davidson. I read this whilst I was walking the Rabbit-Proof Fence. It's about a woman, Robyn Davidson, who learned to train camels for two years and thereafter walked through the Australian desert with her dog and four camels. The way Davidson described the desert and her environment was exactly how I felt while walking the Rabbit-Proof Fence.

Babel, directed by Alejandro González Iñárritu. This movie made me realize how interconnected we all are and how one society's actions can affect another.

Mental and Physical Health
I don't really have any strategies. I like to stretch and do some yoga poses but wouldn't say I really do yoga. I like swimming in cold water, but don't regularly have cold showers. I sometimes journal, but not every day. I sort of do things when I think about them, but I have never kept to a routine in anything. I'm quite impulsive.

If you'd be obligated to live on an isolated island for the next 10 years, and you're only allowed to take 2 people and 5 objects with you; who and what would you take with you?
I would bring David Attenborough and Michelle Obama. For the objects, I would bring a knife, suncream (I burn, and my lip frazzles easily), a musical instrument (so I could finally teach myself one), a *Kindle* (with an unlimited supply of books), and some sort of ball.

What advice would you give to someone who's stuck in a job they don't like and dreams about being an adventurer?
I'm probably the wrong person to ask this question to, as I've always been a freelancer. The grass is always greener . . . But if you have a burning desire to really want to do something, whether it's an adventure or a dream job, I'd encourage anyone to give it a go. Weigh out the pros and cons. Write a contingency plan for if it all goes wrong, to give you confidence that you've thought everything through. I thought about doing the Rabbit-Proof Fence for eight years. I had no idea if it would be possible to do it, but I wanted to do it so much I just had to give it a go. I told my friends that I'd pull out if it got too difficult. It's been the best thing I've ever done! I'm so glad I pushed my fear and anxiety about it to the side.

What advice would you give to your 18-year-old self?
I took failure really gravely and personally when I was younger. Failing at something seemed like the end of the world. Now I realize that I've learned so much from being thrown off course from my intended path. So, I'd tell my younger self not to worry. Everything works out. You're still young and can do anything you want to do.

Characteristics and Personality Traits

[I asked Lindsey to rank herself from 0 (not like this trait at all) to 10 (very much like that)]

Optimism: 8

Discipline: 2

Courage: 8

Resilience: 8

Stubbornness: 6

Social skills: 8

Creativity: 7

Curiosity: 10

Find out more about Lindsey:

www.lindseycole.co.uk

facebook.com/lindseycoleadventures

instagram.com/stompycole

It Took a Big Dose of Blind Optimism and Faith to Bring My Dreams to Life

CHARLES GIFFORD POST is an ecologist, photographer, filmmaker, and environmental brand consultant. He is also co-founder of 'The Nature Project', a non-profit that gives under-served youth the opportunity to experience nature alongside a collective of like-minded athletes, environmentalists, and philanthropists. Charles is married to adventurer, artist, and environmentalist Rachel Pohl.

"My heroes and mentors remind me time and again that happiness comes from creating a life around the two questions 'Does this fulfill you?' and 'Does this compel you?'"

Growing Up Surrounded By Nature

I grew up at the foot of California's coast range, just north of San Francisco, in a small town surrounded by nature and just a stone's throw from the Pacific Ocean. Redwood trees and bay laurel, sycamore, and oak threw shade over the small creek that flowed just over the back fence. The creek sustained wild coho salmon up until I was in high school. I was raised by a family that appreciated time outside. My dad is an avid fisherman and hunter, and my grandmother was a passionate birder. Every spare moment was spent either off on some sort of wildlife focussed outing or in our big garden, which had an orchard and sprawling veggie patch. On many nights, my brother and I would pile into my dad's old *Volvo*, and my dad would drive us into the forests in search of animals along the road or venturing into the meadows in the cover of darkness. We would see deer and bobcats, coyotes and foxes, skunk and opossum. I learned about caring for the land at a young age by tending to our backyard ecosystem. I also witnessed its demise as the backyard creek was transformed into a storm drain and the salmon stopped showing up, marking the end of an ancient migration.

By the time I got into high school, I had the surfing bug. I lived to surf, and so I spent all of my spare time traveling up and down the California coast in search of waves. Most of the time, I ended up in the Golden Gate National Recreation Area and Point Reyes National Seashore, regions among the most biodiverse in North America. At times we would be surfing amongst migrating gray whales or have to pick our way through a flotilla of surf scooters or a colony of wintering elephant seals. Surfing on the productive north coast was exciting and filled with life. It was during these adventures that I started carrying a camera. The trips that married adventure with wildlife and some outdoor pursuit became my passion and ultimately led me to a career as a creative and ecologist studying wildlife.

Doing What Seems Like Madness

I was first introduced to ecology as an 8th grader when I spent my last semester of middle school volunteering with the National Park Service. I helped pull invasive ice plants from coastal dunes and replant native lupine and coyote brush. The next year, I volunteered at a marine mammal rehabilitation center. Later, I took my first environmental science courses as a sophomore and junior in high school. Ultimately, all of these experiences pushed me down a path of science and ecology. I was guided by a deep curiosity about the natural world. When I discovered there was a field of study focusing on these pursuits, I jumped in. Having an interest in writing and photography, I often journaled and took photos from my surf trips or forays into the field to watch animals like the tule elk that roam the foggy headlands of Point Reyes. My long-time best friend, Cole Barash, a professional photographer, really pushed me to use my camera as a tool. So, I took photos nearly every day for years. I only had a 50mm lens, and so I had to work for all of my shots. This forced me to be patient, a skill that would come in handy as I began working as a research apprentice during my college years at UC Berkeley. It wasn't until I started studying under scientists who had an acute appreciation for visual storytelling as a complement to the empirical sciences that I really began focusing my energy on the confluence of these approaches. These influential scientists include Dr. Mark Moffett, National Geographic photographer, and Dr. Todd Dawson, UC Berkeley professor and scientist who helped discover the tallest trees on earth.

The biggest challenge for me was finding the support and mentorship to shift from a traditional science career to one that was equally weighted with storytelling. I was three years into a Ph.D. program at UC Berkeley when I realized that I was no longer fulfilled by the work. I had spent nearly a decade earning my B.S. in Ecology and holding various field research positions at this point. To leave Berkeley was the hardest decision I have ever made simply because, outside of the efforts I poured into my graduate work, I had never worked harder for anything. So to ask my advisory committee, composed of some of the world's most inspiring ecologists like my mentor Dr. Mary Power, seemed like madness. But thankfully, they recognized my passion and gave me their support to depart with a Master's Degree in Ecology after submitting my thesis on the American Dipper, North America's only fully aquatic songbird. They cheered me on as I ventured off campus to pursue a career that blended science and storytelling.

Leaving academia was very hard. The new chapter in my life required a lot of patience, honing my voice and skills, and saying 'yes' to just about every opportunity that came my way. I took a huge leap of faith to try and build a totally new and unique career. It left me feeling unmoored, to say the least. It took many years before I felt like I had truly made the right decision. I was running on a dose of blind optimism and faith up to that point when the work I had dreamed of doing really started to come to life.

You are married to adventurer and landscape artist Rachel Pohl. What makes Rachel and you a great couple?
We both live for the beauty of the natural world. I notice the wildlife, the comings and goings of songbirds, the tracks in the snow, or the tendencies of the deer that frequent our fields. Rachel, on the other hand, sees the light and colors that punctuate these moments. Her eyes pull out the hues and patterns that I miss or just simply don't have the eyes to see. When we met and started spending time together, especially outside, we realized that we allow one another to experience aspects of nature that we had been missing all along. Now, life is all the richer, all the more complete in the sense that we are tapped into a much bigger spectrum of experience than before. And perhaps most importantly, we admire one another deeply. I think

that's a hugely important quality that has galvanized our relationship. We push each other, and also hold each other accountable. She's a wonderful communicator, and also sweeter than any human I've ever known. She makes me a better person and appreciates the nerdy tendencies I have, which I realize takes a special person. After all, not just anyone would happily sit on a riverbank while I explain what's so cool about a particular aquatic insect I've found beneath a river stone or indulge me while I gawk at a passing western tanager or some other brilliant songbird.

Likewise, I try my best to give Rachel the support and attention she needs so she may thrive as an artist. We often stop and watch the sunsets so she can study the colors and the way the light comes and goes. I know how much these moments mean to her, so I'm happy to prioritize a hike or ski that affords a certain vantage point, knowing that she has her muse picked out. I asked her to marry me only a few months after we met. I'd say a key influence was the fact that we felt something that we'd never felt before. I'm not sure there are words for that, but in truth, we couldn't have imagined life going any other way. And while that's a bit gushy and romantic, I think the saying of "when you know, you know" is something that truly speaks to our experience.

If Warren Buffet would write you a check of $10 million and a note that says "to be used to do good", how would you spend the money?

I would donate half to conservation efforts with a focus on wild salmon, songbirds, and pollinators, and the other to organizations that provide community-based support services for autistic youth. My little sister, a personal hero of mine, is autistic among many other inspiring qualities and characteristics, including bravery and courage beyond measure. I've seen firsthand the horrible treatment she has received from the public school system, and more generally the public and her peers simply because many perceive her to be different. I've been disgusted and heartbroken so many times. Although, she's resilient and has defied all the odds and criticism others so unfairly placed on her. I've also seen how incredible and life-changing organizations that specialize in supporting autistic youth can be. The phrase that is well known in these circles, is "different not less." My sister is like that. She has benefited tremendously from organizations that all too often are grossly underfunded and underrecognized. In light of this, I would donate half the funds to those groups so that more autistic kids can have better support and ultimately a higher quality of life.

If you'd be invited to give a College commencement speech, what would you talk about?

The theme of my talk would be the importance of living a life that fulfills you, one defined by experiences and work that compel you. To be compelled and fulfilled are two experiences that I often reflect on as I say 'yes' or 'no' to opportunities. As I get older, I can't help but notice that all too often people find themselves with lifestyles, circumstances, or occupations that don't fulfill them, and by work or tasks that don't compel them. My heroes and mentors remind me time and again that when we create a life around the two questions "does this fulfill you?" and "does this compel you?" happiness and contentment often follow.

Social Media Isn't Everything

Today, Rachel has over 150 thousand followers on Instagram, I have over 100k. Both of us grew our Instagram accounts organically. We just started publishing the things that were meaningful to us. Time did the rest. And truthfully, our voices and the content we post adapt as we grow and experience new things. But, the essence of our content has stayed true to my passion for ecology and science, and Rachel's passion for art and the journey as an artist. I'd like to think our passion and authenticity have helped fuel our growth more than anything.

Social media can be a major time drain and distraction. Over the years, we have learned how to steward our accounts while also being very clear that it is just one tool in our toolbox. Truthfully, and contrary to what some may suspect, social media work comprises maybe 5% of Rachel's business. A majority of her work and revenue come from fine art sales and the products she designs. The same goes for me. 95% of my work revolves around my creative endeavors like filmmaking or writing and, more predominantly, my ecological brand consulting commitments. I often work with well-known outdoor brands and run various internal and consumer-facing programs that hinge on my experience in ecology, marketing, and brand strategy.

There's a misconception that social media is everything. In truth that's just not the case for most. Sure, some are living exclusively on social media-generated income. But how sustainable is that? What's next? Rachel and I have always had career goals that have been complemented by our social media platforms but have never been defined by them. And lastly, it's easy for people to correlate engagement (number of likes & comments) with influence. In truth, you can have 10k random people like your work, or you can have 20 of the right people – your heroes, potential clients, peers, collaborators – like your work. The two are very different.

What are you grateful for?
Health, happiness, my family and friends, and access to nature.

Recommended Books
The Great Animal Orchestra, by Bernie Krause
A Sand County Almanac, by Aldo Leopold
Braiding Sweetgrass, by Robin Wall Kimmerer
The Shepherd's Life, by James Rebanks
The Outermost House, by Henry Beston
Adventures Among Ants, by Mark Moffett
Dark Emu, by Bruce Pascoe
Arctic Dreams, by Barry Lopez
The Wayfinders, by Wade Davis

On top of this, I would suggest that anyone interested in conservation and/or living a meaningful life study the words and work of Kris Tompkins. She's a personal friend and one of my greatest sources of inspiration. Together with her husband, Doug Tompkins, she has done what was once thought to be impossible; creating or expanding 15 terrestrial and two marine National Parks in Chile and Argentina, effectively protecting over 14 million acres of terrestrial habitat and 30 million acres of marine habitat. She is brilliant and incredible.

What is your definition of a life well-lived?
To give more than you take, uplift others, have a positive impact on our planet and community, find and steward happiness and fulfillment, and do so by altruistic and synergistic means. Our puppy Knute (@mr.knute on IG), makes us happy beyond words, so he gets some credits to my 'life well-lived' too.

Find out more about Charles:
www.charlespost.com
instagram.com/charles_post

I Continuously Try to Expand My Understanding of the Human Condition and Our Relation to the Natural World

FOREST WOODWARD is an internationally recognized and awarded photographer and filmmaker. His work focuses on human connection and environmental protection. In his free time, Forest loves to go trail running, rock climbing, or mountaineering.

"The passion-projects for which I can't find fundraising and thus have to rely on the engagement and creative brilliance of friends and volunteers are often the best experiences – both from a creative standpoint and a community-building standpoint."

Natural Curiosity

I grew up in rural Appalachia. As a homeschooled child of alternatively minded parents, I was given freedom from an early age to explore the world through a creative and inquisitive lens. I loved getting to row the oar rig on our family rafting trips through the Gates of Lodore, learning to read white water and navigate the canyons of the southwest. Growing up, we were encouraged to entertain ourselves outside. I relish the memories of building trails and forts and creating imaginary worlds in the woods and along the mountainsides behind our home in North Carolina. Already as a kid, I developed a passion for photography and would become the youngest student ever to attend the *Rocky Mountain School Of Photography*.

I spent my twenties and early thirties living in communities that drew my interest all around the US; from New York City to a roadless rural community of 100 residents in the North Cascades. During those years, I also went traveling to over 50 countries on 6 continents, seeking to better understand the human condition and our relation to the natural world. Interactions with people who live and think differently from me have always been a part of how I learned to see the world. These interactions have also always been an integral part of my art as a photographer and filmmaker. I like listening to other people, trying to expand my understanding of the fabric of the country and planet I inhabit. My degrees in Sociology and Spanish certainly underpin some of that curiosity. The ability to speak across language barriers has also been helpful while traveling. Throughout those many years of the geographic movement, I continuously evolved my craft as a storyteller; expanding into the fields of film and prose, and supporting my personal projects through commercial and editorial assignments.

Blessings in Disguise

It can be frustrating to look around at the landscape of "content" in the current day and to feel that the stories that get funding are not always those with the most social impact. However, it can also be a blessing in disguise to have those sorts of personal projects that bring you into contact with yourself and your community in a meaningful way. *Rural Runner* was a short movie about my brother Canyon, who's a climate advocate and trail runner. Despite many efforts, I couldn't find any fundraiser for the project. But, I deeply believed in it and my friends rallied around me. I had a dozen friends and brilliant creatives volunteer their time to make that film a reality. I also worked on another film over the past few years, *Strong Winds*, a short piece, and call to climate action co-produced by my friends from *The Pacific Climate Warriors* and my brother Canyon. That project was another example of no one wanting to fund it, but us feeling passionate about the story and investing our own time and resources to get it out there. Honestly, these are often the best experiences – both from a creative standpoint, and a community-building standpoint.

If you could step into someone's shoes for one week at any place in the world and at any point in history, who would you choose?

Yours. The kid who works the window at McDonald's. My Mom's. Anyone really. I don't presume to think that anyone's experience is more valuable than another one's.

Who and what are you grateful for?

I'm grateful for my family, for all of the friends with whom I have gotten to share time in this world, for the strangers who have welcomed me into their homes, and for all those who have shared parts of their stories with me, however humble.

Recommended Books

Underland, by Robert McFarlane
Beauty in Photography, by Robert Adams
The Lord of the Rings, by JRR Tolkien

If you could rewrite the Ten Commandments, what would they be?

I think everyone should live on their own and rewrite them often but mostly, live them. Don't worry about writing them or externalizing them for others. Let your life be the writing.

What advice would you give the 20-year-old Forest?

Worry less about what other people think.

What is your definition of happiness?

Being able to hold grief and joy in the same hand, to be at peace with yourself and the imperfections of the world.

Find out more about Forest:

www.forestwoodward.com
instagram.com/forestwoodward
facebook.com/forest.woodward

Say Yes More

At age 25, **DAVE CORNTHWAITE** *decided to quit his job and skateboard the length of Great Britain. Two months after crossing the finish line, he flew to Australia and broke the Guinness World Record for the longest skateboard journey, having skated 3,618 miles from Perth to Brisbane. Since then, the craziness has never stopped.*

"I just always did what felt right."

Expedition 1,000

At age 25, I felt unhappy in my corporate job and decided to go on an adventure. I think I was mainly looking for an identity that felt right. So I learned skateboarding, rode from John O'Groats to Lands End, and thereby became the first man to have skateboarded the length of Great Britain. That was June 2006. From there, I went to Australia and skateboarded from West to East, the longest journey someone had ever conducted on a skateboard. In 2009, I went back to Australia and kayaked the Murray river, good for 1,476 miles. After every adventure, I experienced a sense of depression. The reason was, I hadn't planned my next adventure, there was just this empty space . . . Coming back from the Murray River, I thought about setting a long-term goal in order to counteract this post-adventure blues. At the same time, it would be a sort of bucket list that would set me up for continuous growth and learning. I came up with the idea to undertake 25 journeys of at least 1,000 miles, each journey by a different non-motorized means of transportation.

Today I have completed 15 of my journeys. Amongst them, I kick-scooted in Japan, water-biked across Norway, drove on an Elliptigo through Western Europe, sailed the Pacific, swam the Missouri River, and supped the Mississippi River. For each adventure, I block out one to three months on the calendar, way in advance. Then, about 3-4weeks before departure, I look at the country map and a list of potential vehicles I made. At that moment, my gut feeling tells me which challenge to do. As a result, I often get to the starting point with very little specific training, if any. For example, when I was putting on my wetsuit at the banks of the Missouri River, I didn't know how to swim . . . I learned it along the way.

Community Builder

In 2012, I started sharing a personal motto: "Say Yes More." It was a message encouraging people to get out of their comfort zones, try new things, and say "Yes" to adventure. Nowadays, it's so easy for most of us to stay in our comfort zone all the time. It has become very easy not to stretch ourselves. But we shouldn't forget that we've always been evolving creatures, there's an innate curiosity in all of us. The danger of staying in the comfort zone too long is that life starts feeling like a rud. Adventure is a great way to break through the rud, to discover the possibilities in life, and experience what we're actually capable of.

During my adventures, I've met so many incredible people along the road. I would talk with them for one minute and get invited to their house. I have experienced unbelievable hospitality and friendliness. I wanted to experience this feeling of connection with like-minded people in Britain as well. So, one day in 2015, I posted on Facebook: "Come camp with me." That weekend, 19 people turned up to camp with me. We took a train, got to know each other around a campfire, and slept under the stars. The next week, 25 people came. Before long, we were trying to hide 50 wild campers away for the night. We called the community *The Yes Tribe*. At the end of that summer, we organized our first *Yestival*. Today, there are over 20,000 *Yes Tribe* members all over the world.

What advice do you give people who come up to you, telling you that they would also like to turn their passion for adventure into a career, but don't know where to start?
Well, this is indeed a very difficult step to take. I had saved money for 1,5 years before I went skateboarding. Once that money was gone, it was mostly a matter of reducing day-to-day spending. The first years of being an adventurer, I got by with only £4000 a year. The biggest cost for most people is rent or a mortgage. So try to find a solution so you don't have to pay for housing. For a couple of years, I spent 100 nights a year wild camping around London. For the last couple of months, my wife and I have been house and pet sitting in different countries.

It took me about 7 years to make my adventurous lifestyle sustainable. Today, I have around 20 different small streams of income: filmmaking, books, speaking engagements, organizing workshops, etc.

The biggest thing standing in the way of most people is the fear of letting go of security. I encourage them: "Just get started, take the first step." And when it comes to money, think about this: if you quit your job, you'll have 24 hours a day to find a way to make a living by doing something you love. That's a lot of time and there are many ways to earn money.

Out of every 100 comments I get on my adventures, there's probably 99 positive and 1 negative. But, it's the negative ones that seep into my mind. In order to deal with it, I created a page on my website called 'They Need a Hug', where I post the negative messages I receive from jealous, pessimistic, or judgmental people. Actually, I know I shouldn't bother at all about these attacks, because people that went on their own journey, faced difficulties, and got on a big adventure would never tear someone else down . . .

Book and Movie Recommendations
Not really any books or movies actually. Nevertheless, I like the character of Forrest Gump. That guy just went out, did what he loved, had so many great encounters, and touched so many people in small and big ways. I have the same idea about life and adventure. I just always did what felt right to me. By the way, there's a scene in the movie where Forrest Gump gets injured and can't run anymore, so he starts playing ping pong in the hospital and becomes a master in no time. That's exactly what I did when I got limited in my possibilities to go outdoors during COVID-19. I started playing table tennis and got really good at it.

Characteristics and Personality Traits

[I asked Dave to rank himself from 0 (not like this trait at all) to 10 (very much like that)]

Optimism: 9

Discipline: 9

Courage: 7

Resilience: 7

Stubbornness: 10

Creativity: 7

Sense of humor: 8

Self-Propelled

I host a podcast called *Self-Propelled*, where I interview people that go their own way in life. In order to be a good podcaster, first of all, you need perseverance. About 92% of all podcasts don't make it to the 8th episode. You also need really good audio equipment. And then, you just have to be generous with your guests. Give them the openness to tell their story. A couple of questions I like to ask are: "What are you afraid of?", "What does a good life look like to you?", and I always finish with "What are the most important things in your life?"

What are the most important things in the life of Dave Cornthwaite?

Love, happiness, and creativity.

What's your definition of happiness?

It's not just joy. It's also finding out the things you don't like to do and then don't do them.

What are the most important life lessons you'll teach your kids?

It's probably gonna change somewhat once I'll have them, but for now, I would say: "You don't need much material stuff to be happy. Connect with nature, be grounded. Don't spend much time with people you don't feel good about. Most importantly, believe in yourself."

Find out more about Dave:

www.davecornthwaite.com

facebook.com/davecornthwaite

instagram.com/davecorn/

Time Slows Down in the Wilderness

MIRIAM LANCEWOOD is a former Dutch pole vaulting champion who has been living in the wild for the last 11 years, together with her partner Peter. Living a simple, nature-connected life is the way in which they find great happiness and mental and physical strength.

"I think anyone could lead this way of life. Hunting and gathering are in our genes, in our blood, in our instincts. It is the way our ancestors survived for thousands of years."

Living Without Having To Work

I grew up in the Netherlands in a normal loving family. I have two sisters. One is older, one is younger, and we are each 18 months apart. Every summer, we went wild camping in France, where we enjoyed playing in the forest, building tree huts, and swimming in rivers. At age 7, I joined the scouts. That's where I learned navigational skills, making fire, setting up a tent, etc. I also enjoyed soccer, athletics, and playing music. When I was 13, I was discovered as a pole vaulting talent and I would become a National Champion 6 times. Because of my passion for sports, I decided to study Physical Education in College. After graduation, I volunteered for a year in Zimbabwe as a teacher. Unfortunately, I didn't like it. I felt lonely and I missed freedom . . . I had just spent so many years at school as a student, and there I was again in a school! I decided I wanted to feel free and do something fun: I wanted to travel. I had very few savings, so I chose a country where I could live very cheaply: India. I traveled around the country alone for 5 months before I met my future husband Peter.

Peter is a highly educated, intelligent New Zealander who had been living in India for 5 years at the time of meeting him. He told me it's actually possible to live without having to work. That idea sounded fascinating to me. We started traveling together through South-East Asia and Papua New Guinea. Despite Peter being 30 years older than me, I fell in love with him. We had the same view on life. We didn't care about a car, a house, possessions, or a career. Both of us wanted an adventurous life in the wild. We decided to give it a try in 2010 and spend four seasons in the mountains in New Zealand. When I told my parents about my relationship with Peter, they were quite shocked. Peter was almost as old as they were, so in the beginning, it was difficult to accept. On the other hand, when I announced that we would live in the wild, they were very supportive.

Discovery

As a premise to receive a residence permit in New Zealand, I had to be a school teacher for one year. During this year, I prepared myself for hunting with a bow. Every day, I shot arrows at a target. By the end of the 12 months, I had become an accurate archer, so I went into the wild quite confidently. Too confident, as it would turn out. Hunting in the wild is extremely difficult! You hardly see any animals, because they're on their guard. The rare times I had the chance to spot a wild goat, deer, or pig, it would run away as soon as it smelled me. It took me 6 months before I shot my first goat. I still carry its horn on a string around my neck as a souvenir. For me, it's the symbol of the cycle of life and death. We survive in the mountains by hunting. Death gives birth to life.

The first weeks in the wilderness required a lot of adjustment. On the first day, Peter and I were euphoric. We had this immense sense of freedom. The second day, we looked at each other and said: "Oh my god, what are we going to do?" It was day two and we were already bored. As it would turn out, you need about two weeks of boredom before reaching a state in which you are in sync with nature. Once this happens, life goes much slower. You stop identifying yourself with the past and future. You lose your sense of time. We didn't have a clock, we didn't have contact with our family, so it felt as if we had left the past behind. We had burned our bridges, so to say.

Our relationship is very harmonious because we are living a life we both really want. We also complement each other. I am physically stronger, so I hunt and I carry most of the load when we're moving from one place to another. Peter is better at navigation, reads the weather like a book, gathers the best firewood, and knows more about edible plants. We always have a chessboard with us, as well as some philosophy books, Nietzsche for example. This allows us to read for many hours and discuss the work afterward.

Despite getting along with each other very well, it's not easy to live with someone 24/7. I'm often surprised by how deeply rooted our conditioned responses are. For example, I get grumpy and silent when Peter makes an insulting comment. Then I ask myself why. Is it to punish him so he knows never to make such comments again, even though I know there might have been some truth in what he said? . . . Our relationship is a way to discover and understand ourselves and our cultural conditioning. Every now and then, I go for a hike for a couple of days without Peter. When being alone in that deep silence, sometimes there are moments of great connectivity. Thoughts seem less dominant for a few hours and there is just clarity that is not based on knowledge from the past. When that happens, I feel I'm walking in the wisdom of the forest.

Healthy Living

We left civilization 11 years ago. After our first year, we saw no reason to return to a house. We decided this was the life we wanted to live, so we've been living this nomadic life for seven consecutive years in New Zealand. Every couple of months we came back into "the human world" to buy lentils, rice, flour, and salt. In the Alpine Mountains where we live, there are very few plants to eat, so we need to have these basic supplies to survive. Sometimes I borrow a guitar and sing songs in town to earn some money. Our total yearly budget is between €3,000 and €5,000 for two people. Considering our lifestyle, that might still seem like quite a lot, but that's because food is very expensive in New Zealand.

For the past few years, I no longer hunt with a bow and arrow, but with a gun. This makes it a lot easier. At the same time, it's better for the prey. When you hit an animal with an arrow without killing it immediately, it will often continue to suffer for hours or even days, slowly bleeding to death. Each time we kill a big animal (a goat, for example) we have to eat it as fast as possible, before flies arrive and the meat gets filled with maggots. Sometimes we smoke the meat to preserve it, but the blowfly lays its eggs horribly quickly. We eat quite irregularly. I think that the typical meal-planning of breakfast, lunch, and dinner is good if you work in a school or another institution. But, without a clock, these 3 meals don't make sense. With hunting, it's always feast or famine.

Our sleep rhythms are very different from most people's. We live according to daylight. This means that our nights are quite short in summer, especially because I prefer to hunt in the twilight, but very long in winter. In winter, we can sleep up to 14 hours a night! The first thing I notice each time we come back to the city is how tired people look. People underestimate the importance of sleep. After a long night of sleep, I feel so much happier, more joyful, and more energetic. Living in the forest also rejuvenates me. In the city, there's constant noise, light everywhere, and our sleep gets disrupted. As a result, I wake up tired and I reach for sugary food which makes me feel even worse afterward. We never get sick in nature, but we often do when we come back to the "normal" world.

Wild at Heart

During the first 7 years living in nature, we did something slightly different each year. For example, one year we walked 3,000 kilometers in New Zealand, from North to South. In all those years, we never encountered other people who lived like us. After a while, the media heard about our nomadic lifestyle and one article spiked the interest of a book publisher. This way, I got to write my first book *Woman in the Wilderness*, in which I told the story of self-discovery, love, and survival of our first years in the wilderness.

Thereafter, Peter and I decided to go overseas. For two years, we walked 1,000 kilometers through Europe. We started in France, went all the way up to Austria, and then took a bus to Bulgaria. From there, we walked another 1,000 kilometers until we finished in Turkey. Europe was different compared to New Zealand. We didn't have a rifle with us or a license to hunt. But, on the other hand, we found a lot more edible plants, nuts, and fruits. After those two years, we returned to New Zealand where I organized a female expedition. I hiked with another Dutch adventurer, Tamar Valkenier, through the Alps in New Zealand, living only by what we could hunt. It was very hard physically, as well as mentally. There wasn't a hiking trail. We had to pick our own route and be careful not to fall into crevasses. At times we were ravenously hungry. After 10 weeks though, we felt incredibly lean and strong. People can read about the trips through Europe and the adventure with Tamar in the Alps in my second book *Wild at Heart*.

Happiness

I find it striking that no one ever told me it is possible to live in the wilderness, as if that's not a real option to live a life. In primary school, they don't teach us the primary skills of life. We don't learn how to survive, how to grow a vegetable garden, how to milk a goat or cow, how to light a fire, which plants are edible, which herbs are medicinal . . . Teachers don't tell us that you can live without a normal job, off-grid, offline, and self-sufficient. Recently, I was talking to a classroom in Hong Kong about our way of life. The eyes of the eight-year-olds I was talking to went open, some of them might even try to live for some time in the wild themselves one day.

What I notice is that the education system sets us up for a life of constraints. Get a job, buy a house, and pay the mortgage. That sounds like a trap to me. The price to pay for security is not worth my freedom! I experience so much more happiness and health when I'm in the wilderness. In my late teens and early twenties, I was always in a hurry, always stressed, there was always a next thing to do. Living in the mountains made it possible for me to leave behind this part of my personality. I think that, for a lot of people, their past is what is stopping them. Sometimes, you need to leave everything behind you in order to move forward, in order to become another person, in order to set yourself free.

I would encourage everyone to just try and live for two weeks in the wild and see how it changes you. For me, this life is a timeless existence. In the silence of the mountains, I find grace.

Find out more about Miriam:
www.miriamlancewood.com

If You Bring Passion, Purpose, and the Right People Together, Amazing Things Happen

*A climbing accident at age 21 paralyzed **KAREN DARKE** from the chest down, but it didn't stop her from being adventurous, let alone from dreaming big! Over the last 2 decades, she has (amongst many other feats) hand biked across the Himalayas, kayaked from Vancouver to Alaska, traversed Greenland on skis, climbed El Capitan, and won a Paralympic gold medal.*

"My friends call me the master of reframing. As soon as a problem arises, I turn it into something good."

How did you get into adventure?

My parents were school teachers and thus had a lot of vacation time. As a result, we spent most of our summers in France, camping and hiking in the mountains. I grew up in Yorkshire, a region well known for fell running and bouldering. At age 14, I started climbing myself, with friends from school. When I was 16, a regional organization was looking for youngsters to go on an expedition in China. We could choose from different activities: scientific research, climbing, mountain biking . . . I applied for the mountain bike group and got selected. For one year, we went mountain biking every week as preparation for the actual expedition, one month of cycling in remote China. After this experience, I knew that I wanted to make adventure a big part of my life.

After high school, I went to University and studied geology and chemistry. During summers, I always went on a long holiday. I cycled across Corsica and Iceland, and went mountaineering in the Alps with a couple of friends. Looking back, we were a bit naive or irresponsible. We knew almost nothing about mountaineering. We had taken some photocopies of a crevasse-rescue handbook, tested the techniques on the glaciers without any guide or experienced mountaineer, and next thing you know, we were climbing Mont Blanc and Matterhorn.

When I was 21 years old, I was doing my Ph.D. in Geology at a University in Scotland. I had to go to Bolivia for scientific research for 2-3 months a year. Just a week before leaving for the first time, I fell off a sea cliff in Scotland and broke my back. I got paralyzed from the chest down. Later on, I went to Bolivia in a wheelchair, in order to finish my scientific research project, riding through the Andes in a jeep instead of hiking my way through.

When my accident happened, I was in intensive care in Scotland for a month. Then I was moved to a special hospital for spinal cord injuries in Yorkshire in order to be closer to my family. A good friend from uni visited me almost every day up there. But, 3 months into my rehabilitation, a tragedy happened: while climbing in Wales, this friend also fell from a cliff and died. When I heard the news, I could no longer feel sorry for my own situation. At least I was still alive. So, I decided to make the most of my time on this planet.

Gold

During my rehabilitation, I got the opportunity to do sports like shooting and archery. I found them quite boring, and so was very happy when one of the physiotherapists proposed to go sailing together. That's where I started dreaming about adventure again. Three years after the accident, in 1996, I went to the Himalayas and hand-biked from Kazakhstan to Pakistan. It felt like a rite of passage. I was doing something I hadn't considered possible after the accident. It made me dream about what more would be possible.

Another rite of passage was sea kayaking from Vancouver to Juneau, Alaska in 2003. This was a 3-month Odyssey over 1,000 miles. During these 3 months, I didn't have my wheelchair, so I was dependent on my teammates to get me in and out of the kayak. Physically, it was one of the hardest adventures I've ever done. It was also a huge challenge when it came to body care. Since I'm paralyzed, I can't control my lower body temperature, bladder, and bowel movements, so we had to be very careful that my legs and abdomen stayed dry and warm enough.

Traversing Greenland on skis involved even more preparation and vigilance. We had to ski for at least 10 hours a day, with only 5 minutes of rest each hour. Since I can't feel it when my legs get cold, there was a huge risk of frostbites and undercooling. One of the many practical preparations was to have a special sleeping bag manufactured. One of my teammates in Greenland was Andy, and he's a very experienced climber. He said to me: "You should try to climb El Capitan," something he had done himself 12 times before. So, I agreed, and one year after crossing Greenland (this was 2008) we were at the bottom of the world's most famous rock wall. From a physical perspective, climbing El Capitan wasn't that hard because we had a very good pulley system. The biggest challenge was my mindset and managing the fear that emerged for me.

I had never been attracted to Paralympic sports. The idea of racing on an athletics track sounded boring. I loved spending my time in the Scottish hills, camping and hanging out with friends, instead of training on tracks and traveling to crowded cities to race. However, when I heard that the Olympics in 2012 would be organized in London, it triggered me to give it a shot. I thought it would be amazing to participate in the Paralympic Games in my own country! I trained really hard, made it to the Olympics, and finished second in the para-cycling time trial. Four years later, I went to Rio and won the Olympic para-cycling time trial! It was quite symbolic; I had been a geologist in search of gold in South America, and all those years later I had a golden paralympic medal around my neck on the same continent.

Master of Reframing

Over the last decades, I've studied a lot about health, well-being, personal transformation, positive psychology, hypnosis, etc. This, in combination with my adventures, causes me to have immediate power over negative feelings, almost every time they rise up. My friends call me the master of reframing. Whenever a problem arises, I always look at how I can turn it into a challenge or an opportunity. For example, there were a lot of reasons not to go to Greenland: there were tremendous risks for my health and safety. So in advance, I made a list of all the things I was worried about and then figured out a solution for each one of them. For example, if our group encountered a polar bear, I would probably be the most vulnerable and the first one to be attacked, so I googled ways to scare off polar bears. I discovered that they don't like loud noises, so I took a rape alarm with me to scare them off. Another example: in 2013, I was hit by a car and got severely injured. I couldn't move my right arm, but I made a construction out of *therabands* in my hospital bed, which allowed me to move my arm without having to use muscle force. This way, I would keep my nerves and tendons in shape.

I do use a combination of meditation, visualizations, and self-talk to be as mentally strong as possible. I record my own hypnotic visualizations, which can either be relaxing – for example before bedtime – or pumped up as before a race.

People, Passion, and Purpose
I did quite a few of my adventures with people I didn't know that well. My closest friends – the ones I have had since high school or University – are perhaps less into adventure. Or they're too busy, or they can't leave their kids. So often, I end up with friends of friends, or with people I met just briefly before. Sometimes, it's funny when I'm doing adventures with men. I can go for many, many hours without getting tired. And often, the men joining me start asking me "are you alright, Karen?", "tell us if you want to take a break", "we can stop any time you want." They are too proud to admit that they're actually the ones who need a break. (laughs)

For me, a perfect day is to be active in nature with friends. A day of sea kayaking or handbiking in a beautiful environment, while making fun with people I care about.

I was on a podcast the other day, and I was asked about my legacy. I don't really feel like I have a legacy, I don't feel that air of grandiosity. That being said, I hope that some of the things I've done have given people the spark to undergo their own challenges, pursue their dreams, and live a life full of passion.

In my early twenties, I worked for a renowned company and had a decent salary. From an outer point of view, it looked perfect. But I felt half-dead inside. And I think that a lot of people feel kind of dead in their job or even their entire life. That's a shame. The world would look a lot better if we could all do something we love doing.

I try to live a life of purpose. With all the knowledge about psychology and transformational change I've built up over the years (through courses, degrees, adventures, podcasts, and books) I'm now guiding people in finding their own purpose and living a life of passion. I do this through coaching and retreats called 'Your Inner Gold'.

My next big project is to create a new Pole on Antarctica: the Pole of Possibility. The Pole of Possibility will be created at 79° latitude and longitude because 79 is gold's atomic number. With this expedition, I also want to create extra value. I'm raising 79,000 pounds for the Spinal Injuries Association and I would like to couple this expedition to a project by which we'll encourage young people to go out, dream big, and discover what's possible for them.

If you bring passion, purpose, and the right people together, amazing things happen.

Find out more about Karen:

www.karendarke.com

facebook.com/karenquest79

instagram.com/handbikedarke

Dream Bigger Than Yourself

HOLLY BUDGE skydived above Mount Everest and also climbed to its summit. She raced semi-wild horses 1,000 kilometers across Mongolia, and she has patrolled with female anti-poaching groups in Zimbabwe and South Africa. Her contribution to the world today has been the result of more than two decades of developing and honing her skills in adventure, design, and conservation.

"I struggled for years to figure out how my passions could connect and work together, but now the stars are aligned and one passion feeds the other."

The Day Everything Changed

I was adventurous from an early age. I rarely watched TV and spent most of my free time outdoors and in nature. My parents have always been supportive, emotionally. As a child, I competed in tetrathlons: a combination of running, target shooting, swimming, and equestrian jumping. I competed in events during my adolescence and even represented Great Britain a couple of times in international competitions. I was very driven and dedicated. The sport taught me a lot. I learned that you can't be good at everything and you have to work together as a team to succeed. The sport's spirit 'when you fall off the horse, pick yourself up and get back on' also toughened me.

After school, I went to University in Manchester, but I felt trapped in a concrete jungle. I was studying while a lot of my friends were taking a gap year and having much more fun traveling. So, after several months, I decided to pack my backpack and head to Australia and New Zealand, which is where I did my first tandem skydive. That 60 seconds of adrenaline (and terror!) completely changed the course of my life. Not only was I blown away by the experience, but also by the fact that people were getting paid to jump out of airplanes. My career adviser at school hadn't mentioned this to me . . .

There and then, I decided that working as a skydiving camerawoman was what I wanted to do. Several months later, after lots of hard work and dedication, I landed my dream job and got the chance to jump out of airplanes up to 10 times a day! On reflection, I like to refer to this as the 'boldness of youth'. I knew nothing about skydiving. I knew nothing about filming. I knew no one in New Zealand. But, none of that mattered because I knew I could learn all the necessary skills, or at least have a go! Most often, the older we get, the more we tend to overthink and procrastinate. I try to maintain that same boldness I had in my early twenties.

Seeing the Opportunities

After a couple of years of being employed as a skydiving camerawoman, I returned to the UK and studied for a degree in Interactive Media Production. This involved learning design, animation, and film. During this time, I developed a skydiving online training program. When I was skydiving in New Zealand, I used to see students coming in and being handed big, dusty manuals. But who wants to sit down and read an old textbook when you're learning how to skydive?! So I spotted a niche in the market, invested a huge amount of time in developing the e-learning program, got investors onboard, and even won a prestigious award for it.

In 2008, I heard about a world-first expedition called 'Skydive Everest'. It sparked my passion for adventure again after having spent most of my time looking at a computer screen during my studies. I contacted the organizer and it quickly became apparent that I was the only woman to show interest at that point. I knew that was my hook to get sponsors on board. So, I said to the organizer "count me in" and started looking for the £24,000 of sponsorship needed. I knew I couldn't afford this personally, but I had nothing to lose trying to get sponsors to buy into my dream. And I succeeded.

People look at my life now and think it's amazing. What many people don't see is the hundreds of doors closed in my face along the way. On many occasions, I've been knocking my head against a brick wall. Being an entrepreneur doesn't come with a road map! Building a portfolio of adventures over two decades, including two World Records, and at the same time building a conservation campaign has increased my confidence bit by bit. This makes approaching sponsors a less daunting task today. But still, for me, there's no such thing as a life-work balance! I love what I do, but I'm constantly pushing myself and self-motivating. My brain never stops. I keep putting pressure on myself to keep going because I know that's what is needed.

Dealing With Fear

I've led mountaineering expeditions in the Himalayas and summited Everest recently. Everest is a beautiful mountain but a strange place too. Up there I met wealthy box tickers who had never put a foot on snow before, and they were trying to climb the biggest mountain on earth . . .

I climbed Everest as a two-man team. We had a rare privilege of sitting on the summit for over half an hour, with no one else there! It was a bluebird day and the views were awesome. However, on the way back down, we got caught in a storm and had to spend the night at 8,300 meters. It was brutal. Our tent was shaking all night long. We didn't sleep a wink. The next morning, we noticed there were only 3 tents left standing in the camp. Everything else had been blown away. Fortunately, we were the only climbers in that camp at that time, and we had been very lucky . . .

A way to deal with fear, whether it is in skydiving, mountaineering, or horse riding, is by keeping my mind calm and visualizing the best and the worst outcome. Then taking steps to make the best outcome a reality. Obviously, this doesn't always go to plan but 'hope for the best, prepare for the worst' is a well-used motto of mine.

Aligning Interests

When I was studying for a Master's degree in Sustainable Design, I founded my charity 'How Many Elephants'. It's a design-led campaign raising awareness for the African Elephant ivory trade.

I have taken scientific data and used design to turn this data into a visual exhibition.

I'm using design as a powerful communication tool to bridge the gap between scientific data and human connection. The current annual poaching rate in Africa is 35,000 elephants per year. This number is too big to visualize in our minds, so my exhibition showcases 35,000 elephants on a wall. To see and connect with this data visually is highly impactful. I've literally seen people crying at my exhibition, telling me: "I had no idea this was happening to elephants!" I have purposely avoided using any gruesome or gory images, which has allowed me to work with many children and schools. Children are an important audience, as they are the change-makers of tomorrow. I use my adventures to raise money for my charity and other charitable initiatives. To date, I have raised over £400,000.

I've experienced how impactful adventure, art, and design can be. And above all, being out in nature and developing skills is tremendously important for our sanity and well-being.

How Many Elephants
Through my charity, I support several all-female anti-poaching teams in Africa. One of them is 'The Black Mambas', a group of South African women protecting elephants against ivory poachers. In 2008, I discovered a material called vegetable ivory. It's a nut that can be found in the South American rainforests and has a material similarity to elephant ivory. I have worked with it for over a decade in jewelry design. In 2013, whilst studying for my Master's, I built a necklace of 96 elephants cut out of vegetable ivory. The number 96 represents the number of elephants poached each day in Africa. The necklace went on to win five design awards and is a truly striking piece of art.

The necklace forms part of my design-led exhibition showcasing 35,000 elephant silhouettes on a wall. As more people learned about my work and my campaign, the wheels started to turn. I got invited to give a TEDx talk in 2018, followed up by an invitation to speak at a well-known international conservation conference in Cape Town. I'm now speaking at events around the world. I keep experiencing that when you are able to get momentum on your passion, more opportunities present themselves. For example, I earned a rare privilege of spending time on the front line with The Black Mambas and more recently with another all-female anti-poaching team called Akashinga, in Zimbabwe. Recruiting women as rangers has been a game-changer in the world of conservation. Not only are they working on the front lines of conservation, but they are also the breadwinners of their families. They are role models in their communities and are changing attitudes towards the role of women in Africa and beyond. Becoming a ranger has given them skills, knowledge, and hope.

Should everyone follow their passion?
'The day I started to think big and dream bigger, my whole life changed' are the words written on my website. This is in reference to the day I took a leap of faith and threw myself out of a perfectly good airplane, which completely changed the course of my life. I wouldn't advise people to mindlessly follow their passion. Do your research first, then acquire the skills you need to turn your passion into a reality and a paid job. Over the years, I've acquired a broad set of skills that has allowed me to be independent. For example, I have the design skills to build my websites, I have film-making and photography skills too, plus speaking skills to pay the bills! Often, learning new skills is terrifying. I remember when I gave my first keynote presentation my hands were shaking, much like when I first jumped out of an airplane! It

really is incredible what you can achieve with the right skills, passion, and sheer determination. My daily motto is 'Think Big, Dream Bigger'.

What's your definition of a life well-lived?
Thinking bigger than yourself and making a difference in this world.

Find out more about Holly:
hollybudge.com
facebook.com/hollybudgeadventure
instagram.com/hollybudge

Conservational work:
howmanyelephants.co
facebook.com/howmanyelephants
instagram.com/howmanyelephants

My Lifestyle Is Freedom, It's Happiness, It's Choice

SARAH WILLIAMS *cycled from Vancouver to Mexico, ran the Marathon des Sables, walked the Appalachian Trail, and summited Mount Kilimanjaro. But, more than anything else, she's known as the host of the Tough Girl Podcast, on which she has interviewed more than 300 high-achieving women in the worlds of sports and adventure.*

"We work 40-50 years in a lifetime, so I think it's extremely important that we're happy with what we're doing."

Role Models

I grew up in a small town in the North-West of England. In my teenage years, I went to boarding school where I had many opportunities to spend time outdoors and do different sports; netball, hockey, lacrosse, running . . . After boarding school, I took a gap year and went traveling. I started off with a friend in South-East Asia and continued alone to Australia and New Zealand. Finally, I ended up in the United States, where I got a job as a children's camp counselor for Camp America. After the gap year, I went to Durham University to study Business and continued doing a lot of sports in my free time. Once my bachelor's degree was obtained, I started working in banking. I would run the three miles from home to work and back again. As time passed, I started increasing my mileage until I did my first marathon in London, in 2007.

When I was growing up, I had no idea that there were female adventurers. There weren't any role models. It was only in my mid-thirties that I realized it is possible to earn a living and make a career as an adventurer.

One of my biggest motivations with the work I'm doing is leaving a legacy, in the sense of building an enormous resource of stories, advice, and tactics of strong women doing impressive things. My vision is to continue the podcast until there are a few thousand interviews . . . As a result, in a couple of years, I will have helped diffuse the stories of thousands of adventurous and athletic female role models . . . It would also make me very proud and happy if, at age 80, I can listen back to my podcasts and look back at my vlogs and say: "Look what I did, look what I've achieved!"

Back to Square One

Starting '*Tough Girl Challenges*' was extremely difficult. I had a well-paid job in the banking sector. I was recognized as an intelligent woman. I enjoyed the money and the status. But, I didn't like my job and I didn't like the toxic, competitive, male-dominant environment. I had a clear vision of what I wanted to achieve with *Tough Girl Challenges*: an online business I could run from anywhere in the world, getting in touch with incredible women, and being a source of inspiration. I even thought through style aspects like how I wanted the logo to look and what colors I wanted on the website, and of course the vibe and the energy I wanted it to spread out. I had the costs calculated, as well as the possible streams of income. In fact, I had written a 200-page long business plan which included a 6-month plan, a 1-year plan, a 3-year plan, a 5-year plan, a 10-year plan . . . Eventually, most things turned out to take much longer than expected. For example, I had planned to move in with my parents for 4 weeks. 6 years later, I'm still living with them!

The early stages were difficult in all aspects. For the first 2,5 years, I was mainly blogging and earned no money at all. Things only started to change when I focused on the podcast, although very slowly. I discovered that it's extremely hard to get cold, hard cash out of companies. In those early days, I would wake up, immediately grab my laptop and work for 15 or 16 hours a day. I remember one day crying, asking myself the question: "Why is this so hard? I am doing everything and not getting any results! What more can I do, I'm already using all the time available?!"

There was also a lot of self-judgment. While my peers continued progressing in their careers, I went back to square one. When I put out the website for the first time, I was embarrassed. I was afraid that my former colleagues would think: "Who does she think she is, going from banking to being an adventurer?!"

Another difficult aspect of the early years was loneliness. When I was working in the financial world, I could chat with colleagues at any moment. After my career shift, I was talking with incredible women on the phone, but my daily conversations were limited to those with my parents and the members of my gym. I didn't allow myself to have social interactions with friends, because I felt guilty. I was saying to myself: "If you want to build this brand, this company, you have to give it your all and you can't afford to go out. You can't afford to spend money in bars and restaurants and have fun." After a couple of years, I acknowledged that I had to rebalance my life and started working in a coffee bar as a side job. Not only to earn some extra money but just as importantly, to have social interactions again.

Happiness
When I started Tough Girl Challenges 6 years ago [At the time of interviewing Sarah in spring 2020], a lot of the people around me laughed at me, not understanding what I was trying to do. But at the end of 2019, I looked back at the past twelve months. I had spent January and February in Australia, then one month in India to become a certified yoga instructor. Next, I walked the Camino Portugués, followed by the Lycian Way in Turkey. At the end of the year, I got to spend the holidays with my family in Australia again. The *Tough Girl Podcast* won its second national award and surpassed 1 million downloads. While a lot of the people who laughed at me 6 years ago were still stuck in an office eight hours a day, I had experienced an amazing year!

We work for 40-50 years in a lifetime, so I think it's extremely important that we're happy with what we're doing. If you're living for Friday night, constantly longing for the weekend and a yearly 2-week holiday, then you're not actually living. You're just existing. You don't want to wake up after 40 years of hard work and ask yourself why you did this to yourself.

When I look at my life now, I'm so happy, so content, and so incredibly proud of what I've achieved. My lifestyle today is freedom, it's happiness, it's choice. I get to spend time with some of the most incredible women in the world. A lot of those women have become friends. They send me emails and follow up on my adventures. When you connect with other bloggers, podcasters, and adventurers, they get the struggle you've gone through. They know what your life is like, that's amazing.

Some Practical Advice on Quitting a Job and Starting an Adventure Career

It's important to consider where you are in life. If you're a single, 23-year-old with a bit of savings, then fully go for it. If you're 40, have a partner, kids, a mortgage, parents growing old . . . then it's much more difficult. In that case, try to do your job on autopilot, this way you can save energy to work on your adventurous side-projects in your free time.

Save up as much money as you can, because if your passion turns into a job, there's the risk of losing the passion. Some people crack and choose to go back to a 'normal' job.

Don't care about other people's opinions of you, do not listen to your parents or your closest friends. As much as they love you, they're not going to get it. They'll pass on all their fears to you, which can shatter your dream even before it starts.

There are different ways of storytelling. Ask yourself what suits you best: are you a writer, a podcaster, a vlogger, a public speaker? Be deliberate about your medium. When I started, the worlds of YouTube and blogs were overcrowded. It would have been hard to stand out. My choice to focus on podcasts led me to have over 1 million downloads in 174 countries around the world, over the course of the years. That only happened because I put the podcast first and do my blogs and vlogs on the side.

I got advice from Gary Vaynerchuk about what to share on social media. Vaynerchuk says: "Document your life, don't create it . . . don't try to make every video you're posting something original. Just share what you're doing in your life." I've been documenting my adventures ever since hearing this advice. I simply share my day on social media. It has made creating content so much easier.

Do research: look at other adventurers, other bloggers, other podcasters . . . What has made them special? What is their story?

Start thinking about your niche, your brand, your unique selling position. What makes you interesting?

Know that it takes time to develop and grow, there's no such thing as 'the one moment where you get discovered'.

Tactics Sarah Uses to Keep in Mental and Physical Shape

I do a lot of yoga. It's my way of meditation, as is running. Sometimes, I tap into the fabulous flow states where I think: "Where have the last 8 miles gone!?"

Cold and heat sessions: after a workout, I often take a hot bath followed by a cold shower. I believe there's a lot of restorative power in thermic therapy. It detoxifies the body as well. I love saunas too.

Intermittent fasting: most days I don't eat before 10 am. I feel good about it.

I used to maintain a low-carb diet in 2015-2016, while training for the Marathon des Sables, because I wanted to make my body get used to burning fat. Lately, I've read scientific articles debating whether the ketogenic diet is advised for women. It might not be the best idea for all of us.

Every important thing I achieved in life, I had visualized beforehand. From wearing the finisher's medal of the Marathon des Sables to touching the sign indicating the end of the Appalachian Trail. I believe visualization is an incredibly powerful tool!

Journaling has been extremely important in my life. It helps to process negative thoughts. When I was preparing for the Marathon des Sables, I got heavily overtrained, with all sorts of physical issues: I lost a lot of weight, my hair started to fall out, I was cold all the time, my left eye started to deteriorate. I felt like a wreck. Journaling helped me pass through this difficult phase.

Self-talk: I always try to be positive and grateful. During the hardship of the Marathon des Sables, I started to become irritated and think negatively, asking myself why I was doing this to myself. I had to consciously switch my thoughts: "Hold on, Sarah. You've paid a lot of money to be in this race. You love running. You are in the very process of living your best life. Enjoy this, be happy to be here." Gratitude has now become my attitude to life.

Who are you grateful for?
My family, in the first place. My mom and dad are incredible, just like my brother Christopher and his wife Julia and children Grace and Charlie. I adore spending time with them every time I'm in Australia. I'm also grateful for my sister Caroline who is very positive, very inspiring. She's a big goal setter and goal achiever. She really gets shit done. Often, in difficult situations, I ask myself: "What would Caroline do?"

On a professional level, I wouldn't even know where to start. There have been so many people helping me out. Every month, 270 people from around the world donate/support me with a small amount of money, mostly 5 or 10 dollars on a crowdfunding platform called *Patreon*. I can't express how thankful I am for these people supporting me and giving me the opportunity to call 'bringing female role models into the media' my job.

Recommended Books
Awaken the Giant Within, by Tony Robbins. Tony Robbins has been a huge inspiration for me. I absolutely love what he does! I once attended a seminar with Tony in London. In these seminars, you put into question your values, your beliefs, your identity, what you want to achieve, and how you want to achieve it. It's life-changing on all levels: emotional, physical, financial . . .

The Secret, by Rhonda Byrne. This book explains how thoughts become things. It's about having an idea in your mind and then setting the steps to actually realize the idea.

Everything from Tim Ferriss; his books *The 4-Hour Workweek, The 4-Hour Body, Tools of Titans,* and his podcast in which he interviews world-class performers from all over the world and distills the tactics that make them successful.

The Slight Edge, by Jeff Olson. A book about the principle of compound interest. For example, if you exercise 20 minutes today, you won't see any changes in the mirror. If you do it for one week, it still won't lead to big results. But exercise 20 minutes a day over a one-year period and you'll definitely feel the difference. But also the opposite: yes, you can have a burger today and it won't make you fat, but if you eat a burger each day of the year, you'll definitely gain weight. If people tell me: "I don't have the time to read," I advise them: read 10 pages a day and you'll probably have read 10 to 12 books before the end of the year.

Characteristics and Personality Traits
[I asked Sarah to rank herself from 0 (not like this trait at all) to 10 (very much like that)]
Optimism: 10
Discipline: 7-8 (I'm 10 for laziness, but if I need to have something done, I can get very disciplined)
Courage: 6
Resilience: 9 (You develop it. The more you have thrown at you, the more resilient you become)
Stubbornness: 0 (I don't like the word stubborn. I prefer to change it to focus and give myself a 10. If I have a goal, I'm very focused to achieve it, but I'm not stubborn in the sense that I'm very flexible to change my approach if necessary)
Social skills: 10 (I have no problem talking to anyone)
Creativity: 10
Intelligence: 7 (I'm intelligent but more than anything else, I'm a hard worker)

Find out more about Sarah:
www.toughgirlchallenges.com
facebook.com/ToughGirlChallenges
instagram.com/toughgirlchallenges

I'm an Idea-Generator

DEREK LOUDERMILK deserves to be named the 'Tim Ferriss of Adventure'. Not only is he the host of the popular podcast 'The Derek Loudermilk Show', previously named 'The Art of Adventure', he's also the best-selling author of 4 books, a public speaker, the organizer of adventure retreats, a quantum business coach, and father of two kids. In between, Derek is completing his ultimate 123-item rich-life bucket list.

"Learning and having new experiences are my top values."

Kinesthetic Learner

I've always been an active kid. I grew up in Missouri, and as far as my first childhood memories go, I was a boy scout. The scout's troops had an amazing property where we could camp any time we wanted to. So, for 6 years, I did that at least twice a month. It's also in the boy scouts that I learned skills like building an igloo in winter, orienteering, making a hut out of tree branches . . .

Also, in school, I was quite active. Too active to sit still all day long. I remember having a teacher in second grade who let me walk around the classroom. This was great because I'm a kinesthetic learner, I have to move to be efficient. Nowadays, I do most of my phone calls while walking, and a lot of computer work at a standing desk. I think that there are a lot of kids suffering at school because teachers don't understand that they have different methods of learning.

My company, *The Art of Adventure,* has been my third attempt to earn a living in the field of adventure. At first, I tried to make it as a professional cyclist. When I understood that this wouldn't work out, I started an academic career as a scientist. I did research outdoors, trying to find new species in Yellowstone National Park for example. At a certain moment, I bumped into Tim Ferriss' *4-Hour Workweek*. This way, I started thinking about becoming a digital nomad. I came up with the plan to move to South-East Asia and calculated that my living expenses would be about $1000 per month. So, in order to make the math work, I set up my own cyclist' training company. I trained four ambitious American cyclists for $250 a month each. This way, I liberated a tremendous amount of time to enjoy life in Bali and develop other streams of income online. I also dove into the system of saving air miles. After a while, I managed to fly to Asia for free in business class. It was the best flight ever, including a 13-course meal and french champagne! Eventually, I would travel for 6 years as a digital nomad and live on four different continents.

Steal Like an Artist

Throughout my life, I've read more than 500 books. One book that inspired me a lot is *Steal Like an Artist,* by Austin Kleon. Kleon explains that great artists steal from other artists. I put the lesson into practice by stealing Lewis Howes' podcast concept. Howes is a former pro football player who started a podcast several years ago named *The School of Greatness*, in which he interviews high performers in various areas of life. *The School of Greatness* also inspired Tim Ferriss to start his own podcast. In Howes' and Ferriss' footsteps I started off with the idea to interview successful adventurers and entrepreneurs, and I expected to become a millionaire just like them. I called my podcast *The Art of Adventure*, which I renamed in 2020 as *The Derek Loudermilk Show*. However, pretty soon I figured out that rich and successful people with a podcast were already successful and rich before starting it. Their podcast is just a marketing tool. So my podcast didn't make a millionaire out of me, but it paid off in other ways. By listening to entrepreneurs, I essentially 'pick their brains'. I "steal" the knowledge they've gathered throughout years of experience, in a one-hour timeframe.

Another project I developed, over the course of time, is *The League Of Superconductors*, which is a high-level mastermind for thought leaders. Over 150 people have participated in the program, with a lot of different backgrounds: authors, coaches, influencers, podcasters, speakers, YouTubers, and retreat hosts. A lot of the people taking part in the program had formerly been a guest on my podcast.

The Adventure Mindset

Nowadays, my biggest stream of income comes from *The League Of Superconductors* or 1-on-1 business coaching. My books also give me some income. In 2017 and 2018, I also hosted two retreats called *Adventure Quest*. The first one was in the Ozarks mountain range of Missouri and Arkansas, the second was in Bali. The principle of these retreats is to alternate between one day of adventure – think about canyoning, caving, climbing up a volcano – followed by a rest day. On the rest days, I hosted a business workshop in the morning, followed by a relaxing activity in the afternoon, massage for instance.

I've seen some special things happen on these retreats. When entrepreneurs are put in a harness and invited to climb up a rock wall or rappel down a waterfall, they're forced to step out of their comfort zone. By doing things previously perceived impossible, their confidence grows. I remember one day we hiked up one of Bali's highest volcanoes. We had to go up for six hours and step down for four hours. For some managers in the group, it was the hardest thing they had ever done, physically. One guy said to me: "Derek, I've been hesitating to ask my wife to marry me for a couple of months, but I'm always getting stuck in doubt and overthinking. This experience gave me the confidence that I can do it." Today, they're still married and travel a lot.

In my coaching programs, I teach entrepreneurs the 'adventure mindset'. I use Indiana Jones as an example. He always immediately starts acting in the desired direction, without too much over-planning or over-thinking, and with full enthusiasm. 'Taking the bull by its horn' is a mindset that can be useful for entrepreneurs. But, adventures teach us much more; you learn to be resourceful (to figure things out with what you already have), to trust the goodwill of strangers, and to be uncomfortable. Physical challenges also improve your focus, stamina, and energy.

Creativity, Stillness, and Presence

If you look at creative people like Picasso, Michelangelo, or Shakespeare . . . they've produced a tremendous amount of artwork. For instance, Picasso made over 50,000 pieces of art throughout his life! Therefore, it's really important for me to have at least three hours a day in which I try to be 100% focused on putting out high-quality creative work. The rest of the time is just about building a support structure that allows me to do this in the long term. I do yoga, meditation, journaling, and deep breathing exercises to keep my body, mind, and spirit in excellent shape. I exercise every day, I have quality time with my children . . . Most of these activities have become a habit, a routine. This way, they don't demand much of the precious brain power I need during my three hours of productive creative work.

Creativity is like a muscle, everybody has it, but you have to train it. There are two exercises I suggest people try out. The first one is *mind mapping*. Let's say the people reading this book decide they want to bring more adventure into their lives. What they could do, then, is take a sheet of paper and put the word 'adventure' right in the middle, encircle it in a bright color, and then start writing down everything that comes up in their mind. At a certain moment, they'll discover that they can cluster some items, or that some words lead to a whole new idea . . . The benefit of a mindmap over making a list is that there's no hierarchy. If you make a list, your subconscious mind will believe that what's on top of the list is the most important. That's not necessarily true . . .

The second exercise is *freewriting*. Freewriting can be used when you don't really know what direction to go. Take a couple of sheets of paper, and on top of the first one, you ask the question: "What should I do with . . . my career path, my relationship, my next holiday, my health, situation X, whatever . . . Then, set a timer for 15 minutes and start writing down everything that comes up in your mind, in a full-text format. Don't think about what you're writing down, and never stop writing . . . This exercise also lets your subconscious mind speak . . . but often, it takes time to get past the gatekeeper of your all-day life thoughts, the conscious mind. I mostly find that the best ideas come up in the second half of my scribblings.

As I told you, I worked as a biologist for a while. That's where I learned awareness in nature, noticing the beauty of small things like an insect or a flower. Nowadays, I still walk outside in the woods barefoot and try to be really aware of what I see around me. People have lost their connection with nature. I think that's a major cause of issues like pandemics, wildfires, and chronic diseases. We have to learn again that we aren't separate from nature, we are part of it. Walking barefoot helps with that, just as stillness. If you shut off all the distractions – by means of meditation, for instance – you give your body and mind the opportunity to reset. All the noise gets cleared; stillness and awareness bring to the surface what's really important in life.

This being said, being present is still a daily practice for me. I'm an idea generator, I very much live in the future. My wife is totally different, she's very present. Often, when we see each other at the dinner table, I start talking about new things I've learned that day, who I spoke to, what plan came up in my mind, how cool it would be to do X, Y, or Z . . . Then she answers: "That's nice Derek, but I'm just appreciating my pasta right now."

My children are one and three years old now, and they've influenced the way I do business. I have unconditional love and attention for them. I've been applying this attitude in my professional relationships. I've noticed that people, as soon as they feel accepted and listened to, will feel safe to be themselves. They're more vulnerable, more creative . . . If you can avoid judging people, you get to the real stuff. Eventually, this will make you more successful.

How Breaking a World Record Became a Spiritual Ceremony

Breaking a *Guinness World Record* was one of the items on my bucket list and in 2016, I gave it a shot in Bali. With a group of 7 people, we would try to break the speed record of the *Three Peaks Challenge;* climbing up the 3 highest volcanoes on the island. Our plan was to walk up the first and most difficult volcano during the night and the other two after daylight. So, at midnight, we gathered at the foot of the first volcano. After a couple of hundred meters, we had to walk behind a temple . . . all of a sudden, thousands of people, dressed in white, appeared on our path. We couldn't believe our eyes. There were priests, old people, children . . . They were walking up the mountain as well, so our only choice was to get in line and climb our first volcano at a moderate pace. Once we got down, we were two hours behind schedule and we knew it would be hard to break the record. But from there on, everything went smoothly. While hiking up our third mountain, rainfall replaced the hot and burning sun. After all, we broke the record by 3,5 hours.

We were curious about what had happened that night and found out that these people were conducting a ceremony meant to evoke the start of the rain season. I couldn't grasp my mind around the fact that only some hours later, without any clue, it had indeed started raining and it would continue to rain for 5 months. Then I did some research and I found out that science can explain what had happened that day. Apparently, the thoughts of people – the Balinese asking the Gods for rain – can evoke subatomic changes in the environment which can lead to rainfall. There's a physical explanation for it. In fact, I believe that every experience we call religious or spiritual is explainable by physics. It's all part of a knowable Universe. We just don't know this part yet.

The One Question to Ask Yourself

A question people that are bored, stuck, or lost should ask is: "Who would I be if I already had what I want?" . . . If you want to be a millionaire, then show up as a millionaire would. If you want to be a polar explorer, then show up as a polar explorer would . . . People often believe that a lot of time is required to develop a thing that will make them happier. However, we already have the opportunity today to feel what we would feel if we achieved our goals. When you're calling up this feeling and then going out, it'll be easier to develop the thing . . .

Who would Derek Loudermilk be if he already had what he wanted?

I know that my full expression is already in the seed I am today. I want to allow my life trajectory to emerge effortlessly, instead of forcing it all the time. I would love my life to be a co-creative process, where I can push things in a certain direction, but also allow the natural thing to happen.

Find out more about Derek:

derekloudermilk.com
instagram.com/derekloudermilk
facebook.com/derekloudermilkshow

Never give Up Exploration

JONATHAN RONZIO and EMILY HOLLAND are two friends, adventurers, and hosts of the podcast 'The Stokecast'. With the brand 'Explore Inspired', they want to inspire people to pursue their passion and make a positive impact on the world. On The Stokecast, they have had amazing guests such as Chris Burkard, Jeremy Jones, Emily Harrington, Mirna Valerio, and Ami Vitale.

"There's no secret sauce to getting well-known people on the show, it's just about Emily being annoyingly perseverant."

Getting Into Adventure

Emily: I grew up on a Christmas tree farm in upstate New York. My mom was very creative with our childhood activities and always took me and my sisters into nature. She took us on some boy scout-like excursions in our backyards where we identified everything we could encounter. She and my dad also ran the Christmas tree farm. So, from a pretty young age, I started helping my parents on the farm, getting my hands dirty in the ground. Also, our holidays were often centered around activities in nature: boating, fishing, hiking, sleeping in cabins . . . All of these wonderful childhood experiences definitely made me appreciate the natural beauty of the Earth.

Jonathan: My story is the opposite. My parents were not at all outdoorsy people. We never went camping – we went to Disney. But my parents gave me nothing but confidence and love, enabling every passion and idea of mine. My dad taught me the value of hard work, my mom taught me empathy and kindness. We also moved around quite a lot because my father's job required him to. Before arriving in 3rd grade, I had already lived in 4 different states. This way, I learned to be adaptable and to be okay with getting uprooted from my current environment. I think this influenced my optimism in exploration later on; I know I can go in every direction and figure it out. I'm able to adapt. I can fit in everywhere.

When it came to sports, I continued carving my own path throughout my teens. For some reason, I felt the need to step away from the traditional path of highly competitive, strictly defined sports. I wanted more freedom, more creativity, more fun. I found that in skateboarding, snowboarding, and hiking.

It's also in my character – once I find something really enjoyable – to get quite addicted to it and push my limits as much as possible. I always want to know how hard I can go, how fast, how long . . . This way, I can go very fast from a beginner's level to quite advanced challenges. The addiction to the outdoors went to a whole new level when I went studying for one semester in New Zealand. Over there, I discovered surfing, skydiving, rafting . . . and I started dreaming about making a career in the outdoors industry . . .

How did the two of you meet?

Emily: We met in a climbing gym called *Brooklyn Boulders* in Boston. My boyfriend wore a t-shirt that said 'Aspen Brewing' and Jonathan yelled across the gym: "Hey, Aspen Brewing!"

Jonathan: Although every person in a climbing gym shares the same passion, you can still feel quite isolated there. When you go climbing, everyone is there with their own group of friends. It is not that often that different groups interact and get to know each other. I had moved from Aspen to Boston only two years earlier and still felt as if I had not yet really found my tribe. So, as soon as I saw Andrew's t-shirt, it was like a marker saying "yes, that's my mate".

Emily: Jonathan and Andrew got along very well immediately. They had lived the same minimalistic lifestyle in Aspen and had had some similar experiences over there. Soon, they went trail running and climbing together. This way, Jonathan became a friend of mine too.

Bringing the Show to Life

Jonathan: In the early 2000s, I had already started working for my brother's video production company. This experience collided with my studies in marketing and my obsession for the outdoors, in the summer of 2010. I won an internship with *Old Spice* and they sent me to Zermatt, Switzerland to make content for a product launch. That's where it became clear to me that companies were actually willing to pay for what I could offer them with my combined experiences in adventure, video production, storytelling, and marketing. When I came home after the internship, I started brainstorming on that idea. I worked one year as a snowboard instructor and bartender in order to save up some money to go to South America with two friends of mine: Ethan Lee and Ryan Sarka. Our goal was to climb the tallest mountain of the continent, Aconcagua, and to travel from there all the way up to Alaska in order to climb the highest mountain of the North American continent: Denali. Along the way, we wanted to engage in a volunteering project in every country. Unfortunately, after four months of traveling and volunteering, we were completely broke and didn't make it to Denali. Nonetheless, the film we made about the project, called 'Between the Peaks', became a massive hit. It gave me the desire to inspire more people to pursue their passions, while also thinking about ways to give back. That's how I started my company '*Explore Inspired*'.

Emily: While Jonathan was developing *Explore Inspired*, I had started writing a blog about the outdoors. He then invited me to contribute articles to the *Explore Inspired* website. Two years into our collaboration, we were sitting at a bar outside the largest outdoor industry trade show in the US brainstorming about what we could do next. We wanted to talk with really cool people about really cool things and that's how we came up with the idea to start *The Stokecast*.

Not Being Free, in Order to Be Free

Emily: I still have a conventional full-time job. Not having to rely on my work as a content creator in the adventure industry is a privilege to me. For a while, I had the idea to follow Jonathan's example, quit my 9-to-5 job, and live my most adventurous life possible. But, I changed my tune to it. I work for a market research company, which has given me tremendous flexibility. They gave me the chance to move to Boulder and work remotely. I also have a lot of flexibility in organizing my working hours. This way, I still have enough time to enjoy the great outdoors around Boulder and to build my own creative projects based on what I truly want, without the pressure of said creative projects having to generate revenue. This combination of freedom and security is quite awesome, especially this year [Emily refers to the insecurity on the job market in 2020 as a result of COVID-19].

Jonathan: I agree with Emily. *Explore Inspired* is an awesome lifestyle company. Thanks to it I've gotten a lot of free gear and I've connected with amazing people. It also provided a little amount of money, but not enough to live from. What was paying the bills was the marketing work I was doing for other brands. From an ROI perspective, it would have been smarter to stop *Explore Inspired.* Nevertheless, I kept it going as a creative outlet. It didn't seem to make sense. But, because I kept on doing the work, I learned a bunch! I used this knowledge to launch a small business software company called '*Trainual'* in 2018, which has really taken off in the last couple of years. This way, just as in Emily's case, I now have the freedom to do the adventures and creative projects I really want, without having to think "is this adventure marketable?" or "will someone pay me for this?" or "will some company be willing to put their logo on this?" I just pursue the ideas I want to.

How do you balance your professional career with your own creative projects, adventurous pursuits, and social life?

Emily: I'm aiming for flow states during my work. So, I use a structure that enables me to tap into those states. I get up at 5 a.m. and use that as quiet time for yoga and reading. At 6.30 a.m. I start working until 3.30 p.m. In the late afternoon, it's time to go outdoors; that can be skiing, hiking, climbing, or walking the dog. On Sundays I have a 'come to Jesus meeting' with my boyfriend to reflect on how our weeks went and how we can improve certain things. We also check in with the goals we've set for our different pursuits at the beginning of the year.

Jonathan: I work with 90-day benchmarks. Each quarter, I set myself goals in business, fitness, relationships, and creative work. For example, this quarter my relationship goal is to have 12 date nights with my wife, and my creative goal is to release a song that I've been working on for several years but never managed to finish.

What advice would you give to an upcoming adventurer or athlete?

Jonathan: Don't start by chasing the sponsors or the audience/fame. Start by chasing your adventure dreams. I think the biggest mistake people make is to think too much about making it a career too early. When you focus on an authentic pursuit and share along the way because you just love it, doors will open.

Nowadays, more than ever, it's important to not only create great content but to build a community too. Also, when it comes to community building, you have to stay true to yourself. Don't try to become an Instagram hero just because Instagram is popular right now. If your favorite medium is writing or making videos or recording voice notes on the trail, focus on that. Find the creative outlet you're passionate about and can keep up with consistently because you have to put out episodic content continuously to start to build some traction. If you have no love for the medium you choose, you most likely won't succeed because you'll burn out when it feels like a chore to create.

The Secret to Getting Stars onto a Podcast

Emily: There's no secret sauce, it's just me being annoyingly persistent in emails (laughs). When we started out, we made a dream list of people we absolutely wanted to have on the podcast. From that point on, the most important thing was persistent outreach. I don't think there's a secret language that convinces people to say yes. It's really about having the discipline to dig the internet for email addresses, contact talent agencies, and send out many, many, many emails. In the worst case, if I don't find someone's email address, I send a DM on Instagram. But that's something not very much appreciated by most people, asking for one hour of people's time via Instagram is not seen as professional.

We use a project management software called *Trello* to keep up with where we are: Who have we contacted? Who said yes? Who said no? When is an interview planned? Who do we have to contact back? . . .

I send up to three emails to one person in a 2-to-3 week window. If I don't get a response, I reach back out to them a couple of months later. Sometimes, people don't take the time to answer their emails because they're on an expedition, or they are working on a book or preparing a big project . . . 6 months later their life can be much calmer and they may get back to you immediately. After all, people in the outdoor and adventure industry want to promote themselves, they like to get exposure.

Jonathan: There's also some luck involved. For example, when we were able to have photographer Chris Burkard as a guest for our 14th episode, it increased our credibility and became a catalyst for growth. We had tried to contact Chris by mail several times but repeatedly hit a wall at his gatekeepers. Then we met him in person at a live event, got our courage together, stepped up to him, got into a nice conversation, and asked if he wanted to come on our podcast. He said: "Sure, send another email to my team and tell them I said it's ok."

Which have been your favorite guests, who blew you away?

Jonathan: For me personally, I had a lot of fun interviewing Jeremy Jones, who had been a hero of mine for many years. As well as Chris Burkard. A person we both loved to talk to was photographer Ami Vitale. When that interview was finished, Emily and I both took a deep breath and said "wow! That interview checked every box: it went deep, it went emotional, it went strategic, it went tactical . . . We talked adventure, we talked branding, we talked business, we talked purpose . . .

Emily: She opened up the conversation talking about the emotional power of trees, how trees take care of each other by their underground root system. She compared that to the interconnection of people. Talk about setting the tone . . . During the interview, she was very empathetic and kind, but at the same time she gave real actionable takeaways: "If you want to be a photographer, this is what you have to do, this is the price at which you should sell, this is how to negotiate . . . "

Mirna Valerio and Emily Harrington have been two favorites of mine too. Emily was the one person on top of my list of people I absolutely wanted to talk to. I still remember what clothes

414

I was wearing the day we interviewed her (laughs). She also came with some very deep insights.

If you'd have the chance to go and drink a beer with three people, dead or alive, who would you choose?
Emily: Ariana Grande and Adèle. For the third person either Rosa Parks or Martin Luther King or Malcolm X.

Jonathan: Richard Branson, Bear Grylls, and Will Smith.

What is your definition of a life well-lived?
Jonathan: A life without judgment or regret. Saying yes to what you feel inspired by, intuitively.

Emily: Never giving up exploration; whether that's exploration in the outdoors, exploration of knowledge, or exploration of yourself. When I face difficult choices in my life, I often use the deathbed rule: "When I'm lying on my deathbed, will I be happy to have done this or not?"

Find out more about Jonathan and Emily:
www.exploreinspired.com
instagram.com/jonathanronzio
instagram.com/emilylaurelholland
instagram.com/thestokecast

Storytelling Can Be a Powerful Way to Educate People

LESLEY PATERSON is a five-time professional World Champion off-road triathlon, screenwriter, and film producer. Her husband, Dr. SIMON MARSHALL, is a Professor of Exercise Science and Performance Psychology at the University of California, San Diego. Together, they coach endurance athletes in a holistic way.

"Having a purpose beyond ourselves, sharing our knowledge, and helping others out is what makes us happy."

Lesley, you're living your second triathlon career, why did you stop competing in 2002?
At the time, triathlons in the UK were mainly focused on Olympic distance. I was doing everything I possibly could to make it to the Olympic team, but I just couldn't get my swimming speed to the desired level. Little by little, I got disillusioned and gave up my dream. Another important reason is that the coaches I worked with were very science-driven. Everything had to be timed and measured, it had to be executed perfectly as the coaches planned. I felt that this was a way of training opposed to my nature. I grew up as a wild, free-spirited girl doing rugby and fell-running, I'd always been an outdoor person. After a while, this way of machine-like training was no longer heart-driven, it was no longer fun . . .

I quit triathlon and I started pursuing my other passion: film. I've always been a creative and artistic person and I love both acting and producing. I got a Master's degree in *Theatre*, acted in several independent films, and eventually started a film production company with my producing-partner Ian Stokell. This artistic expression helped me in finding out who I really was and opened up the way I looked at the world. I got to capture the idea that there are many different ways to the top. I started running again and really enjoyed it, even winning some races. This way, the desire to compete in triathlons grew more and more. Only, this time, I decided to focus on off-road triathlons, which are more in line with my talents and nature than Olympic Distance was.

Since then I have always continued to combine my producing work with my triathlon career. People ask me how I'm able to handle the combo, but in my experience both passions fuel each other. I can transfer the discipline and structure I require to be a successful athlete to my work in films, opposed to a lot of creative people who're having trouble staying focused and getting things done. At the same time, having trained my creativity-muscle by acting and producing allows me to see the sport in different ways. It allows me to think out of the box, to be more flexible in the face of problems. The best example of this is the creation of my alter ego 'Paddy McGinty'. Paddy is a persona which is fearless, sharp, and extremely confident. I get into the skin of Paddy McGinty before races or even before training sessions, which has been proven to be an incredible tool in dealing with self-doubt, race stress, and anxiety.

What makes you a good duo in the coaching of other athletes?

Lesley: We have different skill sets. Simon has a huge institutional and scientific background in physiology and psychology. I have a lot of experience as an athlete. I know what goes on in the athlete's body and mind from my own experience and from witnessing other athletes.

Simon: Actually, I rather rarely get to see the athletes of *Braveheart Coaching* – which is the name of our company. Lesley takes care of their training schedules. They only come to me either if they want to finetune their performance by improving their mental skills, or if they have an issue to deal with, like a lack of motivation, willpower, or confidence. Or something more concerning; a subclinical eating disorder, or struggling with a behavioral addiction.

Do you see a place for coaches and psychologists in the adventure world as well?

Lesley: I think it very much depends on the type of coach. Most coaches are very performance-orientated. They like to plan, measure, and monitor meticulously. This runs counter to the innate character of the typical adventurers, who value freedom and exploring their boundaries.

Simon: A psychologist can be beneficial for everyone. Nevertheless, only a very small percentage of people seek out professional psychological help. There is still a long way to go, as very few athletes seek out the help of a sports psychologist today. Adventurers have to deal with the same challenges as athletes and then some, so they could definitely be useful in the assistance of adventurers.

Nature

Lesley: I have a huge relationship with nature. As a kid, I struggled at school and with friendships. Nature was my place of happiness and it still is today. Nature is where your primal instincts come to the surface. It's where you get to enjoy the sweat and the mud on your face and you can just go wild.

Simon: For years, we've known that our physical environment has a powerful effect on our body and mind. This was first discovered scientifically over a half-century ago, when they found that hospital inpatients with a bed next to a window had better health outcomes than those with no window. Today, we know that being in nature stimulates the release of neurotrophic factors, which regenerates neural connections and thus improves our mental capacities. It also stimulates the release of serotonin, which improves our creativity and makes us feel grateful and happy. Recent studies show that the connections between our visual system and the brain play an important role as well. When our neural retina detects we are moving through time and space, the brain's threat detection centers calm down, leaving us feeling calmer and less stressed. The sensory distraction in nature – hearing the birds singing, seeing wonderful landscapes and so on – also runs interference on the sensation of pain and stress. When you couple that with the scientific finding that being in nature reduces rumination and worry centers in the brain, it leads to an important conclusion: GET OUTSIDE AND MOVE!

What is your definition of happiness?

Lesley: Having passion and drive, and family and friends to share it with.

Simon: For me, it's having a purpose and meaning bigger than myself. I have a lot of intellectual curiosity, I love to learn about science, health, psychology . . . and I love to communicate my knowledge to help others. Another aspect of happiness is having a sense of control over your life. As in choosing to do the activities you truly enjoy. For me, that's writing, physical activity, and communicating.

Lesley: Adding to Simon's ideas about purpose and meaning, I experience that my underlying motivation in triathlon has changed a lot over the course of my triathlon career. In the early days, it definitely was a selfish pursuit. But, I noticed that even big achievements didn't give me the happiness I was looking for. I learned that true fulfillment comes if you can share your knowledge and passion to help other people out.

Impactful Books and Movies

Lesley:

Saving Private Ryan, directed by Steven Spielberg.

Warrior, directed by Gavin O'Connor.

These are just two examples of a whole list of movies we enjoy. The overarching characteristic of a good film, to us, is a strong message told in a powerful way. The strength of the medium of film is that it can capture the viewer and teach important lessons without them being aware. This way, if people can relate to a powerful character, they are likely to become inspired to seek out their own inner strength.

Simon:

Man's Search for Meaning, by Viktor Frankl. It's a very impactful book about how to find reasons to stay alive in the most difficult circumstances imaginable.

The Chimp Paradox, by Steve Peters. This book explains, in a playful way, how our human brain works – often against us – and how to manage it.

Mindset, by Carol Dweck. It's a book that motivates the reader to take a different approach to failure, to look at failure not as something bad, but rather as a chance to learn and grow. Dweck explains the distinction between a 'fixed mindset' and a 'growth mindset', and how adopting the latter makes us much more resilient and successful.

And of course, in a shameless self-plug, our own book '*The Brave Athlete, Calm the F**k Down and Rise to the Occasion*'.

What's a simple thing people who want to develop a growth mindset can do?

Simon: Let me give you two things. First, start by adding 'yet' to your self-talk. "I am not as skilled as my opponent YET, I am not good at swimming . . . YET, I don't have enough confidence . . . YET." Scientific research has shown that this simple trick really changes our brain chemistry for the better. The second piece of advice is to reward yourself, as well as others, for the effort instead of the result. If you put in the work needed, but you don't get the result you had hoped for, then it makes no sense to blame yourself. Congratulate yourself for the endeavors instead. Teachers, parents, and coaches should also apply this effort-based-rewarding to their education and coaching.

What advice would you give the 18-year-old Simon and Lesley?
Lesley: Be content in the present moment, enjoy the journey.

Simon: The human brain is wired to never be content. We're always chasing the next goal. We're born horizon-seekers. It's a real task to learn to enjoy the present.

Lesley: I guess that is what makes sports so exciting and fun. It forces us to be concentrated on the task at hand and thus to be present. Besides sports, we can practice awareness and presence by seeking out moments of quietness and by being fully engaged in the conversations we have with others.

If you could be the 'President of the World', what would be the first thing you'd change?
Lesley: The education system, for sure. It is really letting us down right now. There's way too much polarization nowadays, while we don't learn important skills such as communication and self-assessment.

Simon: I agree. I'd make a four-year college degree FREE to anyone who wanted it, paid for with taxes. I'd also encourage educational opportunities that focus more on developing critical thinking skills over just job vocation training.

What is the biggest gift someone can give you?
Lesley: Unconditional love. Unconditional love gives you the space to challenge yourself and face your fears. My parents, family, and Simon have always given me unconditional love. This has allowed me to go full-in on my careers in film and triathlon since I knew that someone would be there to catch me if everything goes wrong.

Simon: Their time. In this 21st century, time has become so costly. It's the greatest commodity we possess.

Lesley and Simon, thanks for your big gift.

Find out more about Lesley and Simon:
www.braveheartcoach.com
www.lesleypaterson.com
facebook.com/lesleypatersonic
instagram.com/lesleydoestri

I Had to Learn to Become Responsible

MAHSA HOMAYOUNFAR grew up in Iran, studied in Germany, and lived in the UK, Canada, and Spain. Since 2011, she's been traveling all over the world on her motorbike, meanwhile leading a travel company called 'Not Just a Tourist'.

"Being a digital nomad on a motorbike is really hard, but the rewards make this lifestyle absolutely worth doing."

A Nomadic Lifestyle

In 2017 I left my apartment in Seville, Spain. Since then, I've been living on the road full-time. I believe everybody should try to live like a nomad for a while. It's how humans lived for hundreds of thousands of years. It's our natural way to live. Our species has always traveled because of climatological reasons, or in order to find more food or a better living environment . . . It has only been since the agricultural revolution "only" 12,000 years ago that we've been able to stay in one place. But, the danger is that this gets people stuck in a comfort zone, which can make us closed-minded.

The nomadic lifestyle also has benefits for our physical health. Most city people can get through the day without moving their bodies that much. But, when you're commuting from place to place as I do, your body is obligated to move in a wide variety of motions . . . walking, unpacking stuff, washing the bike . . . On top of this, riding a motorbike is a very physical activity. Actually, I'm working out all of the time without having to hit the gym. And that's a good thing because I'm really lazy. This being said, I try to fit in a supplementary 20 minutes of yoga and 20 minutes of pilates each day. I compare my body with my motorbike: in order to make the best use of it, I have to maintain it.

Riding a motorbike is dangerous. You have to be concentrated all the time. I think that's why it's so hard to combine with a business. When I'm riding 7-8 hours a day, I'm exhausted, physically and mentally. On top of this, I'm constantly searching for something on the road: water, food, gasoline, an internet connection . . . At the end of the day, I don't feel like calling clients, sending emails or doing paperwork. But I don't have a choice, it's my company, it's my responsibility.

On the other side of the coin of being a digital nomad, there's freedom. The world is literally yours. Every day is surprising. Even though you're missing out on a lot of deep, long-term connections at home, you're creating new, interesting conversations and relationships with people on a nearly daily basis. And, although being on the road is energy-draining, the fact of having new experiences all of the time is also energizing. Finally, probably the biggest upside, is that you learn a lot. Traveling is like a University.

Cultural Diversity

I grew up in Iran. My father was always very eager to learn, and my mother loved traveling. So, my destiny to become an adventurer can probably be, for a large part, explained by my genes. Part of my family lived in Germany. At age 17, I joined them to learn German literature and psychoanalysis. Just like my father, I'm always looking for new learning opportunities. I followed courses and obtained degrees in various fields and in various countries. I started studying Journalism in Iran. I did one year of Film Studies and Art History in the UK. I have a B.A. in *Art History and Theater, Film, and Media Studies* from Germany, a Master's degree in *Translation and Interpreting* in German and Spanish, and another Master's degree in *International Commons and Asian Studies* in Spain. Along the way, I also became a massage therapist and Pilates instructor, speak five languages fluently and know the basics of two others. I've tried to immigrate to Canada, but I retreaded because I realized that I need cultural diversity around me. In contrast to Canada, in Europe people from a wide variety of nationalities and cultures live very close to each other, and we're just a couple of hours of traveling to the Middle East, Africa, and Asia.

The idea of traveling on a motorbike came in 2009. I was on holiday in South-East Asia and was on the lookout for a way to be an independent traveler, instead of a dependent backpacker. Traveling on a motorbike seemed to be a great way. The only problem was that I did not know how to ride one. Another female traveler told me about how she started riding a scooter and suggested that I try that. So I did, but I had a couple of little accidents and found out small scooters are very unhealthy for the back. I decided to take things seriously and obtain a driver's license in Spain. Together with my partner at the time we took courses, I bought a motorbike, and we left that same year (2011) towards West Africa. Actually, before leaving, my partner and I split up, but we stayed friends and decided to hit the road together anyway. Surprisingly, this trip brought us back closer together. We cleared up all the problems of our relationship, it was really healing. Nevertheless, after coming back, it was clear that we had different expectations of the future. I wanted to keep on traveling, he wanted to settle down. So, in the end, we separated anyway. But today, I'm again traveling with an adventurous boyfriend, which is great.

I'm always traveling with a purpose. I want to discover how countries really are. Often, the media shows the wrong picture. The combination of traveling and studying different cultures made me get rid of all racism. When you travel, you have to be able to trust people everywhere.

Success and Setbacks

In 2012, '*Not Just a Tourist*' started operating. The spark for the creation of the company came from being disappointed by the poor and non-personalized tours that were offered by most mass tour companies. I was looking for something personable, honest, and free of lies. Something with respect for the outsider/traveler/foreigner, something for somebody who is *not just a tourist*. In the start-up phase of the company, I got a lot of help from my ex. We worked great together, we were very complimentary. But, then we split up as a couple and I had to run everything by myself. At first, I thought this would mean the end of the company. But, I switched my mindset and said to myself: "Well, let's see what you're capable of Mahsa, let's just try this!" This has been such an empowering situation; I didn't only get through it, I got better results than before! I got more clients, more collaborators, and more revenues. Since then, I try to look at every problem as a solution. I always keep the positive energy. That's probably one of the most important traits one needs as an entrepreneur.

One of the biggest setbacks I had was in 2013. I had planned a trip through Iran, Pakistan, India, and Nepal. Mostly out of curiosity to discover the fairly unknown Pakistan, and to learn more about Persian culture and music around the Persian Gulf region. While I was riding on the northern shore of the Persian Gulf in Iran, a car hit me and broke both my legs. It was a very long revalidation; I spent five months in a wheelchair, completely dependent on other people. I couldn't go to the bedroom by myself, couldn't shower, couldn't drive . . . The physical pain at the time of the accident, and the first week, was devastating. As soon as I got out of the wheelchair, I climbed up onto a motorbike as a passenger. Nine months after the accident, I started riding by myself again. One thing kept me going during this difficult process: a longing for my next trip through South America, with a new motorbike.

The Art of Asking
As I said before, I'm extremely eager to learn. Traveling brought me into contact with amazing teachers. Two friends of mine have been extremely important: Fernando Sanchez, from whom I learned a lot about nutrition, nature, and well-being, and Sourena Parham who helped me with entrepreneurship, principles of a business-minded approach, and obtaining success. I think it's important to look for mentors when you're young. Reach out to people who inspire you, who have done the things you want to do, and learn from their expertise.

A second thing I'd say to young people looking for a direction in life is to try out a lot. Many people stop themselves because they overthink. But actually, you can't lose anything by going out there. I think I'm lucky with my genes. When I was young, I just wanted to have fun. I was quite careless. I was and still am very curious. On the other hand, I really had to learn to become reliable, responsible, and resilient. By traveling and starting a company, I had no choice but to make this change. Traveling made me learn. It made me grow. It made me the person I am today.

Find out more about Mahsa:
www.notjustatourist.com
instagram.com/mahsa.homayounfar
facebook.com/mahsita

Life is One Big Chaos, Just Flow With It

PETER EBERLEIN skated 4,000 kilometers in South America as a part of 'Blade Ventures', a street inline skating brotherhood. Apart from skating, Peter is an interesting and curious soul who is grateful for the beauty of life, the company of others, and the ability to learn and grow.

"Paulo Coelho wrote a book called 'The Warrior Of the Light'. Warriors of the light are the ones who appreciate the miracle of being alive, the ones who accept failure, and the ones whose quest leads them to become the person they want to be. I recognized myself a lot in this book."

An Active Youth

My first adventurous memories are when my father took my brother and me out into the woods to make a fire, roast some sausages, and throw knives and axes at a tree. I must have been around seven at the time. During my adolescence, there were always renovations going on at home. That was a kind of adventure for a youngster as well, using hammers and drills to construct and deconstruct. On top of this, my parents encouraged me to play sports from very early on. I tried out many sports: acrobatics, Go-Shin-Jitsu, BMX, hiking, skateboarding, motocross . . .

I dropped my first mini ramp on inline skates when I was only 6 or 7 years old. I didn't get really hooked on it until I was 14 though, thanks to a classmate named Alex. After half a year of asking me to go out skating together, I finally went with him to the skatepark and learned my first soul-grind. Afterward, Alex showed me a skate video called *Fruitbooter*, about a group of friends doing crazy skate stunts in the streets. From that moment on, all I wanted was to skate more and more. I've always been a curious child and skating just lit the spark even more. My friends and I continuously looked for new grounds. On weekends we would go to other cities and make friends with fellow skaters all over Germany, and later on all over the world.

Blade Ventures

One of the friends I made in Germany is Marian. In 2018, Marian set off on a trip across South America on roller blades, together with a friend of his, Santiago. Santiago was born in Colombia and nowadays lives in Germany. Before Marian and Santiago left for their adventure, Santiago had already hitchhiked across South America and had financed that trip by selling handmade jewelry.

When I graduated as a Geographer, Santiago and Marian had already skated from Rio de Janeiro to Buenos Aires. I was inspired by the trip, talked to them on FaceTime, and impulsively decided to join them. I remember I handed in my thesis on a Tuesday and took the flight to Buenos Aires the following Saturday. Together, we skated some 4,000 kilometers on the South American continent and were joined by two other inline skaters who also felt inspired by Marian and Santiago. It was the inline skating version of *Forrest Gump*.

Today, we're in the production phase of a movie about our trip. We sometimes joke about giving it the title '*Por Qué?*' (which means *Why?* in Spanish) because each time we were suffering on an uphill, we were asking ourselves "Por qué?" Why are we doing this to ourselves? The answer to our question always came clear during the thrills of the downhill, as well as when we experienced great hospitality from the local people at the end of the day. Eventually, we titled the film 'Obvio', which means obvious, and yeah that was our answer when people told us we were a bit crazy.

Skating With Bandits
Overall, the trip to South America was amazing. People were very generous and friendly. In areas that are well known to be dangerous, we took the bus. Nevertheless, while traveling through Peru, we got into a tricky situation. It was night and we had hopped on an empty truck that would take us to our destination. All of a sudden, some girls on the road stopped the truck and, out of nowhere, 6 glue-sniffing football hooligans showed up. Before I knew it, I had a big knife in front of my face. Luckily, I had stored all my valuable stuff in my socks, so I handed them my hip bag without anything worthy in it. Then, my friends started talking to the bandits in Spanish. They told them that we were just simple skaters, boys from the street like they were, traveling with no money. The leader of the group understood our situation and incited his gang members to give back our bags – loco!

A couple of days later, we found ourselves in a skate park with these same bandits, shaking hands and giving high-fives. We had to grin and bear it, just to stay out of trouble. For two weeks, I kept playing the story of what happened in my head. I was terrified in a way. Now I'm over it, but it made me more conscious of this kind of danger. I feel like I have another pair of eyes on my back now. *No de papaya*, they say in Colombia. Never give others the chance to rob you.

Opening the Mind
The first rule of geography states: Everything is related to each other. And so it is in life. My bachelor's degree at uni was about a Community Gardening project called Transition Town. *The Power of Doing Stuff* was the credo of this grassroots movement. Doing the garden work, I was embodying the first rule of geography: feeling connected with the earth, something most of the students only read about in textbooks. When finishing my bachelor's degree, I laid aside the following master's degree because I wanted to experience more in real life, instead of consuming more books. I wanted to truly live the life I was craving for. I think that it's always better to be a good example to people instead of trying to convince them with arguments.

The trip to South America itself also changed my perception of everything. Hanging out with so many Latinos helped me to be more relaxed. I stopped overthinking things and nowadays try to simply flow. In our secure and analytical societies, people are so used to sticking to straight plans. But, life is different, it is full of surprises. The best is to know what a good life means to you and try to live up to it. As a result, you will automatically learn, develop, and do the right things.

Connecting with nature and people and learning new things are the most fun things about adventure. It's not about certain tricks, achievements, or being famous. Just do what you love to do, at the moment, that feels right to you! The bigger goal of adventure is the never-ending self-development, especially learning to be more supportive of the people around you!

Book and Movie Recommendations

Some books and movies have also been very influential and opened my mind to new ideas: The self-made documentary *Cabin Alone in the Alaskan Wilderness* by Dick Proenneke made me realize that you can do everything in life on your own if you want. But, for sure, you need to learn from others before you can. It's about a man living alone in the wilderness, building his own wooden cabin, having almost no possessions and nearly no human contact. It's a kind of lifestyle I would like to try out once for a couple of years.

The movie *Fear and Loathing in Las Vegas*, adapted from Hunter S. Thompson's novel. A very influential movie for me, as it showed me a very important perspective on life: throw yourself into crazy situations and survive them.

The classic *1984*, by George Orwell. On the level of social criticism, this book is super important. Many people do not realize how much they are influenced by all the capitalist propaganda around them – that just makes you work like a robot, consume, and live in the fear of not fulfilling that goal. That fear makes people enslave themselves.

Siddhartha, by Hermann Hesse. I wasted so many years in public schools and the University. I felt like I just did stuff for other people all the time and had to fit into a certain desired frame. I put a lot of pressure on myself, as did the people around me. This way, I was losing the ability to have fun in life and I almost stopped skating. *Siddhartha* changed me as a person. It made me get out of the matrix of life. The book gave me more confidence and it no longer made me feel as if all the time in formal education had been a waste of time. Sometimes taking the long way is worth all the time, since you learn so much along the way. Just like Siddharta, I now try to look at the river of life more often and wait for my opportunities to come. I believe that everything in the Universe got its direction already. So trying to change things or put yourself in the way of something spontaneously happening would alter it in a way it's not supposed to be. Life is a big chaos, just flow with it.

Warrior of the Light, by Paulo Coelho. This manual for life is a good book if you are having a loss of motivation or self-confidence. Warriors of the light are the ones who appreciate the miracle of being alive, the ones who accept failure, and the ones whose quest leads them to become the person they want to be. I recognized myself a lot in this book.

What's the hardest thing about being a warrior of the light?

Motivation is the most important part of this kind of life. If you are doing something for yourself, you are responsible for getting your butt up from the couch every day. It's not only going out skating, it's being in a mental state to be creative and free of fear without forcing yourself too much.

Patience is also a big deal. Often, the expectations we put on ourselves are too high, with the risk of losing the fun and motivation. It can take a long time before you satisfy your own demands and get the emotional satisfaction you desire.

Another difficult aspect of being an adventurer is making money. I still do a 'normal' job from time to time to pay the bills. Now that I'm living in Barcelona – Europe's capital city for skating – I'm moderating German spoken videos. Eight hours a day on a screen, it's not my cup of tea. In the future, I'm aiming to create passion projects in geography. I'm also building a website by which I want to teach people rollerblade tricks and stunts. This being said, it's possible to travel really cheaply. In South America, each one of us spent €200 in an entire month. We found lodging at people's homes almost every day, which often came with a free meal. And although finding sponsorship isn't easy, it is possible. Before setting off to South America, Marian and Santiago skated from Germany to Copenhagen as a preparation project to gather a following, show potential sponsors that they were physically capable of doing so, and make some cool YouTube videos. They also launched a crowdfunding campaign which allowed them to buy professional filming equipment, which will hopefully lead to a good return on investment when our film comes out.

Another issue is injuries. Altogether, I've been 4 years off skating due to injuries. I had two knee surgeries, and both of them left me uncertain whether I would ever be able to skate like before. Mentally, this was a double fight because you not only have to start from scratch again, you have to restart more frightened. It really ate me up at some point, being stopped from what I love so much. I almost gave up skating because of it, but I found myself lost without my passion. At that moment I heard about Marian and Santiago's rollerblading project in South America. The rest is history.

Today, I feel that I have a stronger body and more energy than five years ago. But, it takes effort. You have to eat healthily and work out regularly. I try not to consume pre-processed food, in order to cut out any artificial additives. I am also eating hardly any meat and aim to become a full vegetarian. A lot of fruits, vegetables, and water is what I go for. When it comes to training, I do yoga and body-weight exercises and I do most of my daily transport by bike. I'm also a big fan of cold showers and saunas. Taking care of your health occupies time, energy, and money, but it's absolutely worth it.

Do you also train yourself mentally?
Yes, I do. I make use of visualizations and I meditate sometimes. Visualizations are quite important for doing tricks in the streets, like grinding down handrails. You should be able to really imagine yourself doing the trick standing at the sideline. Normally, if I want to train a new trick or try a new spot, I try to visualize the movements at home before sleep or in the mornings. This way, the muscle memory gets stimulated, and I can even feel the mere fear of wanting to do something dangerous.

I try to meditate to be more focused and block out unnecessary thoughts. Breathing techniques are also part of it. Also during skating, I try to be aware of my breath more and more. All of these mindfulness techniques are self-taught with the help of friends.

But when it comes to the mental side, I believe that being surrounded by good people is still the most important thing. The people around me motivate me every day to live up to my dreams. Alone, I would be nothing. I learned everything I know from somebody else.

Characteristics and Personality Traits

[I asked Peter to rank himself from 0 (not like this trait at all) to 10 (very much like that)]

Optimism: 10 (my friends in Germany always hated me for my optimism in our teenage years)

Discipline: 6 (if I force myself, I can be disciplined on doing something specific. But, when I focus on something, I will lose discipline in other areas in the meantime)

Courage: 10 (always holding it down for the friends!)

Resilience: 10 (the South America trip on skates showed me that, together with friends, I am able to do almost anything I can imagine)

Stubbornness: 8-9 (I can be so stubborn if I want something! This can be a good motivation, but sometimes I get too excited and then I overshoot the goal)

Social Skills: 7 (I am very open to people, but sometimes shy at first)

Creativity: 6 (I'm still in the process of opening up my creativity, I guess.)

Curiosity: 10

If you'd be obligated to live on an isolated island for the next ten years, and you're only allowed to take 2 people and 5 objects with you; who and what would you take with you?

My girlfriend Théa and her dog Gaia for sure. My girlfriend always helps me to believe in my path when I cannot see clearly. And Gaia, yeah she is just too funny to not have her around. With a partner, you can share deep emotions. Which is quite important, I guess, when you're stuck somewhere. I would take my best friend Alex with me as well – big shoutout to him here because he was always holding it down for me throughout the years when I was in trouble. When it comes to the objects: a pair of skates (obviously), an instrument, a knife, a steel bottle/pot, and an ax. All you need to survive.

What advice would you give to someone who is stuck in a job he/she doesn't like and dreams about being an adventurer?

You should stop caring about what other people think about you. In our society, which is dominated by people being employed full time in a strict routine, you may face some sort of discrimination being an adventurer. They may tell you that you are lazy, ask why things take so long, or ask where the product of your work is. Many people do not understand that the process is the product itself. You have to trust in yourself. Forget all your fears and doubts, those emotions only stop you from shining. Look for people who support you. That keeps you motivated and inspired! Start to maneuver yourself in the direction of your dreams. The first step is the hardest one to take – always! Keep your eyes open for the little signs in life that will offer you opportunities to step further. In the end, it's all about mindset. You have to believe that you're the one creating the reality you are living in.

Find out more about Peter and Blade Ventures:
www.blade-ventures.com
facebook.com/bladeventures
instagram.com/bladeventures
instagram.com/fruitbooter55

The Key to My Success is That I've Stayed True to Myself Along the Way

BEX BAND discovered the world of adventure, but not before her late twenties. A 1,000 kilometer-long hike through Israel immediately convinced her to take her career in this direction. Today, she's a full-time blogger, the CEO of 'Love Her Wild' – a company organizing team adventures for women – and an ordinary adventurer.

"Adventurers don't need to be tough, bearded white men. I'm female, pretty unfit, not very rugged, and still make a living out of it."

How did you come to the point of making adventure a major part of your life? Was there a one-moment decision, or a gradual process?

It was both a gradual thing and a split-second decision. I'd never really had the opportunity to get outdoors, or to try adventurous pursuits beyond a few activity days, in my school years. As a result, getting outdoors, camping, and hiking were something that I started to take a back-seat interest in, in my late twenties. I began following outdoor bloggers and attending events, slowly dipping my toes into hiking and camping. I became fixated on a trail in Israel I'd heard about. The trail was 1,000 kilometers long. It would take me two months to complete, which meant uprooting my career and the life I'd built myself in London. One day, I made an instant decision to make it happen.

Really it wasn't the decision that was the key part, but the small proactive steps I took afterward to start making it a reality – handing in my notice, booking the flight, and buying a tent. It turned out to be the best thing I have ever done. I came out of that expedition a changed person. A lot of the confidence that I had lost in my childhood and early adult years was built back up. For the first time, I was free from societal pressures. I had no bosses breathing down my neck or expectations to look or act a certain way. It was like I could breathe for the first time in my life. While in the desert, I found out who I was as a person. The creativity came flooding back and all these new ideas started brewing. I came up with the idea for *Love Her Wild*, a women's adventure community, and got started on it immediately after. Not only did I make a dream come true by completing the hike, but I also went on to build a career for myself as an adventurer and now live a life very much on my terms. Meanwhile, *Love Her Wild* has grown bigger than I could ever imagine.

What are the difficulties that an adventurer has to deal with?

When I started out, it was a serious struggle; practically, physically, financially, mentally, and socially. It takes a lot to step out of the 9-to-5 way of life that is expected for all of us and instead pursue a career that very few have made a success of. If I was to pick the biggest barrier in getting to where I am now, I would say it was myself. It took a huge amount of confidence and bravery to take the steps towards making my dream a reality. Ignoring all the external criticisms and, even more so, the internal criticism. I have a fundamental belief, that stems from my school days, that I am not good enough in whatever it is that I am pursuing. It's taken a lot of being proactive, counseling, and coaching to get myself to a place where I can override the feeling that I will fail and am not good enough.

I'm not attached to physical possessions and things, so living with less stuff has suited me well. There have been some sacrifices along the way. Mostly, that was in terms of not being able to afford a full-time base to come home to in-between the travels and adventures. It took me three years, but eventually, that changed and I am now able to afford a modest rental home in the UK to come back to in between trips. This has made all the difference as I can finally maintain a steady community and a better work/life balance.

My path as an adventurer and my lifestyle is very different from a lot of others. It can be a bit of a juggling act, maintaining social life alongside being away on lots of adventures and having a busy career. Sometimes I feel a bit disconnected from the world, this can be difficult at times. I can relate to my friends' struggles with work and office politics, but when I have something that is difficult, not everyone can understand. I've definitely lost friends in the process, but equally have made some of the best friends of my life. Many of them because we've shared adventures together.

How do you cope with danger?

All adventures come with some kind of risk. Some of the risks can be expected (like being on the road and having the potential of a truck hitting you) and some are not (like camping one night and having a drug user threatening to shoot you because he thinks you are bigfoot, true story!). The key to managing danger is to be prepared. I went on many courses, from navigation to first aid, so I feel like I am in a good position to make rational decisions when danger strikes. A lot of it comes down to staying calm and trusting your instincts.

I don't like to put myself in dangerous situations, but there have been a couple of moments where I thought I was going to die. The most vivid memory that comes to mind was being just meters away from a giant redwood tree as it fell to the ground. It certainly shook me and made me feel vulnerable. When this happened, I had a strong urge to be with loved ones and to let them know how much they mean to me. That's always ultimately the most important thing in life.

Health & Family

I never put a lot of focus on training. I generally don't like structured exercise, so I try to take on challenges where I can get in shape while on the actual adventure. This being said, I do put a lot of emphasis on leading a healthy lifestyle, both physically and mentally. My diet is plant-based – one of the best decisions of my life, both for sticking to my environmental morals, but also in terms of my health. Meditation is something I try to do most days, even if just for ten minutes, as this keeps my mental health in check. I believe it's very important to keep your mind healthy and to work on good habits – like meditation, a morning routine, and continued personal development – to ensure you are as efficient as you can be.

My husband has been the most incredible person in my journey to where I am today. I'm very fortunate that we have a great relationship and are very close. He supports me in achieving all my dreams and I reciprocate that. I think we have a very good balance in our relationship of knowing when to push the other person and when to spot when it's time for them to slow down.

This year [at the time of interviewing in 2020] will be the ultimate test as we are expecting our first child. While I know that adventures will need to become less extreme, I won't suddenly stop and stand still just because I have a baby in tow. I will just adapt, switching wild camping for campsites, long-distance hiking for hut to hut hiking – whatever needs to be done to make it work.

How do you get your projects financed?

I've been able to create a career for myself from the adventures I have been on either through motivational speaking, writing, or organizing and leading expeditions for others. Because I've grown a following for myself, through my blog and on social media, funding projects is now relatively easy. It can be a slow process to build a following for yourself. The key to my success was being honest and true to myself along the way. I'm very different from a lot of other typical adventurers in that I don't come from an outdoorsy background and was never exposed to adventure pursuits through my schooling, I'm still pretty unfit and not very rugged. In most cases, I will look to find a brand that will financially cover the costs of any adventure in exchange for exposure on my channels, or with other benefits like photos from the trip.

Tip: Bex shares a lot of advice about finding sponsorship, earning money online, building a brand, etc. on her website: www.theordinaryadventurer.com/be-your-own-boss

Lessons for Wannabe-Adventurers

We all have inner demons and critics. If you don't tackle those, then your success will always be limited by your own restrictive beliefs.

I constantly push myself out of my comfort zone in all areas of my life. Even if it's just something as simple as sending an email that makes me feel nervous. I find this keeps me in a good place to adapt to challenges and also feeds my creativity.

Start practicing minimalism. This leads to learning to live with less stuff and spending less money. With few ties and some savings in the bank, traveling and adventure becomes a whole lot easier. The world of opportunities really does start to open up.

I try to live my life to the fullest so that if I die next week, I would feel happy that I was focusing on the important things and had made the most of the privilege and opportunities I've been awarded.

The more time you dedicate to pursuing interests, the more likely you are to find out what it is that you enjoy doing in life. Don't worry about moving between jobs too much. I switched jobs a lot and, despite external criticisms that this would make me look unreliable, it actually helped me develop a lot of skills and ultimately let me discover my dream job.

There's so much to be gained from going on adventures and for many you won't know what that is until a long time afterward!

The setbacks are endless and just when you think you've covered them all and you think you are prepared for anything that comes your way, a pandemic hits [Bex refers to the COVID-19 pandemic in 2020; which forced Bex to cancel all the adventures planned with 'Love Her Wild']. Building a career for yourself in any field is tough. You've got to learn how to deal with adversity and how to be flexible to the inevitable problems that will come your way. There are a few things I've learned along the way to deal with this: how to set aside emotions, think with logic, and act professionally. Using every mistake and mishap as an opportunity to learn and to change something next time to prevent the same problem from repeating. Understanding that the end product is rarely how you imagine it will be. The more flexible and adaptive you are the more likely you are to succeed.

What's the impact you want to have on the world?
We protect what we love. My hope is that the more people I can encourage to get outdoors and go on adventures, the more people will reconnect and learn to love our natural spaces. We've got a long way to go in the field of conservation and I hope this is a positive impact I leave behind.

Find out more about Bex:
The Ordinary Adventurer
www.theordinaryadventurer.com
facebook.com/bexband
instagram.com/Bex_band

Love Her Wild:
www.loveherwild.com
facebook.com/LoveHerWildUK
instagram.com/loveherwilduk

99% of People are Willing to Help You, Try to Avoid the Other 1%

PATRIK WALLNER is a Hungarian/German filmmaker and photographer. He has worked for companies such as Adidas and Red Bull. Two red lines go through all of his work: skateboarding and traveling.

"What I enjoy the most is being and shooting in the middle of nowhere."

When did your passion for traveling and filmmaking start?

Early on, I yearned for moving images to the extent that I created a replica of a television set out of paper at the age of 6. Films and photography were a way to document events. I took an early appreciation of this form of art while growing up in central Europe. Skateboarding fused well with my passion since I became obsessed with filming my fellow friends on and off the board. What really took my skill to the next level was completing a train journey on the Trans-Siberian Railroad from Moscow to Hong Kong. I documented the journey in my skateumentary; *10,000 Kilometers (2009)*. During our eight-week journey, we were tested with unusual circumstances. This is when I realized that I wanted to do more, go further, and dig deeper with film-making.

What's the hardest thing about becoming a travel/adventure photographer and filmmaker?

In the beginning, I felt like nothing could stop me. Later on, while traveling through more dangerous regions of Afghanistan or Iran, I had developed more anxieties. I started asking myself "What happens if I get arrested?" or "Could the mosquito who bit me have had malaria?" During my early twenties, I couldn't sit still. I was on the road more often than not. I didn't spend more than ten days in one country. Financially, I was lucky to have worked for clients who could afford to pay me accordingly. Also, I was just constantly working back to back, so I had spare change to work on personal projects; which meant heading into the unknown.

What's the most beautiful thing about your lifestyle?

I am grateful for the lifestyle I have created, by a combination of hard work and luck. What I enjoy the most is being in the middle of nowhere. Shooting photos somewhere in a remote little village within one of the countries ending in '-stan' or taking a morning dip into clear blue water off the coast of the Horn of Africa. During the post-production periods, I love the feeling when the edit starts binding well with the song I have selected. That feeling when you get sucked into the edit and you actually enjoy the painstaking process of editing.

How do you deal with danger?

I tend to push my luck on occasion. I push the envelope until I get the slight feeling of danger and then I usually back off. Luckily, by good fortune and destiny, my crew and I were safe over the years of traveling to over 120 countries. A lot of trips could have gone wrong. Death or imprisonment was lurking around the corner not rarely; especially by skate-filming when property gets destroyed. There were moments in Mongolia, North Korea, or India that could have ended badly. I usually like to forget those memories though.

Are you a spiritual or religious person?

I grew up in a Hungarian household where Christianity has been passed down for dozens of generations. I must admit, I am not very actively practicing nor preaching it. But, I think in the end it is all defined with the balance and relationship one finds with the higher being. I appreciate the traditionalism within religions. I have witnessed and met with so many people practicing various forms of beliefs throughout the continents, and there is something magical about faith and the fable explanation of mankind. It just appeals and fascinates me more than atheism.

Who have been and currently are the most important people in your life?

Family and friends. Anyone who motivates me to reach further. In photography, Sebastio Salgado and Steve McCurry. In filmmaking, I was struck by the amazing editing and filming which went behind '*Wax & Gold*'; a short visual feature in Ethiopia.

What were your biggest sources of inspiration?

Baraka (1999), a silent narrative by Mark Magidson and Ron Frickie, has been hands down the biggest inspiration since I was eighteen years old or so. It opened my eyes to capturing visuals without having anyone speaking; letting your moving images speak for themselves. Their newer piece '*Samsara*' (2012) was also an instant winner in my opinion.

There are a bunch of tactics athletes and adventurers make use of to train their minds and spirit. Which strategies do you use to optimize your mental and physical performance?

I can't help but shake my head thinking of all the failures I have experienced trying different techniques. I have also succeeded in some, but don't find myself religiously applying these measures throughout my life. When in ex-soviet nations, I jump in freezing waters and heat up in the Sauna. In Tibet, I tried to cope with high altitude, but found myself buying oxygen from the receptionist downstairs. Meditation is hard for me, since too many thoughts rule my mind. However, eating a plant-based diet is something I would like to totally adapt to my life, but found myself being more lenient and letting myself slip away with around two to three meat days a week.

Highlights

Halfway through 2013, I won an award naming me the '*Best Videographer of Europe*' at the Bright Tradeshow. I felt very honored and fortunate to have won such an award, considering I haven't shot a single film/documentary within Europe and was mainly roaming around Asia. The reward entailed a trip to any destination I would like to film a skateumentary at. I picked Madagascar, since I knew skateboarding would probably never take me there on another scale. We ventured to the remote island at the edge of the Indian Ocean and even deeper into the western side of Madagascar, to skate through the stunning Baobab trees. That entire morning was just an unforgettable sequence of events. We taught the tribespeople to push on a skateboard, we hugged the thickest and most obscure looking trees on this planet, roasted coffee beans with locals while listening to the late Wilko Grüning play the stunning ufo-like instrument called the 'hang'.

What advice would you give to someone who's stuck in a job he/she doesn't like and dreams about being an adventurer?
Don't buy into the typical clichés, which are typically brushed on by various cultures. Go into everything with an open mind and just take the leap forward without much hesitation. 99% of the people anywhere are humble and willing to help you on most occasions. Try to avoid the other 1%.

What advice would you give to your 18-year-old self?
Do more exercises for your lower back. After all these years of filming, I should have started working on my core a bit earlier. Besides that, I would have given my 18-year-old self a bit of financial credit on my 33-year-old behalf so I could have shot more trigger-happy analog films back in the early 2000s.

Characteristics and Personality Traits
[I asked Patrik to rank himself from 0 (not like this trait at all) to 10 (very much like that)]
Optimism: 9. Everything can be worse, always like to look on the bright side!
Discipline: 9
Courage: 8
Resilience: 8
Stubbornness: 8
Social skills: 8
Creativity: 8
Intelligence: 8

Find out more about Patrik:
www.patrikwallner.com
instagram.com/patrik_wallner

Adventure as an Antidote to Today's Instant Gratification

MELANIE WINDRIDGE is a physicist, writer, and public speaker with a taste for adventure. She has traveled the world, gained a doctorate in fusion energy, made inventions for technology companies, climbed Mount Everest, and written books, most notably 'Aurora: In Search of the Northern Lights', about her Arctic journey to find the science and the stories of the aurora borealis.

"When I first held a copy of Aurora in my hands, I remember thinking that there was so much of me in such a small package."

The Crossover of Science and Adventure

I have always loved the outdoors. As a child, I loved climbing trees and visiting the Lake District with my family, where we would scamper around in the hills. We went skiing and I just adored it. As a student and then gap-year traveler, when I was making my own way, I knew I wanted mountains in my life.

I chose to spend the third year of my University degree in Grenoble, France, so that I could go skiing at the weekends. During my travels, I hiked the Inca Trail in Peru, skied for a month in Whistler, and trekked the month-long Annapurna Circuit in Nepal, as well as scuba diving in South America, Australia, and Asia.

Back in Europe in 2005, before starting a Ph.D. in Plasma Physics (working on fusion energy), I spent 7 months as a work experience student at the Swiss plasma physics research center in Lausanne. The lab was on the shores of Lake Geneva and I could see Mont Blanc from my window. I applied there because I wanted to study fusion physics, speak French, and be in the mountains. It was the perfect place and I was very happy there. When the time came to leave and return to London for my Ph.D. studies, I remember looking out my office window and telling myself that if I couldn't live in the mountains, I must prioritize them in my life. That was one turning point.

A few years later, I started spending January each year in the mountains of France. A few more years later, I was spending Augusts there as well. That was the recreational side, but soon the outdoors started coming into my work too. By the time I was finishing my Ph.D. in 2009, I was realizing that if I wanted to do more interesting stuff in the mountains, then I needed to learn climbing skills. So I did. First, through the Imperial College Outdoor Club, then the Jonathan Conville Memorial Trust alpine skills course, then with friends and some commercial expeditions. I joined the Alpine Club of which I am now currently Vice President.

All this time, as well as my outdoor's experience increasing, I was also evolving my academic interests. As well as my physics work, I became fascinated by exploration, the nature of reaching into the unknown, and achieving hitherto impossible things, such as reaching the summit of Everest or the Earth's poles. I saw scientific research as an exploration too. So, for me, all these things were linked.

As a plasma physicist, I wanted to see the northern lights – the most spectacular natural plasma phenomenon – and as a skier/climber I wanted to visit the Arctic. I realized that with my understanding of plasma physics, my outdoor skills, and my keenness to learn, there was a story to be told. This trip was combining the science of the aurora with the people, the places, the landscapes, and the stories of the Arctic, alongside a little adventure for me! So, the idea for my book *Aurora: In Search of the Northern Lights* was born. This was another turning point in my life, opening gates that enabled me to climb Mount Everest in 2018. I have since written a book about the science of Mount Everest too, looking from a historical and contemporary angle at the science and spirit that enables humans to achieve such a feat as going up to 8,848 meters altitude, and how the same factors that held the early pioneers back are what still kill people on the mountain today.

Looking for a Solid Backbone

I'm a scientist and writer first, not an adventurer. Since finishing my Ph.D. degree, I have worked on the communications side rather than in research. This transition from a Ph.D. student to a freelancer was the hardest part of building up my current lifestyle. When I started out, I was just a youngish school lecturer and wannabe writer. I felt unsure of my identity and value and it was a struggle financially. But I had a mixture of speaking and educational work and I was building up experience.

Then in 2013, I began working on fusion energy communications with a small start-up called *Tokamak Energy*. This gave me more stability financially, but still enough flexibility to pursue my interests in the aurora and Everest on the side. Another important thing it gave me is the ability to take time out for research, travel, and expeditions.

Nowadays, I make some money back as income from books and speaking, but in order to fund my *Aurora* and Everest projects, I had to work and save. I'm not good at fundraising. My main problem is that I don't like asking! And I don't like putting so much effort into something with such an uncertain outcome. Fundraising takes a huge amount of work for no guaranteed return. Whereas, if I put that effort into the solid backbone work of a fusion scientist, I can save the money and spend it on the projects I want, free from the constraints of sponsors.

Skiing More Than Two Weeks a Year Isn't Excessive

I believe that life is about sacrifices – what you choose and what you choose to live without. I didn't necessarily say 'no' to anything; I just made choices that took me in a particular direction and not another. I know that I could make more money by doing a full-time, more corporate job, but that isn't me. I value my freedom, both personal and academic, very highly. I lost a boyfriend, potentially a husband, who told me that I 'didn't conform' and that more than two weeks of skiing a year was 'excessive'. Staying together seemed like a negotiation for which a mutually-agreeable compromise could not be found. I don't regret the decision.

However, it's true that being a writer and adventurer is a selfish existence. Traveling requires family members to accept time away. Writing a book is a long-term commitment, a multi-year obsession. I like to remind myself that people are more important than work when I'm in the obsessive writing phase. I'm not planning any more big adventures for a while.

Which experience made you grow the most as a person?

I'd say *Aurora* is still a pivotal one for me. I used to say that it was a beautiful adventure, and it was. Of course, the northern lights and the Arctic are beautiful in themselves, but the journey was beautiful too. I did things that pushed me out of my comfort zone; not just the more difficult expeditions, but even the solo traveling. I learned that traveling with a purpose was so much more rewarding than the undirected tourism of earlier years. I grew in confidence. I expanded my mind around physics in a new context. I learned about how to take care of myself in extreme environments. I learned about simplicity and priorities. I learned about anticipation, the vagaries of nature, and the appreciation of wonders that are outside our control, perhaps an antidote to today's instant gratification. And I learned about the generosity of the human spirit.

When I first held a copy of *Aurora* in my hands, I remember thinking that there was so much of me in such a small package. That book changed my life. Not because it is famous or was a best-seller, but because of the beautiful people that I met – and still meet – because of it, and for the personal growth and the beautiful adventures that it gave me.

Giving Back

My family has always been incredibly supportive of me, even when I was putting my own life in danger, which was obviously really tough for them. There have been so many other people who helped me along the way as well; from supportive employers to expedition leaders to interviewees for book research or YouTube videos or blogs. When I wrote *Aurora* – a completely unknown writer approaching people with a dream – I was overwhelmed and humbled by the number of those people who gave so freely of their time, their knowledge, their stories, and their friendship. I try to be mindful of that when students, writers, bloggers, podcast hosts . . . ask me for interviews, tips, or advice. It can be tough when there are so many requests and a lot going on in life, but I wouldn't be able to have done what I have done without the generosity of others, so I try to pay it forward when I can.

How to Follow Your Passion

I'm very determined when I care about something enough. I take the long view and patiently work towards an objective. I'm optimistic, highly motivated, and not easily discouraged. There are downsides to these traits too – I'm working on acceptance and letting go! I don't think these traits necessarily set me apart from others. I think many people share these qualities and we can all cultivate them, particularly in areas where we have a genuine passion. You just have to go out there and do things that are hard. It's ok if people think you're crazy. At the same time, be smart and be realistic. Build skills and experience, ask for help, learn, and figure out where you can add value to the world.

Find out more about Melanie:

melaniewindridge.co.uk
facebook.com/DrMelanieWindridge
instagram.com/m_windridge

Fear and Insecurities are My Driving Forces

LAURA BINGHAM has sailed across the Atlantic Ocean, cycled 6 months through South America without any money, and led an expedition to discover the source of the Essequibo river in the Amazon, followed by its first kayak descent. Laura is also a public speaker, writer of a children's book, mother of three, and married to fellow explorer Ed Stafford.

"I left on an expedition only 4 months after our first child's birth. I was terrified that being a mother would make me lose my own identity, I just had to go on a scary adventure again."

A Turbulent Youth

I grew up as the youngest of four sisters. They're much older than me, and honestly, I was quite spoiled as a child. My dad has family in South Africa and each year we would fly over there to meet his family and have an adventurous holiday. We went on safari, paragliding, wild water rafting . . . All of this sounds cool, but it didn't really appeal to me. I preferred to stay inside. I remember that one year I asked my dad – who's very outdoorsy – if I couldn't have a television instead of going to South Africa. He looked at me baffled, his facial expression saying: "Who are you?! It's not possible you're my daughter!"

My parents had a very painful divorce during my teenage years, and the unhealthy interactions I noticed at home set me up with emotional trauma. I had periods of extreme anxiety and self-doubt. By the time I was 17, I had an eating disorder, took way too many drugs, and got drunk very often. In some way, that is what sparked my interest in travel. I looked in the mirror and knew something had to change. One reason was to limit my options for damaging behavior. If I would be traveling, it would be harder to get drugs and because I would stay in hostels, the barrier to go puking in the toilets would be much higher than it was at home. Another reason was that I felt that I had to punish myself in some way. I felt that I had to go through pain and suffering in order to be able to cope with who I was.

Remember, I wasn't comfortable at all. As a result, my first travels – at age 18 – were in Europe. I knew that I would be in a safe environment, able to catch a flight that would bring me home in just a couple of hours at any time. I first went to Greece, where I spent a couple of weeks with a friend and a couple of weeks alone. Thereafter, I went to live in Belgium for a couple of months. Next, I went to South America alone. A big step, but I still had my dad's family nearby. Those trips eventually gave me the confidence to go to Mexico. For half a year, I worked there as an English teacher and for the government's jaguar conservation program. Instead of flying back home, I chose to join the crew of a trimaran and sailed across the Atlantic Ocean.

The Essence of Laura

Looking back at my early twenties, I noticed that every trip was a new, small step out of my comfort zone. Every other trip, I experienced "wow, I'm capable of doing this," and my confidence grew a bit more. After sailing the Atlantic Ocean, I wanted to stretch my comfort zone some more and came up with the plan to cycle across South America . . . without money. It would mean that I would depend on the generosity of strangers and my own ability to find food. I could use some help for the latter, so I wrote an email to Ed Stafford, a famous English adventurer who had walked the length of the Amazon and had survived 60 days on a desert island.

Ed then Googled my name and decided I was good-looking enough to reply. In the following weeks, we kept sending each other text messages. After a while, we met up. Three weeks later, I moved in with him. Three months later, we were engaged. One year later, we were married. Nine months after the marriage, we had our first child, Ranulph.

Ranulph was only 4months old when I left on another expedition; searching the source of the Essequibo river in the tropics of Guyana, and kayaking the river down to the Ocean. A lot of people don't understand why I left my son behind when he was so young. But, I was terrified that being a mother would make me lose my own identity. I just had to do something scary again. Hence, again fear. Again fear, and not innate desire, was my prime motivation for adventure, just as it has always been. Maybe I'm still that teenage girl who prefers to watch television over wild water rafting in South Africa.

If I would have to describe the essence of who I am, in all honesty, it's still fear and insecurity that's driving me. But, I do try to own this fear to the best of my abilities, by trying to become better than my history. I want to be at a much higher level in life than my parents have been, I want my children to be very proud of me. Personal growth is a major value in my life, but it comes with a catch. If you focus on constant improvement, you might always feel as if you're not good enough yet. Some people look at me as an exceptional adventurer, while I feel as if I've achieved nothing – I should be climbing Everest and building multi-million-dollar businesses.

So therefore, it's important to regularly get grounded again and remind myself that it's about the joy of exploration, not about the achievement. In some way, I'm constantly developing myself in order to find answers to the questions I sit with. But, most often, I don't find answers and only more questions arise . . . "A fool thinks he knows everything, a wise man understands he knows nothing." Luckily there's a lot of fun in the process of thinking, searching, and learning.

Heart vs. Brain

In 2019, Ed and I went to live on a desert island with our then 2-year-old son Ran. We filmed our adventure and it got broadcasted on *Discovery Channel*. A lot of people have this as a romantic dream; running away from all obligations, experiencing full freedom. Well, let me tell you: it was awful! The main reason is that as long as we're safe, people are longing for freedom. But, humans also crave routine and structure, and that's even more important when in a hostile environment. When we were on the island and stepped out of our daily routine, I would get crazy. For example, by sunset I wanted all three of us to be in the camp. If by the time darkness set in, Ran wouldn't be lying in bed, or Ed would still be somewhere hanging out on the island, I would freak out. I think that our daily routine was the only sense of security I had on the island, so it couldn't be broken.

Nevertheless, the island experiment was interesting in itself. We showed the people watching that children can be perfectly happy with less stuff, it's most important for them to have their parents with them. I hope we inspired people to not put a hold on their adventures and travels because they have kids, and might have opened the debate whether we're not overprotecting our children as a society. And it made me extremely grateful to have a nice bed and a fridge full of delicious foods at home.

In 2020, we had our twin daughters Milly and Molly, and I'm still feeling the desire for a fourth child. I think it's human instinct to reproduce plentifully. But, I have to admit that there's a battle between the brain and the heart. The brain says that our planet is already overpopulated and that our kids are going to face huge environmental challenges. But, the heart, working in alliance with our instincts, urges us to have children. It feels like our life's purpose. And in our case, the heart has been more powerful than the brain. But, I do think that a lot of people should be forbidden to have kids. It might sound harsh, but I really believe that the government should deliver a license that does or doesn't allow people to have kids. Because a whole lot of people are not capable of being healthy parents. Such a license would solve a lot of problems society is facing today.

As opposed to most adventurers, you choose television as a medium to interact with the audience. What are your reasons behind that choice?
I do think that a lot of adventurers would want to be on television, but they don't have the opportunity. I've been lucky that Ed was already a well-known TV personality. The fact that he was familiar with the world of television definitely made it easier for me to get in. Ed and I count our blessings every day because it's television that allows us to have a rather fruitful career as adventurers, while a lot of people in this niche are struggling to get by.

However, television is a double-edged sword. I think that the real puristic adventurer really wouldn't want to be on it, because in the end what people want to see on the screen is drama and entertainment. It's a difficult juggling act to stay true to yourself and yet provide what the broad audience wants to see. That's why charismatic storytellers have far more chances to get a television contract than the elite-athlete type of adventurer who is boring to watch and listen to.

Can charisma be developed, or is it something you're born with?
I think it's both nature and nurture. As a child, I was very charismatic. I was always joyful, always telling stories, making people laugh. Then, as a teenager, I completely turned inward and got very socially anxious. I had to relearn to become charismatic in my twenties. Ed, on the other hand, has plenty of natural charisma.

Besides storytelling and being charismatic, what other advice could you give to people who want to make a career as an adventurer?

If you rely on speaking engagements, television contracts, and sponsorship, your income isn't very predictable. That's very stressful, so you might search for a way to have a basic secure income. Either you get a job part of the year, or you try to make passive income. Ed and I are now looking to find a way to make passive income from real estate. But, of course, that's not for people starting out with little or no money.

I would also say to think thoroughly about the media value of the expeditions you plan. A 'world's first' is always a good idea. Also: The pictures are just as important, if not more important than the actual expedition. It's better to go on a great expedition and have very great footage than to go on a very great expedition and have average footage. An odd thing that might make a big difference is to try to finish your expedition in July or August. During summer there are fewer news facts because a lot of people are on holiday, so you have a bigger chance to make it to the news report on national television.

We do also believe that working with a professional publicist is one of the best investments you can make. When Ed walked the length of the Amazon river, he employed a publicist. She got his adventure covered in all newspapers and magazines. When he arrived at the mouth of the river, BBC and CNN were waiting for him. Ed calculated the total media coverage he got was worth £25 million of commercial value.

From personal experience, I don't think that organizing courses is a good idea. A couple of years ago, I put together a bushcraft course. It was tremendous work in preparation and I got almost no money out of it.

Social media has become very important. I think everyone has to find his own ways of using it. Personally, I'm very open about my personal life on Instagram. I show pictures of me crying or breastfeeding for example. It's a conscious choice. A lot of people are looking up to public figures like us. I want to show that we are human. I want to show the bad and the ugly, the good and the bad days. A lot of people only show the glitter of their life with the result of their followers envying them and wishing they had an amazing life themselves. By showing that I'm also full of flaws, fears, and insecurities, I try to prevent my followers from feeling jealous of me or bad about themselves.

What are the mental techniques you use to cope with doubt, fear, or stress?

I usually ignore the problem until it goes away. If that doesn't work, I try to react in a conscious way instead of in 'fight or flight' mode. Journalling or seeing a therapist helps with that. Ed meditates, but for me, it's too boring. But honestly, one of my most used coping techniques is crying. I cry a lot.

If you would be an angel who can enter every mother's house in the UK and stick a post-it on their fridge, what would you write on it?

Nobody said it would be easy, but it's worth it!

What's your definition of a life well-lived?

Being 90 years old, looking back at everything and saying to myself: "My dear, you've put yourself out there and did everything you possibly could!"

Find out more about Laura:

www.laurabingham.org
instagram.com/laurabingham93
facebook.com/laurabingham93

Every Loss is a Chance to Dive Deeper Into Who You Are and What You're Capable Of

ERIK WEIHENMAYER climbed El Capitan and the Seven Summits. He has also kayaked down the Grand Canyon and hiked the length of the Inca Trail. Impressive feats, especially if you know that Erik is completely blind. With his organization 'No Barriers', Erik helps people from all walks of life reconnect to nature and unleash the beast inside themselves.

"People asking me to join them on a trip, putting their lives in my hands, trusting me, that's really the biggest gift someone can give me."

A New World Opening-Up

I was 4 years old when I got diagnosed with a rare eye disease called retinoschisis. I progressively lost eyesight and by the age of 14, I was completely blind. I felt helpless and sad because I couldn't do activities with my friends or take girls on dates. But, as I started walking with a cane and learned braille, my world slowly opened up again. I joined the high school's wrestling team. That's where, for the first time, I no longer felt like I was just 'the blind guy', because my capabilities matched those of the wrestlers with eyesight. Wrestling gave me a sense of purpose. I became better and better at it and even made it to the Junior National Championships. During my teenage years, I also joined a month-long skills camp for the blind in Massachusetts. The camp involved skill training in all kinds of situations, including the discovery of several sports, such as rock climbing. Climbing up the first rock faces made me extremely proud and I fell in love with the sport.

After high school, I went to Boston College in order to become a schoolteacher. During the summer holidays, my dad and my brothers Mark and Eddie and I completed a couple of longer treks together, such as the 60-mile-long Inca Trail in Peru. Meanwhile, I always continued rock climbing. After graduating from college, I became a school teacher and wrestling coach at Phoenix Country Day School in Arizona. For 6 years, I combined my adventurous pursuits with my day job as a schoolteacher. I really loved the job. I found very interesting ways to interact with a group of children as a blind teacher and I even got to know my future wife in school.

Nevertheless, after reading Dick Bass' book about *the Seven Summits*, I started thinking about making a life in the mountains. If it wouldn't work out, I still could go back to teaching. When I spoke about my intentions with my dad, he immediately offered to be my manager. In the beginning, it was quite hard. I managed to get a lot of gear for free and went speaking for schools and organizations, for which I got paid a small amount of money. Yet, financially, I was very much dependent on the income of my wife Ellie. It's only after climbing Everest that the ball started rolling. The idea of a blind man climbing Everest caught people's attention. People were fascinated by it and all of a sudden, I couldn't keep up with the speaking requests. My biography, *Touch The Top Of The World,* also sold very well. We're twenty years later now and I'm still fortunate to make a living out of my adventures, and my 80-year-old dad is still my manager!

What advice would you give to people who also want to make a career as an adventurer?
I get this question a lot and honestly, I have no idea. A blind man climbing is kind of like a Jamaican bobsled team. It's so rare, so unique, so unbelievable that people are captivated by it. Nowadays, we're bombarded with people going on big adventures. But the fact is: nobody cares. It's only every now and then that a very impressive feat breaks through and makes it to the mainstream media (like the first winter ascent of K2 or Tommy Caldwell climbing the Dome of El Capitan) because they're groundbreaking. So honestly, I don't know how a starting-out adventurer can get sponsorship. That's why I wouldn't recommend quitting your job to become an adventurer. Instead, keep your job and patiently build your brand and your following on the sideline. Maybe then, over time, you'll manage to become well-known and make adventure your career.

If your guide dog Zena could talk, how would she describe you?
She would probably say I'm fun but quite intense. We hike and run a lot together. I take her out on climbing trips too. I take Zena everywhere with me, except for the high mountains because I'm worried something could happen to her up there. She's very important in my life. She shows me the ways to doors and escalators and navigates me around restaurants. I couldn't imagine living without a guide dog.

No Barriers
'No Barriers' is the name of the non-pro it organization I founded. With it, we take 20,000 people a year outdoors. People from all walks of life, from amputees and people in a wheelchair to people dealing with anxiety to kids who are in the foster care system. With *No Barriers,* we aspire to build hope, optimism, and resilience for the future. A central pillar of the programs is showing the participants what they are capable of when they're surrounded by a great team. It's something I've experienced as an athlete myself: without the great training partners and expedition team members that have backed me, I'd never have been able to climb *the Seven Summits* or kayak the Grand Canyon. Those people asking me to join them on a trip, putting their lives in my hands, and trusting me; that's really the biggest gift someone can give me. This way, I've been able to achieve my dreams. With *No Barriers,* I try to offer the same gift to others.

I have two kids, Emma and Arjun, who are at the beginning of their adult life. Typical for that age, everything I try to teach them back ires. They want to go their own way, ind their own truth. Nevertheless, I'm happy to see they have adopted the 'No Barriers lifestyle'. They have seen Ellie and me putting it in action for many years. They understand the template; ind a purpose, make a plan to go forward, and surround yourself with a great team.

Dealing With Loss

People sometimes ask "What's the point of climbing mountains if you can't see the surroundings?" I answer them that despite the fact that I'd love to see the natural landscape, I do experience its beauty too. Feeling the ice, experiencing sound vibrations, or hearing the magma moving while climbing an active volcano, are very beautiful and intense ways in which I experience the mountains. And because I don't have eyesight, I pay more attention to those senses than other climbers.

The way I experience the mountains is illustrative of how I deal with loss. It's making the most out of what you have. When I was 12 years old, the story of Terry Fox was deeply inspiring to me. Fox ran across America on a prosthetic leg. "What a great reaction to loss," I said to myself. Getting bigger as a result of loss, instead of smaller. Expanding instead of shrinking. I have carried Fox's example with me ever since. Every loss is a chance to dive deeper into who you are and what you're capable of, it's an opportunity to tap into the potential that's inside of you.

In my lifetime, I not only have to deal with the loss of eyesight but also with the tragedy of losing several loved ones. Also in these situations, I use the same coping strategy; the best way to honor those people is to not let their loss stop us from who we are, but to make the best of our own lives.

If you could turn back time and relive one day of your life, which one would you choose?
I remember one day my kids were playing in a lake, climbing on and jumping off a raft all the time. It was joy in its purest form. I said to my wife, I wished I could lock that moment in and experience it for our entire life.

There have been many days I'd like to relive and be more present. For example, birthday parties of my kids where I was present, but I was also planning the next expedition. As a result, I wasn't fully aware. I wasn't fully enjoying the moment. Expeditions are always future-oriented and often that's hindering full engagement in the present moment. It's something I'm still struggling with up until today.

Don't Feed the Monster

I've been surrounded by a great team, not only in my adventurous pursuits. Also as an entrepreneur, amazing people are helping me out. They take care of management, communication, and social media. Especially for the latter, I'm grateful. I'm too lazy – or maybe too old – to be willing to spend hours a day on social media. In my opinion, it's often a monster we keep on feeding endlessly. We want to feed it until we have 10,000 followers. When we arrive at 10,000 we aim to go to 50,000 followers. Then to 100,000 . . . It makes me think 'what's the point of it?' I very often scratch my head about its value. Recently, I posted a picture where I was doing a very complex climbing move – I was hanging on my ingertips on a sloped rock – and expected people would be impressed by it. But, I only received a couple of comments from people saying "Good job, Erik!" A couple of days later, I posted a simple picture of Zena and got 1,000 likes . . .

Alchemy

A life well-lived is not about climbing mountains or kayaking rivers. As adventurers, it's tempting to have some secret ego or snobbery about our accomplishments, because we're doing things most people aren't capable of. But actually, in the overall scheme of things, it doesn't matter at all. Therefore, I think that a life well-lived is much more about being authentic and living a 'No Barriers life' according to your own definition. Understand that it's not all about you. Don't take yourself too seriously. Make it a priority to be of positive influence in the community; to take care, lift others up, and give love. A life well-lived also involves consciousness and understanding of your own capacities to create alchemy by taking on a challenge and turning it into something good.

Find out more about Erik:
www.erikweihenmayer.com
www.nobarriersusa.org/
instagram.com/erikweihemayer
facebook.com/erik.weihenmayer

The World Needs More People
Who Love Their Job

*When **BELINDA KIRK** was 18 years old, she took a gap year in Africa and came back as another person. Since then, Belinda never stopped traveling and going on adventures and expeditions. Over the last decade, she's been focusing more and more on giving back.*

"Breaking a Guinness World Record is amazing, but it doesn't change other people's lives. Today, I try to change society, I want to be a service to the world."

Grandfather's Stories

I grew up on one of the Channel Islands between England and France and got immediately exposed to the outdoors. I was a pretty wild kid and the seed for adventure probably got planted during my childhood. One of the most inspirational persons throughout my life has been my grandfather, who had worked as a zoology professor in Africa. His stories gave me the desire to go to Tanzania when I was 18 in order to study the food patterns of monkeys for three months. Thereafter, I traveled around the continent for about eight months. This trip opened my eyes to the world and myself. I came back as another person; emboldened, confident, and open-minded. I knew I had discovered something I needed in my life. If my grandfather wouldn't have triggered me with his stories, I might have been a lawyer or accountant today.

Expeditions

Throughout my twenties, I did adventure merely for myself. I was a filmmaker and expedition leader. I worked on expeditions organized by private companies, as well as the television industry. I was abroad for at least 6 months a year and most of my expeditions took place in remote jungles or deserts. On the big expeditions, I was mostly surrounded by experienced, competent people. Along the way, I also got involved in projects run by the *British Explorers Society* or *Youth Adventure Society*. My task was to take youngsters aged 16 to 21 on an expedition. This could go from discovering rock paintings in Lesotho to conservation work in Alaska. At age 26, I was the chief leader of a group of 100 youngsters conducting biological research in the Amazon forest. I was the youngest person ever in such an important position. However, at this moment I had already 8 years of experience as an adventurer, so I was perfectly ready for the job. By now, I've guided about 15 of these youth expeditions. They have been very important in my life. I've seen so many changes happening in the youngsters who participated. These adventures gave them the confidence to go for the job they really want, to ask out the girl they're dreaming of, to go on another, bigger adventure . . . etc. Each time I see people who have been on these expeditions again, they talk to me about 'a life before' and 'a life after' the expedition.

Another turning point in my career has been when a good friend of mine asked me if I wanted to cooperate in a BBC documentary called *Beyond Boundaries*. In the documentary, a group of disabled people – blind, deaf, people in a wheelchair, etc. – would try to walk across Nicaragua. My role was just to help out the team with equipment and logistics, I wasn't actually helping them while walking. This documentary had an incredible impact on the watching public. It was literally telling them "What's your excuse not to get out of your chair and move?"

Rowing Great Britain

By my late twenties, the expeditions I was doing weren't that special anymore. I'd gone to deserts and jungles for 10 years, there was not that much left to learn. I started thinking about a new adventure that would take me out of my comfort zone again. I wanted to get in touch with adventurers from other fields, so I came up with the idea to build a community of adventurers and created *Explorers Connect*. This way, I very rapidly got in touch with some ocean rowers. They told me that one of the most difficult ocean rows in the world is the circumnavigation of Great Britain. It's the most difficult for three reasons: there are a lot of conflicting currents causing big waves and unpredictable streams, you have to row close to the coast (which involves the risk of collapsing against the rocks), and lastly there's a lot of sea traffic. Many teams had tried to row around the country, but only one had succeeded. My idea was to build the first female team that would aim to do so. I used *Explorers Connect* as a platform to find the right crew members. After one year of learning sea navigation skills, physical training, and practical preparations, we set off under the approving eye of Sir Richard Branson – his airline company *Virgin* was the head sponsor. 52 days of suffering later, we had circumnavigated Great Britain as the first team of female rowers and got rewarded with an official *Guinness World Record*.

Explorers Connect

I'm still in touch with the women with whom I rowed around Great Britain 12 years ago. During big expeditions, you often undergo very transformational changes together. These experiences tend to create a very strong bond amongst each other. Despite the beauty of these grand expeditions, today I'm only consulting adventurers and explorers in undertaking them. I no longer go on big expeditions myself. The main reason is that I wanted to build a family, and it's fairly hard to be a good mother if you're away several months a year. Besides, as *Explorers Connect* got more and more known, I increasingly received requests to organize small, easily accessible adventures. So, about 6-7 years ago, we started organizing adventures that lasted only a couple of days to a maximum of a couple of weeks, often in Great Britain. I soon discovered that they're much more fun than long expeditions. The organization is much easier, there isn't the stress to find the finances, and you can really make people happy. Accomplishing a big expedition comes with a lot of pride, and it surely inspires friends and family to be more active outdoors, but it's not really having an impact on society. Breaking the *Guinness World Record* of circumnavigating Great Britain was great, but it didn't change people's lives. The work we're doing with *Explorers Connect* is much more meaningful. Next to our small adventures, we help people find a job in the field of adventure, we organize workshops, we have a yearly adventure festival, and we created a national night of adventure called 'Wild Night Out'. Through all of these channels, *Explorers Connect* has encouraged over 30,000 people to discover a world of outdoor challenges over the last decade.

Jackson

I met my partner, Jim, 18 years ago during a youth adventure program in Lesotho. In 2017, we got our son Jackson. He's by far our biggest and best adventure. Before being a mother, I always commented on our society for being over-protective. My opinion was that parents don't allow their children to take risks, and therefore children wouldn't learn to cope with adversity and wouldn't be ready to go out into the world. Today, I've muted my discourse a bit, because now I feel the emotional conflict myself. We live in a National Park and Jackson is always outdoors. As a result, he's much more physically capable compared to most children of his age. But, I admit, that it's scary to see him climbing in trees. It makes me a bit fearful to think that soon I'm gonna have to let him go to school on his bicycle . . . This makes me feel a bit like a helicopter parent, but I know I have to let him discover, take risks, and make mistakes. It's necessary for him to be able to cope with adversity and build his resilience.

What makes you a good entrepreneur?

I do not consider myself a real entrepreneur. Entrepreneurs are most often interested in making money, I'm not. I started *Explorers Connect* as a passion project. In my opinion, our society is too obsessed with making just a little bit more money, only to consume more. What the world really needs is people doing jobs that they love. You will have to work for many, many hours over a lifetime, so if you're not passionate about what you're doing, what's the point in doing it? I've always just done what I'm interested in. Whenever I see an opportunity, I go for it. But it's not easy to follow your passion. You have to be determined, but at the same time be flexible as well. One thing that has helped me a lot is that I genuinely care about other people. If I didn't care about people, I wouldn't be able to lead them.

What's your biggest dream left?

I would like to change society, motivate even more people to be active outdoors. I believe that everyone has an innate sense of adventure. It's in our DNA. But, because of society, rules, and the ease of modern life, a lot of people have lost it. It's only by experiencing that being cold, wet, and hungry can actually be fun – what makes us feel more alive than that? – that people will reconnect with nature and get outdoors more often. Too many people have lost their inner child. It is important to keep a level of child-like curiosity and excitement in order to be happy.

Being a service to the world, truly impacting people in a positive way, is becoming increasingly more important in my life. For the last couple of months, I've been sitting around the table with governments to discuss how we can bring back more adventure into people's lives. I also published on a book titled *Adventure Revolution*. I've gathered all of the scientific evidence that proves the benefits of adventure on our mental health status. The last decades have delivered us some terrible statistics. For example – to come back to parenting – the lack of coping strategies as a result of an overprotective upbringing is a major causal factor for suicide. One of the best ways to build resilience is by adventure. I'm happy to see that, over the last 5 years, more and more adventure communities have arisen. But, we still need much more change!

What's your definition of happiness?
Having good people around you.
Doing something meaningful.
Being silly and having fun.

Find out more about Belinda and Explorers Connect:
www.explorersconnect.com
www.belindakirk.com
facebook.com/ExplorersConnect
instagram.com/explorersconnect

BACK TO BASECAMP

If your dream is also to live a life full of adventure, then my hope is this book has inspired you to take the next steps in your journey, and has given you some specific tools to fasttrack your progress. If you really want to take things to the next level and are serious about making a career in the field of adventure, then hurry up and go to *www.professionadventurer.com* where I have a unique offer for you!

Acknowledgements

Building a career as an adventurer isn't an easy task. Let alone if a pandemic hits, totally out of your control, and you're forced to cancel your planned expedition, scratch your head and ask yourself the question how you're going to feed your kids if this Covid-thing isn't going to pass by soon.

Still, during the most difficult times imaginable for someone who makes a living out of adventure and travel, 100 amazing people were generous enough to give 1, 2, 3 or in some cases even more hours of their time to a naive, unknown 29-year old guy with a big dream. My thankfulness for each single one of these inspiring individuals can not be put into words, so this is only a humble attempt to honor each one of these amazing adventurers:

Merci, Alban
Thank you, Alex
Thank you, Alice
Thank you, Alison and Don
Merci, Antoine
Dhan Ya Baad, Apa
Thank you, Belinda
Thank you, Ben
Merci, Bertrand
Thank you, Bex
Merci, Brian
Merci, Brieg
Thank you, Cameron
Merci, Caroline
Thank you, Charles
Thank you, Charlie
Danke Schön, Christian
Thank you, Dakota
Merci, Damien
Gracias, Dani
Thank you, Darcy
Thank you, Dave
Dhan Ya Baad, Dawa
ευχαριστώ, Dean
Merci, Delphine et Maxime
Thank you, Derek
Thank you, Dimitri
Bedankt, Dixie
Merci, Dylan
Thank you, Emily and Jonathan
Thank you, Erik

Merci, Ewen
Takk fyrir, Fiann
Thank you, Forest
Bedankt, Frank
Merci, Fred
Thank you, Geordie
Thank you, Graham
Bedankt, Gregory
Thank you, Hazel
Thank you, Hilaree
Thank you, Holly
Thank you, James
Thank you, Jamie and Jamie
Bedankt, Jelle
Bedankt and Grazie, Jente and Alessia
Thank you, Jenny and Jenny
Thank you, Jill
Danke Schön, Jonas
Shukran, Joyce
Thank you, Julie
Merci, Julien
Thank you, Justine
Thank you, Karen
Thank you, Kit
Tack, Kristina
Thank you, Krystle
Thank you, Lael
Thank you, Laura
Thank you, Lesley and Simon
Thank you, Lindsey
Merci, Liv
Takk, Liv
Danke Schön, Lorraine
Mam'noon, Mahsa
Merci, Marie et Nil
Merci, Marion et Erwan
Merci, Marc
Thank you, Mark
Merci, Matthieu
Thank you, Matty
Thank you, Melanie
Grazie, Michele
Tack, Mikael
Thank you, Mike
Bedankt, Miriam
Merci, Olivier

Köszönöm, Patrik
Thank you, Paula
Thank you, Peter
Danke Schön, Peter
Thank you, Rachel
Thank you, Rebecca
Thank you, Rickey
Thank you, Roz
Thank you, Sara
Thank you, Sarah and Sarah
Thank you, Sean
Bedankt, Siebe
Bedankt, Stef en Sofie
Thank you, Steven
Merci, Thomas
Thank you, Tim
Dhanyavaad, Vasu
Dhanyavaad, Vedangi
Merci, Victor
Bedankt, Wim
Merci, Xavier

Two people from this long list deserve some supplementary words of thanks. Firstly, Karen Darke. Karen, ever since I got to know you, we've been engulfing each other with complements. Yet once more I want to acknowledge you for the kindness you've been spreading ever since our first call. I'm truly honored to have you as a friend and I can't wait to make many more friends together with you.

Secondly, Derek Loudermilk. Derek looks at the world through a different lense than 99,99% of people. There's not a single individual on this planet who taught me more useful, interesting and sometimes insane things about business, human interactions and the universe. Derek, it has been a pleasure to be mentored by you and subsequently backing you as your personal assistant. I'm truly honored to have you as a friend and can't wait to create much more magic together with you.

Furthermore, I want to thank Anthony Ripoll, Eline Declerck, Donavan Leyn, Carl Salomez, Robin Schuermans, Hanne Benoit, Steven Vervaecke, Steven Vandersyppe, Guido Lazeure, Nancy Dehouck, Matthew Valentin and Johan Valentin for being a witness and emotional support during my space hopper adventures. I want to thank all of my other friends for cheering me up in all the challenges I push myself through, even though they're often beyond the conventional.

About The Author

Hi there, Glenn here, the author of the book. I hope you enjoyed reading the stories of the 100 adventurers in this book. I started writing this book in March 2020, a couple of days after the start of the first global COVID-19 lockdown. As I did my first 5, 10, 20 interviews during those first quarantine weeks, they only confirmed to me that writing, adventures and doing sports outdoors was what I wanted to dedicate my life to, and that my physiotherapy job was standing in the way of that.

I made a drastic decision that changed the direction of my life completely: I resigned from my job. I had the intuitive feeling that I needed to burn my boats and focus fully on finishing this book and go on adventures that would give me media-exposure.

For the next 8 months, I lived on my savings while sending out over 1000 emails to adventurers from all over the world. I spent months in isolation in the cheapest flat I could find in the Pyrenees, spending 12-16 hours a day doing nothing else than working on the book, trail running, cycling and pulling tires. While I collected the interviews little by little, I also managed to get in the spotlight as an 'adventurer', first by climbing The Col du Tourmalet – an epic 19km-long mountain pass well known by the Tour De France – on a spacehopper. Subsequently, by becoming the first person ever to cross a mountain range with a unicorn.

By the time my 100 interviews were finished, my bank account was empty. In order to be able to pay for a cover designer, proofreader, editor and book formatter, I went back to taking a job as a physiotherapist. But, only for a short period of time, because one of the adventurers in this book, Derek Loudermilk, offered me to become his personal assistant in the autumn of 2021. As thus, this book-project paid me dividends in ways that I could not have expected. I am now living as a digital nomad and preparing my next adventures. Meanwhile, I also broke a Guinness World Record, started a YouTube-channel and launched a clothing-brand.

Although the last 2,5 years have been extremely hard – emotionally, mentally, physically, socially, and financially – , the feeling of finally having started my hero's journey, following my heart and living my purpose, has been well worth all the hardship. And today I feel I'm only inches away from becoming a "Professional Adventurer" myself.

Continue The Journey

If you enjoyed reading the stories in this book, then I would be deeply grateful if you could help me out by conducting 1, 2 or 3 of the following small acts of appreciation:

1. Take a selfie of yourself with this book and post in on social media with the hashtag #professionadventurer

2. Send a direct message to two people who you think will enjoy reading this book!

3. Go to Amazon (scan QR code below) and leave me a review!

Continue the journey:

Become a professional adventurer yourself: *www.professionadventurer.com*

Find out more everything about me: *www.glennvalentin.com*

Send me an email: *glenn@smileplaygive.com*

Printed in Great Britain
by Amazon

82363995R00273